VINEGAR HILL

Vinegar Hill

The last stand of the Wexford rebels of 1798

Ronan O'Flaherty and Jacqui Hynes

EDITORS

FOUR COURTS PRESS

Set in AGaramondPro 10.5pt/13.5pt by
Carrigboy Typesetting Services for
FOUR COURTS PRESS LTD
7 Malpas Street, Dublin 8, Ireland
www.fourcourtspress.ie
and in North America for
FOUR COURTS PRESS
c/o IPG, 814 N Franklin St, Chicago, IL 60610

© The various contributors and Four Courts Press 2021

A catalogue record for this title is available
from the British Library.

ISBN 978-1-84682-962-8

All rights reserved. No part of this publication may be reproduced,
stored in or introduced into a retrieval system, or transmitted, in any form
or by any means (electronic, mechanical, photocopying, recording, or otherwise),
without the prior written permission of both the copyright
owner and publisher of this book.

SPECIAL ACKNOWLEDGMENT

The volume derives from the Longest Day Research Project,
funded by Wexford County Council.

Printed in Spain by GraphyCems, Navarra.

Contents

FOREWORD: Vinegar Hill and its international legacy — vii
Tony Pollard

1. Preface: the Longest Day Research Project — 1
   Ronan O'Flaherty and Jacqui Hynes

2. Who fears to speak of '98? A review of the sources — 10
   Rory O'Connor

3. Command and structure: the crown forces at the Battle of Vinegar Hill — 34
   Chris Robinson, Barry Walsh and Jacqui Hynes

4. Command and structure: a rebel republic? — 62
   Brian Ó Cléirigh

5. Testing the theories of why the Hon. Major General Francis Needham was 'late' for the Battle of Vinegar Hill — 88
   Jacqui Hynes and Barry Walsh

6. The field of battle — 105
   Ronan O'Flaherty and Rory O'Connor

7. The architectural landscape of Enniscorthy in 1798 — 141
   Edmund Joyce

8. Investigating potential mass graves on Vinegar Hill — 157
   James Bonsall and Cian Hogan

9. The underwater surveys — 171
   Niall Brady and Rex Bangerter

10. Picking up the pieces: the archaeological survey of Vinegar Hill — 190
    Damian Shiels and James Bonsall

11	Archaeological monitoring and licensed surveys at Vinegar Hill and Clonhasten *Catherine McLoughlin, Emmet Stafford and Colm Moriarty*	205
12	Oral histories of the 1798 rebellion in Enniscorthy and surrounding areas *Jacqui Hynes*	219
13	From Vinegar Hill to Knightstown Bog: the last march of the Wexford pikemen *Ciarán McDonnell*	249

APPENDICES 261

1(a)	Details of garrison in Enniscorthy	262
1(b)	Numbers killed and wounded in defence of Enniscorthy on 28 May 1798	263
2	Extracts of Jane Barber's diary	264
3	Extracts of Barbara Lett's diary	273
4	Extracts of Alicia Pounden's diary	275
5	Details of trials of those court martialled for participation in the rebellion of 1798	277
6	Numbers of government troops in Ireland, 1796–9	280
7	General Needham's force at the Battle of Arklow	281
8	Government troops (field army) for the Battle of Vinegar Hill	282
9	General orders for the Battle of Vinegar Hill	284
10	Eyewitness account of William Kerr of the Midlothian fencible regiment	286
11	Government casualties at the Battle of Vinegar Hill	289
12	Extract from letter of 21 June 1798 from Lake to Castlereagh	291
13	Ranges for guns used by government forces	293
14	Daily rates of pay for the British army in 1800	294
15	Extracts from folk narratives	295

LIST OF ILLUSTRATIONS	301
LIST OF ABBREVIATIONS	306
LIST OF CONTRIBUTORS	307
BIBLIOGRAPHY	309
INDEX	321

FOREWORD

Vinegar Hill and its international legacy

TONY POLLARD

PROFESSOR OF CONFLICT HISTORY AND ARCHAEOLOGY, UNIVERSITY OF GLASGOW

The Battle of Vinegar Hill should loom large in the popular imagination. For one thing, it is a classic story of the underdog suffering at the hands of a more powerful establishment. It also includes many of the elements of a classic last stand, like an Alamo (1836) or a Rorke's Drift (1879), but in this case the bulwark held by the defenders was not a fortified mission station, as it was with both of those later battles, but an unfortified hill. The reality is, however, if you were to ask the average person outside of Ireland whether they had heard of the battle, the answer would likely be no. Perhaps a film would help with its international profile, it certainly deserves one, but the battle today, and indeed those others that punctuated the Irish rising of 1798, are not remembered far outside of Ireland, and no doubt not universally even there.[1] This was not always the case though, and the name of Vinegar Hill as a symbol of the price paid in the fight for liberty made its presence known across the globe.

In 1804 there was a convict rebellion in New South Wales in Australia, when a number of inmates of Castle Hill Convict Farm escaped and encouraged others to join them while attempting to seize arms with which to defend their new found freedom. It was the first time Europeans fought one another in what could be described as a battle in Australia (Anon., n.d.). This was a planned rebellion, and around half of the more than 200 convicts were Irish, with some of those having been transported for their involvement in the 1798 rebellion. Around 39 rebels were killed, most in the battle, which resulted in no deaths on the side of the crown forces, while nine, including the rebel leader Phillip Cunningham, were hanged without trial. The engagement was referred to as the 'second Battle of Vinegar Hill' and the connection between the two places and events was marked when a stone from the original Vinegar Hill was incorporated into the monument to the Australian battle in 2004. Fifty years after Castle Hill, in 1854, Australia witnessed another rebellion, this time of gold miners at the Eureka Stockade. Here again the memory of 1798 was invoked, when the rebelling miners used 'Vinegar Hill' as a password.

[1] At least three films have been made of the Alamo fight, and the popularity of the Anglo-Zulu War among military buffs has much to do with the iconic status of the 1964 film, *Zulu*.

There are several places which came to be named Vinegar Hill in the USA, including a neighbourhood in Brooklyn, New York City. This Vinegar Hill was so named because of the high number of Irish immigrants who became residents, presumably remembering that other hill in Wexford where so many of their countrymen had also gathered. However, there is no battle associated with the place and it is uncertain how many people would today associate the name with events taking place across the Atlantic over two hundred years ago.

There is also a Vinegar Hill in Charlottesville, Virginia, and although not the scene of a battle, it was in 2017 the scene of an act of violence that once again brought the name into the headlines, when a peaceful anti-racism protester was deliberately run down by a car during a white supremacist rally (Newkirk, 2017). Vinegar Hill had long been a black neighbourhood that suffered enforced urban 'renewal' in 1965, a process which resulted in evictions, the closing of businesses and the dispersal of the community. The origin of the name is uncertain and a story is told of a barrel of vinegar spilling its contents after falling from a wagon, with the smell lingering long enough to inspire the toponym. Such retrofitting of the past is a common theme in folklore accounts – there is a Vinegar Hill in New Zealand that shares the origin story of a barrel of vinegar falling from a wagon. However, in the case of Vinegar Hill, Charlottesville, there is another suggestion (Saunders & Shackelford, 1998), that the name was transported from Ireland by a group of Irish merchants who set up shop there in the early nineteenth century, in which case it is very likely a direct reference back to 'our' Vinegar Hill.

Both parts of the place name have been rolled into one in my own hometown of Glasgow. Vinegarhill is a neighbourhood at Camlachie on the east side of the city that was once open fields and showground, and which from the 1870s attracted travellers and hosted Glasgow's annual carnival. Once again, an association with 'our' Vinegar Hill has been suggested, but as before there is also the now familiar and more mundane explanation of a firm of vinegar producers being located close by (its origins being in the first couple of decades of the nineteenth century). The only known association of the location with a battlefield seems to be the presence of replica 'Ypres Trenches', at the carnival in 1917 – 'including Dugouts, Periscopes, Trench Hospitals, and Dressing Stations, Trench Mortars, Ruined Farm Houses, etc.' (Anon., 2011).

The nearby presence of a malting plant, or vinegar factory, has also been noted in the case of Vinegar Hill in the estuary town of Bideford in Devon. Here, however, the name is associated with a narrow lane or alley which runs parallel to the river, close to where troops would have embarked for the Irish campaign of 1798. On their return it is said that the route along which they marched was named after the recent victory. This association with the Irish battlefield seems a credible one given the association of the town with the rebellion. Another connection was reported in the *Bath Chronicle and Weekly Gazette* in August 1799, when the local South Devon militia, under Lord

Rolle, was granted the freedom of Bideford, 'as a mark of esteem for their patriotic services in Ireland' (Kirby, 2018, p. 80).

It is apparent from the foregoing that during the nineteenth century and beyond, the Battle of Vinegar Hill did have a resonance on a global scale, stretching as far as Australia and the USA. Despite a recent resurgence of interest in the first and second Battles of Vinegar Hill (in Ireland and Australia, respectively) the possible association of these other place names with the site of the 1798 conflict has weakened over time, and it might be in some cases that rival origin stories for these place names have taken primacy. It is therefore very gratifying indeed to see the results of the Longest Day Project published in a volume which will hopefully get the wide circulation and international readership it deserves, and in doing so will help to once again give Vinegar Hill a global profile.

My own association with Vinegar Hill dates back to late 2013, when I was invited to attend a meeting at the National 1798 Rebellion Centre in Enniscorthy. The first meeting of what would become the project's steering group took place in late January 2014, with the extensive programme of archaeological fieldwork and historical research which is reported here being formulated at those meetings. The project engaged the expertise and passion of a large team and the scope of their individual and collective researches are contained in the chapters which follow. Unfortunately my commitments elsewhere, which included the archaeological investigation of the battlefield of Waterloo with Waterloo Uncovered, prevented me from playing an active role in the project, but it has been a pleasure to see the results of the work as it has progressed.

There are of course connections between Vinegar Hill and Waterloo, with a number of the British army regiments engaged in Ireland later going on to fight at one of the world's most famous battles. These included the 1st, 2nd and 3rd Foot Guards, now known as the Grenadier Guards, the Coldstream Guards and the Scots Guards. All three of these regiments took part in the defence of Hougoumont Farm, which has often been described as a battle within a battle. Since 2015, the archaeological investigations of Waterloo Uncovered have focused on Hougoumont, and buttons from the 2nd and 3rd Foot Guards were found close to the gate that famously was closed against the French by men from both of these regiments. The recovery of the Scots Guards buttons was especially rewarding, as the Coldstream Guards dominate the retellings of that episode.

The metal detector survey at Vinegar Hill has also come up trumps, and some of the finds made are to be envied by those working even at Waterloo. As pointed out in these pages, the metal detector results are the richest from any battlefield archaeology survey in Ireland, and the importance of this project in the history of battlefield archaeology in Ireland cannot be exaggerated. It is however the combination of archaeological and historical research which has reaped the greatest reward at Vinegar

Hill; it was a similar holistic approach that worked so well at the site of the 1746 Battle of Culloden (Pollard, 2009). The last battle of the Jacobite wars had, at least on the surface, some similarities with Vinegar Hill, with both the Irish rebels and the Jacobites in Scotland making a stand against a professional foe made up from British army regiments supported by volunteer and militia units. The comparison must be a limited one though, as the Jacobites at Culloden had more experience in battle and were better armed than the rebels at Vinegar Hill.

With their home-made pikes, the United Irishmen (and women) perhaps had more in common militarily with the various Radical movements active in England from the late eighteenth century and into the post-Waterloo period. The same types of weapons, their simple iron spearheads hammered out on the anvils of local blacksmiths, were also used by the insurgents in the Scottish Radical Rising in 1820 (Craig, 2020). Not far from Glasgow, the skirmish known as the Battle of Bonnymuir was fought, and here a small force of pike-armed rebels faced a yeomanry cavalry charge, playing out almost like a Vinegar Hill in miniature; like the 1798 rebellion it too resulted in executions and transportations to Australia.[2]

There is no suggestion on the part of the contributors to this volume that this is the final word on the Battle of Vinegar Hill, and that is the wonderful thing about this project – there is still work to do, not least in testing the geophysical anomalies to confirm if they do indeed represent mass graves. I look forward to a continued association with Vinegar Hill and those who have done so much to tell its story, but in the meantime this volume represents a vital stepping stone on the road to a fuller understanding of 1798, and I wish it all good fortune.

---

[2] One unit of Scottish fencible cavalry and one of infantry fought at Vinegar Hill. These were the Midlothian corps of fencible cavalry and the Dumbarton fencibles, the latter being a unit which impressed Sir John Moore, who deployed them elsewhere in Ireland as light infantry after the rebellion (McGuigan, 2008).

CHAPTER ONE

Preface: the Longest Day Research Project

RONAN O'FLAHERTY & JACQUI HYNES

A wet winter, a dry spring, a bloody summer and no King.
—Irish prophecy for the year 1798

The rebellion of 1798 is the most violent and tragic event in Irish history between the Jacobite wars and the Great Famine. In the space of a few weeks, 30,000 people – peasants armed with pikes and pitchforks, defenceless women and children – were cut down or shot or blown like chaff as they charged up to the mouth of the cannon.
—Thomas Pakenham, *The year of liberty* (1969)

INTRODUCTION

The Longest Day Research Project was born out of a chance encounter in a supermarket aisle in 2013 between the second named author (then manager of the National 1798 Rebellion Centre in Enniscorthy) and Tony Larkin, Director of Services, Wexford County Council. In this unlikely venue the germ of an idea was planted for a programme of interdisciplinary research to establish what really happened at Vinegar Hill on that fateful day of 21 June 1798.

However, first a little background about the Battle of Vinegar Hill itself. The latter half of the eighteenth century saw a wave of revolution sweep through North America and Europe. The ideas of democracy and self-determination that had fanned the flames of revolution in America and France found a ready audience in Ireland. The Society of United Irishmen was established in Belfast in October 1791 by a group of men whose aims were based on the French ideals of liberty, equality and fraternity for all citizens (Graham, 2000, p. 55). Driven underground, it re-formed in 1795 as a secret oath-bound society, determined to achieve full independence from Britain through armed rebellion. After the disappointment of a failed landing by a French expeditionary force in 1796, plans for a general uprising were devised and revised into the early months of 1798. However, the government struck first, arresting many of the leaders in March that year. A patchy uprising followed in May, fizzling out almost everywhere except Antrim, Down and Wexford. The rebellion in Wexford began on 26 May and was by far the most successful, with the entire county falling into rebel hands, a surprisingly effective rebel army taking the field and the establishment of what became known as the 'Wexford Republic'.

The enduring symbol of the rebellion in Wexford was and is Vinegar Hill. Standing just 120m above sea level, Vinegar Hill commands extensive views over the surrounding countryside and the town of Enniscorthy. It is the highest point of a ridgeline that runs in a north-west/south-east direction above the River Slaney. Near the summit, the ruins of a windmill are a familiar landmark on the northern approach to the town. However, what makes it special is the place it holds in Irish history, folklore and song as the scene of the most famous battle of the 1798 rebellion.

WHAT HAPPENED AT VINEGAR HILL?

On 21 June 1798, a camp of 20,000 insurgents on Vinegar Hill was surrounded and attacked by a force of between 13,000 and 15,000 government troops. In command of these was General Gerard Lake, supported by no less than three other generals and sixteen general officers. By this stage, the United Irishmen rebellion had been quelled everywhere else and only Wexford remained under arms. Lake had planned this battle as the final destruction of the rebel army, carefully manoeuvring his troops so that there could be no escape from the hill. A well-armed force, including both cavalry and infantry, with some 26 artillery pieces and a baggage train almost 7km long, Lake's army was the most formidable to take the field in Ireland in a century. By contrast, the rebel camp included large numbers of non-combatants who had taken refuge there. Those defending them and the hill were armed mainly with pikes and had only two rounds for their cannon. The line of command on the hill is unclear, as democratic principles applied even to that. However, the leaders included Anthony Perry, Miles Byrne and the charismatic Fr John Murphy of Boolavogue.

Lake was taking no chances. He gave the signal to advance with a gun at 4.00 a.m., by which time General Johnson seems already to have been engaging the rebels to the west of the town. When all contingents had moved or were en route to their assigned positions, artillery bombardment of the hill began, around 7.00 a.m. Lake had at his disposal a new exploding shell, used at Vinegar Hill for the first time. This was an anti-personnel weapon, designed to explode above the enemy or seconds after landing. It was shock-and-awe warfare of a kind never seen before in Ireland. Bombardment of the hill was combined with an infantry assault, and this deliberate orderly attack continued for perhaps two hours. Contemporary accounts talk of the rebel defenders being slaughtered where they stood in their trenches.

Meanwhile, in the town, General Johnson had pushed the defenders, led by William Barker and Fr Mogue Kearns, back into Market Square, where desperate house-to-house fighting continued throughout the morning. The rebels gradually yielded ground until they reached the bridge across the Slaney. Here they made a last stand. Despite overwhelming odds, they held the bridge – this was to prove crucial later.

On the hill, a multi-pronged attack was yielding results: Lieutenant General Dundas had made ground on the right flank, while Major Generals Loftus and Duff were pressing heavily on the centre and left. The rebel command began to contemplate a general retreat. They noticed a gap in the encircling forces to the south – a gap that was supposed to have been closed by the the Hon. Major General Needham. Fortunately for the rebels, a change to the orders issued by Lake meant that Needham was delayed in taking up his position, leaving that crucial gap open and earning himself a place in history as 'The Late General Needham'. Sometime after 9.00 a.m. the rebels began to flood through 'Needham's Gap', protected to the west by their comrades holding the bridge and by an extraordinary rearguard action led by Fr Thomas Clinch. Once the main body of rebels had made good their escape, the defenders at the bridge made a successful retreat themselves. However, the rearguard led by Fr Clinch was overrun and Clinch himself killed.

All might yet still have been lost, for as the rebel force flooded back towards Wexford town, Major General Needham finally came into sight and began a pursuit that could have inflicted terrible casualties had not the long-awaited relief force from Wexford under Edward Roche arrived on the scene. Roche and Needham engaged each other until, eventually, Needham withdrew. Some miles further south, the tattered remains of the rebel army limped into the temporary safety of Wexford town.

ATROCITIES

The rebellion in Wexford and elsewhere was marked by atrocities committed by both sides. In the lead-up to the rebellion, pitch-capping, flogging and half-hanging were all-too-common punishments meted out by the authorities. Once the rebellion was underway, the erstwhile victims were not slow to take revenge. While occupying the hill, summary execution of loyalist prisoners by the rebels was an almost daily occurrence, with the windmill used as a temporary prison. The worst excesses only stopped when the rebel command in Wexford town despatched a special armed guard of 130 men to Enniscorthy to take control of the situation and put an end to the atrocities, which had appalled many on the rebel side. However, some executions continued even after that.

On the crown side, beatings, torture and even rape were used to terrorize and dominate suspected rebels and their sympathizers in the local population. When crown forces retook the town of Enniscorthy on 21 June 1798, the rebel hospital was deliberately set alight, burning alive the wounded rebels inside. Many of those killed during the battle for Vinegar Hill were camp followers, women, children and the elderly. In all, it is reckoned that some 1,500 'rebels' were killed during the assault on the hill, while fatalities on the crown side were only 22. Sir Jonah Barrington, visiting the site shortly after the battle, said that the 'numerous pits crammed with dead bodies … seemed on some spots actually elastic as we stood on them'.

HISTORY OF RESEARCH

The events of 1798 have not wanted for either commentary or commemoration. There are significant historical accounts of the battle, including first-hand accounts, along with a plethora of other tomes compiled during the nineteenth century. These were often written to a specific political agenda, be that loyalist or nationalist, reflecting the social and political climate of the time – Musgrave's *Memoirs of the different rebellions in Ireland*, from 1801, Maxwell's *History of the Irish rebellion*, from 1803, and Hay's *History of the insurrection of the county of Wexford AD1798*, also from 1803, are all good examples of the genre. Later again, Fr Patrick Kavanagh's *A popular history of the insurrection of 1798*, first published in 1870, became the primary source for a nationalist interpretation of the rebellion in a newly independent Ireland. Fr Kavanagh's work played down the role of the United Irishmen, viewing these with a certain suspicion as members of a secret, oath-bound society. Instead, he portrayed the rebellion as an almost spontaneous peasant uprising in defence of the Catholic religion by an oppressed and tortured people, while carefully avoiding any suggestion of atrocities on the rebel side. For many even today, that remains the narrative of 1798.

Thomas Pakenham's seminal *The year of liberty*, first published in 1969, delivered a more balanced analysis of 1798 and remains one of the best overall introductions to the period for the general reader. The approaching bicentennial commemorations in 1998 sparked renewed interest in the rebellion, its origins, sponsors and international context. Some of the most important publications on the rebellion emerged around this time, including Dickson et al. (1993), *The United Irishmen: republicanism, radicalism and rebellion*, Bartlett et al. (2003), *1798: a bicentenary perspective* and a little later Guy Beiner's *Remembering the Year of the French* (2007) focusing on the importance of folk history and social memory. More recently, there have been a number of archaeological surveys of particular areas of the Vinegar Hill battlefield, specifically linked to the expansion of local schools and property development over the past ten years. These reports (pertaining to school expansion and development) show little evidence of battlefield archaeology, and there appears to be an absence of any archaeological research undertaken prior to domestic house constructions for this area as well. The (then) Department of the Environment, Heritage and

Preface: the Longest Day Research Project

Local Government, also commissioned a report on Vinegar Hill as part of the Irish Battlefields Project (Cronin, Fitzsimons & Shiels, 2008) and, while unpublished, this report was very generously shared by the department with the project team. This was a seminal report, and many of its insightful suggestions were to be confirmed or reinforced by work undertaken under the present project.

All of the work carried out to date has added immeasurably to our understanding of the wider context in which Vinegar Hill sits. However, despite that, critical details about the battle itself remained elusive, including just how many people were involved, the dispositions and movements of the combatants, the progress of the battle and the burial of the dead. It was to answer questions like this that the Longest Day Research Project was established.

THE LONGEST DAY RESEARCH PROJECT

This was a multi-disciplinary research programme funded by Wexford County Council. The overall objective was to undertake a programme of historical, archaeological and geographical research into the events and extent of the battles of Enniscorthy and Vinegar Hill (28 May and 21 June 1798, respectively). A total budget of €50,000 was made available to the project over a four-year period by Wexford County Council, which met the cost of commissioned specialist reports as well as some initial conservation of finds.

A project team was put in place, led first by Jacqui Hynes, then manager of the National 1798 Rebellion Centre in Enniscorthy, and then by Dr Ronan O'Flaherty, an independent researcher. Other team members included Rory O'Connor and Kieran Costello (both of the 1798 Rebellion Centre), Graham Cadogan (an independent researcher and 1798 re-enactor) and Tony Larkin (Director of Services, Wexford County Council). A steering group was also established to lend consultative supports to the project team, and help ensure that the research would be undertaken to the highest standards. Membership of this group included Professor Tony Pollard (Centre for Battlefield Archaeology, University of Glasgow), Paul Walsh (Department of Environment, Heritage and Local Government), Ian Doyle (the Heritage Council) and Robert Shaw (the Discovery Programme). The key stakeholders were identified as Wexford County Council, as one of the main owners of land on Vinegar Hill, Enniscorthy Town Council (now Enniscorthy Municipal District), the National 1798 Rebellion Centre, landowners in the vicinity of the research zone and the people of Enniscorthy – Vinegar Hill is 'their' hill and they are immensely proud of it. The investigations would also involve local historical and archaeological societies, re-enactment groups, community groups and local schools.

Much of the research was to be desk-based, looking at and analysing historical, cartographic and topographic information. An architectural survey of Enniscorthy town was also planned, focusing on the surviving architecture of 1798. The archaeological programme was designed to be non-invasive, relying on geophysical survey and a carefully planned metal-detection programme (which would involve recovery of finds). An underwater survey of the area around the 'old' bridge in Enniscorthy town (the William Barker Bridge), which saw heavy fighting, was also envisaged. The overarching objective was to locate as much as possible of the underlying archaeology, including any graves or burial sites, both to enhance our understanding of what happened at Vinegar Hill and to ensure that the battlefield, with its surviving lanes and ditches, could be properly protected into the future. No specific programme of excavation was planned, although this was not ruled out for any future investigative phases. All archaeological work was fully licensed through the relevant state authorities.

Between 2014 and 2018, the project team undertook or oversaw all the work that had been planned in its initial research design. This included historical research, folklore studies and outreach programmes undertaken by the team itself, along with commissioned reports including an architectural survey of Enniscorthy (by Edmund Joyce of Carlow IT), underwater investigation at the old bridge in Enniscorthy (by ADCO Ltd), a photogrammetry survey of the Windmill (by Coastway Ltd), geophysical surveys of areas of the hill (initial survey by LGS, followed by detailed surveys by Earthsound) along with an extensive programme of licensed metal detection (Rubicon & Earthsound). A novel field experiment was also undertaken in 2017 with the assistance of the Reserve Defence Force to find out just why General Needham was late. In addition to the project, some limited excavation was also carried out by Stafford McLoughlin Archaeology in 2014 in advance of work onto paths across the hill, the results of which were generously shared with the project. Highlights to emerge from the research include:

- the rediscovery of the notorious rebel prison 'Beale's Barn' – still standing and intact on a local farm;
- identification of a shortlist of candidates for the all-important 'Green Hill', whose early capture by crown forces dictated much of the subsequent course of battle;
- proof that 'The Late General Needham' could never have arrived at his assigned position on time, and was not motivated by any desire to prevent a massacre, as believed by many at the time (and even today);
- location by geophysics of a series of very large dug pits, just below the summit of the hill – strong candidates for mass graves;
- the discovery of a previously unknown older structure beneath the 'old' bridge across the Slaney;

Preface: the Longest Day Research Project

- an incredibly rich assemblage of finds from the metal-detection programme – the richest in fact from any battlefield as yet investigated in the state, and of a level of detail that allows key phases in the battle to be reconstructed.

PRESERVATION OF THE BATTLEFIELD

The work carried out under the Longest Day Research Project has confirmed the immense value of that very first report on Vinegar Hill which was commissioned as part of the Irish Battlefields Project (Cronin, Fitzsimons & Shiels, 2008). Similar comprehensive baseline research has now been completed on most other Irish battlefields as part of that wider project, and our experience at Vinegar Hill shows how this research can act as a catalyst for more detailed archaeological and historical investigation. The various reports produced by the Irish Battlefields Project allow local authorities and local communities to consider and plan the future management of their battlefields, armed with a solid body of initial research.

What makes Vinegar Hill so special is that the landscape of the core battlefield, the lanes, fields and ditches, has remained largely intact since 1798. Much of the area near and around the summit is owned by Wexford County Council and is maintained and protected by them. Other land on the hill itself is in agricultural use, as it has been for centuries, and as it was in 1798. However, even on these lands, at the heart of the battlefield, there are threats, chiefly in the form of illegal metal detection. Metal detectorists, some travelling for this purpose from abroad, have already stripped some parts of the hill of finds, with the loss forever of information that is crucial to our understanding of the battle. Increased vigilance by local users of the hill has frustrated more recent illegal activity, which shows the important role that the local community plays in protecting sites like this. However, areas slightly further afield that people have not traditionally appreciated to be part of the battlefield are also at risk, this time from inappropriate development. Other areas closer still have already been destroyed without any archaeological information being recovered.

Aside entirely from the archaeological impact of large-scale development on the hill, what is not fully appreciated is the *visual* impact that accompanies this, which intrinsically alters the landscape setting of the battlefield, and indeed of the windmill on its summit which is, of course, a national monument. Leaving aside the moral imperative of preserving for future generations a site that has passed to this generation virtually intact, there are also economic benefits to the preservation of the battlefield. These include its tourism value – yet to be realized, but real nonetheless. Battlefield tourism is a major industry internationally and Vinegar Hill, with its ease of access and intact landscape, is a unique tourism offering for Enniscorthy and Co. Wexford. The fact that so many of the participants on the crown side are names that won fame

1.1 Members of the steering group and others on Vinegar Hill, 31 Jan. 2014. *From left to right*: Tony Larkin, Robert Shaw, Graham Cadogan, Tony Pollard, Ronan O'Flaherty, Jacqui Hynes, Rory O'Connor, Kieran Costello, Ian Kidd, Cathy Keane, Damian Shiels. Photo by Patrick Browne. Courtesy of the National 1798 Rebellion Centre.

or notoriety in the American War of Independence and the Peninsular Wars, while a rebel leader went on to a prominent position in the French Army, adds immeasurably to the 'saleability' of this product. Large-scale development within the core area of the battlefield, no matter how well designed, will bring permanent, negative results and will permanently disfigure what is for many hallowed ground. However, Wexford County Council have shown vision and determination in their efforts to both understand and protect this special place, and there is every reason to hope that Vinegar Hill will stand witness for generations to come to the ambition and tragedy that was that first 'year of liberty', 1798.

ACKNOWLEDGMENTS

So many people have helped this project in so many ways. First and foremost, we thank Tony Larkin, deputy CEO of Wexford County Council, for the faith he has always shown in the project team and for having the courage and vision to support such an ambitious programme of research. We acknowledge with pleasure the gentle historical guidance of Brian Ó Cléirigh and the military knowledge shared so freely by Lord Edward's Own and the Napoleonic Association re-enactment groups. We are deeply grateful to Stafford McLoughlin Archaeology, Catherine Kavanagh of Wexford County Council, Wexford County Archivist Grainne Doran, members of Enniscorthy Municipal District, District Manager Liz Hore, the local community, local landowners, local schools and all our commissioned providers (who were always so much more than that). Very special thanks must go to Professor Tony Pollard of the Centre for Battlefield Archaeology, University of Glasgow, for his constant support and encouragement, and to battlefield expert Damian Shiels, without whose commitment, knowledge and friendship this research programme would not have achieved half of what it has.

James Bonsall and Damian Shiels would particularly like to acknowledge the archaeological metal detection and geophysics teams who carried out the licensed fieldwork and reporting on Vinegar Hill, particularly Michael Cahill, Ciarán Davis, Heather Gimson, Cian Hogan, Byron Jones, Enda O'Flaherty, Darren Regan and Hilde van der Heul. Conflict Archaeologist Sam Wilson acted as the metal-detection supervisor for the project, and his expertise in that role proved invaluable.

A special word of thanks is owed to the team at Four Courts Press, especially Sam Tranum, Martin Fanning and Anthony Tierney, for their support, attention to detail and patience throughout the many iterations of this volume. Finally, we cannot end without thanking the individual contributors for all their work in researching, drafting and perfecting their own chapters. This book belongs to them.

CHAPTER TWO

Who fears to speak of '98? A review of the sources

RORY O'CONNOR

INTRODUCTION

The epicentre of the 1798 rebellion in the south-east of Ireland was Enniscorthy town. Its strategic location in the centre of Co. Wexford, overlooked by the eminence of Vinegar Hill, made it an obvious tactical choice for the rebels in their campaign for control of the county. Richard Musgrave (1802, i, p. 430) describes it as

> a market, a post, and a borough town, which returned two members to parliament. It is divided into two parts by the river Slaney, over which there is a stone-bridge. The market-house, the court-house, and the principal streets are on the south side of it. Two suburbs called Templeshannon and Drumgoold lie on the north side, and at the foot of Vinegar-hill, a mountain which is quite close to the town. It is about twelve miles from the town of Wexford, sixteen from Ross, eighteen from Gorey, eight from Taghmon, six from Ferns, and nine and three quarters from Newtown-barry [Bunclody]. As the tide ebbs and flows to it, which makes the river navigable for barges of some burden, it was a place of considerable trade; and the inhabitants were between four and five thousand, before the desolating spirit of rebellion banished or destroyed a great portion of them.

The town witnessed two battles during the rebellion of 1798, generally recorded as the 'Battle of Enniscorthy' (28 May) and the 'Battle of Vinegar Hill' (21 June). Despite its title, the latter was actually fought over two locations – over the town itself and around and over the adjacent Vinegar Hill. In the period between these two battles, Enniscorthy and its surrounds were under insurgent control. Miles Byrne (1863, pp 69–70) notes the 'immense importance' of the first battle in his reflections, commenting that, had it been rapidly followed up by one or two more [victories] which at that time could have been so easily obtained victory would have been secured for the rebellion across Leinster, if not Ireland.

EXAMINING THE SOURCES

Although the Battle of Vinegar Hill was by no means the last engagement of the 1798 rebellion, it is remembered as the symbolic 'last stand' by many. Edward Hay (1803, p. 228) recalls how the rebels 'displayed vast courage and intrepidity before they abandoned the hill', while loyalists (Musgrave, 1802, ii, p. 12) recalled the 'peace and good order' that was restored once the insurgents were defeated on Vinegar Hill. These diverse viewpoints of the battle have ensured that Vinegar Hill has become one of the most discussed and debated battles over the past two centuries.

There are numerous accounts of the 1798 rebellion in Enniscorthy and its environs, with significant diversity of opinion and often lack of consensus, reflecting political or religious affiliations of the various authors. Given this, there is value in identifying, examining and further analysing some of the most significant and influential first- and second-hand accounts. This also offers the potential to pinpoint areas within the landscape that may contain material culture relating to the conflict or surviving built-heritage used during the rebellion – all of which helps to guide fieldwork in this area.

As mentioned, the Battle of Vinegar Hill is one of the most discussed engagements of the 1798 rebellion. However, many authors, particularly during the middle and latter half of the nineteenth century, simply regurgitated accounts first compiled by their predecessors. The statement 'history is written by the victors' is particularly applicable in this case – many prospective authors among the rebel leadership were either killed during the rebellion or executed afterwards. This meant that memoirs of the leaders on the rebel side are limited to accounts from Miles Byrne, Thomas Cloney and Edward Hay. From the perspective of the crown forces, however, there are letters, diaries and memoirs of the various battles from generals and officers alike, while from a civilian perspective the diaries written by 'loyalist' women of the town offer impassioned details. The transcripts of the trials of those accused of crimes perpetrated during this period also give first-hand information that is of immense value.

It is essential, however, to be attentive to the limits of these historical accounts. Many authors and eyewitnesses recalled only the significant events associated with its leaders, infamous deeds or the main proceedings of the battle. Lacking were exact locational references to areas of intense fighting, defensive structures or the burial of the dead, and this requires piecing together from a range of written, oral and cartographic sources. Thus, through examining the wide variety of available material, the opportunity for further archaeological, historical and geographical investigation and discovery is refined and directed.

The various written sources available to us are collated and discussed in this chapter, while the oral tradition is reviewed in chapter 12. First, however, an outline summary of the events themselves is provided.

HISTORICAL BACKGROUND OF REBELLION IN ENNISCORTHY

After the United Irishmen movement was outlawed and driven underground by the establishment, who saw its members as potential French allies, and after it re-formed in 1795 as a secret society, Theobald Wolfe Tone and other leading members travelled to France to seek aid for their planned uprising. This appeal for support first resulted in the failed French landing at Bantry Bay, Co. Cork, in December 1796 (Clements, 2011, p. 69). During the following eighteen months, the United Irishmen continued their plan for insurrection, while the establishment tried to brutally suppress the movement.

The rebellion was initially planned for April 1798; however, in March of that year, many leading members of the United Irishmen were arrested during a government raid on the Dublin house of one of their leaders, Oliver Bond (Jeffrey Jarrett, 2006, p. 162). As the Wexford delegate was late for this meeting, the level of organization in Co. Wexford remained unknown (Byrne-Rothwell, 2010, p. 53). Following these arrests, the rebellion was postponed until 23 May, when the entire country was expected to rebel. However, many counties only achieved what amounted to sporadic skirmishes before the mobilization dissipated. The insurrection in Dublin was suppressed within the day and although there was some success in Cos. Meath and Kildare, the United Irishmen in these areas were swiftly defeated by the crown forces, under the command of General Gerard Lake. The United Irishmen in Co. Wexford were slower to mobilize, and the rebellion didn't begin in the county until 26 May.

THE BATTLE OF ENNISCORTHY, 28 MAY 1798

The Battle of Enniscorthy, fought on 28 May 1798, was the first urban engagement during the rebellion in Co. Wexford. Hostilities had broken out in the county two days previously (26 May) at The Harrow, where, after a brief skirmish, some villagers from Boolavogue parish, led by Fr John Murphy, killed two members of the Camolin yeoman cavalry. This event is commonly identified as the beginning of the rebellion in Co. Wexford (Furlong, 1991, p. 50). Following this, historical accounts observe that United Irishmen in the north of the county began to assemble their forces on pre-determined hills.

On 27 May there were two brief engagements between the insurgents and the crown forces, on Kilthomas Hill and Oulart Hill. The former resulted in a victory for the crown forces while the latter witnessed the insurgent army orchestrating an effective ambush, which left 105 North Cork militia dead as opposed to only six rebels (Cleary, 1999, p. 87). Following their victory at Oulart, and with their numbers continuing to grow, the insurgent forces made their way the next day (28 May) to another pre-agreed assembly point at Ballyorill Hill. This hill lay only 4 miles north-west of Enniscorthy town (Gahan, 1995, p. 46).

The main rebel command at this point consisted of Reverend Fathers Michael and John Murphy (no relations), Miles Byrne and Edward Roche. Of these, Roche had some military experience and may even have been in overall command. The insurgent force was estimated to number 6,000–7,000, with approximately 600–1,000 bearing firearms. Facing this significant rebel army was a much smaller collective of crown forces. It comprised 70 North Cork militia, 100 members of the Enniscorthy yeoman infantry, 80 from the Scarawalsh infantry and fifty of the Enniscorthy cavalry (Dickson, 1955, p. 71). The defending forces were under the command of Captain William Snowe from the North Cork militia, boosted by several loyal Enniscorthy inhabitants who offered their assistance to defend the town.

The rebels planned to attack the town at various locations. The main body of pike and musket men would attack the defenders around the Duffry Gate area, while large flanking parties would extend to their right and left and attack the town from the Irish Street and St John's Street directions (Byrne, 1863, p. 42). Captain Snowe anticipated that the main rebel attack would come from the direction of the Duffry Gate and consequently placed 100 Enniscorthy yeoman infantry to defend that area. He also stationed the Enniscorthy cavalry and Scarawalsh infantry directly behind them in reserve. Small detachments of sharp-shooters were placed on prominent buildings in the town such as the Market House, while loyalist townspeople took positions in the upper floors of many of the buildings that lined the street. Captain Snowe decided that he himself should stay with the North Cork militia on the bridge which would be the last line of defence if the rebels broke through the town (Gahan, 1995, pp 47–8).

As the rebels made their way towards the Duffry Gate, the Enniscorthy yeomen advanced to intercept them. By the time both sides were within range to engage each another, the rebels split, as planned, into three groups. Upon seeing this, the crown forces deployed their cavalry, in the hope of disrupting the rebel lines. The cavalry, however, were met by a barrage of rebel musket fire, which left a number dead and the remainder in retreat (Hay, 1803, pp 139–40). In response to the rebel flanking manoeuvre, the Scarawalsh infantry were redeployed to defend against their left flank on Irish Street, while the rebel right flank was making steady progress towards the south of the town. The insurgents also made various attempts to wade across the River Slaney, eventually doing so at Blackstoops (to the north of the town).

In the meantime, the battle around the Duffry Gate became a stalemate, broken only when the rebel commanders orchestrated a stampede of cattle into the ranks of defenders. The crown infantry were sent into disarray and the rebels pressed their advantage by sending a full pike charge at the retreating soldiers (Field, 1851, p. 230).

After receiving desperate pleas for reinforcements, Snowe began to march his North Cork militia from the bridge towards Market Square. However, he then decided to divert them from this course and instead engaged those rebels attacking from St John Street. After a futile cavalry charge, Snowe and his men again retreated to the bridge, leaving those in Market Square to fend for themselves (Beatty, 2001, p. 77).

By this stage the battle had continued for almost two hours. Both sides had suffered significant casualties and, to compound matters, the thatched cabins along Irish Street had caught fire, either deliberately or from the musket volleys. The rebels had now pushed their opponents from Irish Street and the Duffry Gate to the area of Market Square, while the insurgents who had successfully crossed the river were now engaging the North Cork militia on the east side of the Slaney (Furlong, 1991, p. 68). With the town now engulfed in fire and smoke, Snowe realized he could not defend Enniscorthy indefinitely and decided to rally his men in a retreat along St John's Road. The rebels seem not to have recognized that their opponents were now in retreat and therefore did not pursue them to complete the rout. Musgrave (1802, i, p. 437) records that 73 members of the crown forces lost their lives in defending the town, while some 17 were injured. It is recorded that rebel casualties were some five times higher (Gahan, 1995, p. 54).

FROM 28 MAY TO 21 JUNE: THE COURSE OF THE REBELLION IN CO. WEXFORD

As news of the rebel success in Enniscorthy filtered through the surrounding countryside, the rebel forces established their camp on Vinegar Hill. Throughout the next day, insurgent leaders from surrounding parishes gathered their forces and proceeded to Vinegar Hill, considerably swelling the numbers there. The camp also acted as a place of refuge for families and other 'non-combatants' with rebel sympathies, as it was believed to be one of the few places, for the interim, unlikely to suffer an attack from crown forces (Cloney, 1832, p. 16).

The rebel leadership then considered which town to attack next. Many opted for New Ross in the belief that a successful outcome there would result in United Irishmen from neighbouring counties joining the rising. Others wanted to attack a town in the north of the county for similar reasons. It had also been decided to march on the garrison at Wexford town, but the garrison unexpectedly released senior members of the United Irishmen leadership (Edward Fitzgerald and John Henry Colclough) from prison, with the intention of negotiating with the insurgents in Enniscorthy. Fitzgerald and Colclough brought news that many other senior figures were still imprisoned in Wexford town and consequently it was decided that the focus should be on freeing these leaders. Late in the afternoon a force of up to 10,000 rebels left Vinegar Hill en route to a camp at Forth Mountain, with the intention of attacking Wexford town (Byrne, 1863, p. 66).

While encamped on Forth Mountain, the insurgent forces became aware of a column of Meath militia travelling near to their location on their way to reinforce the garrison defending Wexford town. After quick deliberation, rebel leaders from the barony of Bantry[1] sprang an ambush on these reinforcements and annihilated the column at the Battle of Three Rocks on 30 May 1798, capturing two howitzers in the process. After hearing of the ambush, the 1,200-strong Wexford garrison, under the direction of Colonel Maxwell, abandoned the town and retreated to the military fort of Duncannon. Later that same day, 30 May, the rebel army entered Wexford town. Almost all of Co. Wexford was now under rebel control (Cloney, 1832, p. 21).

Over the subsequent days, and following deliberations by the rebel commanders, it was decided to divide the army into two attacking groups, commonly referred to as the 'North Division' and the 'South Division'. The latter, under the leadership of Bagenal Harvey, would march west to attack New Ross. The former would further sub-divide, and a detachment, led by Miles Byrne, would attack the town of Newtownbarry (now Bunclody), while a larger force, under the leadership of Anthony Perry, would attack the towns of Gorey and Arklow (Gahan, 1995, pp 31–2).

On 1 June a 5,000-strong rebel force, under the joint command of Miles Byrne and Fr Mogue Kearns, attacked the garrison town of Newtownbarry. Positioning an artillery piece on the outskirts, the rebels forced the crown forces back into the town. This was followed by pikemen driving most of the defenders across the bridge into Co. Carlow (Byrne, 1863, pp 64–5). However, crown sharpshooters, still within the confines of the town, caused havoc among the rebels and upon hearing the gunfire, the retreating crown forces returned and inflicted 400 deaths among the insurgents, ultimately forcing the rebels to withdraw (Bartlett, 1997, p. 279).

On 4 June, a column of 400 crown forces, consisting of cavalry, yeomanry and militia and led by Lieutenant Colonel Walpole, were successfully ambushed as they traversed a narrow pass at Tubberneering, Co. Wexford. This was at the hands of the Northern Division under the command of Fr John Murphy. Walpole himself was slain along with 100 of his troops (Byrne, 1863, p. 73). The insurgents also captured three guns, which they would soon put to use at the Battle of Arklow. On learning of the rebel victory at Tubberneering, the crown forces abandoned the nearby important town of Gorey. The way was now clear for the United Irishmen to engage the crown forces at Arklow, and if successful, march on to Dublin.

Meanwhile, further south, rebel forces were closing in on the town of New Ross, where battle commenced at dawn on 5 June. Crown forces, expecting the rebel assault,

---

1 Located in the west of Co. Wexford. A barony is a sub-division of a county – there are eight baronies in Wexford.

had prepared defences in advance. They had a complement of 2,000 soldiers under the command of General Johnson. Bagenal Harvey, leading approximately 10,000 men, divided his troops into three groups. There was some initial success for the rebels when a force led by John Kelly (later made famous in the ballad 'Kelly the Boy from Killane') succeeded in breaching the Three Bullet Gate and seizing two-thirds of the town. However, in the early afternoon the crown forces rallied, and re-took all of the town (Alexander, 1800, pp 55–6). The remaining rebels withdrew to the east, having sustained approximately 2,500 casualties. Crown losses were roughly 250 personnel (Dunne, 2010, pp 267–8).

Early in the afternoon of 9 June, rebel forces, primarily commanded by Fr Michael Murphy, Anthony Perry, Edward Roche and Billy Byrne, commenced their assault on Arklow, Co. Wicklow. They began with cannon fire from various strategic points around the outskirts of the town, and the crown forces, under the command of General Needham and numbering 1,700, returned artillery fire from the fortified barricades they had constructed at all main entry points. The rebel forces, numbering approximately 10,000, and divided into separate contingents, advanced towards them but were repelled at all locations. Although a cavalry charge across the Avoca River was repulsed by the rebel forces, defeat overtook the rebels and at nightfall they withdrew under cover of darkness, unaware that crown forces throughout the town were almost out of ammunition. Fr Michael Murphy lost his life during the battle along with almost 500 of his men. The losses on the crown side were approximately 100 dead, and many were wounded.

With the losses at Arklow, New Ross and Newtownbarry, everything would soon change for the United Irishmen (Gahan, 1995, pp 154–5). Their initial successes would give way to a reassertion of government control over the county in a most definitive and authoritative fashion.

For an interim period, the insurgent forces of Wexford were not drawn into any significant further confrontations with the crown forces, whose attention was diverted towards rebels in Cos. Kildare and Meath, and in the Ulster counties of Antrim and Down. These uprisings were progressively suppressed by a significant force under the leadership of the commander-in-chief, General Gerard Lake (Chambers, 2003, pp 122–36). Once the insurrection in the other counties was stifled, Lake turned his attention to Wexford, and moved to crush the rebellion there.

On 16 June, General Lake issued his general orders for the Battle of Vinegar Hill. With enough reinforcements stationed in Dublin, Lake implemented his strategic offensive against the rebel forces in Co. Wexford. He intended to mass his strength along the northern, north-western and western borders of the county in order to begin his assault on 19 June. In preparation, the other main contingents of the crown forces began to move into position. General Moore broke camp at Clonmel, Co. Tipperary, and made his way to New Ross via Waterford, where he joined forces with Generals

2.1 'The [Rebel] Camp on Vinegar Hill', by George Cruikshank (Maxwell, 1866, p. 99). Courtesy of Wexford Public Library Service, Local Studies Collection.

Johnson and Eustace. Simultaneously Sir James Duff began to move through Co. Kildare, making for Newtownbarry, while Lake himself linked with General Dundas at Baltinglass, Co. Wicklow, and together they pushed southwards towards Carnew in Wexford. General Loftus, who on 17 June was stationed at Tullow, Co. Carlow, was instructed to combine his force with that of Dundas and Lake at Carnew, while General Needham awaited his orders in Arklow (Gahan, 1995, pp 179–82).

On 19 June, Gorey was re-taken by crown forces. On 20 June, crown and rebel forces engaged at the Battle of Foulksmills (or Goff's Bridge). In a decisive battle, the crown forces under the command of General Moore secured a hard-won victory. The defeated rebels flooded back to their camp at Three Rocks on Forth Mountain, just outside Wexford town. On the same day, followers of the rebel Thomas Dixon massacred 90 loyalist prisoners on Wexford Bridge, despite attempts by the rebel leadership to enforce better discipline and prevent atrocities.

The pieces were now in place for a final attack on the rebels on Vinegar Hill. In the interim, the situation for the inhabitants of Enniscorthy town and its environs remained perilous, with murders, attacks and plundering continuing to take place (see appendices 1–3 for further details).

THE BATTLE OF VINEGAR HILL, 21 JUNE 1798

The crown forces advancing on Vinegar Hill are generally believed to have numbered between 13,000 and 15,000 men fully equipped with muskets and artillery, and may even have numbered as many as 20,000 (see chapter 3). The commander-in-chief, General Lake, had planned to surround the rebels on all sides and prevent any escape from the hill. Each of his commanders had been designated a particular position to take up in advance of the assault. However, by nightfall on 20 June General Needham, who was to close off the route south from Vinegar Hill, had not yet arrived and this was to prove crucial later. The numbers of rebels on the hill may have been as many as 20,000, mainly armed with melée weapons such as pikes, and including many thousands of women, children and older people. To compound their woes, Edward Roche and promised reinforcements from Wexford town had not yet rendezvoused with them at the hill (Gahan, 1995, pp 205–6).

The battle began at dawn on 21 June, around 4.00 a.m., when General Lake gave the signal to advance. Crown forces under General Johnson may have already engaged the rebels to the west of Enniscorthy by this stage. Artillery bombardment of the hill began around 7.00 a.m. using a new exploding shell which caused havoc among the defenders. The bombardment was combined with an infantry assault on the hill that appears to have been fiercely resisted. Meanwhile, in the town, General Johnson had pushed the defenders, led by Barker and Kearns, back into the Market Square, where desperate house-to-house fighting continued throughout the morning. The battle raged for several hours across the town and hill but by 9.00 a.m. it was clear that the rebel cause was lost. The rebel forces in the town still denied Johnson the bridge, preventing him from crossing the Slaney and joining the general assault on the hill, and while they did so a general retreat commenced from the hill. General Needham, who was still to take up his intended position, had left a crucial gap open in the crown assault lines and through this the defeated rebels flooded down the road south towards Wexford. A fierce rearguard action held back the pursuing crown forces and prevented the retreat from turning into a rout. For a fuller account of the battle, see chapter 3 and for an analysis of why General Needham was late, see chapter 5.

MILITARY EYEWITNESS ACCOUNTS

Substantial eyewitness accounts survive of the battles of Enniscorthy, Vinegar Hill and the intervening period. From the insurgent viewpoint the three main military authors are Miles Byrne, Edward Hay and Thomas Cloney. From the government perspective, three significant eyewitness accounts survive in the form of the recollections of Archibald MacLaren and William Kerr and correspondence between General Gerald Lake and Lord Castlereagh (acting chief secretary for Ireland).

Miles Byrne

Of the three rebel leaders noted here, Miles Byrne was the only individual to fight at both Enniscorthy and Vinegar Hill. Therefore, his memoirs offer the only first-hand account of the course of these battles from an insurgent perspective.

Byrne was born in the townland of Ballylusk near Monaseed in 1780. He joined the United Irishmen in 1797, apparently influenced by another rebel leader, Anthony Perry of Inch. Byrne participated in the rebellion when he was only 18 years of age, fighting at the battles of Enniscorthy, Bunclody, Tubberneering, Arklow and Vinegar Hill. After the latter, he accompanied Fr John Murphy on the advance to and retreat from Castlecomer, Co. Kilkenny. He continued to lead his men until the end of the rebellion and eventually escaped to Dublin where he remained undetected from 1799 to 1803. He met Robert Emmet in Dublin and became one of his lieutenants. After the failure of Emmet's rising in 1803, Byrne once again escaped, this time to Paris. He was commissioned as an infantry officer in the Irish Legion of the French army and fought in the Napoleonic Wars, having a very distinguished career. He died aged 82 in Paris in 1862. Before his death, he compiled, with the assistance of his wife Fanny, his memoirs of the 1798 rebellion in Ireland.

Of the Battle of Enniscorthy on 28 May, Byrne recalls the now famous incident of the rebels driving a herd of cattle through the crown forces and the town itself:

> Every disposition that could be thought of was now in readiness, and at half past one o'clock, father John at the head of his little army left the hill and marched to attack Enniscorthy. A small advance guard of two hundred men with fire arms flanked by some pikemen, preceded him. They were met at the Duffrey gate, outside of the town, by the whole military force of the garrison, composed of several corps of infantry and cavalry, commanded by captains Pounden, Cornocks, Richards, Jacobs, etc., with the exception of captain Snow of the North Cork militia, who did not think it prudent to quit the town and march with the infantry under his orders: probably in consequence of the severe lesson which his regiment had received the day before on Oulard Hill.
>
> Father John fearing it would be very difficult to get his pikemen to attack this mass of infantry so well posted, flanked on one side by the river Slaney, and on the other by houses and walls, from which a continual fire was kept up, and many of his men killed when they advanced, bethought himself of a stratagem, after consulting with the other leaders; it consisted, in getting some thirty or forty of the youngest and wildest of the cattle brought from the rear of his column goaded on by some hundreds of brave, decided pikemen, which immediately threw the Enniscorthy infantry into the greatest confusion.
>
> The more they fired, the more the cattle and their drivers advanced through the smoke and balls, until the line was completely broken, and all forced to

retreat precipitately into the town, where captain Snow and his infantry had remained on the bridge and secured thus the passage to this panic stricken army, that boasted in the morning they would never return until all the insurgents were exterminated. They now however betook themselves to the houses, from which a tremendous firing was kept up from the windows and doors on the insurgents, who bravely pursued them into the town. Though exposed to the greatest danger, under the terrible fire, and seeing their comrades fall dead by their side, yet the people set to work calmly and determinedly to besiege every house where the enemy took refuge. Such perseverance and courage finally succeeded. (1863, pp 58–60)

He also implores:

I trust that one day, when poor Ireland will be free, that there will be a monument raised to the memory of those brave men who so heroically contributed to gain the battle of Enniscorthy: to Thomas Synnott, who with his little band waded the river Slaney, above the town, under the fire of the enemy; and to those fine fellows in the suburbs, who set fire to their own houses in the rear of the king's troops, and made them thereby suppose that they were surrounded on all sides, and caused them to fly with confusion in every direction. (1863, p. 63)

With regard to the later Battle of Vinegar Hill, Byrne's initial feelings of the impending battle were that

We were doomed to fight the battle of Vinegar hill in the absence of general Edward Roche and his brave division of five thousand strong, and the best marksmen of the Irish army.

He also recalls how the rebels had failed to make defensive preparations in advance of the battle:

I had not seen Vinegar hill since the morning after the battle of Newtownbarry, the 2d of June, and I was surprised to find that scarcely any thing had been done to make it formidable against the enemy; the vast fences and ditches which surrounded it on three sides, and which should have been levelled to the ground, for at least a cannon shot, or half a mile's distance, were all left untouched. The English forces, availing themselves of these fences, advanced from field to field, bringing with them their cannon, which they placed to great advantage behind and under the cover of the hedges and fences; whilst our men were exposed to a terrible fire from their artillery and small arms, without being able to drive them back from their strongholds in those fields. (1863, pp 169–72)

2.2 The charismatic rebel leader Miles Byrne. Having avoided arrest after the rebellion, he joined Robert Emmet's failed rising in 1803, escaping then to France, where he pursued a long and distinguished military career. Photograph taken in Paris in 1859.

Edward Hay

Edward Hay was born at Ballinkeele (Co. Wexford) into a Catholic family of large land owners. His brother John was a rebel leader (and was executed for this afterwards) and his brother Philip was a member of the crown forces. Although Edward himself had no active involvement in the fighting, he was tried (and acquitted) for involvement in the rebellion. Due to his brother John's prominent position in the leadership, Edward was most likely privy to the directives of the insurgent commanders. He was the first author to publish a history of the rebellion from a nationalist perspective. This was in 1803, just five years after the rebellion, and of necessity his approach, while sympathetic, remains cautious, presumably to protect his own position.

As mentioned, Edward Hay was not present during either battle in Enniscorthy, although he does comment upon both, and did witness the aftermath of the Battle of Vinegar Hill as part of one of the delegations that sought terms of surrender from the crown forces on 22 June (Hay, 1803, p. 234). Of this he notes (1803, pp 234–5):

> We then hoisted a white handkerchief as our flag; and could descry the country all along between that and Enniscorthy in a most dreadful situation; houses on fire, dead men and women strewed along the road, and in the fields; while the soldiers were hunting for such as might be concealed in the ditches, and bringing down every person they met; in fine, it was altogether a dreadful picture, exhibiting all the horrors of war! … the town exhibited a dreadful aspect, as the greater part of the houses, which had escaped until the arrival of the army, were still on fire; and the house which had been used as an hospital by the insurgents, and which was set on fire with all the patients in it, continued burning until next morning, when I saw a part of a corpse still hissing in the embers.

Thomas Cloney

Cloney, although forwarded for court martial, was one of the fortunate rebel leaders who avoided execution after the rebellion. He was condemned to death, but that sentence was later commuted to banishment for life to the penal colony in New South Wales. After spending some time in gaol, he was released on the condition he leave Ireland for a period of two years. He published his memoirs in 1832, recalling how he had joined the rebels on Vinegar Hill the day after the Battle of Enniscorthy (1832, p. 16):

> The innocent and guilty were alike driven into acts of unwilling hostility to the existing Government; but there was no alternative; every preceding day saw the instruments of torture filling the yawning sepulchres with the victims of suspicion or malice; and as a partial resistance could never tend to mitigate the cruelty of their tormentors, I saw no second course for me, or indeed for any Catholic in

my part of the country, to pursue. I joined the people and took an affectionate farewell of my father and sisters, when he, as I before stated, was in a dying way, and my sisters quite unprotected. Their distraction of mind at my parting is not to be described. This was not a moment for indecision. I proceeded as a Volunteer, among many others, to Enniscorthy, without authority or command. I belonged to no Society under the United Irish organization, and possessed no claim to distinction, or any right to command; and I believe it is a matter of rare occurrence, that those who are invested with power, willingly submit to have that power abridged, or usurped by one who had not the slightest pretensions to seek it, even did I seek for such an unenviable distinction.

He describes his attempts to calm the situation on Vinegar Hill on that day:

My mind occupied with reflections, such as the melancholy scenes before me had suggested, I ascended Vinegar Hill, wishing to turn my eyes from those sickening objects which none but persons divested of all humanity could take pleasure in beholding …

On the hill were assembled some thousands of people, inhabitants of that part of the county north and north-east of Enniscorthy, many of whom bore evident marks of the dangers they had encountered in the two preceding days – some recounted the actions they had performed against the enemy, and showed wounds that proved them not destitute of courage; others mourned their children, brothers, relatives and friends, who fell in the late engagements, or who had suffered death previously by torture …

I soon found my situation among the people rather perilous; how indeed could it be reasonable under such strong excitations to fury and revenge, and owning no obedience to any controlling power, to expect that they would stop to listen to the sober advice of a stranger. Their passions could not then be soothed, nor their anger appeased. I had very few acquaintances in that part of the county from which those people came, yet I expostulated with them on the impropriety of their indulging in a spirit of revenge; that their actions should be deliberate if they hoped for ultimate success; and that as persons of every religious persuasion were embarked with them in a common cause, they should be particularly careful to abstain from any acts of violence that would give their proceeding the character of a religious war, and thereby alienate men from their cause.

The result of my interference soon convinced me how futile is the task of attempting to subdue the disorderly passions of an enraged multitude. (1832, pp 17–18)

Having participated in the battles of the Three Rocks, New Ross and Foulksmills, Cloney was part of the delegation dispatched to seek terms of surrender from General

Lake at Enniscorthy on 22 June. Of their hazardous journey accompanied by Captain O'Hea of the North Cork militia Cloney recalls (1832, p. 66):

> Very different were the dangers which I had to encounter, in conveying an officer dressed in full uniform through the entire body of retreating Insurgents, maddened by defeat and despair … But as neither Captain Hea nor myself put on a disguise of any kind, it was to the interposition of providence we owed our lives on that eventful day. Many guns were presented at him, and the murderous trigger about to be drawn at different stages of the journey from Wexford to Enniscorthy; yet some friend, some acquaintance, or person whom the leaven of mercy had not yet abandoned, would stay the upraised and hostile arm … but on my explaining to them the objects of our journey, or on the kind interference of some humane friend, of whom I had many among the retreating Insurgents, our lives were preserved.

He gives a vivid description of the carnage he perceived along the line of the rebel retreat from Vinegar Hill (1832, pp 68–9):

> On coming within about a mile of Enniscorthy town, we could perceive many of the soldiers still engaged in the work of slaughter. The dead and dying were scattered promiscuously in fields, in dykes, on the roads, or wherever chance had directed their last steps, and where their barbarous butchers hastened to put a period to their miseries. In one place we beheld some men with arms, and some with legs off; and others cruelly mutilated in various ways; horses, with their necks broken, and their cars, with women and children under them, either dead or dying in the road and ditches, where, in their precipitate flight, they had been upset. The town and environs of Enniscorthy presented to the view such a picture as no pencil could attempt to draw.

From the government perspective, we have three main accounts to draw upon, i.e. those of Archibald MacLaren, William Kerr and the commander-in-chief himself, General Gerard Lake. As these accounts are analysed in considerable detail in chapter 6, only a brief overview is provided here.

Archibald MacLaren

MacLaren was under the command of General Needham during the Battle of Vinegar Hill and because of the later arrival of General Needham to his designated position, he did not actively participate in the battle itself. His account, from his removed position, serves to outline the effectiveness and impact of the artillery in any battle. It also helps to pinpoint areas in which the crown force's infantry assaults took place (MacLaren, 1798, pp 27–9).

William Kerr

William Kerr, aide-de-camp to General Loftus, details the role of the artillery during the battle and helps identify the likely location of the 'green hill', the area in which Loftus placed his guns during the battle, and which allowed them to enfilade the rebel lines. Kerr also outlines the sequence of the infantry assault and failed rebel counter-attacks (Bartlett, 1988, pp 82–5).

General Gerard Lake

In the immediate aftermath of the Battle of Vinegar Hill, General Gerard Lake composed a report of the battle for Lord Viscount Castlereagh (then acting chief secretary of Ireland). The report outlined the formation of the crown forces during the battle and highlighted the significant contributions of the light infantry and the artillery. The report also includes the return of ordnance seized from the rebels after the battle (Musgrave, 1802, ii, pp 440–1). Lake appears to have been somewhat concerned himself at the actions of some his troops and the potential for atrocities by government forces. In a letter written to Castlereagh from Enniscorthy on 21 June 1798, Lake commented, 'The troops behaved excessively well in action, but their determination to destroy everyone they think a rebel is beyond description and wants correction' (Castlereagh, 1848, i, p. 221).

CIVILIAN EYEWITNESS ACCOUNTS

Contemporary accounts of the rebellion in Enniscorthy also survive in the personal diaries of those writing at the time, or in post-rebellion accounts of insurgent court martials. The diaries available in the historical record are written mostly by women, who were both civilian witnesses and profoundly impacted by the course of the rebellion. The recollections of Jane Barber, Barbara Lett and Alicia Pounden offer first-hand accounts of Protestant women during the rebellion. There appear to be no surviving diaries or narratives written by those considered civilian 'rebel' supporters. Additional extracts from the diaries mentioned here can be found in appendices 2, 3 and 4.

Jane Barber

Barber was born about 1783 and describes herself as follows:

> My father's name was Samuel Barber. He held a small farm within two miles of Enniscorthy, called Clovass; it contains but twenty-one acres … It had been in our family since the Battle of the Boyne, for I am descended from a Williamite … We had four milch cows and sent milk and butter to Enniscorthy; several

dry cattle and plenty of pigs and poultry, in particular we had a great number of geese, for a beautiful trout stream ran through our ground. Besides working horses, we had two very excellent ones, one which we thought good enough afterwards to mount a rebel General.

We kept but one servant girl, for both my mother and myself were active and hardy; and we kept one labourer in constant employment – poor faithful Martin. Our kitchen was always open to the poor travellers and many a handful of meal and boiling potatoes as my dear father encouraged me to bestow on those that wanted. It was not in this world he met a return for it....

My father was advanced in life when he married, indeed upwards of forty, but my mother was much younger and I was their second child. He had five more at the time I speak of, the eldest William, was a fine, well grown boy of sixteen or upwards; I was eleven months younger, not much above fifteen, but I was considered a cute and sensible girl for my years. I had two sisters, one eleven, the other six, a brother of four, and my mother had lain-in another little boy only six weeks before the fearful times which I am now endeavouring to describe. (Beatty, 2001, pp 70–1)

Details from her diary are reproduced in appendix 2 (based on Beatty 2001, pp 70–89). Barber recalls in traumatic detail her experiences over the next six weeks and offers the most sobering description of the rebellion in Enniscorthy.

Barbara Lett

Barbara Lett of Killaligan, Enniscorthy was born in 1777. Her father was a surveyor of excise in Enniscorthy, and he was among the Protestant prisoners piked to death on Wexford Bridge on 20 June 1798. In 1859, at the age of 82, Lett wrote down her experiences of the rebellion, expressing the bitterness she felt at her family's mistreatment. She recalled many details of the rebellion, but more specifically the names of those she encountered and their actions during this time. Her story reflects a 'large farmer' loyalist perspective but is a balanced one as she offers opinion, both positive and negative, of actions from both sides of the conflict. See appendix 3 (based on Beatty, 2001, pp 117–44).

Alicia Pounden

Alicia was the wife of John Pounden of Daphne and was born in 1772. She married John in 1786. As magistrates both he and his brother Joshua showed kindness to their Catholic tenants and allied themselves with the liberals on Catholic issues. Both men served in Solomon Richard's Enniscorthy yeoman cavalry. John and Joshua fought in the defence of Enniscorthy on 28 May and John was killed in the fighting. Alicia's diary reflects the views of a liberal gentry family, but like Jane Barber's diary, it also records the conditions suffered by Protestants in the wake of the Battle of Enniscorthy, where liberals and conservatives alike suffered significant losses. See appendix 4 (based on Beatty, 2001, pp 145–52).

George Taylor

George Taylor was a travelling preacher of the Methodist Church and was the author of *A history of the rise, progress, and suppression of the rebellion in the county of Wexford, in the year 1798*, first published in 1800. He lived in Ballywalter in the parish of Ballygarret. The historian Charles Dickson says of Taylor that he was a zealous 'loyalist' with obvious evangelistic leanings. Seamus de Vál (1998, p. 49) describes his work as 'chiefly valuable where he describes events of where he was an actual eye witness, particularly in the Gorey neighbourhood and in Wexford town where he had a very narrow escape from death on Wexford Bridge'. He also comments on the battles of Enniscorthy and Vinegar Hill, and of the establishment of the rebel camp there and their 'Tree of Liberty', shouting '*Vive la Republique*' and '*Erin go Braugh*' (Taylor, 1800, p. 146).

Witness evidence from the trials

The *Report on Irish prisons* for 1798, published in the *Commons Journal* in 1799, shows that between August 1798 and February 1799, nearly 400 people were tried by court martial and of those 131 were executed. The unremitting hunt for former rebels began in the immediate aftermath of the defeat at Vinegar Hill and, over the subsequent days, the court martials were brief and sentences carried out immediately. These swift trials continued until Lord Cornwallis intervened in late July 1798, ordering that all sentences with supporting documentation were to be forwarded to him for confirmation or disavowal of sentence (Sweetman, 2013, p. vii).

Vinegar Hill and Enniscorthy are mentioned extensively in witness evidence from these court martials, with some twenty-seven men 'tried'. Of these, two were found 'not guilty'; eleven were sentenced to death; eight had their sentences to death commuted to 'transportation' for a defined period (usually for life) and six accounts gave no verdict, or the trial appears not to have concluded. A full list is recorded in appendix 5.

SECONDARY SOURCES

There are numerous publications by those commenting on the course of the rebellion in Enniscorthy and its environs, and a scan of the bibliography at the end of this volume will illustrate the diversity of those used as part of our research. These are merely the 'tip of the iceberg' in a sea of published works pertaining to this period both nationally and internationally and spanning some 220 years. Some are written with political or religious biases, whereas those written from the time of the bicentenary to the present day attempt a more impartial historical analysis and reflection. In addition, there is also an extensive body of folklore to be considered: on this point Guy Beiner comments that 'the history of the 1798 rebellion in Ireland can benefit from an examination of oral traditions, which need to be located within a larger context of Irish folk history' (Beiner, 2006, p. 81). The folk tradition is considered in detail in chapter 12.

In terms of the historical narrative then, there are two significant accounts from the 'loyalist' perspective and two from the 'nationalist' perspective that provide a starting point for our study of the secondary sources. The accounts of Sir Richard Musgrave and James Gordon offer the loyalist perspective. Fr Patrick F. Kavanagh and Brother Luke Cullen offer details from the nationalist perspective. These, coupled with many others, when combined together, offered invaluable information in our search for the course of events and remaining traces of the rebellion in Enniscorthy.

Sir Richard Musgrave composed one of the largest accounts of the 1798 rebellion in his two-volume work *Memoirs of the different rebellions in Ireland*. According to Gibney (2009) his publication is completely biased towards the side of the crown and built around an anti-Catholic framework. However, for a contemporary author, he went to great lengths to collect first-hand accounts and testimonies even while the rebellion was still ongoing, and he gives full accounts of both the Battle of Enniscorthy and the Battle of Vinegar Hill. Musgrave's accounts were so substantial that his work was plagiarized by authors well into the nineteenth century, including W.H Maxwell, whose account had the addition of illustrations by the illustrator George Cruikshank.

Reverend James Gordon, rector of Killegney, wrote his own history of the rebellion in 1803, but his moderate interpretation provoked animosity between himself and Musgrave. The second edition of his publication included 'a reply to the observations of Sir Richard Musgrave upon his work' (Gordon, 1803).

Father Patrick Kavanagh's account is undoubtedly the main force behind the elevation of Fr John Murphy to prominence in the public awareness of the leaders of the 1798 rebellion. The tone for his work is set in his preface to the first edition:

> The heroic men who took part therein have, indeed, passed away to that happier country where the tears of the oppressed are dried – where might is no longer the enemy of right, where no tyrant threatens, and no slave weeps in fetters; but their memory still remains, a bright light to guide us through darkness to the holy Temple of Freedom.

Brother Luke Cullen, throughout the mid- to late 1800s, collected a large number of folk memories from both participants and civilians during the rebellion. For this study, the significance of his work comes in the form of an account given by a Wicklow insurgent who participated in the defence of the bridge during the Battle of Vinegar Hill (Cullen, 1959, pp 26–7).

A very interesting account also comes from John Jones in his book *An impartial narrative of each engagement which took place between His Majesty's forces and the rebels during the Irish rebellion, 1798, including very interesting information not before made public carefully collected from authentic letters.* It offers a vivid insight to the battle of Enniscorthy town, with particular details of the engagement that took place around what is now the William Barker Bridge (Jones, 1834, p. 57), which may help inform archaeological research around this area.

The bicentennial of the rebellion in 1998 generated new interest in the period, resulting in a flurry of new analytical and synthetic publications, revisiting and sometimes challenging earlier conceptions of the rebellion. While it is not possible to consider these works here (the purpose of this chapter being to elucidate the path of the Battle of Vinegar Hill, not the origin or philosophy of the rebellion), the interested reader will enjoy exploring the many publications to emerge around and after this time. Of particular interest will be Bartlett et al. (2003), *1798: a bicentenary perspective*; Keogh and Furlong (1996), *The mighty wave*; Keogh and Furlong (1998), *The women of 1798*; Beiner (2006), *Remembering the Year of the French*; and from 1993, *The United Irishmen*, edited by Dickson, Keogh and Whelan. A visit to the National 1798 Rebellion Centre in Enniscorthy – itself a legacy of the bicentenary – will also bring the story vividly to life.

GRAVES OF THE FALLEN

An important aspect of the literature review was to source information that could potentially identify sites of mass graves from the period, and although the Battle of Vinegar Hill features prominently in nineteenth-century Irish historical literature, burial accounts of the deceased in these contemporary records are, on the whole, scarce and lacking specific locational details.

While trying to identify possible locations on Vinegar Hill, we need to be mindful of two distinct 'phases' of burial activity. The first encompasses the period between 28 May and 21 June, where current estimates suggest up to a hundred 'loyalist' prisoners were executed by rebels on the hill (Gahan, 2010, p. 148). The second phase incorporates the immediate aftermath of the battle, where possibly hundreds of 'rebel' dead, including non-combatants, were either buried in mass graves or left (for an unknown period) where they fell in the adjacent fields, roads and ditches. Recent estimates suggest that approximately 1,500 insurgents and camp followers died at Vinegar Hill, most of whom were presumably buried on site. By contrast, only 20 members of the crown forces are recorded as killed during the battle (two subalterns, two serjeants, sixteen rank and file) (Musgrave, 1802, ii, pp 440–1). What records exist suggest that these were removed from the hill and buried in local graveyards.

Contemporary accounts of the fate of rebel victims identify a variety of disposal methods. It appears that, initially, the rebels made little attempt to bury their bodies, as testified by three separate eyewitnesses (Gurley, Magee, Whitney – see Gahan, 2010, pp 145–7). They recount seeing dozens of bodies lying unburied 'outside the mill' (Whitney) or 'along the hillside' (Gurley). However, over the intervening weeks, most likely due to health and safety and sanitation concerns, bodies were buried in a variety of ways, either individually, in small groups or in mass graves at the same site.

There are numerous accounts of single burials, but one interesting one is of the 'miraculous' survival of the Enniscorthy glazier Charles Davis. He fought in the defence of Enniscorthy on 28 May, but was subsequently captured by rebel forces. He was shot at least twice and suffered numerous pike wounds. Laid in an individual shallow pit and covered lightly with sods, Davis was still alive the following morning. With the aid of a priest he was brought home to his wife, who nursed him back to health (*Protestant Advocate,* 1813, p. 653). Also there is the story of William Reynells, who was executed by the rebels on Vinegar Hill. His body was subsequently retrieved by his family for re-burial in Monart, Enniscorthy, Co. Wexford, where his tomb still stands. This story is discussed in greater detail in chapter 12.

Still other accounts suggest that the bodies of several victims may have been drawn to the River Slaney and disposed of there. This has parallels with the aftermath of the Battle of New Ross. An anonymous chronicler cited by Taylor describes the bodies of the executed at Enniscorthy as being

> reduced to a state of putrefaction, that at length became so offensive to the murderers, who drew them to the waterside, where they covered many with the sand and threw others into the river (Taylor, 1800, pp 153–4).

Jane Barber also makes similar claims, stating that bodies from the Battle of Enniscorthy 'had been thrown into the Slaney' (Beatty, 2001, p. 86).

In the weeks following the Battle of Vinegar Hill, two contemporary authors referred to bodies and graves there. General Sir John Moore wrote during a halt in Enniscorthy on 10 July 1798 that 'Vinegar Hill stinks of dead bodies half buried' (Moore, 1904, p. 305). Sir Jonah Barrington wrote that there were 'numerous pits crammed with dead bodies on Vinegar Hill … seemed on some spots actually elastic as we stood on them' (Barrington, 1827, pp 274–5). The latter could easily be referring to the graves of prisoners executed by the rebels rather than those of the rebels themselves. Of particular interest in these accounts is the mention of 'bodies half buried' and 'pits crammed with dead bodies' being described as 'elastic' which may allude to the difficulty experienced in the burial of the dead due to the underlying geology of the site, with rock lying close to the surface at many points. This point is exemplified in an extract from a letter to the editor of the *Missionary Magazine*, composed two years after by a travelling preacher, William Cooper, concerning rebel massacres during the rebellion. Cooper writes:

> I walked one evening on Vinegar-hill; I had to move the earth with my foot, and the sculls of the buried slain appeared in almost every part, not entirely rock; tufts of human hair lay thick on the surface of the earth, and on the bushes and crags of mountains …

Enniscorthy inhabitants would recall similar experiences to William Cooper's over the subsequent decades and generations, as recorded by Dick Donohoe:

> The old people of the area close to the hill and many of whom I was well acquainted with would tell of cart loads of the fallen being buried in shallow graves in the small fields under the hill overlooking Enniscorthy. One account was of the Whiteness of the fields, with upturned bones, which remained for years after the rebellion … (Donohoe, 1998, p. 62)

There are three accounts which offer pointers to a potential mass-grave site and although recorded sixty years apart they do seem to corroborate each other. The first account is an extract taken from a letter penned in Waterford dated 18 July 1801 by Anthony Sinnot to the editor of the *Gentleman's Magazine*, 'Sylvanus Urban'. It concerns Sinnot's description of Vinegar Hill, Enniscorthy and New Ross. In relation to Vinegar Hill, Sinnot writes:

> At the declivity of the hill there is a vast pit, in which the bodies of the unfortunate men who were killed in this ruinous and fatal contest are deposited, to the number (as I was informed) of five hundred. The south side of the hill next [to] Enniscorthy is for some yards covered with the bones of men and animals, which are bleached as white as ivory by the weather. Near the summit of the hill is a gibbet, on which the bodies of three men who were active in the rebellion are suspended; this sight is very disgusting to the inhabitants, as the bodies can be very distinctly seen from the town; and a certain description of persons, yelep'd [called] Orangemen, amuse themselves by firing at the gibbet, and running their bayonets through the bodies.

The second extract is taken from a letter dated Enniscorthy, 14 December 1801. Its author, an Enniscorthy inhabitant signed 'Normannus', composed the letter as a rebuttal to Sinnot's earlier publication in the *Gentleman's Magazine*. Normannus writes:

> That the hill or any part of it is covered with bones, is totally and notoriously unfounded. Equally so is the assertion that the bodies of the gibbeted malefactors can be distantly, or at all, seen from the town; when the avarice or superstition of their wives and children had stripped the miserable culprits of their clothing after execution, a subscription of the loyalists of this town was made to cover the disgusting carcasses with pitched bags, and such bags were actually put upon them within 48 hours after the sentence of the law had been carried into effect. Neither has the story of Orangemen firing at the bodies a more justifiable foundation; had such an occurrence taken place, had it ever happened, I as an inhabitant must have heard it …

This account is particularly interesting in that through its rebuttal of Sinnot's letter it only discounts aspects of the account, leaving the initial elements of Sinnot's account – describing a vast pit at the declivity of the hill containing the bodies of 500 individuals. It also seems to accept the presence of a gibbet on the hill.

The third account suggesting the presence of a mass grave on Vinegar Hill is recorded by Michael Banim in the notes to his novel *The croppy*. The book was originally published in 1828, before which Banim visited Vinegar Hill and received the following account from 'a respectable, well-clad peasant of advanced age'. Banim writes:

> This man described the scene of slaughter, perpetrated on Vinegar-Hill, and pointed out to me how the burial of the slain was effected. A deep trench was dug at the base of the eminence, the bodies were laid therein, and the earth and stones from above, tumbled down to fill the excavation. (Banim, 1865, p. 432)

Banim's and Sinnot's accounts provide corroborating evidence that a mass grave or graves were dug on Vinegar Hill to take the bodies of the rebel slain. The two accounts may even refer to the same grave. For example, Banim describes the mass grave as a 'deep trench' while Sinnot describes it as a 'vast pit'. Both writers also locate the grave(s) quite similarly: Banim puts it 'at the base of the eminence' while Sinnot points to it being at 'the declivity of the hill'.

The above accounts make it clear that Vinegar Hill was the site of considerable burial, all of which seems to have been carried out relatively close to the summit or in fields directly below. This information helps define a general area over which geophysical research can be carried out, for the purpose of locating these graves. It is also possible that the results of such a survey could differentiate between burials of rebels by crown forces and burials of prisoners executed by the rebels, due to the likely dimensions and morphology of the graves in each case. The very limited geophysical survey undertaken as part of the Longest Day Research Project may have located the first of these mass graves: working on the basis of the various pointers provided by the literary accounts of the day, an area of land just below and to the east of the modern car park was selected for survey. The results, discussed in detail in chapter 8, were remarkable including identification of a series of pits in this area, one of which was 17m long. Is this a mass grave, perhaps even that recorded by Banim and Sinnot? It may well be.

CONCLUSION

It is true to say that any study of a historical period that has evoked such diverse opinions and passions is akin to having a jigsaw puzzle with the pieces scattered over a wide area. The review of the literature presented here has been no different. There are accounts that show political and religious bias, that (understandably) try to portray one side as more heroic, valiant or resilient than the other, and the challenge is always to look beyond the rhetoric and posturing and see the kernels of historical fact. There is also the fact that even some of the eyewitness accounts were only written down long after the events took place and their accuracy may have suffered as a result. To take this information and try to plot it to a timeline or map is fraught with danger and yet is also filled with the potential to significantly inform our understanding of what happened in Enniscorthy and its environs during the 1798 rebellion. This is a piece of work that can only continue to evolve as we, and others, learn and discover more.

CHAPTER THREE

Command and structure: the crown forces at the Battle of Vinegar Hill

CHRIS ROBINSON, BARRY WALSH & JACQUI HYNES

Over the town of Enniscorthy rose the United Irish camp of Vinegar Hill. This station, which will be ever memorable in the annals of Wexford, is situated on the eastern side of the Slaney, a noble river, dividing a great portion of the county of Wexford into east and west, and taking in its course the town of Enniscorthy, which stands on either bank. This town, which was stormed by the United Forces on 28 May, and carried after a desperate conflict, remained, together with Vinegar Hill, in their undisturbed possession until the 21st June, when the Royal army, under General Lake, commenced its operations. (Teeling, 1832, p. 132)

INTRODUCTION

The Battle of Vinegar Hill was the scene of significant milestones for the crown forces in Ireland. It saw the first use of the drastic and devastating explosive shell and the early use of the rifle in any field of combat by a regular unit of the British army, having previously employed German mercenary rifle units, particularly in the American War of Independence (1775–83). It saw the first use of military instead of civilian drivers for the Royal Irish Artillery (RIA) and the first engagement of the newly raised Royal Horse Artillery (RHA). The suppression of the rebellion was also the last major field engagement of the crown forces in Ireland, and the last major engagement of the separate Irish establishment of the British army. After this, the kingdom of Ireland was joined with the kingdom of Great Britain under the Acts of Union 1800 to form the United Kingdom of Great Britain and Ireland, greatly diminishing the independence of the army stationed in Ireland (Keogh & Whelan, 2001).

To quell the rebellion that raged in Co. Wexford from 27 May 1798, General Gerard Lake required, and had at his disposal, significant numbers of men and quantities of ordnance. Various historical accounts suggest that between 13,000 and 20,000 men (cavalry, infantry and artillery), at least thirty-three guns and 'four hundred carriages laden with provisions and ammunition' (Musgrave, ii, 1802, p. 8) were required to complete his task. Kavanagh (1918, pp 206–7) suggests that:

> twenty thousand English troops, led by six chosen generals, and practised in every military manoeuvre, furnished with that great arm of war, a formidable artillery, and aided by many corps of yeomen cavalry, might promise themselves an easy victory over enemies so unskilfully led and so poorly armed as the insurgents. Moreover, the royal troops were fresh from the repose of the camp, and vigorous as men should be who never suffered from the want of fitting food or drink. Sir Jonah Barrington estimates the number of the royal troops at 20,000. Mr Hay agrees with him in this statement.

This chapter explores the preparation, progression and aftermath of the Battle of Vinegar Hill from the perspective of the crown forces. It investigates on a macro level its structure, organization and administration during combat and on a micro level the composition, distribution and movement of this apparently synchronous and cohesive force along multiple fronts during the battle. It recounts orders given to ensure generals were 'in place', and undertook battleplans as directed, while also recording the aftermath, including casualties and ordnance returned.

It undoubtedly shows a structure that is regimented, ordered and meticulous in recording and reporting. This contrasts with rebel accounts and consequently has given a wealth of knowledge on the progression of the battle from the perspective of the crown forces. The research team did encounter 'gaps' in information, but, like any jigsaw, hopefully, over time, further information will come to light which will continue to expand our knowledge and understanding.

THE IRISH ESTABLISHMENT OF THE BRITISH ARMY FOR THE KINGDOM OF IRELAND

Prior to the Acts of Union of 1800, Ireland was a distinct kingdom with its own parliament, government and 'division' of the British army. The king (George III), as head of the government, was represented in Ireland by the lord lieutenant (or viceroy), who was head of its executive. Reporting directly to the lord lieutenant was the commander-in-chief of the Irish establishment of the British army for the kingdom of Ireland. During this time, General Charles Cornwallis simultaneously held both the positions of lord lieutenant and commander-in-chief (Nelson, 2007, pp 30–4). With charge of the Irish War Office, he was responsible for the army in Ireland, and all matters pertaining to the defence of the kingdom of Ireland. This office, while quite separate and nominally independent of the British army headquarters in London (Horse Guards), kept in close communication to ensure co-ordination of activities.

ORGANIZATION AND STRUCTURE OF THE BRITISH ARMY

The organization of the British army in both kingdoms during this time was split into two departments. The first, under the command of the commander-in-chief, was the War Office. It had responsibility, on-the-whole, for the field army, comprising the regular army, the militia and the yeomanry. The second department was the Irish Board of Ordnance. The Ordnance, as it was known, was the technically qualified branch of the military, and had control of all fortifications, artillery, engineers and the supply of 'hard goods' to the army, such as guns, muskets, water bottles and other necessary equipment.

The garrison or field army

In times of relative peace, the Irish establishment of the British army formed a garrison for the purpose of defence and keeping order in the kingdom. This garrison was paid for by the Irish treasury. As the administration learned of the likelihood of a widespread insurrection, the commander-in-chief directed the garrison forces under his command to move into the field and appealed to his London counterpart for reinforcements. The reinforcement of the field army continued almost to the eve of the Battle of Vinegar Hill, with the arrival of Lord Dalhousie in Ballyhack, Co. Wexford on 19 June 1798.

The field army was made up of various types of troops drawn from the regular army, militia and yeomanry, each of which had different levels of professionalism and terms of service.

Regulars: Full-time professional soldiers, enlisted to a particular regiment, fighting for the king for a shilling a day (hence the expression to 'take the king's shilling'). The 1768 Army in Ireland Act permitted some 15,000 regulars (potentially coming from anywhere within Britain, Ireland or possibly the colonies) to be stationed in Ireland for the security of the Anglo-Irish establishment in peacetime. However, it appears that in January 1798 there were 18,377 stationed here, the dramatic increases prior to this year reflecting increasing anxiety and preparations for any impending rebellion. (Soulsby, 2018, p. 114 citing Bartlett & Jeffery, 1996)

Cavalry: Organized as regiments, squadrons and troops. The regular cavalry in Ireland was of two types – 'dragoons' and 'light dragoons'. Dragoons rode larger horses and were armed with a straight sword to charge through the enemy, using shock tactics to inflict maximum panic and injury. The light dragoons were a reconnaissance force, on lighter horses and ponies, used for scouting, flanking and communications duties. Light dragoons used the sabre or curved sword. Both also carried carbines or pistols.

Infantry: Organized into battalions, which usually consisted of eight centre or battalion companies and two flank companies. All were armed with Brown Bess muskets. Their tactics were to fight in ranks from which they could fire volleys from their muskets. The flank companies comprised the 'grenadier company', made up of the taller, 'finer' soldiers of the regiment, and the 'light company', which consisted of smaller, more nimble and more 'intelligent' soldiers, who fought using skirmishing tactics to screen the movement of the battalion on the battlefield.

Rifles: The British army had previously employed rifle units as mercenaries during the American War of Independence, where they realized the value of sharp-shooting on the battlefield. The 60th (Royal American) Regiment of Foot (5th/60th battalion) was the first ever regular-rifles unit of the British army. Raised in 1797, they were usually assigned at a divisional level, to provide sharp shooters in advance of the brigades of infantry. They saw their first combat at Foulksmills, Co. Wexford, on 20 June 1798. The rifle was a significant improvement upon the musket. Unlike the smooth-bore musket with accuracy at up to fifty paces, the rifle, with its spiral grooves, could spin the bullet, meaning it was accurate at up to three hundred paces.

Fencibles: Light cavalry and infantry regiments were raised from volunteers who enlisted for three years, or the duration of the war, for the defence of the kingdom against invasion, hence the name (de)fencible. They filled a niche between the regulars and the militia. Unlike the militia, they volunteered to serve and did so in their own area, but unlike other regulars, they could not be sent out of the kingdom to serve in war without their agreement.

Militia: To supplement the regulars, each county raised a regiment or battalion of militia. Service in the militia was decided by ballot, with authorities using parish records to decide, at random, the names of all eligible men to join for service. The militia were organized like regular infantry battalions, consisting of a number of companies, the number depending on the population of their county. Militia battalions tended to be deployed in a county other than their own, with the individual companies dispersed to various posts to perform garrison and policing duties. Due to the population profile of Ireland at the time, their composition was mainly Catholic. The number of militia in Ireland rose from zero in January 1793 to 22,358 in January 1798, increasing again to 32,583 in January 1799 (see appendix 6).

Yeomanry: With rising tensions, and the threat of rebellion becoming increasingly likely, the government authorized trusted Protestant landowners to raise corps of yeomanry from among their families, tenants or other loyal subjects in their area. In contrast to yeomanry in England, where the term exclusively means light cavalry and the term 'volunteer' is used for light infantry, in Ireland yeomanry referred to both light cavalry *and* light infantry (the use of 'volunteer' having unpalatable political overtones for Dublin Castle). Again, reflecting hastened preparations for an impending rebellion, the numbers of yeomanry in Ireland rose from zero in January 1797 to 36,854 in January 1798 to 43,221 in January 1799 (see appendix 6).

Mercenary units: Historically the British army had used mercenary units, especially from Germany, who had skill and experience using rifles. One such unit was the

Hompesch Mounted Rifles, raised in January 1798 by Colonel Ferdinand von Hompesch. They were contracted to the British army on 17 April 1798 and sent to Ireland, where about fifty men saw action at Vinegar Hill.

FIELD FORMATIONS OF THE REGULAR ARMY

'Field formations' are groupings of units that manoeuvre on the battlefield together. They are described below in ascending order of size.

Company: A company was the smallest tactical unit of the British army. It was commanded by a captain, with a lieutenant as second in command and one or two subalterns (second-lieutenants or ensigns) in junior leadership positions. Three to four sergeants armed with spontoons (pikes or half-pikes, each having a pointed blade with a crossbar at its base) 'dressed the ranks' to keep order. Orders were transmitted by beat of drum.

Battalion: A battalion was made up of a number of companies. Under the command of a lieutenant colonel, these were the basic fighting unit of the army in the field. Two officers with the rank of major assisted the commanding officer, along with support from the surgeon, responsible for treating the wounded, the adjutant, usually a captain, responsible for day-to-day administration, and the quartermaster, charged with ensuring sufficient supplies and logistics. Eight of the companies in a battalion were termed 'centre companies' or 'battalion companies'. These were the standard type of line-infantrymen armed with a Brown Bess musket and bayonet. They fought in line and directed their fire by volleys. The strength of a 'centre company' was around seventy private men but was often smaller.

In battle, the lieutenant colonel commanded the battalion from the centre of the line, where a 'colour party', consisting of two flags carried by two ensigns and some sergeants charged with protecting them, was also located. The 'colours' served as a rallying point on the battlefield (see also separate section below on the colours). Each battalion also had two 'flank companies', so called because they were deployed on the right and left flanks of the battle line. On the right of the line (which marched at the head of the column when the battalion moved any distance) was the 'grenadier company'. In the seventeenth century these men threw grenades during battle. However, by the eighteenth century this role was no longer relevant, and these grenadiers were chosen for being the most physically powerful soldiers, who would lead assaults in the field of battle. The 'light company' composed of smaller, faster and fitter men was drawn up on the left of the line, although they were often sent out ahead to form a skirmish line to screen the movement of the battalion, act as scouts and counter-reconnaissance. Light companies were often detached from their parent regiments and formed into a 'battalion of lights'. We know that the three 'light battalions' of the 1st, 2nd and 4th (Nelson, 2007, p. 165) were at Vinegar Hill.

3.1 British uniform style of the day.

Regiment: An administrative unit that could be considered as a 'family unit', sharing the same uniform and traditions. The officers of a regiment belong to that regiment but may be assigned to other battalions or staff duties, detached, on half-pay or semi-retired. During this period, most regiments had only one battalion, but a few had two or more (e.g. the 60th had five battalions). A regiment was commanded by a colonel, and often had a traditional recruiting area.

Brigade: A group of four battalions fighting together, usually commanded by a major general or brigadier general. At Vinegar Hill there wasn't time to form proper brigades, so the term 'column' is more appropriate to denote a formation of similar size but made up of a variety of smaller units acting together on a temporary basis.[1]

Division: Consisting of one or two brigades, usually commanded by a lieutenant general. Not applicable to the Battle of Vinegar Hill, but the term is used in the references to General Needham's troops (see appendix 7).

REGIMENTAL UNIFORMS

The crown forces in Ireland are inextricably linked with the 'redcoat' uniform which was the traditional regimental coat of the infantry and heavy cavalry. The light cavalry

[1] The terms brigade, corps and column are used interchangeably throughout the first-hand accounts, but we have chosen to use the term 'column' to standardize references to troop formations or movements.

and artillery had dark blue uniforms, while the 5th/60th (the new specialist rifle unit) wore green. To identify the numerous regiments from one another, the colour of the facings (the strip of material on the cuffs, collar and behind the front fastening buttons) on the coat were different for each regiment and matched the regimental 'colours' (see appendix 8 and fig. 3.1).

THE ORDNANCE

The Board of Ordnance was responsible for providing guns, ammunition and other war materials to both the army and the navy. It was headed by the master general, who issued contracts for the construction of guns and supervised the gunpowder mills. Everything supplied by the Ordnance carried its 'crowsfoot' mark. The artillery and engineers were also under the responsibility of the Ordnance, as their officers had to be technically qualified to perform their duties. Prior to the union of 1800, there was a separate Irish Ordnance department and RIA regiment, responsible for fixed and field guns (cannon) in Ireland. Comprising twenty companies in total, of which five were based in the West Indies, they were primarily based in Chapelizod, Dublin, but had other detachments across the country (Crooks, 1914, p. 309).

The Royal Artillery (RA) was much larger, with five battalions. Styled as a single regiment, it had two main elements – the 'foot artillery' (or siege artillery, who served at home in garrisons in larger forts) and the 'horse artillery' who operated field guns (pulled by horses to fight alongside the army in the field). Although no foot batteries of the RA operated in Ireland during 1798, smaller units were attached to the regular infantry regiments and had been rushed from England to reinforce the field army in time to see active service at Vinegar Hill:

> The detachments of the Royal Artillery, which were present with the battalion guns attached to the regiments from England, were six in number, each detachment consisting of 1 non-commissioned officer and 9 men. The whole were under the command of Captain Henry Geary, assisted by three subalterns. The regiments to which they were attached were the Guards (three battalions),[2] the Queen's, 29th and 100th Regiments. A reinforcement of two companies was asked for by General Lake, but the successes at Wexford rendered it unnecessary to meet his demand. (Duncan, 2012, pp 78–9)

Another first for Vinegar Hill, and the campaign in Wexford, was the change from the longstanding practice of hiring civilian drivers for the limbers and wagons. From

---

[2] The Grenadiers, Coldstream and 3rd Foot Guards.

December 1797, three hundred dragoons were permitted to volunteer to the RIA as drivers (Crooks, 1914, pp 304–6). This, for the first time, militarized the role of artillery drivers and was followed by the RA in due course.

Field artillery

On the battlefield, the role of the artillery is to support the other elements of the army in a planned attack. This could be either at the start (to initially inflict maximum injury to the enemy in the safest way possible to one's own forces, thereby reducing their numbers in advance of an infantry attack) or during the battle (where this process is repeated in reaction to a resurgence from the enemy). The artillery batteries on Vinegar Hill (drawn mainly from the RIA but reinforced by a contingent of Royal Foot Artillery and RHA rushed across from Great Britain) used two types of ordnance – guns and howitzers. Guns (cannons) fire round-shot on a flat trajectory or case-shot in a shotgun-like spread. Round-shot is a cast iron ball and case-shot (or cannister) is a tin containing iron balls, whose number depend on the calibre of the gun. Case-shot is used at short range, as upon leaving the muzzle of the gun the case disintegrates and the balls continue on, spreading out to inflict injury on the massed ranks of the enemy. In contrast, howitzers fire shells on a high arching trajectory. Shells are hollow globes of iron, filled with gunpowder, exploded by a fuse.

The majority of RIA artillery and the RA was attached as 'battalion guns' to the regular infantry and militia battalions, consisting of a pair of light 3-pounder or 6-pounder guns commanded by RIA gunners and crewed by trained infantrymen.[3] The RIA also employed 'flying artillery', light guns, including 1-pounder curricle guns, that could be moved quickly about the battlefield by just one or two horses. The RHA deployed 6-pounder, 12-pounder and 5½-inch howitzers, pulled by large teams of horses, which could move rapidly on the battlefield in support of both the infantry and cavalry.

> At this time, H.R.H. the Duke of York ordered two 12-pounder guns to be attached to each troop of Horse Artillery … Two guns, from four troops respectively, went to Ireland to assist in quelling the rebellion, but only those involved in A, B, and C Troops took part in the active operations … The strength of the Horse Artillery sent to Ireland was as follows – 177 horses (and 13 from Driver Corps), 8 guns, 15 ammunition wagons. N.B. – the guns were two twelve-pounders, two five ½-inch howitzers, four six-pounders. (Duncan, 2012, p. 79)

The disembarkation order for the RA (HO/100/11, National Military Archives, London) shows their arrival in Dublin in December 1797.

---

3 'Pounder' indicating the weight of shot being fired.

Infantry weapons

Brown Bess musket: Refers to a family of muskets in service over the course of 175 years. With detachable bayonet, these were the main weapon of the foot soldiers on Vinegar Hill, the majority being of the Short Land pattern (produced from 1730 to 1797). They were slow to load, but Lender and Stone (2016, p. 52) suggest that a well-trained soldier could fire three or four shots per minute, with two being normal for less experienced soldiers. They were most accurate at distances of fifty paces or less. To overcome the high risk of inaccuracy, musket soldiers fired en masse in a volley or in regulated rolling fire.

Rifle: These were accurate at greater distances, but they did take longer to load. The Battle of Foulksmills (20 June) and Battle of Vinegar Hill (21 June) are significant for the first use by the British army of rifle-equipped troops using rifle or light infantry tactics, which would become revolutionary for them during the subsequent Napoleonic Wars. The regiment used was the 60th (Royal American) Regiment of Foot, 5th Battalion.

Sword: Usually the weapon of officers and non-commissioned officers, it was as much a badge of rank as a weapon.

Spontoon or pike: Used by the sergeant to 'dress' the ranks and keep order.

Pistol: Many officers carried pistols and these were used for close-quarter engagement.

Cavalry weapons

1796 Heavy Dragoon Carbine: Similar to the Brown Bess musket and firing the same 0.76 inch calibre ball, it was however much shorter, which allowed it to be carried and used on horseback.

Other carbines and pistols: A wide variety of other weapons were used by members of the crown forces, including some older patterns being phased out of service with the regulars or weapons from private purchase (especially for officers).

Swords: Light cavalry used the 1796-pattern light-cavalry sabre, while the heavy cavalry (dragoons) used the 1796 heavy-cavalry sword.

COLOURS

An essential element of each battalion was their 'colours' or flags, of which there were two. One was a 'king's colour' (the Union flag, with a regimental device and number on it), and the second a 'regimental colour' (bearing the same colours as the regiment's unique facing colour). Ensigns usually carried the 'colours', and it was not unknown for them to be as young as 15 years of age. The flags themselves were 6ft (1.8m) by 6ft 6in (2m) and hoisted on a 15ft (4.6m) pole. Defending them was the role and

Command and structure: the crown forces at the Battle of Vinegar Hill   43

3.2 Representation of 'defending the colours' at a Battle of Vinegar Hill re-enactment in 2013. Courtesy of the National 1798 Rebellion Centre.

responsibility of the colour party, comprised of older, steadier sergeants, who were appointed to the position of colour sergeant.[4] Losing a regiment's colours was a great shame, and to be avoided at all costs.

THE BATTLE OF VINEGAR HILL

Preparation for battle: Sunday 17 to Thursday 21 June

In a letter dated 8 June 1798, Viscount Castlereagh told Thomas Pelham (2nd earl of Chichester and Irish chief secretary) that

> The rebellion in Wexford has assumed a more serious shape than was to be apprehended from a peasantry, however well organized. Their numbers are very great, their enthusiasm excited by their priests, and the face of the country

---

4 Colour sergeant as a rank came in around 1803.

so broken and enclosed that regular formations are impracticable … The enemy are in great force at Vinegar Hill, within half a mile of Enniscorthy, and at Carrickburne, near Taghmon. Their numbers consist of the entire male inhabitants of Wexford, and the greatest proportion of those of Wicklow, Kildare, Carlow, and Kilkenny. From Carlow to Dublin, I am told, scarcely an inhabitant is to be seen. (Gilbert, 1893, pp 130–1)

Hence the need to prepare for this 'final' battle became ever more pressing.

Troop movements

According to Maxwell (see appendix 9), general orders for the Battle of Vinegar Hill were issued on 16 June, for the period 17–21 June. It gave instructions for the movement of senior officers, both outside and inside the county, and their regiments comprising 'a force of above thirteen thousand effective men, with a formidable train of artillery' (Gordon, 1803, 2nd ed., p. 171) to positions that would facilitate a 360-degree assault on Vinegar Hill on the morning of 21 June. There was also a second ring of support at strategic locations around the county, including at Forth Mountain (outside Wexford town), Newtownbarry (Bunclody) and the Barrow valley.

Usual practice was to form three or four infantry battalions into a brigade (standard manoeuvre unit on the battlefield). However, in response to the evolving rebellion, it appears commanders added troops to their ranks as they hastily moved through areas. This led to sections of regiments with different commanders, sometimes simultaneously. Also occasionally regiments were not always billeted or garrisoned in just one town, but divided into its constituent companies, lodging in various towns within that county to police the population. This was especially true of the militia who were dispersed in small numbers around a county. This is referred to by Musgrave (1802, i, p. 490) recounting General Lake's orders to Lieutenant Colonel Walpole to proceed from Dublin to join General Loftus 'with what troops he could procure from General Dundas at Naas, Kilcullen and Baltinglass … with two number six-pounders and a howitzer'.

Officers for Battle of Vinegar Hill

The aggregate force under the command of General Lake, approximating to Twenty Thousand men. (Teeling, 1832, pp 123–4)

Within the army, rank denotes the seniority of the officer or soldier and position (or command) defines the duties the soldier was performing. Some positions, however, required a certain rank – for example, an officer commanding a regiment was always a colonel. They are divided into three grades: general officers (all generals including lieutenant general, major general and brigadier general); field officers (those from the

Command and structure: the crown forces at the Battle of Vinegar Hill

ranks of colonel and major) and company officers (including captains, lieutenants and subalterns). Below, in order of seniority, are the ranks of officers that formed part of the battle plan for Vinegar Hill on 21 June 1798, along with their names where known.[5] Their ages in 1798 are also included where known (Soulsby, 2018, p. 47).

Commander-in-chief and general: Gerard Lake (54), commander-in-chief of the Irish establishment of the British army for the kingdom of Ireland, April 1798–9.

General: Richard R. Wilford (28).

Lieutenant general: Ralph Dundas (60/1) ('Dundas of Manour', 2020).

Major general: Sir Charles Asgill (36), John Francis Cradock (39), Sir James Duff (46), Charles Eustace (61), Hewitt, Henry Johnson (50), William Loftus (46), Francis Needham (50).

Brigadier general: Lords Ancram, Blaney, Glentworth, Sir John Moore (37), Lord Roden.

Colonel: Barry, Campbell, Sir James Foules, Charles Handfield (46), King, Thurles (also noted as captain), Vesey (also noted as major), Sir W. Wynne.

Lieutenant colonel: Blyth, Cole, Read, Stewart, Williamson.

Major: Aylnier, Daniel, Dewar, Elrington.

Captain: Bloomfield, Crawford, Duncan, Dunn, Geary, Ledwell, Manus, Schneider.

Lieutenant: Baines, Barker, Hill, Sandys (also noted as Sands).

Second lieutenant: (also called ensign/subaltern)

Aide-de-camp (ADC): Any officer attached to a general, whose role is to undertake tasks for the general. General Lake notes that his ADC was Captain Nicholson, while the ADC of Major-General Johnson was the 15-year-old son (William Cornwallis Eustace) of his second in command, Charles Eustace (Eustace, 2009), and Captain Hugh Moore of the 5th dragoons was ADC to General Needham (Musgrave, 1802, i, p. 404)

Non-commissioned officers (NCOs)

Regimental sergeant majors

Sergeant: Johnson, M'Laren

Corporal/bombardier

Private/fusilier/guardsman/rifleman/gentleman: The same role, depending on the specific unit.

Order of battle

We know from records that there were elements of at least four cavalry, ten infantry, one rifle, six fencible and twenty-nine militia regiments, as well as one mercenary unit and both the RHA and RIA participating in the battle (see appendix 8). During

---

[5] It has been noted that accounts often use different ranks to describe officers. We have opted to use the names and ranks outlined in the first-hand accounts contained in this chapter. Differences in rank or spelling are also noted. This list reflects research findings to date.

our research we have attempted to identify how these groups were distributed to form light battalions that headed each column, and these columns themselves, that functioned as ad hoc brigades. This continues to be an evolving process as further sources of information and details become available.

We know there were four 'light battalions' (formed in January 1797) drawn from an array of militia light companies (Nelson, 2007, p. 165), three of which fought at Vinegar Hill. The first light battalion, under the command of Colonel Campbell, comprised a nucleus of regulars from the 65th Foot and the light companies of Cork city, north and south Co. Cork, Downshire, King's Co. (Offaly), Longford, Louth, South Mayo, Tyrone and Wicklow. The 65th comprised 210 men and the battalion overall comprised 910 men. The second light battalion, under the command of Lieutenant Colonel Williamson, comprised a nucleus of regulars from the 30th Foot (259 men) and the light companies of Cos. Dublin, Fermanagh, Galway, Leitrim, Limerick, Londonderry, Meath, Roscommon, Sligo, Waterford, Westmeath and Wexford, some 1,099 men in total. The fourth light battalion, under the command of Lieutenant Colonel Stewart, comprised a nucleus of regulars from the 89th Regiment of foot (342 men) and the light companies of Antrim, Clare, Donegal, Kildare, Kilkenny, Limerick city and North Mayo and Queen's Co. (Laois) – a total of 902 men.[6]

These light battalions were then combined with other regiments to form (based on the general orders of General Lake) five 'ad hoc columns', under the command of Generals Duff, Dundas, Johnson, Lake, Loftus and Needham, and supported outside Enniscorthy by Moore and Asgill. General Wilford's brigade is noted in the casualties list but not in the general orders for the battle. He and his men are in proximity to Generals Dundas and Lake. We hypothesize, and this is a work in progress, that they commanded the following:

Centre Left Column (Generals Lake, Dundas, Wilford): Nelson (2007, p. 209) states that General Lake had the first and fourth light battalions, in addition to the Armagh, Antrim, Cavan, Londonderry and Tyrone militias. We note from 24 May he also had the 9th Light Dragoons, the Romneys (New Romney fencible cavalry) and Suffolk fencibles (Musgrave, i, 1802, p. 319).

Centre Column (General Loftus): Musgrave (1802, i, pp 489, 492, 500) notes that on 29 May, Loftus had within his column two hundred of the Dumbarton fencible infantry, and fifty of the 5th Dragoon Guards. He also received further reinforcements from Lord Ancram's detachment, consisting of two hundred and fifty men from the King's Co. militia and Ancram's own detachment of dragoons. This includes eighty Midlothian Dragoons, and a detachment of Meath and Donegal militia, who were designated to General Johnson but 'diverted' to General Loftus. This also includes the RHA, who are operating with the Midlothian Dragoons.

6 The third battalion, which was not at Vinegar Hill, was commanded by Lieutenant Colonel Innis of the 64th Foot and comprised companies from Armagh, Carlow, Cavan, Dublin city, Kerry, Monaghan and Tipperary. This battalion had fewer men than others, with only 605 men.

Centre Right Column (General Duff): There appears to have been a very fluid interchange of men between Generals Loftus and Duff, with no specific reference found to date of named regiments under his direct command.

South East Column (General Needham): A full account of the regiments, comprising some 1,800 men, is recorded by General Needham following the Battle of Arklow, 9 June. It included the men from the Royal Irish Dragoons, Ancient Britons, Antrim, Armagh, Tyrone, north Cork, Cavan and Londonderry militias, and Durham, Dumbarton and Suffolk fencibles (appendix 7). It can be assumed that this changed little over the intervening twelve days.

Western Column (General Johnson): We note from an account in *Bell's Weekly Messenger* (no. 114, 1 July 1798) that he had (at least) the Royal Meath Regiment, Dublin County Regiment, Roscommon Regiment and the Midlothian fencibles. We also observe the Donegal and Sligo militia, 5th Battalion, 60th Regiment and four sections of the RA, who were split between Generals Loftus and Johnson. It is most likely that the RIA was also operating the guns with each militia column.

Supporting Column at Taghmon (General Moore): Sir John Moore (Moore, 1904, pp 296–7) records that on the 19 June, he was to be reinforced by the 2nd (Queen's), 24th and 29th regiments of foot. The 4th Dragoon Guards (2,000 men) had also landed in the city of Waterford and were marching to reinforce him (HL 100/National Archives, Kew, London). He further notes that he had 'the 60th Yagers, 900 light infantry, 50 Hompesch Cavalry, and six pieces of artillery'.

Field artillery for the battle

As mentioned, it is most likely that the guns at Vinegar Hill fired predominantly round-shot (never shells), the howitzers fired mostly shells (and sometimes round-shot) and both are equally likely to have fired case-shot. We suggest that at least thirty-three guns (cannon) were involved in the general orders for the Battle of Vinegar Hill, including Moore, stationed at Taghmon. These include one curricle gun (1-pounder); one flying artillery (3-pounder); four 5½-inch howitzers (including two from the RHA); twenty-five 6-pounder cannon (including four from the RHA) and two 12-pounder cannon (from the RHA). The guns were assigned to the columns under the command of the generals as listed below:[7]

Centre Column (General Loftus): Six guns (most likely all 6-pounders). Musgrave (1802, ii, p. 6) notes that:

> General Loftus surprised the rebels by the celerity of this movement, because the hill was steep; and the ground which he occupied there was divided by stone walls; but by breaking open gaps, he had two guns carried over at first, and soon after four more, by having untackled them from the horses.

[7] Note: The locational positions noted are as observed from the perspective of the crown forces.

Additionally, William Kerr notes 'Gen. Loftus was fortunate enough to find a very advantageous [position?] for the four guns attached to us' (*JWHS*, 1988–9, pp 82–3). This includes, most likely, the four 6-pounder guns from the RHA as we note Musgrave's report of the guns being 'untackled from the horses.' These guns were brought close to the action by their drivers, untackled and put into action by their crews, acting together as a battery.

<u>Centre Left Column (Generals Lake/Dundas)</u>: Four guns (one curricle – inference of more; one 5½-inch howitzer, two 6-pounder). Maxwell (1866, p. 138) notes that on 17 June in Hacketstown, Co. Carlow, 'a body of regular troops under General Dundas, assisted by an irregular corps, called the True Blues, with two pieces of cannon' were in pursuit of a group of rebels in the vicinity. We assume that these pieces were still in their possession four days later. William Kerr (Earl Ancram, 6th marquess of Lothian and commander of the Midlothian fencible regiment) also notes:

> On seeing Gen. Dundas's light companies moving up towards their right the rebels began to file off in considerable numbers in order to line the hedges and ditches. They were gallantly attacked by the light infantry and stood their ground very well for about twenty minutes notwithstanding that a howitzer from the front of Gen. Dundas's brigade was playing upon them the greater part of that time. (*JWHS*, 1988–9, p. 82)

He also notes that the south Cork regiment was also temporarily detained at the battle by an accident when 'one of their currick guns had stuck in a gateway (and) one of the horses was lying in the ditch beside it'.

<u>Centre Right Column (General Sir James Duff)</u>: Eight guns (at least six 6-pounders and two 5½-inch howitzers). William Kerr again confirms that there were 'eight guns belonging to Sir James Duff's brigade which were firing upon them a little to our right' (*JWHS*, 1988–9, p. 83). Maxwell (1866, p. 144) also notes that:

> General Sir James Duff, who advanced by the Ferns Road, with his right resting on the Slaney, and his left flanked by the light infantry under General Loftus, reached the base of the hill with occasional interruptions from rebel pickets, who occupied the high grounds on the line of march, but who were easily dispersed by a few shells from the howitzers.

The fact that this pair of howitzers are operating together attached to Duff's force suggests they are part of the RHA force that contained two 5½-inch howitzers. It is logical their ordinance continued to operate in their established teams rather than being split or mixed with similar ordnance of the foot artillery of the RIA.

<u>South East Brigade (General Needham)</u>: Four guns (most likely all 6-pounder guns). We note from accounts prior to Vinegar Hill that regiments under the

command of General Needham have guns in their possession. From the battle of Arklow we note that:

> The royalists were already in position; the line being slightly curved, the flanks refused, and each protected by battalion guns, with two six-pounders nearly in the centre … while the upper end of the street was barricadoed with carts and lumber, and defended by part of the Antrim regiment, and a field-piece. (Maxwell, 1866, p. 133)

He further notes (1866, p. 71):

> The garrison of the latter town [Naas] consisted of one hundred and fifty of the Armagh militia, with two battalion guns, and seventy-five cavalry, comprising small detachments of the Fourth Dragoons, Ancient Britons, and sixteen mounted yeomen. The whole were under the command of Colonel Lord Gosford.

It is reasonable to suggest that both the Antrim and Armagh militia brought their battalion guns with them to the battle of Vinegar Hill, and we also note that after the Battle of Ballyellis on 30 June, when the crown forces attempted to dislodge the rebels at White Heaps, Needham is reported to have used four cannon against these rebels.

<u>Western Column (Major General Johnson)</u>: Five guns (including one 3-pounder; two 6-pounder and two 12-pounder guns from the RHA). Musgrave (1802, ii, p. 11) notes:

> The main body [of rebels] which marched from the town to attack him, occupied an eminence, on which three or four shots from twelve-pounders were fired; and when the balls lodged on the hill, numbers of the rebels emulously vied with each other to lay hold of them. After that some shells having been thrown on it, and a great body of them having surrounded them for the same purpose, they exploded and blew them to atoms.

He further confirms (i, p. 511) two 6-pounder guns and one piece of flying artillery from the Sligo militia, most likely a 3-pounder, when he notes: 'Next day, colonel King marched with his regiment, to Ross, with two battalion guns and a piece of flying artillery.'

<u>Supporting Column at Taghmon (General Moore)</u>: Six guns (including one 5½-inch howitzer and possibly five 6-pounders). Moore specifically notes that on the eve of the battle of New Ross he had 'the 60th Yagers, 900 light infantry, 50 Hompesch Cavalry, and six pieces of artillery' (Moore, 1904, p. 295). Three of these guns are noted during the Battle of Foulksmills on 20 June 1798. Maxwell (1866, p. 141) notes from Moore that:

I sent my advanced guard, consisting of the two rifle companies of the 60th, to skirmish with them, whilst a howitzer, and a six-pounder, were advanced to a cross road above Goff's-bridge, and some companies of light infantry formed on each side of them under Lieutenant-Colonel Wilkinson. The rebels attempted to attack these, but were instantly repulsed, and driven beyond the bridge. A large body were perceived at the same time moving towards my left. Major Aylmer, and afterwards Major Daniel, with five companies of light infantry, and a six-pounder, were detached against them.

THE SEQUENCE OF BATTLE

An invaluable first-hand account of the battle is given by William Kerr, 6th marquess of Lothian and commander of the Midlothian fencible regiment (see appendix 10). His account is extremely detailed and gives insight into the movement of the various regiments, the locations of some of the guns, the fluidity of the battle, and the need to respond to unforeseen events. Archibald M'Laren, Sergeant of the Dumbartonshire Highlanders, also gives an eyewitness account of the battle (M'Laren, 1798, pp 27–32). Both accounts have informed the reconstruction below. Other writers have also contributed significantly to our understanding of the sequence of the battle, and are noted in what follows.

Eve of the battle, 20 June 1798

Other than some skirmishing, the rebels appear to have decided against taking any offensive action of their own as the forces gathered against them on the eve of the battle. O'Kelly (1842, p. 107) suggests that the possibility of a night attack was put forward but that the majority rejected this:

> On the night before the battle of Vinegar-hill, Mr John Hay, brother to Mr Edward Hay of respected memory, took a command, or at least gave counsel to attack General Lake and his troops, during the night. Finding from an observation which he had made by telescope, on the approach of night, that Lake and his army displayed a loose and irregular encampment, and that the soldiers exhibited marks of fatigue, from the mode in which they lay scattered among the hedges, where the army had pitched their camp, he consequently advised the nightly attack, which he recommended … His counsel now was not attended to, by the united body on the hill, and therefore a defeat of the insurgents followed, by awaiting the attack of the army.

Command and structure: the crown forces at the Battle of Vinegar Hill   51

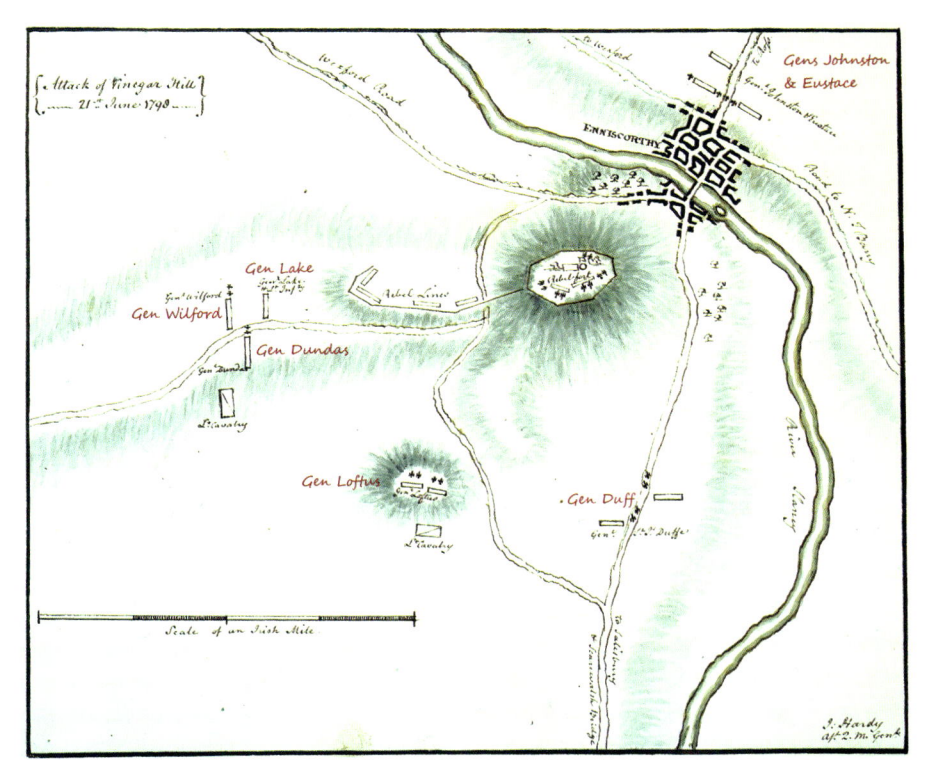

3.3 Sketch plan of the battle, by Hardy after McGurk 1798. PD HP (1798) 21. Courtesy of the National Library of Ireland. (Names of crown commanders added in red.)

The Battle of Vinegar Hill: Thursday, 21 June

> The United forces maintained their position, and, as the enemy expressed it, 'obstinately', for two hours, notwithstanding their want of ammunition, and the disadvantages under which they fought. (Teeling, 1832, p. 135)

Astronomically, 21 June is the summer solstice in the northern hemisphere. It is the longest day of the year, and a day that started particularly early for those involved in the Battle of Vinegar Hill. We have illustrated the battle in phases to highlight the stepped nature of the events. It is divided into 'approach', 'bombardment/assault' and 'mopping-up' phases. An indicative and approximate timeline for the battle is as follows.[8] We do however note that Johnson came under attack on the west side of the town *prior* to the general order to advance.

---

8 Times are approximate and indicate and reflect the 'rolling' nature of battle.

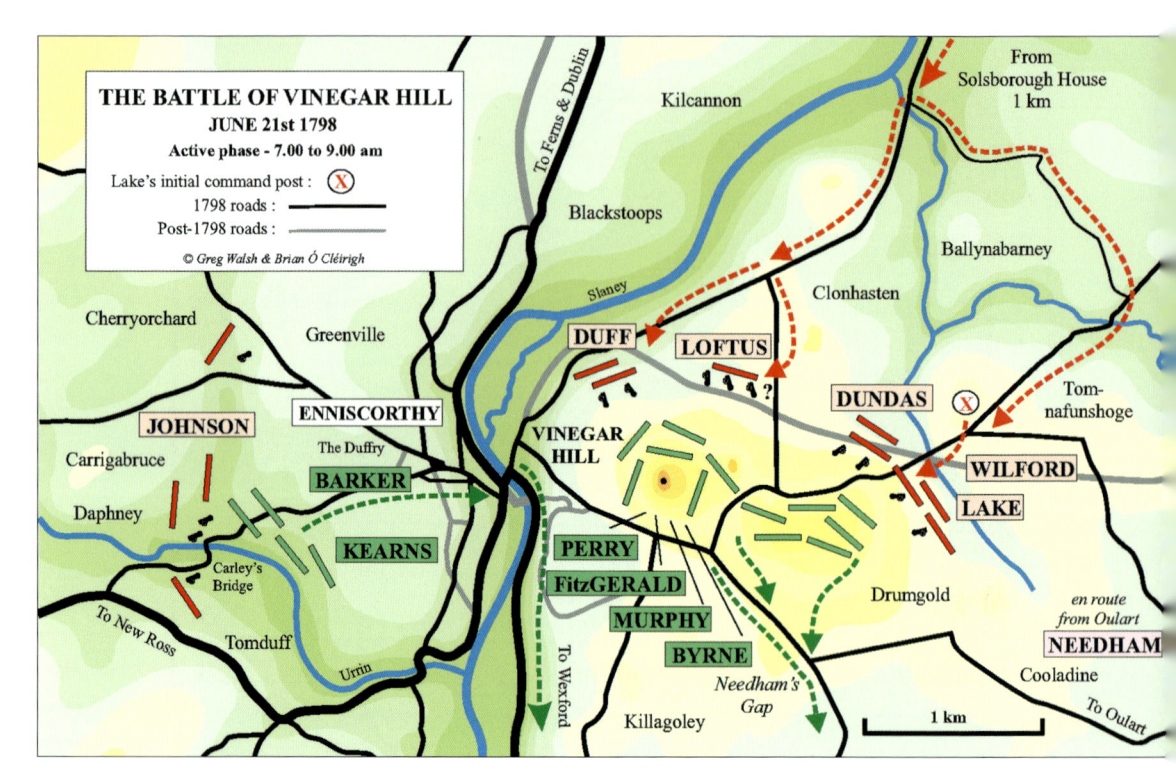

3.4 Illustration of crown forces and rebel positions for the Battle of Vinegar Hill. Map by Greg Walsh and Brian Ó Cléirigh.

Around 1.00 a.m. General Johnson reported his arrival on the west side of the town. However, Byrne (1863, i, p. 167) notes that the General's advance guard had earlier been beaten back by rebel forces defending the approaches to the town:

> General Johnston who had marched from Ross with the king's troops to attack Enniscorthy, had his advanced guard beat back on the 20th by some of our forces … and that the skirmishing continued till night put an end to it.

Approach phase

3.30 a.m.: Signal guns fired. Byrne (1863, i, p. 170) notes that:

> At day break several cannon shots were heard in different directions, from the enemy's camps. These were signal guns, which proved to us that we were now nearly surrounded on all sides, except the Wexford one which should have been occupied by general Needham.

It is most likely that signal guns were fired to inform generals who did not have sight of one another of the need to begin the approach to their designated positions. Skirmishing

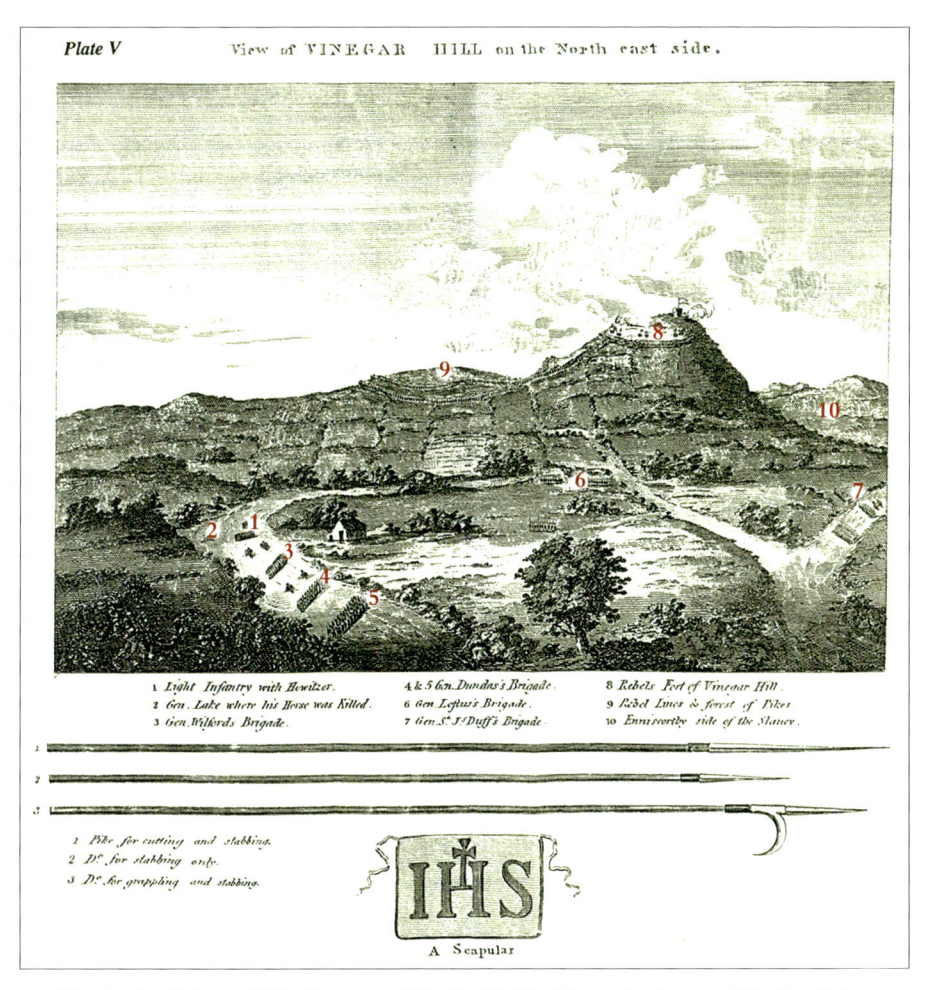

3.5 'The Battle of Vinegar Hill'. Courtesy of Wexford Public Library Service, Local Studies Collection.

of advanced rebel positions also begins with daybreak (around this time). This includes positions around the Duffry Gate, where skirmishes between Johnson and the rebels Barker and Kearns had been taking place from the previous evening. Around the same time, General Needham arrives at Solsborough from Oulart, to receive orders directing him to return to his original position at Darby's Gap. He seeks to delay the advance by an hour to allow his men rest but is informed that Johnson has already engaged the rebels, and therefore delay is impossible. For the next hour 'between 3 and 4 o'clock in the morning … the drums beat to arms.' (Bartlett, 1988–9, p. 82)

5.00 a.m.: After intense artillery bombardment from General Johnson on the west side of the town, the rebel leaders Barker and Kearns order their men to pull back to the Duffry Gate.

6.00 a.m.: General Lake's troops are now almost all in position (save Needham), and are preparing to commence the Battle of Vinegar Hill.

Bombardment/assault phase
7.00 a.m.: Lake's forces engage the first rebel positions at the foot of Vinegar Hill with artillery bombardments. As this area becomes clear of rebel combatants, the infantry were instructed to commence their assault of the hill. The use of exploding shells and canister in this phase is a particular characteristic, and is sometimes termed a 'preparatory bombardment'. The assault phase sees the infantry columns move through the defences at the bottom of the hill and fight their way up. During this phase, the artillery are firing 'in support', picking targets that are a threat to the climbing infantry and negating them with firepower. For accuracy and to avoid hitting their own troops, this would most likely have been done with ball instead of shell. This fluid interchange of artillery and infantry is illustrated by Teeling (1832, p. 135) when he notes that 'the British troops, in their several approaches to storm the camp, were boldly repulsed; but falling back, were protected under shelter of their cannon'.

Corrigan (1844, pp 59–60) describes the progression of the battle in detail:

> When the army had arrived at the beginning of the ascent of Vinegar Hill, General Loftus was detached by General Duff to occupy a green hill in an enclosed park, which was on the side, and compassed a part of, Vinegar Hill. General Loftus surprised the rebels by the celerity of this movement, because the hill was steep, and the ground which he occupied was divided by stone walls; but, by opening breaches, he had two guns carried over at first, and soon after four more, by having them untackled from the horses. From this position he was able to fire into the lower line of the enemy, with such effect, that eighty-five of them were subsequently found in their trenches, killed with grape shot. General Loftus made his movement by a narrow road over the left, diverging from the main one, and then rapidly ascended the hill. At the same time, Generals Lake, Dundas, and Wilford, with Colonel Campbell's Light Infantry, were advancing up the hill, on the south-east side, and were firmly resisted by the rebels, who maintained a very brisk fire on them. On that occasion, General Lake had a horse shot under him. The rebels had not less than thirteen pieces of ordnance, and were well supplied with arms and ammunition. By the well-concerted plans laid down by General Lake, and the gallantry of the various troops under their distinguished leaders, the rebels were soon forced to retreat in great disorder.

There are multiple accounts confirming a start time of 7.00 a.m. General Lake himself confirms this in his letter to Lord Viscount Castlereagh, dated 21 June 1798, stating 'the rebel camp upon Vinegar Hill was attacked this morning at seven o'clock, and carried in about an hour and a half' (quoted in the contemporary periodical *New*

Annual Register or General Repository of History, Politics and Literature for the Year 1798, p. 83). M'Laren and Kerr also confirm that it was around 6.00 a.m. by the time the regiments were in position, while Gordon (1803, p. 171) says:

> The attack began at 7 o'clock on the morning of the 21st, with the firing of canon and mortars and all the armies were in their several posts, except that of general Needham, who arrived not at the appointed position till nine when the business was over.

Miles Byrne, rebel officer (1863, i, p. 170), also notes that 'skirmishing at all our advanced posts commenced with day; however the battle did not become general on the whole line before seven o'clock'. A final account (Jones, 1834, pp 75–6), dated 28 June, written by a soldier signing himself 'W.H.G.' of the Armagh militia, based at the crown forces' camp in Gorey, has an interesting note – that the battle was meant to start at 9.00 a.m.:

> The battle by the command of General Lake, was to commence at nine o'clock. His army took one side of the hill to bombard it, the light brigade, under Colonel Campbell, took another – other commanders were fixed in like manner … The rebels did not wait the appointed time, but commenced cannonading at seven o'clock. They could not tell what to make of the bombs, and said 'they spit fire at us.' – Indeed they answered the desired end, by the numbers they destroyed upon their bursting.

Meanwhile on the opposite side of the town, General Johnson was pushing the rebel defence, led by Kearns and Barker, from the Duffry Gate into Market Square, where intense house-to-house fighting takes place for the next hour.

8.00 a.m.: Kearns and Barker withdraw their men across Enniscorthy Bridge. A stalemate ensues, with rebels and crown forces inflicting heavy causalities upon each another. Rebel leaders realize their defence of Vinegar Hill is increasingly futile without re-enforcements from Wexford town, and with the growing potential of total annihilation, they order a retreat to Wexford town via Darby's Gap, made possible by Needham's absence from his appointed position.

> The rebels after sustaining the fire of the artillery and small arms for an hour and a half, abandoned their station and fled where the passage lay open for them, which passage has been ludicrously termed *Needham's Gap*, most of them directing their course toward Wexford. (Gordon, 1803, p. 172)

8.30 a.m.: General Dundas and his men make significant advances while attacking their section on the centre left. Meanwhile Generals Loftus and Duff were pressing

3.6 'Defeat of the Rebels at Vinegar Hill' by George Cruikshank (Maxwell, 1866, p. 145). Courtesy of Wexford Public Library Service, Local Studies Collection.

heavily on the centre and right flank. However, a near contemporary account of the battle (Anon., 1805, p. 23) notes the strength of the rebel defence:

> But, notwithstanding these formidable preparations, the revolters were enabled from the natural strength of their position to defend the lines during an hour and a half, and it was not until they were outflanked and nearly surrounded, that they at length gave way, leaving behind them thirteen light field-pieces: as civil are always more bloody than foreign wars, the slaughter was immense, for no quarter seems to have been given upon this occasion, as those who escaped the musket when overtaken perished by the merciless bayonet, while so insignificant was the loss on the part of the king's troops, that not above one hundred were either killed or wounded.

'Mopping up' phase

'Mopping up' describes the actions of an army once the assault is successful, when the troops have 'secured' Vinegar Hill and ensured there is no further threat from the rebels. It is also likely that during this phase, crown forces attacked the rebel hospital in the town.

9.00 a.m.: Miles Byrne (1863, i, p. 147) notes that

> the result of the battle of Vinegar hill could not be known before eleven o'clock, [in Wexford town] as it only finished at nine, and the distance is eleven Irish miles.

Whether acting on orders or their own initiative, some of General Johnson's men burned down the rebel hospital in Enniscorthy town, and accounts suggest that seventy wounded rebels perished inside.

Meanwhile, General Needham's cavalry had caught up with the rebels retreating from the hill at Darby's Gap, only to meet, in their turn, the rebel reinforcements from Wexford town. They engage one another until the cavalry withdraw from the pursuit. Needham's infantry was not involved as they were unable to cover the distance in time.

Edward Hay, who was part of one of three delegations dispatched that morning towards the army camps with Wexford town's surrender notice, observes (1803, p. 234):

> We at last arrived in sight of the army at Darby-gap, where captain McManus threw off a great coat which I had the precaution to make him wear over his regimentals. We then hoisted a white handkerchief as our flag; and could descry the country all along between that and Enniscorthy in a most dreadful situation; houses on fire, dead men and women strewed along the road, and in the fields; while the soldiers were hunting for such as might be concealed in the ditches, and bringing down every person they met; in fine, it was altogether a dreadful picture, exhibiting all the horrors of war! A small party of the Antrim militia happened to be among the first of the soldiery that we met, and these hailed their officer with the most heartfelt demonstrations of joy, and conducted us safely to Drumgold, where we met major-general sir James Duff, who led us into Enniscorthy to general Lake the commander in chief, to whom we delivered our dispatches.

The maps at figures 3.3 and 3.4, coupled with the information of William Kerr, provide additional clarity on the structure of the 'net' engaged to surround the rebels on Vinegar Hill. Kerr states that 'Gen. Needham, who we understand had orders to march from Gorey to Olart [sic] so as to intercept them in their retreat to Wexford, was to come in upon their rear and to the right of it' (*JWHS*, 1988–9, p. 82). This confirms that General Needham was to be somewhat distant (1.7km) from the battle, in the area of Darby's Gap, to prevent the rebels retreating along the roads from Vinegar Hill towards Wexford town. The use of the word 'rear' in relation to Needham should be considered in the context of Kerr's reference to General Johnson who 'was to attack on the rear of their left', and we know for Johnson this meant approaching the rebels from the west of the town and pushing the rebels at those outposts through the town and towards Vinegar Hill itself. We also note that Colonel Campbell's force (light infantry, centre left column) attacked the steep eastern side of the ridge, and once in position, the artillery was able to sweep down the rebel lines. The roles of Generals Duff and Loftus were essentially to 'hold' the rebels on the hill front, and make sure, if and when the rebels did break, they did not flee between both.

Richard Musgrave gives considerable detail of the Battle of Vinegar Hill (Musgrave, ii, 1802, pp 1–16), and in this account, recalls an incident from the west side of the town:

> The general then ordered the light infantry to charge over the bridge, and up the hill, which were occupied by a numerous body of rebels; but they having shown an unwillingness to do so, he called on the county of Dublin regiment to perform that service, on which they gave three cheers, and led on by colonel Vesey and lord Blaney, in conjunction with the light infantry, forced the bridge and marched up the steepest part of the hill, driving the rebels before them.

This indicates that by this stage Johnson and his men had taken most of the town and secured the bridge, thereby removing a potential escape route for the rebels to the west side of the river and into Co. Carlow through Scollough Gap, save for those who had already departed before this point. William Hamilton Maxwell (1866, p. 145) also notes:

> The brunt of the action, and the greatest proportion of the loss, fell upon the brigade commanded by General Johnson. On the evening preceding the attack on Vinegar-hill … intending to bivouac in the vicinity of the rebel position … had scarcely, however, piled arms, when the rebels in great force issued from Enniscorthy, and moved forward with the apparent intention of attacking the royalists, and hazarding a general action. They advanced in close columns, covered by a number of sharp-shooters, and connected by several bodies, formed in irregular lines. The rebel skirmishers, after maintaining a sharp fusilade, were speedily dislodged by the fire of the cannon, – and falling back on the supporting column, which had halted on an eminence half a mile from the ground occupied by the royalists, the guns were directly turned upon the height.

'FLIES IN THE OINTMENT' OF A WELL-LAID PLAN

There has been considerable discussion about the 'late' General Needham, and the causes of his delayed arrival. This is explored in depth in chapter 5, but here it will suffice to explore the course of events for General Needham in the lead-up to the battle.

Musgrave (1802, ii, pp 8–9) tells us that following General Lake's orders to move from Gorey to Oulart on 20 June, General Needham, with his long caravan of 'four hundred carriages laden with provisions and ammunition for the army which attended them', travelled 22.5km as directed. He arrived there 'late in the evening … and within six miles of that part of it where he was to take post'. While there 'about half an hour after eight o'clock' he received orders 'signed by the adjutant-general, desiring him to march immediately with the troops under his command, to join general Lake at Solsborough'. As ordered, Needham marched his column to Solsborough, arriving at 3.00 a.m. on 21 June, only to be 'informed by the general himself "that he must immediately occupy the position first allotted to him, in the general orders". Thus after a most fatiguing march, without having had any refreshment for his troops from the time he left Gorey, he was obliged to repair to the post he was to occupy by a circuitous route of eight miles.'

This meant that Needham marched his sleep-deprived men the circuitous route of eight miles (almost 13km) to Darby's Gap, retracing a large portion of their steps, and completing an about turn.

> Needham proceeded, at the head of the grenadier company of the Antrim militia, who led the column, when it was scarcely light; but soon after he discovered that great numbers of the infantry who had been ordered to fall in, overcome with hunger and fatigue, had lain down again.

While returning to Darby's Gap, he observed the rebels' retreat from the hill, and was left with no option but to push forward with his cavalry, who were sufficiently advanced 'to cut down a number of the fugitives' (Maxwell, 1866, p. 144).

Further south, General Moore, with orders to proceed to Taghmon and prevent the rebel escape from Enniscorthy or Wexford, exceeded his orders and began to march to the Three Rocks. His rationale is unclear, but most likely it was to offer re-assurances to the loyalist prisoners of Wexford town, who were becoming anxious as the battle progressed in Enniscorthy. His position on Forth Mountain (where the Three Rocks lie) coupled with Needham's position just below Enniscorthy, meant two large 'gaps' had appeared in Lake's net – one along the east coast of the county and the second between Forth Mountain and Wexford's south and south-east coast. Both gaps were successfully exploited by the retreating rebels. General Moore, from his vantage point of Forth Mountain, observed the rebels leaving Wexford town and heading north, but incorrectly assumed these were town residents fleeing the prospect of an attack. He

3.7 Vinegar Hill, charge of the 5th Dragoon Guards on the insurgents by William Sadler. PD 3176 TX1. Courtesy of the National Library of Ireland.

also missed the second group of rebels escaping south as he had moved too close to the town to observe their departure.

AFTERMATH OF THE BATTLE

The Battle of Vinegar Hill was an overwhelming success for the crown forces. Given the size of the rebel army and the considerable number of men involved in the crown forces, the numbers of fatalities and casualties were miniscule. The rebellion in Wexford was quelled, and the rebel artillery captured. General Lake writes in detail of the victory, casualties and ordnance captured (see appendix 12), and correspondence from the lord lieutenant of Ireland confirms those killed or injured. Maxwell (1866, p. 146) recounts the 'Return of the killed, wounded, and missing of the King's troops, in the attack of Vinegar-Hill and Enniscorthy, June 21, 1798'. We observe ninety-five men were killed, wounded or missing from the battle. These include two field officers wounded, two captains wounded and two killed, two subalterns wounded and two killed, one serjeant wounded and one missing, sixteen rank and file killed, sixty-two wounded and five missing (see appendix 11).

Ironically, an eyewitness account from the otherwise unsympathetic Archibald M'Laren, sergeant of the Dumbartonshire Highlanders, offers us a wider insight into the tragedy of battle:

> As we passed we saw a woman wounded in a ditch, surrounded by three or four children. She told the General and other Officers a piteous tale, how her husband had been forced to join the rebels, and how she herself had been wounded. She begged the soldiers to shoot her, but they would not contaminate their arms with a woman's blood. She asked for a drink of water and they gave her grog which revived her drooping spirits for a little. The General took the children and sent them to Dublin to be taken care of, and death took the mother to be sent to the grave to be buried and forgotten. (M'Laren, 1798, p. 30)

CONCLUSION

At Vinegar Hill there was a series of firsts and lasts for the crown forces, and what is clear is that there was a determination on the part of General Lake to finally quell the rebellion in Wexford. It was also intended to send a clear message to others, both in Ireland and France, that rebellious actions would be met with full force.

We know it was the intention of the rebels after Vinegar Hill to 'hold out' until the French arrived. They endeavoured to do so, but only effectively until mid-July. French forces arrived in August, but were defeated by General Lake at the Battle of Ballinamuck, Co. Longford, a month later. It should be noted also that these victories did not fully allay government anxieties about further outbreaks of rebellion and troop numbers in Ireland continued to rise during 1799.

As for the significance of the course of events in Wexford and on Vinegar Hill, this battle should be considered groundbreaking in a much wider and protracted European context. However, it was also one of appalling bloodshed and atrocities, committed by both sides. We leave the final words to Brigadier General Sir John Moore, in his diary entry of 10 July 1798 (Moore, 1904, pp 304–5):

> I then marched with the rest of the troops to Enniscorthy, where I arrived at eight in the morning. The town had been burned by the rebels, and plundered by us. I visited Vinegar Hill and the position held by the rebels. The town is situated on the Slaney, the country beautiful. Vinegar Hill stinks with dead bodies half buried.

CHAPTER FOUR

Command and structure: a rebel republic?

BRIAN Ó CLÉIRIGH

The rebel army defending Vinegar Hill on 21 June 1798 was no mere hotchpotch of outraged country folk armed with billhooks and scythes. At its heart lay the Northern Army of an ad-hoc Wexford United Army, by this time an experienced and effective force, whose fighting qualities were recognized even by their opponents. The Northern Army, along with its counterpart Southern Army, had been established quite formally by the rebel authorities in Wexford town. But how exactly were these two armies established and what administrative – or even governmental – structure lay behind that? This chapter therefore will attempt to work out how the United Irishmen managed affairs in the town and county of Wexford during the rising in 1798. Evidence is often ambiguous, but nonetheless, when placed together, it points to a historic effort to establish what Sir Richard Musgrave termed an 'embryo republic' (1995, p. 440).

Wexford town was an advanced and aware polity, almost on a par with Belfast and Dublin in the 1790s. It enjoyed the influence of a fairly radical press in the early nineties and the town went through a phase in 1792–3 when the ideas and values of the French Revolution were the talk of tavern and coffee-house (Musgrave, 1995, p. 440). Such was the loosening of established social norms in Wexford in 1792 that Bishop Caulfield caustically remarked that 'it was a happy epoch indeed when the people, the puppies, the rabble dictated' (Cleary, 1992–3, p. 51). However, when it came, the revolution in Ireland did not take place as planned. Like the subsequent popular risings in 1848, 1867 and 1916, which it inspired, 1798 also began in total chaos. The original plan for a nationwide rising by the United Irishmen had failed in Dublin on Wednesday 23 May, and had been cancelled all over the county of Wexford by Friday, 25 May.

But cancellation was easier said than done, at least in North Wexford. There, a quartet of misguided magistrates – James Boyd, Hawtry White, Archibald Hamilton Jacob and Hunter Gowan (bogeyman of later folklore – see chapter 12) – accompanied by yeomanry and militia, had weeks earlier instituted a veritable pogrom, traversing the countryside like madmen, half-hanging, shooting, whipping and burning, in an effort to extract information from people who had none to give, and to intimidate revolutionaries they could not identify (Cloney, 1832, p. 10; Hay, 1803, pp 57–80; Dickson, 1955, pp 35–42).

In The Ballagh on Thursday 24 May, a man was whipped to death for information while water was thrown over his back to get the whip to cut into the flesh (Hay, 1803, p. 99). In Oulart the next day, an old man had to be waked out on the hill for fear of the forces of law and order themselves. People were at breaking point, feeling trapped and fearful. Many had given up their arms to the magistrates in return for a certificate known as a 'protection', which indicated one had returned to one's allegiance. Some even had pikes made just to hand in so as to receive this security (Kavanagh, 1920, p. 88). But this quartet of magistrates rashly ignored these Protections, leaving them worthless and their holders defenceless (Hay, 1803, p. 97). Fear was palpable on all sides as the pogrom continued and the people edged closer to insurrection. As Thomas Cloney pointed out, 'Protection and allegiance are reciprocal obligations … and if one is withdrawn the other cannot be expected to continue' (Cloney, 1832, p. 10).

How the rising actually began is a moot point. The situation was confused. But on Saturday 26 May, after four weeks of arbitrary justice and communal fear, failed by the inability of the paralysed grand jury to impose restraint, angry and fearful at the frightfulness of the forces of law and order and swearing retribution on the culprits responsible, the people were in a state of revolt. It seems most likely that on that Saturday a handful of local United Irishmen from Clohamon to Boolavogue, acting in order to prevent a catastrophe, placed themselves at the head of the people to provide some leadership and direction.

The Rubicon was crossed at The Harrow late on Saturday evening. Local United leader Tom Donovan immediately alerted his counterparts across the district. The Oulart Bell was rung to warn the people as the despatch rider, Donovan's son, having given word to the parish priest, rode on for Castlebridge. The men of each parish were asked to meet the next day on Oulart Hill. The call-up proceeded with such clockwork precision that it must have been following the original local district plan for the nationwide rising cancelled a day or two before. Nothing else could explain it (Cleary, 1999, p. 38). Overnight, the country was up.

However, in origin and character this uprising was no longer the cancelled United Irish revolution nor was it nationwide. Instead of revolution, it was now an insurrection of the people caused by the May pogrom. The rector of Killegny, Mr Gordon, with laudable objectivity in his history of this period, raised the question of whether the rising would have been so forceful or bloody had it not been for the terror of May 1798 in Wexford (Gordon, 1803 cited in Hay, 1803, p. 67). It was this pogrom across north Wexford and around New Ross that lay at the root of the insistent demand for retributive justice by those who had suffered: a demand that was destined to repeatedly thwart, and indeed undermine, the United Irish strategies about to be unveiled in Wexford town four days later. Following the crucial battle of Oulart Hill on 27 May and the capture of Enniscorthy the next day, suspected culprits began to be arrested and executed at the rebel camp on Vinegar Hill for what had gone on before. Over the entire rising up to one hundred were put to death on the hill, some of them with gratuitous cruelty (Gahan, 2010).

The taking of Enniscorthy was a huge shock to the establishment and its psychological impact must have rivalled the success at Oulart Hill. The next morning in Enniscorthy:

> A committee of twelve, consisting of some rebel officers and three priests; viz. Fathers Roche, Kearns and Clinch, and at times Fr John Murphy, continued constantly to sit, and to superintend and regulate the concerns of the camp, and the newly established republic. (Musgrave, 1995, p. 335)

With a tiger by the tail and no firm plan what to do next, a stern summons was sent out on Tuesday, 29 May to all relevant United Irish leaders to appear at the camp forthwith (Hay, 1803, p. 117). Where such men were reluctant to come in (and some were), armed parties were sent out to their homes to collect them. From this point on the rising became a *bona fide* United Irish one, but for many of the rank-and-file insurrectionists who suffered the May pogrom, the leadership would remain on probation. In fact, Hay, Cloney and others fighting for their lives in post-rising courtrooms would argue that the rising was never a planned rebellion but a spontaneous insurrection by an outraged people – and this was technically true. They argued that they themselves were *forced* into positions of leadership, which was technically true also, as many had been summoned to Vinegar Hill. These technicalities were a life-saver to men of firm faith, who found themselves swearing evidence under oath.

DEVELOPMENTS IN WEXFORD

Crucially, unlike in other counties, in Wexford, the rising opened with a string of victories at Oulart Hill, Enniscorthy and the Three Rocks, which forced the military and civic authorities to evacuate Wexford town on 30 May. In this way, the revolution gained critical time and space to establish and consolidate. That Thursday, 31 May, was spent in a plethora of meetings working to develop various committees and make arrangements amid upheaval and confusion as thousands of pikemen flooded into the town, now bedecked with green boughs and other emblems of revolution (Hay, 1803, pp 138, 140–1). Beauchamp[1] Bagenal Harvey was looked up to as the overall central figure. Regarding the actions of the rebels at this point, Musgrave opined that 'their plans appear to have

---

[1] Pronounced 'Beecham'.

been systematic, and guided by policy and foresight' (Musgrave, 1995, p. 366). The most fascinating example of this took place on the evening of 31 May, when a historic meeting was convened, and attended by those whom both Edward Hay and Thomas Cloney called the 'principal inhabitants' from town and country.

The meeting was apparently prolonged and had to be resumed the following day. It was held in the largest premises in the town, Cullimore's premises on Main Street.[2] We do not know how many attended, except that a very big assembly was indicated by General Thomas Cloney, victor of the Battle of the Three Rocks. Writing in 1832 he recalled that his victory was congratulated by this assembly and he names the man who presided over it:

> Of the part I played in this trifling action I will say no more than that I received the thanks of a very general meeting of the principal inhabitants of Wexford on the following night, on which occasion the celebrated Captain Keugh presided. (Cloney, 1832, p. 22)

In this Cloney was confirming what Edward Hay had written in 1803:

> These circumstances produced a general meeting of the principal inhabitants on the first of June, wherein Mr Harvey was called on to act as Commander in Chief, and various other appointments and regulations took place for the maintenance and supply of the country. (p. 150)

This very important quotation shows Bagenal Harvey, who, as we will see, was chosen commander-in-chief earlier that day by the pikemen after a very contentious meeting, was now *formally* confirmed in the command by this meeting of the principal citizens, selected to represent the popular voice. This appointment by the people is crucial: the fact that their approval was necessary at all meant that the ultimate power was being deliberately reposed in this meeting. The United men were laying down a marker that their administration would be governed by a popular parliament as distinct from a military government.

It should also be noted that the statements of both Hay and Cloney are deceptively casual, intentionally playing down events, because their words would be read by English politicians of great influence whose support for Irish objectives in the post-Union Westminster parliament they needed to nurture. We must read between their lines. Hay's narrative was also written to counter the influence of Musgrave's great tome, which cast the rising in a totally sectarian light. While Hay's account of events in Wexford is our richest source by far, he was writing in 1803 – the year of Emmet's

---

[2] Ironically, this premises had also been used as a headquarters by that early 'republican' Oliver Cromwell in 1649!

rising – and could not admit United Irish inspiration lest he incriminate Wexford Unitedmen like Cloney and Gray and put them on the scaffold. Despite his own deep involvement in events he gives the impression that he was merely on the margins, a person on call to help in emergencies.

The first uncompromised opinion as to what the meeting really represented was that of George Taylor, a travelling Methodist preacher from Cahore. His was the first history of '98 in Wexford, appearing in August of that year, two months before several Oulart musketeers and pikemen had made it home from the last days of the campaign in Meath and north Dublin. He writes:

> No sooner had the rebels entered the town than they immediately began to reorganise the state. A Grand National Committee was set up and a Committee of Five Hundred and a Council of Elders; the premises of Mr Cullimore was commandeered and was known as the Senate House. (Taylor, 1800, p. 77)

Taylor's array of structures seems more fitted to a national rather than a county-wide programme. But he correctly identified the meeting as being governmental in character: after all, they now had a county to govern and indeed to defend. And so, with the power now reposed in it, the meeting of principal inhabitants assumed civil and military authority in the county. They then formally established an army and navy and other bodies and committees as well as personnel to lead them, all of which, taken together, bears the unmistakeable mark of a republic, in fact if not in name.

Taylor tells us that Cullimore's premises was 'commandeered' and known as the Senate House. He also uses the term 'rebel senate' in his book (Taylor, 1800, p. 72). The building was used continuously during the rising by various committees and Hay actually calls it the 'Committee House' (Hay, 1803, p. 197). Because of this solid provenance from a valued contemporary source, and even more so because it conveys the democratic essence of what was being done, the term 'Senate' is adopted here to describe this committee of principal citizens in a manner that does proper justice to its place in history. Three meetings of the Senate of 'principal inhabitants' are dealt with in this essay: the first established the new polity; the second established the Council for Directing the Affairs of the People of the County of Wexford; and the third agreed proposals for the surrender of the 'embryo republic'.

THE FIRST MEETING OF THE SENATE

The first meeting, which took place on the evening of Thursday 31 May, four days after Oulart Hill, was given over to military and security matters. It would have discussed, sanctioned or amended proposals brought forward from special groups who had been meeting all during that day. We can see how this worked by looking at the appointment of Bagenal Harvey as commander-in-chief. Edward Hay tells us that earlier in the day:

Command and structure: a rebel republic?

> On this very day Mr Harvey, who had been released from confinement by the people, as soon as they took possession of the town, and was by them appointed, whether he would or no, their commander in chief. (Hay, 1803, p. 138)

Then at the meeting of the Senate that night, he tells us that:

> Mr Harvey was called on to act as Commander in Chief, and various other appointments and regulations took place for the maintenance and supply of the country. (Hay, 1803, p. 150)

This appointment was not so straightforward as Hay suggests. Cloney tells us that it was accompanied by serious difficulties:

> A Commander-in-Chief not yet having been appointed, I waited to learn on whom that high rank and honour would devolve. The cabals and jealousies which arose in the discussion of this question, omened badly for our future prosperity. (Cloney, 1832, p. 32)

All reports suggest that Bagenal Harvey did not want a military post, having no training in that sphere. Who else was being pushed forward and whether Bagenal Harvey was actually a compromise candidate between competing parties we simply do not know. Was Fr John Murphy, victor at Oulart Hill and Enniscorthy, put forward and was this a contentious nomination with the United Irish leaders? Whatever the answer, Cloney felt it was significant enough to mention the challenge.

On Saturday 2 June, the diarist Mrs Brownrigg visited Bagenal Harvey at what appears to be the Wexford Army Headquarters. But she calls it the 'Council', and this raises a question. Was she mistaken in the name or does it reflect the existence of a small but powerful council of representatives from the military and civilian side of the new polity acting as an executive, which one would naturally expect to exist? This will be looked at again later. Mrs Brownrigg had come in order to collect some luggage, and her comment offers a unique keyhole glimpse into the revolutionaries at work at this formative moment when so much seemed possible:

> Arrived at Mrs Lett's, where Centinals [*sic*] were placed, colours flying and all proper dignity preserved. The Centinals stopped me so I asked for Mr Harvey. He immediately came out and took me into a parlour where sat Keugh and Fitzgerald with various papers on a green table before them.[3] Harvey wrote an order for my trunks and I departed. So ended my visit to the Council. (Wheeler & Broadley, 1910)

[3] The Fitzgerald in question is Catholic gentleman Edward Fitzgerald of Newpark, colonel of the Ballaghkeene Unitedmen.

These are three of the most senior figures in the military and security arms of the new polity. Bagenal Harvey was commander-in-chief; Edward Fitzgerald of Newpark, United Irish colonel in Ballaghkeene barony; and Matthew Keugh, governor of Wexford town. The impressive effort to dignify the army HQ as an organ of state is solid evidence in itself.

Musgrave coined the term 'Embryo Republic' to describe these developments (Musgrave, 1995, p. 440). It is a reasonable description of what was emerging. However, there was no formal proclamation of the Republic such as the proclamation of the Republic of Connacht in Castlebar two months later by General Humbert. The reason seems to be expressed in an oft-quoted statement from Keugh: 'We fight with ropes around our necks' (Musgrave, 1995, p. 432) – in other words, as experienced military men, they were aware that with Dublin knocked out it was highly unlikely that they could win in the end, and the less harm done by way of fatuous declarations the fewer people might die on the scaffold when all was over. Hay and Bagenal Harvey were both strongly of this turn of mind.

However, there were other items too that pointed to a republic, in fact if not in name. For instance, Christopher Taylor, a printer in the town and publisher of the *Wexford Herald* weekly newspaper, had the arresting slogan 'PRINTER TO THE WEXFORD REPUBLIC' put in large gold letters on his shop door on Main Street (Whelan, 1998, p. 22). As a witness at the trial of Cornelius Grogan, Christopher Taylor said 'After being some time in prison, I was liberated, upon condition I would print, for the use of the rebels, such papers as they wished for.' He further states that on one occasion some rebels broke into the shop and tried to print a document of their own but bungled the type and that Keugh 'came to me, and asked me not to print anything that did not come from him' (Sweetman, 2013, p. 389). Given this instruction from Keugh, and taking into account that Taylor also said at the trial that at that time he still considered himself 'in some measure a prisoner', his conformity in the matter of such an overt political statement posted on his premises may be reasonably assumed.[4] The slogan was there by order or at least with Keugh's approval and is therefore significant. The papers surviving from the Taylor family's printing shop include travel passes within the town and county from the Public Safety Committee as well as samples of the Commissariat's order slips for goods and rationing coupons used to allocate the appropriate amounts of food to each house in the town based on the number of occupants.[5]

Keugh took his role in Wexford town with the utmost seriousness. He was a republican by conviction although not actually a United Irishman. He had been stripped of his position as a magistrate in 1796 for his political views. He appears to

---

[4] Note from the author. [5] These papers were given in trust by Ms Iseult Taylor to Matthew Maddock of Kilmore Quay, who gave them to the writer, who, in agreement with Iseult and Matthew, lodged them in the National Library.

have been very much the man responsible for establishing Taylor as 'Printer to the Wexford Republic', a role that was essential to transmit public information from the administration. In fact the shortage of such information from the administration to the public during the rising gave oxygen at critical times to the spread of rumour and suspicion, which contributed to instability. Miles Byrne commented on the opportunity offered by Taylor's print shop:

> … a press for printing proclamations, which should have been issued and distributed in thousands, prohibiting pillage or plunder of any kind, but particularly against taking the life of the greatest criminal before he was tried; and for this purpose a special commission or court-martial should have been formed and attached to each army to try all offenders, and have martial justice rendered to all parties. (Byrne, 1863, i, p. 82).

That this could have so easily been done but was not is evidence that the preference was for the administration of justice to remain a *civil* matter and not a military one – an assessment reinforced by the fact that proper trials were already being run by the new administration from its very first days.

Overall, Keugh ran a tight ship in the town and was quite ready to protect his role and execute the functions of the Committee of Public Safety to the full extent. Cloney says of him:

> As a person supposed to be conversant in the practice of military men in the maintenance of discipline, he was called on to assist in framing regulations for the preservation of public order, and for enforcing strict subordination at the different posts which were occupied in the town by the popular force. In the two-fold capacity of a civil magistrate and military commander he acted until the town surrendered to General Lake. (Cloney, 1832, p. 211)

DECISIONS OF THE FIRST MEETING OF THE SENATE, 31 MAY 1798

As already stated, the first meeting of the Senate was taken up with urgent military and supply matters: the establishment of the army, navy, Commissariat and Committee of Public Safety. Behind these were various subordinate bodies that were not necessarily established at the first meeting. However, let us begin with the question of the 'missing' executive committee or council already referred to.

The missing executive committee or council
The evidence for the existence of a 'council' is George Taylor's reference to a 'council of elders' and Mrs Brownrigg's mention of it. Beyond this there is no substantive

evidence of a such an important body until the establishment of the Council for Directing the Affairs of the People of the County Wexford by the Senate on 13 June. Perhaps the Senate left the establishment of such an executive, a necessity for administration purposes, to Bagenal Harvey as commander-in-chief in order to avoid the practical risks attaching to such important personnel being left to the vagaries of a large public meeting. The anonymous *Wexford Freeholder* provides an important clue to the existence of an executive council:

> It is well known that Mr Hay and one Myler, a noted rebel, had been secretaries of state to the republic of Wexford while it lasted … (*Wexford Freeholder*, c.1803, pp 5–6).

A role for Hay as 'secretary of state' suggests some form of executive council and would explain his prodigious involvement in every problem arising, not least his architecture of initiatives like the despatch of an armed contingent to Vinegar Hill to curtail the executions or the later peace moves with Dublin Castle. Hay was the ubiquitous genius of the entire rising, based in Wexford town and dominating the space between the various committees and liaising between them. He was the constant contact between the new polity and society in practically every domain.

The Wexford Army
The establishment of the army was formally confirmed at the first meeting of the Senate and Bagenal Harvey was formally sanctioned as its commander-in-chief. It would comprise over 20,000 men at maximum, including a significant number of Protestants (many under duress). Later on, it was also joined by over a thousand Wicklowmen. The Wexford Army was set up in two divisions, each comprising men from one side only of the River Slaney, which roughly bisects the county, giving us the Northern and Southern armies – Cloney (1832, p. 45) uses the term 'Southern Army'. These functioned as separate field armies capable of independent action and in fact they never fought alongside each other. In all, they fought in over twenty engagements of various sizes and intensities, of which Vinegar Hill was number eleven.

Hay is clear that Bagenal Harvey was appointed commander-in-chief at the meeting in Wexford on 31 May (Hay, 1803, p. 150), notwithstanding that he also says that Bagenal Harvey had been appointed after a fashion by the people earlier that day (Hay, 1803, p. 138, fn 23). It was the sanction of the Senate that mattered. Musgrave, who had access to an official rebel document, says that the appointment took place at a meeting of commanders at Carrickbyrne Camp on 1 June 1798 and that Roche was appointed as a general at that same meeting (Musgrave, 1995, p. 383). Given the sensitivities recorded by Cloney over the army appointments discussed on 31 May, the Carrickbyrne meeting the next day was probably a respectful compromise allowing the army to confirm what the Senate had decided, certainly as regards their commander-in-chief, and in all likelihood the appointment of Roche as a general too for his role on Oulart Hill. A similar approach was used on 21 June to confirm the terms of the surrender agreed with Kingsborough: these were put to the Wexford garrison on Common Quay Street and agreed by acclamation.

The Wexford Navy
Wexford had been the main Confederate port in the wars of the 1640s and the home indeed of the Confederate Navy. It was to assume this role again in 1798. At that time, Wexford was home to large fleet of small ships trading all over Europe. Hay tells us that in June 1798,

> Four oyster boats were fitted out in the harbour, and manned with five and twenty men each, to cruise outside the bay; and these, from time to time, brought in several vessels, mostly bound for Dublin, laden with oats, potatoes, and different other kinds of provisions … and four old sloops were ready to be scuttled and sunk in the channel, to prevent any such armed vessel, in the event of her passing the fort (of Rosslare) from approaching the town.[6] (Hay, 1803, pp 142–3)

John Howlin, a Wexford ship owner who had been a privateer in America under Washington, was appointed admiral of the Wexford Navy. On 2 June, one of the four refitted oyster boats, captained by John Scallan, captured a ship carrying Lord Kingsborough, colonel of the North Cork militia. He was en route to Wexford to join his men after their unhappy excursion to Oulart Hill and was unaware that the town had fallen. This was a significant capture and Scallan was rewarded later by being made the second admiral of the Wexford Navy. Scallan was tried and acquitted after the rising. William Blacker, colonel of the Armagh militia, a serious commentator on these events, noted in his own hand in 1837 on his personal copy of Musgrave's account, that:

> One Scallion had been appointed Admiral to the Republic. He got information on Lord K's being at sea and put out to intercept him which he did with some address. Those who saw the thing gave a ludicrous account of the way in which Lord K threw himself on his back on finding himself suddenly covered by twenty firelocks. He died at sea a few years ago as Captain of a West Indies freighter. WB. [Initials of William Blacker].

The navy also captured a Guinea cutter of forty tons burthen which had struck against the Blackwater Bank. She was armed with six small cannon and carried three barrels of gunpowder, a significant addition to the rebel arsenal. In fact good powder

---

6 The help of maritime historian for Wexford town, Jack O'Leary, on these boats is much appreciated.

was so scarce that only one barrel could be allocated to the Northern Army for the Battle of Arklow. Several cargoes of flour and potatoes en route to Dublin were also brought in and helped considerably.

The Committee of Public Safety

The Committee of Public Safety (its title borrowed from a committee in Paris during the French Revolution) replaced the notoriously sectarian old Borough Corporation (the last in Ireland to admit a Catholic). Matthew Keugh was appointed chairman of this committee by the Senate. He saw to it, insofar as he could, that all was done with democratic liturgical propriety. Very early in the life of the new administration, a special facility was set up by the Committee of Public Safety, to take care of lost or looted property and return it to the owners:

> Various plunder took place on the insurgents taking possession of the town, a great part of which was restored, as orders were issued that all kinds of property not belonging to those in whose possession it might be found, should be returned on pain of severe punishment. The court-house in Wexford was the repository for such property, which the owners recovered on making their claim. (Hay, 1803, pp 175–6)

As chairman of this committee Keugh automatically became commandant of Wexford town. He divided the town into wards, each with its own company of soldiers – the John Street Corps, the Selskar Corps and the Faythe[7] Corps, which between them were a cross section of the business and seafaring communities of the town. Numbering some 600 men in total, these corps elected their own officers and paraded through town twice a day led off by fifes, fiddles and drums (Musgrave, 1995, p. 424). They carried out regular guard duty, with their own passwords, in a town kept orderly day and night except for a couple of sudden outbursts of disturbance. They had a remarkable record in the protection of persons and property in the town. They carried out two official executions: both executed men were Catholics, informers who had been tried and convicted by a court of the new administration (Hay, 1803, p. 173).

A judiciary?

While the new administration did hold courts, there is no evidence that any attempt was made to form a broader juridical structure, the second arm of any state. However, we do know that several perfectly proper trials were held under the new administration. Several of these were referred to at the subsequent trial of Thomas Cloney in July 1799 (Cleary, 1999, pp 41–50), including when Henry Minchin, a witness for the defence, was questioned by Cloney himself:

7 Derived from the Irish word *faiche*, meaning a playing green.

Command and structure: a rebel republic?

>(Thomas Cloney) Did I save you from any and what danger during the rebellion?
>(Henry Minchin) I was taken prisoner by the rebels and put into jail. Shortly after I was ordered down to the gaol-yard to be tried with several others, before Bagenal Harvey, [Edward] Fitzgerald, [Edward] Roache [sic], Nicholas Gray, and others.
>(Cloney) Did you see me interfere to save the life of any other man?
>(Minchin) I heard you say to Mr Harvey, on the trial of one Smithson, who had been a quaker – 'you know Mr Harvey, quakers in general are republicans'.
>(Peter Burrowes to Minchin): Do you believe Mr Cloney said that with a view to saving Smithson's life?
>(Minchin) I believe he did. (Cloney, 1832, p. 257)

In a second example taken from his trial, Cloney questioned defence witness Thomas Greene:

>(Cloney) Did I interfere to save your life and when?
>(Greene) You did the evening of 31st May, 1798. I was brought from on ship-board to gaol, where Mr Harvey and others sat to try me for my life – through the prisoner's interference I was saved.
>(Cloney) Did any other person interfere for you?
>(Greene) No other person interfered for me.
>(Cloney) Did you know those who were present?
>(Greene) I knew Mr Gray, Mr Colclough and the prisoner [Cloney].

These references are clear evidence of trials properly conducted and taken very seriously if we are to judge by the status of the men on the bench. Not only that, but Greene's case was, he says, a capital one. On the trial of Cornelius Grogan immediately after the rebellion, one witness described Keugh as 'Chief Magistrate of the town' which suggests that trials were the business of the Committee of Public Safety (Sweetman, 2013, p. 282). It seems from what evidence we have that the legal process was limited and very ad hoc, which is hardly surprising given the times. But as things turned out, it appears that it would have been for the better had they been continued as they would have acted as a valve to relieve pressure from an aggrieved population and perhaps saved many lives.

Committee of Public Safety in Enniscorthy

Cloney refers to a local 'Committee of Public Safety' in Enniscorthy but it is indistinguishable from the town's administrative council and was possibly one and the same body. In Enniscorthy, the entire context in which the leadership had to manage affairs was very different. It ran a court that passed perhaps as many as a hundred capital sentences. It was described as 'a sham court' with 'summary trials', but it was also claimed that 'regular procedure of some sort appears to have been adopted' (Gahan, 2010, pp 131–65). The reason for the difference between the outcomes in Enniscorthy and Wexford may simply be a reflection of the effect and intensity of the May pogrom. Cloney believed that the reason for the harsh pre-rising oppression in north Wexford was that:

> There was then in the neighbourhood of Enniscorthy, a knot of the descendants of Cromwellian settlers, who were ever tenacious about the tenure by which they held their possessions, and were ever ready to crush the slightest ebullition of popular feeling with a vigour beyond the law … (Cloney, 1832, p. 7)

A definite working relationship between the Enniscorthy committee and the authorities in Wexford is confirmed by evidence given below, but the Enniscorthy council's control of affairs in their own bailiwick was weak. There were many executions carried out on Vinegar Hill from the day Enniscorthy was taken until five or six days into the new administration in Wexford town, when 130 well-armed men under shopkeeper John Murphy were despatched from Wexford to put an end to them. Although they did not cease, they were considerably curtailed.

How this mission came about provides us with our best, if not only, example of co-ordination between Wexford and Enniscorthy for which we have good evidence. Two important letters were found by the anonymous *Wexford Freeholder* in the Council Chamber of Enniscorthy on the day of the Battle of Vinegar Hill. They were addressed to 'Citizen Matt. Sutton, Vinegar Hill', who acted as secretary to the council in Enniscorthy. They were written and signed in Hay's handwriting, and both opened with the republican salutation 'Citizen'. Sutton replied with republican terminology in kind. In the first letter, dated 5 June, Hay tells Sutton that he (Hay) cannot send the reinforcements required by the Enniscorthy council – presumably to prevent the ongoing executions. Hay indicated that he might be able to do so the next day, 6 June. Thus it seems certain that it was Hay who arranged for John Murphy's 130 well-armed men to be despatched right at this time. This was in fact confirmed on the trial of Philip Hay by witness William Carty, who testified that he was at a meeting of

> a good many people who were principals among the rebels, in the house of Peter Redmond in Enniscorthy where it was determined that a letter written by Matthew Sutton be taken to Wexford by the defendant Philip Hay, who put it in his pocket, as he supposes to take it to Wexford.

Carty further testified that this was three or four days after the rebels taking Wexford, which would place this letter leaving Enniscorthy on 4 June. So we can now see the mission of John Murphy and his 130 gunmen actually being arranged between Edward Hay and Matthew Sutton, acting as secretaries of their respective administrations,

Command and structure: a rebel republic? 75

which Sutton certainly perceived as a Republic (*Wexford Freeholder*, c.1803, pp 7–8). After the rising, Sutton was tried and transported to Botany Bay.

Wexford Prisons Committee

In Wexford itself there existed a Prisons Committee chaired by William Kearney. It was a subcommittee of the Committee for Public Safety. The prisons were relatively well-controlled until the day prior to the administration's collapse, when Keugh's entire garrison was drawn off from the town for the Battle of Horetown. This provided an opening for Thomas Dixon and a multitude of people fleeing before Needham's advance southward, who demanded that the jail be opened and were determined to repay the culprits who partook in the May pogrom. More than seventy prisoners were subsequently murdered on Wexford Bridge on foot of the most arbitrary evidence before a sham tribunal. There were several clearly innocent men among the guilty.

The Commissariat

This body was set up to supply the army and navy with food and material, and Wexford town (which had a population of about 8,000 at that time) with food. As already quoted above, Hay referred to it specifically when he says 'various other appointments and regulations took place for the maintenance and supply of the country'. It comprised twelve men in all, businessmen from the town and landed men from the country. Cornelius Grogan of Johnstown Castle was chairman, at least in a titular capacity. Musgrave says Grogan was appointed 'Commissary to the Republic' (Musgrave, 1995, p. 418). He was 70 years old and in poor health. He was chiefly concerned with the food supply function. He had demand notes printed, which the armies presented to merchants for the supply of provisions in specified quantities, and a simple system was introduced to feed the townsfolk. All households were given coupons for food in accordance with the number of residents there. Loyalist households were not discriminated against:

> Among the various duties of the committee one was that of supplying every person in town with provisions. On application to them every house was furnished with a ticket specifying the number of inhabitants, and all persons, even the wives and families of those considered the greatest enemies of the people, were indiscriminately included; and every person sent with a ticket to the public stores appointed for that purpose, received a proportionate quantity of meat, potatoes, and other necessaries free of any expense. The bread in general was bad as no good flour could be obtained. (Hay, 1803, pp 143–4)

Hay described the establishment of the Commissariat during the 31 May, prior to official ratification by the Senate that night:

> The people of Wexford … appointed twelve of the principal inhabitants as a committee, to regulate the distribution of provisions, as well as of all other necessaries in requisition … As whiskey and leather were the articles most in demand in the camps, distillers and tanners especially entreated the committee to issue regular orders for the supplies from their stores … The committee proved the salvation of the country … (Hay, 1803, p. 141)

He goes on to say that the demand from the army for materials was such that 'a separate committee for each article in demand had to be appointed' (Hay, 1803, p. 175). Grogan was later executed for his part in the rebellion. At his trial a Mrs Segrave gave evidence that:

> her family in the town were in want of food, and that she sent to Mr Grogan to give her an order [docket] for some bread – which request to save her family he reluctantly complied with. Through that order she procured some loaves, and supplied her children; and for that benevolent act, and on that lady's evidence, Mr Grogan was sentenced to die as a traitor and immediately hanged and beheaded. (O'Kelly, 1842, p. 110)

The Commissariat nominated two representatives in every parish to take inventories and to organize supplies from the rural areas:

> according to directions from the committee, or the commander in chief, and each of the commissaries had a certain number of pikemen under his command. (Musgrave, 1995, p. 336)

The accompaniment of pikemen, when picked from a locality, ensured the compliance of farmers, supplied local knowledge, helped to network with owners, drovers and butchers and deal with any other matters arising. Several commissaries were court-martialled after the rising (Sweetman, 2013, p. 282). A few documents involving commissaries are given in Musgrave. A receipt to the chief commissary of the Northern Army, John Brennan, shows that republican terms and salutations may not have been uncommon:

> Received from Mr John Brennan, seventeen bullocks, to keep at grass till called for. June 18th, 1798, first year of liberty. Stephen Myler.

The work of the Commissariat expanded to an unmanageable degree as more and more duties were heaped upon it (Hay, 1803, p. 175). A typical example of this was a munitions factory established near the Bullring in Wexford town where every forge was a hive of industry night and day. The overall volume of pike production and repairs in

> *By order of the council for directing the affairs of the people of the county of Wexford.*
>
> *Oaths to be taken by all the united army, in the most publick and solemn manner.*
>
> ### TEST OATH.
>
> IN the awful presence of God, I, *A. B.* do voluntarily declare, that I will persevere in endeavouring to form a brotherhood of affection among Irishmen of every religious persuasion; and that I will also persevere in my endeavours to obtain an equal, full, and adequate representation of all the people of Ireland. I do further declare, that neither hopes, fears, rewards, or punishments, not even death, shall ever induce me, directly or indirectly, to inform, or give evidence against any member or members of this, or similar societies, for any act or expression of theirs, done or made collectively or individually in or out of this society, in pursuance of the spirit of this obligation.
>
> So help me God.
>
> *Oath of a private.*
>
> I, *A. B.* do solemnly and sincerely swear, and take God and his only son our Lord Jesus Christ to witness, that I will at all times be obedient to the commands of my officers; that I am ready to lay down my life, for the good of my country; that I have an aversion to plunder, and to the spilling of innocent blood; that I will fight courageously in the field, and shew mercy where it can be given; that I will avoid drunkenness, tending to disorder and ruin; that I will endeavour to make as many friends, and as few enemies as possible; that above all, I detest a coward, and that I will look upon him as an enemy who will stand back in the time of battle.
>
> So help me God.
>
> *Oath of an officer.*
>
> IN the awful presence of God, who knows the heart and thoughts of all men, and calling my country to witness, I, *A. B.* officer in, &c. do solemnly swear, that I do not consider my life my own, when my country demands it; that I consider the present moment calls for a proof of the sincerity of that sentiment, and I am ready and desirous to stand the test; and do aver, that I am determined to die, or lead to victory; and that all my actions shall be directed to the prosperity of the common cause, uninfluenced by any inferior motive: and I further declare my utter aversion to all alarmists, union-breakers, and cowards, and my respect and obedience to the commands of superior officers.
>
> So help me God.
>
> *Done at the council chamber, Wexford, June 14th, 1798.*
>
> By order of the council,
>
> B. B. HARVEY, *president*,
> NICHOLAS GRAY, *secretary*.

4.1 Oaths to be taken by the United Army – the name of the Council issuing the order makes clear its country-wide ambition and has echoes of revolutionary France.

the Bullring was satisfactory but muskets damaged by inexperienced usage were not always reliable when repaired. Huge efforts were made to increase supplies to both the Southern Army and the Northern Army for the battles of Horetown and Vinegar Hill.

THE WAR

The chain of victories at Oulart, Enniscorthy and Three Rocks was halted abruptly at New Ross and Arklow on 5 June and 9 June respectively. New Ross was a major blow, not only due to the heavy toll of casualties, but also because of the deliberate burning of Scullabogue Barn, not far from the town, by undisciplined elements on 5 June. An estimated one hundred mostly Protestant prisoners – men, women and children – were trapped inside and murdered when the barn was locked and set on fire. This was followed by crown forces at Ross hanging and shooting every straggler they found after the battle there. Two proclamations in quick succession emerged from Wexford. Edward Roche, speaking as general of the Northern Army, issued a proclamation under his own name on Vinegar Hill on 7 June:

> In the moment of triumph my Countrymen let not your Victories be tarnished with any Wanton Acts of Cruelty: many of those unfortunate men now in prison were not your enemies from principle … neither let a difference in religious sentiment cause a difference among the people. (Hay, 1803, p. 168)

This was followed by another proclamation on 9 June, almost certainly written by Edward Hay, promising justice for the aggrieved, in an attempt to assuage the thirst for vengeance arising from the May pogrom:

> PROCLAMATION of the PEOPLE of the COUNTY of WEXFORD
> Whereas, it stands manifestly notorious that James Boyd, Hawtry White, Hunter Gowan and Archibald Hamilton Jacob, late magistrates of this county, have committed the most horrid acts … Now we the people associated and united for the purpose of procuring our just rights … do call on our countrymen at large … to apprehend … the aforesaid and to secure and convey them before the tribunal of the people.
> Done at Wexford, this 9th day of June, 1798.
> GOD SAVE THE PEOPLE.
> (Cloney, 1832, p. 199)

Unknown to anyone, apparently the four magistrates in question were now safely ensconced in Duncannon Fort, as their former handiwork wreaked havoc on both communities across the county.

We have a few intriguing reports from the start of the new administration, when confidence was high and their forces seemed to carry all before them. Musgrave says 'the governors of the newly-established republic prohibited the circulation of banknotes, with a view of injuring the credit of government' (Musgrave, 1995, p. 425). Dr Jacob, the former mayor, then serving as a doctor with the new administration, testified that he 'saw Mr Hay again passing by with Mr Harvey; said they were to give circulation to bank notes' (Hay, 1803, app. XII), meaning that they intended to print their own currency in place of bank notes. The rumour certainly spread abroad.

Command and structure: a rebel republic?

Musgrave speaks of a rebel who 'pulled out of his pocket a large quantity of banknotes, in the street of Wexford, and tore them; swearing at the same time, with much vehemence, that he would ruin all the banks in Ireland' (Musgrave, 1995, p. 425).

Meanwhile, army discipline was perceived to be fraying and the Southern Army was suffering numerically because of men returning to their homes. But change was on the way. On 14 June, Commander Philip Roche wrote to Fr Doyle of Sutton's parish, ordering him

> to order all your parishioners to the camp on Lacken Hill, under pain of the most severe punishment; for I declare to you and to them, in the name of the people, if you do not, that I will censure all Sutton's parish with fire and sword. Come to see me this day. ROCHE. (Musgrave, 1995, p. 406)

Within a few days of the Battle of Arklow (9 June), crown forces, based on Gorey, began to commit a string of atrocities on the Wexford-Wicklow border. There were plenty among the rebel army who could scarcely be restrained from retaliation in kind and this produced a rise in insubordination in the army and among the people:

> So violent was the spirit of retaliation and vengeance, which seemed to actuate the whole mass of the people, that every danger was to be apprehended from it, unless some means were taken to allay the existing ferment. (Hay, 1803, p. 192)

The situation threatened to get out of control and caused particular alarm among the loyalist prisoners in Wexford town:

> Reports of these enormities very much alarmed the minds of the prisoners in Wexford, as they strongly apprehended it might produce an alteration in the conduct of the inhabitants towards them … (Hay, 1803, p. 191)

Into this tense situation two letters arrived from a significant but unknown source in Dublin, apparently military. They were intercepted en route to Wexford by rebel guards at Enniscorthy and delivered to the local council where they came into Secretary Sutton's hands. Sutton duly sent them on to Hay in Wexford as they were addressed to Kingsborough and Lt. Bourke. The anonymous commentator calling himself the 'Wexford Freeholder' described how this worked and what resulted:

> It is well known that Mr Hay and one Myler [sic] a noted rebel had been chief secretaries of state to the Republic of Wexford while it lasted; and therefore it fell to their lot to examine all papers and dispatches which were sent to their mightinesses, and they of course opened the King's Mail; in which having found

> two letters one for Lord Kingsborough and the other for his fellow-prisoner Capt. Burke, … the two secretaries after perusing [the letters] delivered them to his Lordship and the Captain, for which Mr Hay claims much credit: but the fact proves, that he opened the mail, and that he was high in office under the Republic; so much for Mr Hay's loyalty. (*Wexford Freeholder*, c.1803, pp 5–6)

Having perused them Hay delivered the letters to Kingsborough and Lt. Bourke but his apparently secretive conduct in this matter, when it was discovered, was not without consequence. Bourke wrote two years later:

> Mr Hay narrowly escaped with his life, as Captain Keugh, who then commanded in Wexford, expressed great anger on hearing it from Lord Kingsborough, who inadvertently mentioned Mr Hay having done so [delivered the letters], and Mr Hay was afterwards constantly prevented from visiting us by order of Capt. Keugh. (Hay, 1803, app. XI)

Hay, who had been in close contact with the prisoners, says:

> A petition to government, from those confined in the gaol, was accordingly drawn up, expressive of the danger of their situation … They accordingly communicated to me their apprehensions and wishes, and proposed striking out some mode of putting a stop to the violences [on the Wexford-Wicklow border] … Lord Kingsborough was for proposing an exchange of prisoners as the best method of allaying the prevailing alarms … (Hay, 1803, p. 191)

Apart from the growing spirit of insubordination, another and equally pressing worry was the danger that an influential segment of the people would oppose any attempt to open negotiations, for fear it would lead to surrender and to severe repercussions for themselves and the evasion of justice by the culprits they sought to punish. Hay understood the situation, musing that 'how to reconcile the people to the measure, without which nothing effectual could be done, was the difficulty' (Hay, 1803, p. 193). Clearly such a major move required the highest authority if it was to have any chance of securing acceptance by the people or the army, and for this and other reasons the second meeting of the Senate was convened. A further important reason of a different nature was that an honourable proposal would be made in relation to Scullabogue. Thomas Pakenham in *The year of liberty* captured the intent:

> A further attempt was also made to re-shape the government of the Wexford Republic. The system of ad hoc committees with popular representation was too top-heavy and disorganized to handle these delicate negotiations with the Government. (Pakenham, 1972, p. 289)

Command and structure: a rebel republic?

And so the Senate was convened a second time. Hay describes it rather diffidently, as usual:

> On the 13th of June, several persons from the different encampments, led by the most benevolent motives, as if by preconcerted agreement, waited on the commander-in-chief, in Wexford, to consult on the best mode of keeping the unruly rabble in some order ... He immediately assembled those he thought best able to advise him how to proceed, and it was considered fortunate that many respectable persons from the country were then in the town, all of whom approved of endeavouring to forward the sentiments of the prisoners along with Lord Kingsborough's answer ... Accordingly those who had been in consultation with the commander-in-chief proceeded along with him to the house wherein the different committees usually met ... (Hay, 1803, p. 192)

Such an array of respectable people 'from the different encampments' and 'from the country' providentially assembling in Wexford, all at the same time, cannot have been so accidental as all that. Clearly something major was up. No doubt we are looking at a meeting of the Wexford Senate being convened to consider the matters mentioned.

SECOND MEETING OF THE SENATE, 13 JUNE 1798

This critical Senate meeting was held in the 'Senate House' as Musgrave called it. There are no descriptions of the numbers attending, but we know that it sanctioned three proposals: firstly, it approved the establishment of an enquiry into Scullabogue; secondly, it approved the prisoners' embassy to Dublin; and thirdly, it set up a council to oversee affairs and impose discipline.

Although the regime did not survive long enough to initiate the enquiry into Scullabogue, its establishment by the Senate should be noted, because it stands as clear testament that a sectarian pogrom against Protestants was never their policy and would not be tolerated. As to the prisoners' embassy to Dublin, 'the Council immediately proceeded to forward the very plan they themselves [the prisoners] had previously intended to put into operation' (Hay, 1803, p. 193). Lt. Bourke of the North Cork militia set off the next day for the capital, accompanied by the well-chosen Robert Carty of Birchgrove who was both rebel captain and council member, to help Bourke through the rebel lines at Enniscorthy (Sweetman, 2013, pp 102–4). However, they were stopped by some of the people in the town who had been inflamed against the project by Thomas Dixon, who had spread suspicion that a surrender was being considered behind their backs. Bourke was returned to the prison in Wexford the following day. Negotiation with Dublin was now no longer possible, as the Northern Army appeared unable to uphold the writ of the Senate in this matter.

The Council was more successful in its task to impose discipline and improve the governance of the new polity. It had been given a very well-considered name to impress and reassure the army and people of its role. It was named the Council for Directing the Affairs of the People of the County of Wexford. As the name indicates, the authorities in Wexford clearly saw their role as applying to the whole county.[8] The council comprised eight men – four Catholic, three Protestant and one Presbyterian – not elected by the people but probably selected by the leaders and sanctioned by the members of the Senate:

> eight persons, considered the most capable of applying a speedy and effectual remedy to the existing evil, were appointed, and the body so selected denominated 'the council appointed to manage the affairs of the people of the county of Wexford' of which Mr Harvey was chosen president.[9] (Hay, 1803, p. 193)

The Catholic members were Edward Hay, Ballinkeele; Robert Carty, Birchgrove; Robert Meyler, Gurteeminogue; and Edward Kearney, Wexford. The Protestants were Beauchamp Bagenal Harvey of Bargy Castle (president); William Hatton of Clonard and Matthew Keugh of Wexford town. Nicholas Gray of Whitefort, Oilgate, a Presbyterian, was secretary.

Bagenal Harvey was appointed president of the council, but he was removed as commander-in-chief of the Wexford Army with the post given to the then commander of the Southern Army, the redoubtable Fr Philip Roche. The inter-denominational composition of the council was a quintessential United Irish statement that the new order would not be just a change of denominational supremacy, but a new departure where Catholic, Protestant and Dissenter could work together – quite a revolutionary outlook in the Ireland of the time. Significantly, Hay, the most influential man in Wexford, always steering events from behind, was now on the council and bent on working for a negotiated end to the rising.

The loyalty of the army was all important now and they were given the opportunity to object to any member of the new council (Hay, 1803, p. 193). With the embassy to Dublin thwarted, the immediate restoration of discipline to the army and the people was now the main priority for the council and so, on 14 June, a range of compulsory oaths applicable to Wexford Army officers and men, and one for the population at large, were introduced by Bagenal Harvey and Gray (for full texts of oaths, see Taylor, 1800, p. 77). Furthermore, the Council issued a severe Proclamation condemning all

---

8 In an age when Latin was far more widely understood than it is today, the translation of the 'affairs of the people' is *res publica* – a nod perhaps to the idea of a 'republic' operating in the background. **9** Hay inserted 'managing' in place of 'directing', possibly to distance it from the Directory in Paris. Cloney copied it and unfortunately it has spread. But the correct original version, as given above, can be seen on their own proclamation.

forms of indiscipline and prescribing heavy penalties, including the death penalty for insubordination – and none too soon, as the enemy was approaching.

On 16 June, as crown forces began to hover on Wexford's borders, the wind had changed and the first English reinforcements sailed into Dublin. That same day, Secretary Gray sent a reassuring despatch to the new Commander-in-Chief Roche, who was desperate for reinforcements for the much reduced Southern Army. The despatch asserted that the new council would deliver where the old system had failed:

> Dear Citizen,
> … We have, however, now issued orders, desiring all unmarried men to repair to camp immediately: we did so before, but they were not fully obeyed: at the present time particular obedience will be enforced, and we trust you will shortly find at your camp a number of fresh young fellows, as well appointed and provided as our best efforts can accomplish. (Taylor, 1800, p. 166)

Gray had sent men through the southern parishes rounding up young men. Many recruits were also drawn from Wexford town. On 19 June, as events moved inexorably towards the great encounters of Horetown and Vinegar Hill, crown forces were moving towards Co. Wexford from Waterford, New Ross, Bunclody, Carnew, Tullow, Tinahely and Arklow while several British gunships began to muster off the coast.

On 20 June, General Lake ordered a general advance on all fronts from the borders of the county. General Needham began his advance from Gorey towards Oulart, leaving a trail of burning and destruction for a mile on either side of him. No prisoners were taken. The people fled before him on the clogged roads, ending up in the triangle east of the Slaney between Oulart, Enniscorthy and Wexford town. The situation in this area now became wildly unstable and open to manipulation.

The immediate challenge, however, was General Moore, advancing towards Wexford town from the south-west. Very late on 19 June, an order came from the Three Rocks camp for the 600 men of Keugh's Wexford garrison to join them at daybreak. Every available man was needed to confront Moore's advance. Discipline had been enforced with such effect that on 20 June a replenished Southern Army fought the Battle of Horetown – one of the longer 1798 battles – against one of the most experienced British commanders, who would later become a hero of the Peninsular War. On this occasion the battle was inconclusive and only the shortage of gunpowder forced the Southern Army to withdraw. Gray had been as good as his word, although the role of the forceful Commander-in-Chief Philip Roche must also be taken into account in effecting this turnaround.

However, in the meantime, Wexford town had been left open to the multitude fleeing south from Needham's marauding army, outraged by the further death and destruction, and despairing of any justice for their sufferings. The desperate reality of their situation has been largely ignored, even though it was their dark, harrowing experience that provided the insurrectionary impulse that forced the outbreak of the rising, and had remained the primary source of the insistent demand for retributive justice that resulted in distrust of the new rebel administration and its councils, as well as recurrent challenges to its authority during its lifetime. They were the neglected people of the rising.

It appears that no loyalist had so far suffered execution in Wexford town on foot of the May pogrom, and it was possibly this fact more than anything else that was responsible for what was now to happen as the rebel administration's worthy but hesitant policy of due process was overborne. The people took over and some seventy loyalist prisoners were brought before an *ad hoc* tribunal and put to death on the bridge, innocent among the guilty, and Keugh was powerless to prevent it. The manner of their deaths was, in recorded cases, often gratuitously cruel and constituted in itself a human and political tragedy. That evening was one of great drama in a town traumatized by the executions on the bridge. The like had not been seen since Cromwell. A great battle had been fought that day in Horetown and as English gunboats hung offshore, another was preparing for the morrow on Vinegar Hill: two of the biggest battles in Irish history. The faint light of democracy was already flickering to extinction, when about 10.00 p.m. the first returning men brought news of the indecisive result of Horetown.

THE LAST MEETING OF THE WEXFORD SENATE

With the end in sight, Kingsborough sent for Edward Hay to discuss the terms of capitulation to be sent to General Lake, the commander of the English forces at Enniscorthy. Hay insisted the matter be put to the people and he assembled as many of the 'respectable persons' as he could as it was about 8.00 p.m. He was desperate to stall for time as no terms could possibly be agreed before the outcome of Vinegar Hill was known, and so they agreed to meet again early the following morning 'at Captain Keugh's house, where the subject would be taken into consideration by a general assembly, which could not be formed at that time of night'.[10] This would be the last meeting of the Senate.

But at 3.30 a.m., Kingsborough again sent for Hay, and when Hay reached his abode he found him impractically arrayed in his regimentals, ready to go to Enniscorthy. Hay dissuaded him from this foolishness, saying the principal inhabitants were to meet presently in Keugh's house and that he was sure of their concurrence with the plan

---

[10] Keugh lived in what is now Lower George Street. It cannot have been a large gathering and probably comprised no more than 25 persons as the main reception room in Keugh's, the largest room in the building (which is still there today), measures only 25m^2.

Command and structure: a rebel republic?

to capitulate. As Hay left him, he could hear the cannon opening up at Vinegar Hill: probably a reference to those early salvoes fired from Lake's artillery at Ballynabarney.[11]

It was still very early when the final meeting of the Senate opened in Keugh's house. The windows rattled as English gunboats bombarded Rosslare Fort, which a Wexford force had vacated the previous evening (Hay, 1803, p. 226). To the north, the Battle of Vinegar Hill was in progress, from which a well-ordered retreat would ultimately see the greater part of the Northern Army escape, under cover from General Roche leading a fresh force of 5,000 men from Ballaghkeene and Shelmalier baronies. Meanwhile in Wexford, the Senate approved a proposal for terms of capitulation drawn up by Hay in discussion with Kingsborough over the previous hours. The central point of this was

> that they are ready to deliver up the town of Wexford, without opposition, to lay down their arms and return to their allegiance, provided that their persons and properties are guaranteed … and that they will use every influence in their power to induce the people of the country at large to return to their allegiance …
> Signed by order of the inhabitants of Wexford, 21 June, 1798.
> Matthew Keugh. (Hay, 1803, p. 225)

It was also decided that an embassy be sent with these terms along with a letter drafted by Lord Kingsborough to Needham, Moore and Lake, the commanders of the enemy armies at Oulart, Taghmon and Vinegar Hill, respectively. Meanwhile, Kingsborough would stay in Wexford, which would be surrendered to him immediately as military commander. Keugh was anxious to retain the command in the town until the Wexford Army's position was clear, but this was 'most spiritedly opposed by Mr Hay' (Hay, 1803, app. xi). The former Mayor Jacob – who had served the rebel administration as a medical doctor – now resumed his previous office.

Because the numbers in the Senate were depleted; and to reinforce the mandate behind the terms, the Senate decided as usual to put these proposals to the armed corps as a form of wider public and army approval. For this purpose, they assembled the corps on Common Quay Street and approved the terms by acclamation to save the town. With each delegation Kingsborough sent this letter to the approaching commanders

> that the town of Wexford being surrendered to him; and that in consequence of the behaviour of those in the town during the rebellion, they should all be protected in person and property; murderers excepted, and those who had instigated others to commit murder, hoping that these terms might be ratified

---

[11] The writer would like to acknowledge the help of Brian Jordan, proprietor of these lands; Jacqueline Hynes; Gregory Walshe, Taghmon; and Rónán Ó Flaitheartaigh in the identification of this site.

> as he had pledged his honour ... the Wexford-men not being concerned in the massacre which was perpetrated by the country people in their absence. (Hay, 1803, p. 224)

Kingsborough, on accepting military authority over the town, asked the revolutionary commander of the town for his sword in the traditional manner. Keugh, regretting that it could not be surrendered to the approaching armies, presented his sword 'with the greatest formality'. Commander Keugh's insistence on every propriety of the surrender being fully observed is no mere indulgence in ceremony: he was marking, as well as circumstances would allow, the demise of the Wexford Republic.

EPILOGUE

General Lake, still in Enniscorthy, where his men had burned the rebel hospital with seventy wounded men in it, rejected the terms. He wrote on 22 June:

> Lieutenant-General Lake cannot attend to any terms by rebels in arms against their sovereign: while they continue so he must use the force entrusted to him, with the utmost energy for their destruction. To the deluded multitude he promises pardon on their delivering into his hands their leaders, surrendering their arms, and returning with sincerity to their allegiance. (Taylor, 1800, p. 111)

The Northern Army, which had known the May pogrom and experienced the worst of the oppression, also rejected the terms agreed with Kingsborough, preferring to fight on. Having retreated from Vinegar Hill to the camp on Forth Mountain, the Northern Army now divided in two, with Father John Murphy going north-east as far as Co. Laois and Anthony Perry's force going north almost to Ardee (see also chapter 13). They were to know suffering.

Opinions differ as to whether a 'Wexford Republic' ever existed, but there is now a growing acceptance that some formal 'government' was in place. Certainly, as we have seen, the term 'republic' was used by contemporary authors to describe the administration that was put in place, and the institutions that were put in place carry the hallmark of a republic. But where did its authority reside – with the pike or the people?

It comes down to this: if the first great meeting of principal citizens came together purposefully to formally adopt, in the name of the people, the various proposals coming forward from those hurried meetings earlier on 31 May; and if this is why they assembled again for the establishment of the council on 13 June; and if this is why, though reduced in number, they assembled to sanction the terms of surrender, then even the strictest standards of evidence for the existence of a republic ought to be seen to have been met.

If not, then we must answer three questions.

Firstly, for what purpose was a 'very general meeting' (Cloney, 1832, p. 22) of the principal citizens of town and county assembled in Cullimore's on the night of 31 May, and what but the most serious business could require them to resume again on the 1 June?

Secondly, why should Bagenal Harvey and Hay even bother to convene the principal citizens in the Senate House (as Taylor and Musgrave named it) on 13 June to contemplate such already urgent matters as the establishment of the inquiry into Scullabogue, the establishment of the Council for Directing the Affairs of the People of the County Wexford and to permit the prisoners' delegation to travel to Dublin?

And lastly, if not to sanction them, why were the principal citizens required at all, to approve, in circumstances of prodigious urgency, terms of surrender already agreed by Hay and Kingsborough?

Was the answer to all three not because the top echelon of Unitedmen, like Keugh and Bagenal Harvey, in times of even the most appalling difficulty, insisted on having recourse to the people for the ultimate formal authority, because they appreciated that it was this recourse to the people for authority that made it a republican as distinct from a military government? And is that insistence not their gift to our history – and their own greatest memorial?

CHAPTER FIVE

Testing the theories of why the Hon. Major General Francis Needham was 'late' for the Battle of Vinegar Hill

JACQUI HYNES & BARRY WALSH

> If the wholesale destruction of a deluded multitude were a desirable object, certainly the failure of this movement is to be lamented – for the rebels were enabled to get off bodily, whereas, had Needham reached his ground, they must have been so totally *derouted*, that no exertions could have rallied them again, and the flame of rebellion would have been extinguished. (Maxwell, 1845, 148)

INTRODUCTION

For many years a story has endured that the Hon. Major General Francis Needham was 'late' for the Battle of Vinegar Hill through a reluctance to become involved in a massacre of the many thousands of men, women and children who were on the hill that day. The inference was that he acted to deliberately create a gap through which the rebels could escape, therefore preventing a scene of mass slaughter. The research team sought to investigate the validity of this assertion, with the assistance of the Department of Defence, representatives of the Reserve Defence Forces, and members of Lord Edward's Own and Enniscorthy Historical Re-enactment groups, endeavouring to follow the route taken by General Needham as faithfully as possible.

We examined contemporary and modern maps of the locality to identify the mostly likely route, and undertook research of primary and secondary historical sources for references to Needham's participation in the battle, and explanations for his absence from his designated point (the area around Darby's Gap, sometimes called Needham's Gap, on the road from Enniscorthy to Wexford – see fig. 5.3). We also explored what the cause of Needham's absence was, if not compassion. Was it compassion on the part of his commander-in-chief, General Lake, as is sometimes suggested in the contemporary accounts? Or was it the late change to Needham's orders and then Lake's subsequent decision to return to the 'original' plan? Could this, coupled with the time taken to move and reverse the column, including the long, slow and cumbersome baggage train, be the ultimate reason for his delay in arriving at his originally designated position?

Our investigations highlight the confusion at the time as to the reason for his absence, which caused a public disagreement between historians of the day. Our test march also revealed that very little had changed in the intervening 220 years, including public perception of Needham's delay or the length of time taken to make the journey.

HISTORICAL ACCOUNTS

Details of General Needham's participation in the battle are recorded in a variety of sources, including contemporary accounts, biographical memoirs of those present and even woven into a 'spat' between historians, which drew the intervention of Needham himself. The course of events for Needham and his men, from 20 June to the morning of 21 June, is not in doubt, and recalled in great detail in both primary and secondary sources. There is, however, no consensus on the cause of his delay, not even among those who were considered to be 'on the same side'.

The background is neatly summarized by Pearse (1908, p. 104), who tells us that the force was 'commanded by Major-General Needham, an officer who had distinguished himself in the American war and had served with Lake at Yorktown'. Stationed in Loughlinstown Camp in Co. Dublin, Needham was ordered to proceed to Wexford in early June 1798. He commanded the crown forces at the Battle of Arklow on 9 June, and on 20 June received orders to proceed from there to Vinegar Hill, marching, with a significant baggage train, through Gorey and Oulart, with the purpose of participating in what was to be the decisive battle of the rebellion in Wexford.

Primary sources

M'Laren (1798, pp 26–9), a sergeant with the Dumbartonshire fencibles who was part of Needham's column, recalls the timeline for their movements and suggests, interestingly, that some might have considered the resulting delay to have arisen out of concern for the rebels. He specifically records rumours that General Needham 'had orders to let the croppies escape'. However, he dismisses such rumours and, insightfully, he notes that they were 'very immaterial to us whose sole business was to obey':

> We had not been above an hour in Owlart [sic] when an Express arrived from General Lake to General Needham, in consequence of which we were ordered to strike our Tents and begin our march in the dusk of the Evening with positive

injunctions to observe the most profound silence. The occasion of this movement was that the Commander in Chief had designed to collect as many troops as he thought expedient to surround Vinegar-hill …

In order to co-operate with these troops we marched all night and arrived about day-break within a mile and a half of the hill on the left, where we lay for about an hour, rolled up in our Blankets in the ditches by the road's side … When our men (General Needham's army) saw the rebel flag, they showed the most eager desire to begin the attack, but it was near six o'clock before we were put in motion, and even then instead of marching straight forward we were ordered to take a circuit of at least five or six miles which made it impossible for us to be up in time.

This we much dreaded, because ere we had marched two miles from our last ground we heard the cannonading of General Johnson's column …

It was thought by some of the soldiers who are perhaps none of the greatest politicians that General Needham had orders to let the Croppies escape as government might be unwilling to cut off too many deluded wretches in the very midst of their sins. The reason they assign for this opinion is, that had the General advanced a little sooner and drawn a line from the left of General Dundas's column to the river, it would be impossible for the rebels to escape to Wexford, but this is mere conjecture and very immaterial to us whose sole business was to obey. [emphasis added]

Miles Byrne (1863, p. 170), one of the United Irishmen leaders at Vinegar Hill, felt there was a more strategic reason for Needham's diversion to Solsborough:

We were now nearly surrounded on all sides, except the Wexford one which should have been occupied by general Needham, it was said, had he followed his instructions. – This is mere twaddle; he remained in the rear, in reserve, by the orders of his general in chief Lake, to keep the road open to Gory. This prudent English general who refused to fight us at Kilcavin hill, did not like to risk a charge of our pikemen, without having a division in reserve to fall back on, in case of defeat. [emphasis added]

Thomas Cloney, another United Irishman leader, however, states with confidence that the delay was a humanitarian one, and makes no mention of any fear of a resurgent rebel force (1832, p. 71):

General Needham was to occupy a position east of the hill, but he, through some unaccountable cause, did not come up, and it has been confidently stated that he received instructions the evening before the battle to leave a passage, by which the people might retreat. [emphasis added]

Theories of why the Hon. Major General Francis Needham was 'late' for the Battle

Secondary sources

By far the most comprehensive account of Needham's movements during the battle is noted by Richard Musgrave (1802, ii, pp 8–11). He also refutes the assertions of another historian, the Reverend James Gordon, claiming endorsement of his account by Needham himself. Musgrave highlights the part played in the delay by having to turn the huge baggage train around, but his account also agrees with Miles Byrne's in attributing the initial decision by General Lake to call Needham to Solsborough to his commander-in-chief's anxiety about a possible rebel attack:

> As general Needham's column did not occupy the post allotted to it in the first arrangement for surrounding Vinegar-hill, on the south-east side of it leading to Wexford, I think it right to explain the circumstances which prevented it.
>
> He marched from Gorey on the 20th for Oulart, at six A.M. and received orders to halt about a quarter of a mile from that town, where the roads divide, till twelve o'clock, or such time as he conceived colonel Campbell, who commanded the Light Infantry, had made good his march, without interruption.
>
> This delay caused his arriving so late in the evening at Oulart, an inconsiderable village to the east of Vinegar-hill, and within six miles of that part of it where he was to take post.
>
> On that evening, when the troops had taken up their ground, and driven back some advanced parties of the enemy, and made a proper disposition for protecting four hundred carriages laden with provisions and ammunition, for the army which attended them, general Needham received an order from general Lake, about half an hour after eight o'clock, signed by the adjutant-general, desiring him to march immediately with the troops under his command to join general Lake at Solsborough, the seat of Mr. Richards, where he had taken up his head-quarters.
>
> The guide conducted the troops to Solsborough, who passed by the road on the left leading directly to Vinegar-hill; and it was observed by several officers, that the column had lost their road, till they were informed of the order to march for Solsborough. The harnessing and arranging in the proper order of march such a number of carriages, occupied a good deal of time.
>
> Thus incumbered, the movement of the column was slow; particularly, as it passed through deep and narrow roads, with high and thick fences on each side, and in a country so much enclosed as to render it impossible to send out flanking parties; though, from their proximity to the enemy, there was every reason to expect an attack, which, had it been made, might have proved fatal.
>
> However, the column proceeded unmolested, and arrived at Solsborough, about half past three o'clock, on the morning of the twenty-first of July [recte: June]. Major-general Needham, on reporting his arrival to general Lake, was

informed by the general himself, 'that he must immediately occupy the position first allotted to him, in the general orders'. Thus, after a most fatiguing march, without having had any refreshment for his troops from the time he left Gorey, he was obliged to repair to the post he was to occupy by a circuitous route of eight miles.

In obedience to his orders, major-general Needham proceeded, at the head of the grenadier company of the Antrim militia, who led the column, when it was scarcely light; but soon after he discovered that great numbers of the infantry who had been ordered to fall in, overcome with hunger and fatigue, had lain down again. Lieutenant Camack conveyed a message from lieutenant-general Lake to major-general Needham, while on his march, requesting to know if his column would arrive at his destination in an hour; and his answer was, that it was impossible for the infantry to be there in one, or even two hours, but that he himself would proceed immediately with the cavalry, which he accordingly did, and took his post, having ordered the infantry to follow as speedily as possible; but, though they did not arrive until the action was over, it did not arise from the fault of any officer or soldier in that column.* (The reader will find a further explanation of this affair in appendix No. XXVI)

Major-general Needham was but six miles from Oulart to the post of attack destined for him in the original orders; and had the troops under his command been allowed to take proper refreshment and repose, at the former place, they would have attained their position in full strength and vigour, and long before the action began. He was more than eight miles from Solsborough to the post of attack; and the counter-marching his cannon, and the turning and tackling 400 ammunition waggons [sic], in a deep narrow road, which was almost impracticable, caused a very great delay; however, by rapidly advancing with his cavalry, he was able to cut off many of the fugitive rebels; but his infantry could not arrive in due time to share the laurels of that day, the complete and perfect success of which they would have ensured, had they been allowed to move from Oulart to the point of attack, as was first designed.

It is to be lamented, that a large body of rebels escaped at the point which general Needham was to have occupied; but as he acted precisely according to the orders which he received, no censure could be cast upon him, or on any of the officers under his command.

As Mr. Gordon, in his history of the rebellion, differs materially from me in his statement of this transaction, I have made the most sedulous enquiry about it, from the most respectable officers of the king's troops and the yeomen; and I have the concurrent testimony of a great number of them that my relation of it is perfectly correct. [emphasis added]

As mentioned above, appendix XXVI (Musgrave, 1802, ii, p. 546) notes that he now has in his possession a letter from General Needham himself, dated 1 March 1802, which clarifies the reason for his late arrival:

> The reason that lieutenant-general Lake ordered general Needham to repair to Solsborough, from Oulart, contrary to the general orders given to the different columns destined to attack Vinegar-hill, was this: General Lake was very near that mountain, on which there was an immense body of rebels and apprehending an attack, in which the rebels by the great superiority of their numbers, aided by the darkness of the night, in a very inclosed country, might have baffled discipline, he, <u>desirous of strengthening his main body, suddenly changed his orders to major-general Needham</u>, which made it impossible for the latter to be at his post of attack in due time. This contradicts the mistatement of Mr Gordon in page 193. I give this from the *very first authority on that command*. [underlining added for emphasis]

The source of ire to Sir Richard Musgrave and General Needham must have been the suggestion by Reverend James Gordon that he (Needham) was late because of humanitarian concerns (1803, pp 171–2):

> The attack began at seven o'clock on the morning of the 21st, with a firing of cannon and mortars, and all the armies were in their several posts, except that of general Needham, who arrived not at the appointed position till nine, when the business was over. For this the honourable commander can doubtless account in the most satisfactory manner, though the matter is not clear to me.* However, this and other occurrences gave occasion to some ill-natured persons to bestow on him the epithet of the *late general Needham*. The rebels after sustaining the fire of the artillery and small arms for an hour and a half, abandoned their station and fled where the passage lay open for them, which passage has been ludicrously termed *Needham's gap*, most of them directing their course toward Wexford.
>
> *Sir R. Musgrave says, that this piece of conduct of general Needham arose from orders inconsistent, and impossible to be executed, sent him by general Lake. As general Lake is certainly of no such puny intellect as to merit the title of an *old woman*, he had doubtless good reasons for what orders he issued, and knew how to apply each instrument to its proper purpose. <u>The commonly received opinion is, that general Lake, unwilling to permit the slaughter of so many thousands</u>, which would have been horrible; or to urge their despair, which might have been dangerous; and distrusting the discipline of his men, who perhaps could not possibly be restrained from slaughter in case of the surrendry of the rebels, <u>contrived a gap for their escape in the quarter of general Needham, without deigning to confide his plan to that commander</u>. [underlining added for emphasis]

Pearse (1908, pp 106–7), in his memoirs of General Lake, gives an interesting insight into the delay, suggesting that issues in managing the baggage train drivers also added to the time required to travel the route, but asserts that the ultimate goal was the 'total destruction of the rebels':

> The column commanded by Major-General Needham, who had shown both skill and determination at Arklow, was also too late for the encircling movement. Needham had in his charge 400 impressed waggons, carrying the supplies of the whole army. With an enemy in great numerical strength close at hand, and experiencing much difficulty in controlling his drivers, many of whom were disaffected, it will be readily understood that Needham found that his march took longer than the calculated time …
>
> Needham then did his best by throwing his cavalry forward; but although the latter did some execution, the gap caused by the non-arrival of Needham's infantry prevented <u>the total destruction of the rebels that had been intended and would have taken place</u>. [emphasis added]

Contrastingly, Sir Llewelyn Turner, a Welsh politician with an interest in recalling stories of the 1798 rebellion in Ireland from his youth, had a very interesting opinion on General Needham, alluding to 'secret instructions' to deliberately delay his arrival. He also recalls the humorous nicknames of two of the generals (1903, pp 45–6):

> Towards the end of the rebellion, the Government, seeing that the head of the rising was broken, were desirous to avoid further bloodshed as far as possible. A large body of rebels were encamped upon a hill, and the generals, Needham and Eustace, had orders to attack, but had secret instructions from Government that if the rebels gave way they were to let them escape. The public, not being aware of the instruction given by the Government and believing that the generals had been guilty of neglect, transposed their names from Needham and Eustace to Generals Needless and Useless.

As a result of our analysis, we are excluding humanitarian intent by Needham as a cause for his delay, as all accounts confirm that he was summoned to Solsborough by Lake, and therefore was only following orders for his column on the eve and day of the battle. In addition, any of the contemporary accounts that suggest a secret humanitarian intent attribute that intent to the commander-in-chief himself, General Lake – not to Needham. This then transfers the investigation to Lake himself. Did he contrive to leave a gap through which the rebels could flee, and Needham was merely the general chosen to implement his covert plan? This suggestion can also be eliminated based on observations of Lake as a soldier, including his actions while in Co. Wexford. Take, for example, his response to the rebels' request for terms on 21 June:

Theories of why the Hon. Major General Francis Needham was 'late' for the Battle

5.1 British regimental baggage wagons, *c*.1802. Print after W.H. Pyne.

> Lieutenant-General Lake cannot attend to any terms by rebels in arms against their sovereign. While they continue so he must use the force entrusted to him with the utmost energy for their destruction. To the deluded multitude he promises pardon on their delivering into his hands their leaders, surrendering their arms, and returning with sincerity to their allegiance. *Enniscorthy, June 22, 1798 Signed G. Lake.* (Kavanagh, 1874, p. 221 and Musgrave, ii, 1802, p. 34)

These are not the words of a man distressed by the thought of continuing violence. He will not even discuss terms of a surrender.

It is a matter of fact that General Needham was ordered to Solsborough at approximately 8.30 p.m. on the 20 June 1798. Having arrived there at approximately 3.00 a.m., he was then ordered to re-trace his steps and march to his original designated position. Having eliminated any secret humanitarian intent playing any part in the plans, we then examined whether the nature and composition of Needham's column and the baggage train, and the obstacles they faced on their route to and from Solsborough, hindered their arrival at their appointed position in time.

NEEDHAM'S MARCH

We know from manuals such as the 'Rules and regulations for the formations, field-exercise, and movements, of His Majesty's Forces' the expectations and procedures covering all aspects of a soldier's life. This gives invaluable information relating to the requirements of soldiers marching with Needham through Co. Wexford:

- Needham's men would have undertaken a 'long march' or 'route march' from Oulart to Solsborough, a phrase used to describe how the British army of the

1790s covered long distances. Rayner (n.d.) notes that this differs to marching 'on a front', which was used on the battlefield and parade grounds, and is more lenient and less regulated.

- The pace of march is seventy-five paces per minute, and a unit is expected to cover up to three miles per hour at this pace.
- According to Rothwell (1888, p. 40), for each hour of march, a halt to rest of five minutes is allowed.
- It was recommended that the column of soldiers was formed by 'platoon' or 'sub-division', depending on the terrain. This means that the column would have marched either eight to ten men wide if by 'platoon' or four to five wide if by 'sub-division'. It is most likely, given the narrow nature of the roads in the locality, that they marched by 'sub-division'.
- On the march an infantry battalion was led by a vanguard or mainguard. This is the foremost part of an advancing army and consisted of a party of infantry, some horse artillery and cavalry. It would also have included pioneers (soldiers employed to perform engineering or construction tasks and whose chief duty was to remove obstacles for the marching column) and possibly a screen of picquets (a soldier or small group of soldiers assigned to a duty such as being sent out to watch for the enemy). They would have been dispatched to proceed on the side of any expected attack. For example, Alexander (1800, p. 100) comments of the march by General Johnson during the same campaign: 'On Tuesday, the eighteenth of this month, early in the morning, GENERAL JOHNSON, with the whole of the Ross Garrison, marched against VINEGAR-HILL, &c. On this occasion I was ordered to procure 126 men to attend the army with spades, pick-axes, and other implements, to make way for the cannon, and in short, to act as pioneers.'
- The other elements of the column were the main body, the rear guard (soldiers at the rear of a body of troops), a party (under the control of a corporal) to collect stragglers and most likely a bread wagon to carry men who fell out due to illness. There would also have been a detached guard of infantry and cavalry accompanying the baggage. The numbers involved in each element would depend on the circumstances of the column.
- As per the rules and regulations on formations, 'the attention of the soldier is allowed to be relaxed' (Rayner, n.d., p. 369). Soldiers were allowed to talk on the long march as long as they didn't become loud and boisterous. M'Laren (1798, p. 26), however, notes they were asked to observe the most profound silence while making their march, and Musgrave (1798, ii, p. 9) comments that given the topography of the area it was impossible to send out flanking parties.

Knapsacks

It is likely that on their march to Vinegar Hill the soldiers were in 'light marching order' with their packs or knapsacks (leather or canvas envelope type packs) on their backs with blankets rolled and stored on top. This meant they did not carry their camp equipment with them (a billhook, an axe, a camp kettle shared between six men and their greatcoats), instead leaving these with the baggage train. According to Haythornewaite (1999, p. 129), the total weight of this equipment was up to 60lb, including the musket and bayonet (14lb), cartouche containing sixty rounds (6lb), rations in the haversack and a canteen of water (7lb). The soldiers would have marched and gone into combat with these on their backs, and our investigators also carried a knapsack with them for authenticity.

Baggage train

The baggage train is the logistical element of the army's combat units. It carries everything needed to keep them fed and supplied. For the campaign in Ireland civilian drivers with their carts and wagons were hired to transport the vast majority of supplies, but there were also specialist vehicles belonging to the army itself which formed part of the baggage until needed. Most civilian vehicles of this time were two-axle wagons pulled by teams of two, four or six horses (the eighteenth-century equivalent of the articulated lorry). There would also, most likely, have been a number of single-axle carts pulled by one or two horses. The baggage carried items not immediately needed by the combat units such as camp equipment and greatcoats. Officers were allowed to have personal effects carried in the baggage, frequently amounting to a large quantity of luggage and home comforts. Sergeants were allowed to have a box carried in the baggage, but the ordinary soldier carried all his personal possessions in his knapsack. Other military supplies such as ammunition may have been carried in the specialist carts. Spares, materials and equipment for the artillery were also carried with the baggage, and the bulkiest material for transportation would have been the fodder and feed for the hundreds of horses. There were also special travelling forges used by the farriers of the cavalry regiments for shoeing horses. Rogers (1977, pp 85–6) summarizes as follows:

> The type of transport varied of course, considerably because it was made up mostly from the carts and wagons used by the farmers and traders in the theatre of operations … The regimental baggage moved in the army baggage column … and were used for tents and blankets. Every squadron had a forage cart and there are references to farriers' carts, which were presumably the travelling forges … The train was composed of artillery equipment, spare gun carriages, ammunition carts and wagons, pontoons and their carriages, wagons for artillery and engineer stores and specialist vehicles.

5.2 An army wagon train moves along a country road. Print after W.H. Pyne.

There were strict prohibitions on carrying any civilians or camp followers with the baggage, and the only passengers carried were sick soldiers. Commanders knew that the baggage of the army presented a tempting target for the enemy, so it would usually have been guarded by a squadron of cavalry and some infantry.

Overall length of Needham's baggage train

When calculating the length of the baggage train, we know from Musgrave (1802, ii, p. 10) that Needham was responsible for a 400-strong baggage train. Rothwell (1891, p. 37) stipulates the length and distances between each wagon:

> Rough rule: 1 yard for each horseman and for every two foot soldiers; 20 yards for each vehicle. A 2-horse vehicle requires 10 yards; A four-horse vehicle requires 15 yards; A six-horse vehicle requires 19 yards [all including 4 yards distance]. A single horse, mule, or pack animal requires 4 yards, and a camel 5. Minimum width of road necessary for cavalry in sections, 18 ft.; for infantry in fours and Artillery in column of route, 9 ft. Minimum width of opening to allow guns to pass, 7 ft. 6 in. Track of guns and military wagons (normal), 5 ft. 2 in. (outside).

Given the likelihood that a sizeable proportion of the artillery equipment was pulled on vehicles with six horses, occupying a linear space of some 19 yards, we can suggest a maximum length for the baggage train of about 7,600 yards or just over 4 miles (nearly 7km). Depending on the mix between two-, four- and six-horse wagons (see table 1), the very shortest Needham's baggage train could have been was about 2 or 3 miles (3–5km).

Table 1: Length of baggage train

	Yards	Miles	Kilometres
400-strong baggage train (6-horse) x 19 yards each	7,600	4.3 miles	6.9km
400-strong baggage train (4-horse) x 15 yards each	6,000	3.4 miles	5.5km
400-strong baggage train (2-horse) x 10 yards each	4,000	2.3 miles	3.7km

Pace of march

As mentioned, a rate of 3 miles per hour was considered optimum for 'field artillery and train' over ideal flat terrain with military drivers, proceeding unhindered and without interruption (Rothwell, 1891, p. 40). However, as noted above, the terrain surrounding Vinegar Hill was far from optimal, and the long baggage train made its way cautiously through deep and narrow roads, in the dead of night, in areas unknown to the officers, guided by drivers they had not previously worked with and in constant fear of attack from the rebels. Based on these conditions, a potential maximum speed of 1.4 miles per hour is suggested, but this could have been as slow as 0.7 miles per hour, depending on the challenges of the terrain (Sheldon, 1904, p. 6).

Additional constraints

We know from accounts that there were two other issues delaying the departure time of the soldiers and baggage train. Archibald M'Laren (1798, p. 27) says that when the men arrived near Solsborough they slept for an hour 'rolled up in our blankets in the ditches by the road's side', inferring that their preparation for departure only began at approximately 4.30 a.m., and then 'it was near six o'clock before we were put in motion'. This is understandable given that some 1,800 men (infantry and cavalry), combined with a baggage train up to 4 miles long with their supporting drivers and guards, had to be turned and the order of the baggage train and column reversed on very narrow roads before they could even commence their march.

There is no specific reference to the method of turning the baggage train, but Musgrave (1802, ii, p. 10) confirms that it was turned. It appears that the 'order of march' of the baggage train is not of significance, so there may well have been no need to reverse the order of the train, but merely to about-turn each cart. This turning would however have required a turning distance at the side of the road, so possibly

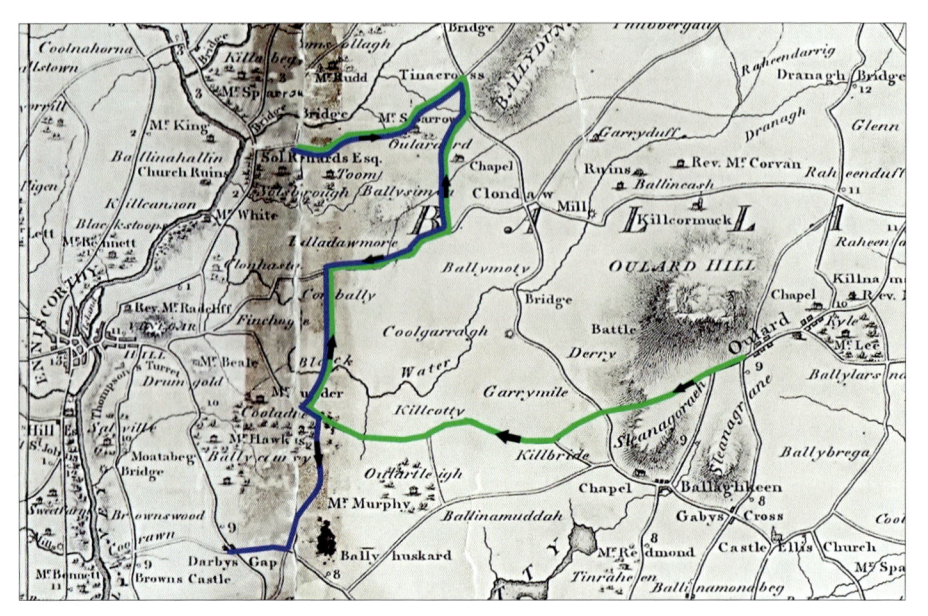

5.3 Route taken by Needham's column from Oulart to Solsborough (in green) and from Solsborough to Darby's Gap (in blue). Base map is by Valentine Gill, 1811. Reproduced with permission of Wexford County Council Archive Service.

wagons were turned in fields on either side of the road. The troops attached to it for defence would then have marched to the reversed head of the column, and adopted their original positions. However, the order of the infantry column did require reversal and they would have been counter-marched (performed a U-turn) to achieve this. They too may have turned in adjoining fields.

FIELD TRIALS

We conducted our test on Sunday, 3 September 2017, departing Oulart Village at 8 a.m. The weather conditions were poor, with a constant drizzle (unlike 21 June 1798, when the weather was notably warm and dry) but improved over the course of the morning and afternoon. The team marched along the route and at Cooladine Crossroads split into two groups – one team going left, and proceeding to Darby's Gap, and the second turning right and proceeding to Solsborough (see fig. 5.4). Both teams marched distinct stretches of Needham's route and the times were then collated at the end of the walk. It should be noted that we did encounter a modern disturbance along our route – an under-construction road bypass, but as it was at the very end of each route, it did not impact significantly on our test or the findings. The results of the field test are summarized in Table 2 below.[1]

[1] Exact times for each section: Oulart to Solsborough, 184 minutes 50 seconds; Oulart to Cooladine

Table 2: March times

Route	Distance	Expected pace	Expected time	Needham's march	Research team's march
Oulart to Solsborough (Green Route)	11.25 miles (18.1km)	3 mph	3 hours 45 minutes	7 hours: 8.30 p.m. to 3.30 a.m., including preparing train for departure	3 hours 20 mins, including a 15-minute rest break
Solsborough to Darby's Gap (Blue Route)	8.45 miles (13.6km)	3 mph	2 hours 49 minutes	4 hours 30 minutes: 4.30 to 9.00 a.m., including turning column and train but later jettisoning infantry and train	2 hours 20 minutes, including a 10-minute break
Total march	19.7 miles (31.7km)	3 mph	6 hours 34 minutes, without breaks	12 hours 25 minutes, had the infantry reached Darby's Gap, including 55-minute rest break	5 hours 50 minutes, including a 25-minute rest break
Total March at wagon speed	19.7 miles (31.7km)	1.4 mph	14 hours 4 minutes, without breaks	12 hours 25 minutes, had the infantry reached Darby's Gap, including 55-minute rest break	

Table 2 is highly instructive. General Needham took almost *twice as long* as the official manuals of the time indicate for a column marching at the expected infantry pace of 3 miles an hour. Why was this? Is the pace set out in the manuals realistic and achievable over terrain like this? Our field test suggests that it is perfectly achievable: as illustrated above, the research team marched the distance at the required pace of the infantry (i.e. 3 miles per hour, if not a little faster). So why did it take Needham so long? The answer must be that Needham's entire column proceeded at the speed

Cross, 89 minutes 28 seconds; Cooladine to Solsborough, 95 minutes 22 seconds; Cooladine to Darby's Gap, 44 minutes 56 seconds.

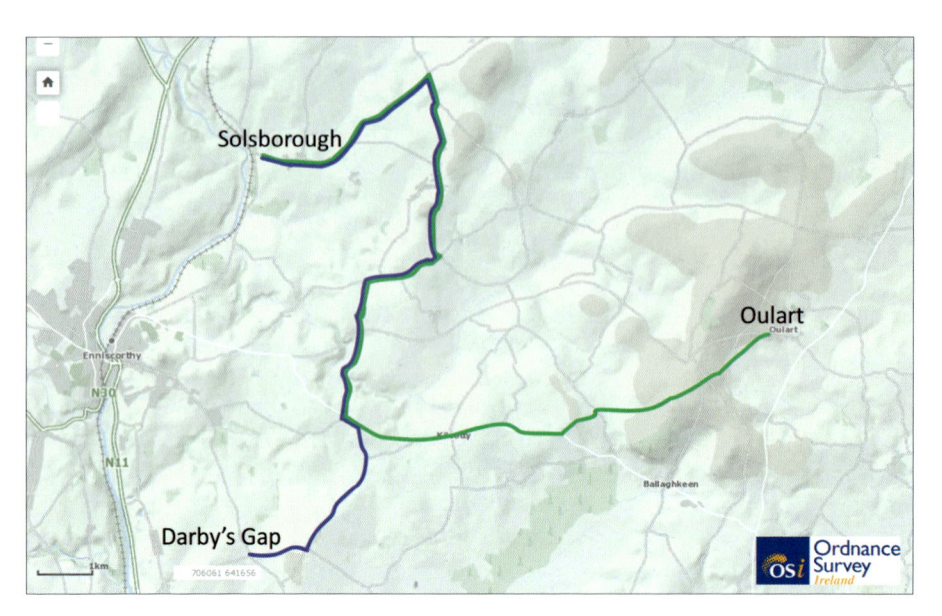

5.4 Route taken during test march on 3 Sept. 2017, reconstructing the route taken from Oulart by Needham in 1798, first to Solsborough (green) and then to Darby's Gap (blue). Base map © Ordnance Survey Ireland/Government of Ireland. Copyright permit MP 001021.

of the slower baggage train, which would optimally have been 1.4 miles per hour. The estimated time for the column to complete the journey to Darby's Gap at this speed should have been 14 hours and 4 minutes without breaks, and our analysis indicates that had Needham remained with the column he would have made the journey in 12 hours and 25 minutes, including a rest-break of 55 minutes. In other words, he was proceeding as fast as he possibly could towards his destination while keeping his column together, until he realized he would have to split off with the cavalry if he was to have any hope of closing the gap. This ties in completely with Musgrave's account (referred to earlier), which has Lake dispatching a rider to Needham while on his march asking him if he could be in his position within an hour, to which Needham replied that 'it was impossible for the infantry to be there in one, or even two hours, but that he himself would proceed immediately with the cavalry'. Clearly, up to this point he had remained with the slower-moving column but, finding that events were now outstripping him, he opted then, and only then, to abandon the baggage train and infantry and try to close the gap with the cavalry alone.

CONCLUSION

Did an act of compassion permit some 20,000 men, women and children to escape the narrowing net of a well-armed and well-equipped army on the field of battle?

5.5 Members of the Reserve Defence Forces, Lord Edward's Own and Enniscorthy Historical Re-enactment Group, who participated in our investigation. Photo by Jacqui Hynes.

Widely held belief claims it did. Research proves it didn't – based on personalities, orders and logistics.

We know from historical accounts that Needham was ordered by his commander-in-chief to march away from his originally designated position and join him at Solsborough. We also know this was then countermanded by a subsequent order to return to his original position, requiring Needham to turn his entire column around on narrow roads and march back the way he came. This added some 14 miles to the journey, one he and his column travelled at the slower speed of the baggage train, winding their way through enemy country at the dead of night. We know the battle was well advanced before Needham ever got close to his position. When news reached him that the rebels were retreating and were now flooding through the 'gap' that he was to have sealed, Needham had no choice but to abandon his infantry and wagons and pursue them with his cavalry instead.

There is no need to look to secret 'acts of compassion' to explain the delay, either on the part of General Needham or General Lake, despite widely held belief at the time that this must have been the case. Unhindered by the baggage train, he could possibly have arrived at Darby's Gap in time for the battle, but a combination of changing orders and the challenge of turning a baggage train that may have been over 4 miles long on narrow country roads, simply made it impossible that he could ever have arrived in time.

ACKNOWLEDGMENTS

Our thanks to Paul Kehoe TD, Minister for Defence, Commandant Enda McDonald, Sergeant John Cooney, Sergeant Dick Martin, Corporal Joe Mullins and Private Paddy Brereton of the Reserve Defence Forces. Barry Walsh and Peter Molloy of Lord Edward's Own and Peter Freeman, Ray and Paul Murphy of Enniscorthy Historical Re-enactment Group. Also thanks to Brian Cleary and Muireann Hynes for their assistance on map interpretation, timings and distances.

CHAPTER SIX

The field of battle

RONAN O'FLAHERTY & RORY O'CONNOR

INTRODUCTION

In a way, we are fortunate that the Battles of Enniscorthy and Vinegar Hill happened when they did. Why? Because we have maps – lots of maps. They are not all of the same quality or scale and are not always accurate – but they are still maps and they allow us to reconstruct the field of battle in a way that would have been virtually impossible had these battles taken place even fifty years earlier. In this chapter we will explore three 'fields' of battle – Enniscorthy town, Vinegar Hill and the wider landscape of the 'Big Houses'.

WHAT'S IN A NAME?

Vinegar Hill's Irish name – Cnoc Fhiodh na gCaor – tells us something about that early landscape. Translated, this is the 'Hill of the Wood of the Berries' (Joyce, 1891–1913, iii, p. 597), but that wood was gone centuries before the battle took place. Grattan Flood (1898, p. 125) translates it as 'The Hill of Judgement', based on what he believed was an anglicized corruption of the Gaelic term *fenecus*. Mícheál Óg Ó Longáin gives us 'Cnoc an bhFinégire, aimsir Cnoc an bhFinchair' (Ní Shéaghda, 1939, pp 191–2), which is just 'vinegar' in Irish, and so a somewhat circular argument. However Joyce delivers the etymology which has won general acceptance as follows:

> Vinegar Hill … This name has never been explained till now. There was formerly a wood around the hill which was well known by the name of Fiodh na gcaor, represented exactly in sound in English letters by 'Feenagare' … This I have ascertained by hearing the name pronounced on the spot, as I did thirty years ago by several intelligent old natives. This name was retained by the old people down to recent times and I believe it may still be heard if rightly searched. Hence the hill was naturally named the 'Hill of Feenagare' or 'Feenagare Hill' as I often heard it called, which got easily corrupted to Vinegar Hill. (Joyce, 1891–1913, iii, p. 597)

6.1 Down Survey map of Enniscorthy showing a walled town at the junction of two rivers. L. Brown Collection of Digital Historic Maps.

However, because the Gaelic version of the name has been 'back-engineered' from a phonetic rendering in English, all Joyce can do is point to a plausible Irish language version of that sound. We cannot say with confidence that this is in fact the name, but Cnoc Fiodh na gCaor – 'Hill of the Wood of the Berries' – seems a likely construction and it is the one that is most generally accepted today.

ENNISCORTHY AND VINEGAR HILL IN 1798

One of the earliest maps that we have of Enniscorthy and the surrounding country was produced as part of The Down Survey, conducted from 1656 to 1658. This map (fig. 6.1) emphasizes the strategic position of Enniscorthy at the junction of two rivers, the Slaney and the Urrin. Interestingly, the town itself is depicted as walled although there is no documentary or archaeological evidence that this was ever the case. However, the fact that some of the hottest fighting during the Battle of Enniscorthy and later during the Battle of Vinegar Hill took place at what is referred to as 'the Duffry Gate' may well recall a time when there actually was a wall or bank surrounding the town. Early road maps, like Taylor and Skinner's from 1777 (fig. 6.2), also make the strategic

The field of battle 107

6.2 Early road map by Taylor and Skinner showing Enniscorthy around 1777, with Vinegar Hill and its landmark windmill clearly visible.

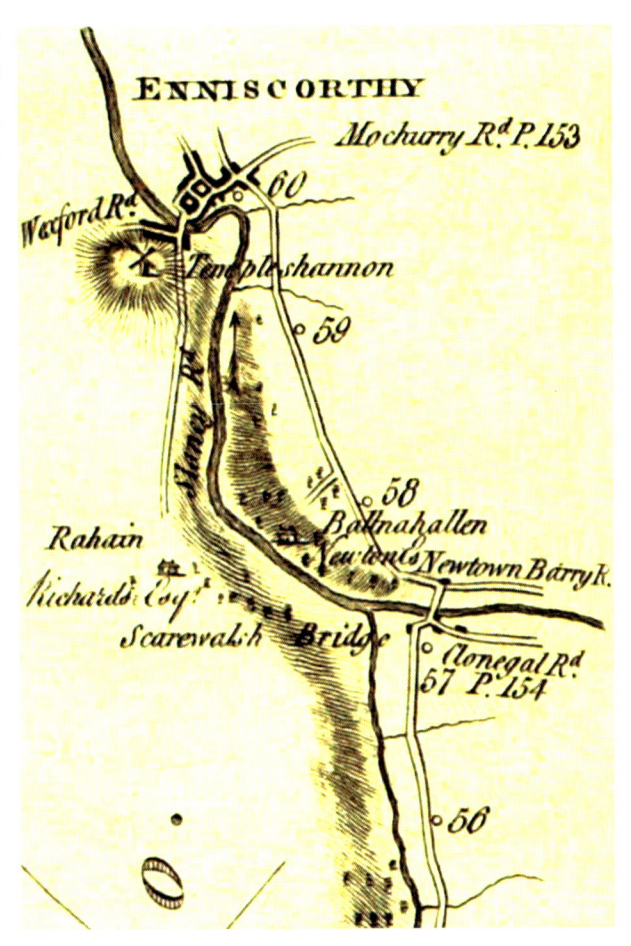

position of Vinegar Hill very clear. It is shown prominently, along with its landmark windmill, commanding the town of Enniscorthy, the road from Dublin to Wexford and the road to New Ross and Waterford.

One of the very best overviews of the entire landscape comes from 1811 in the form of the Valentine Gill map (fig. 6.3). Produced just thirteen years after the rebellion, this map is the closest we have in time to the Battle of Vinegar Hill itself. It provides a wealth of information, showing the layout of the streetscape of the town and, very importantly, the various roads in use at the time, which differ in many respects to those we are familiar with today. A key point to remember in this respect is that the R744, which runs across the northern slopes of Vinegar Hill, did not exist in 1798. The map also names the principal landowners in the area, as well as landmarks like Darby's Gap, the scene of a fierce rearguard action by the rebels.

As for Vinegar Hill itself, even though it is just under 120m, it commands extensive views of the surrounding countryside, stretching north to the Wicklow Mountains

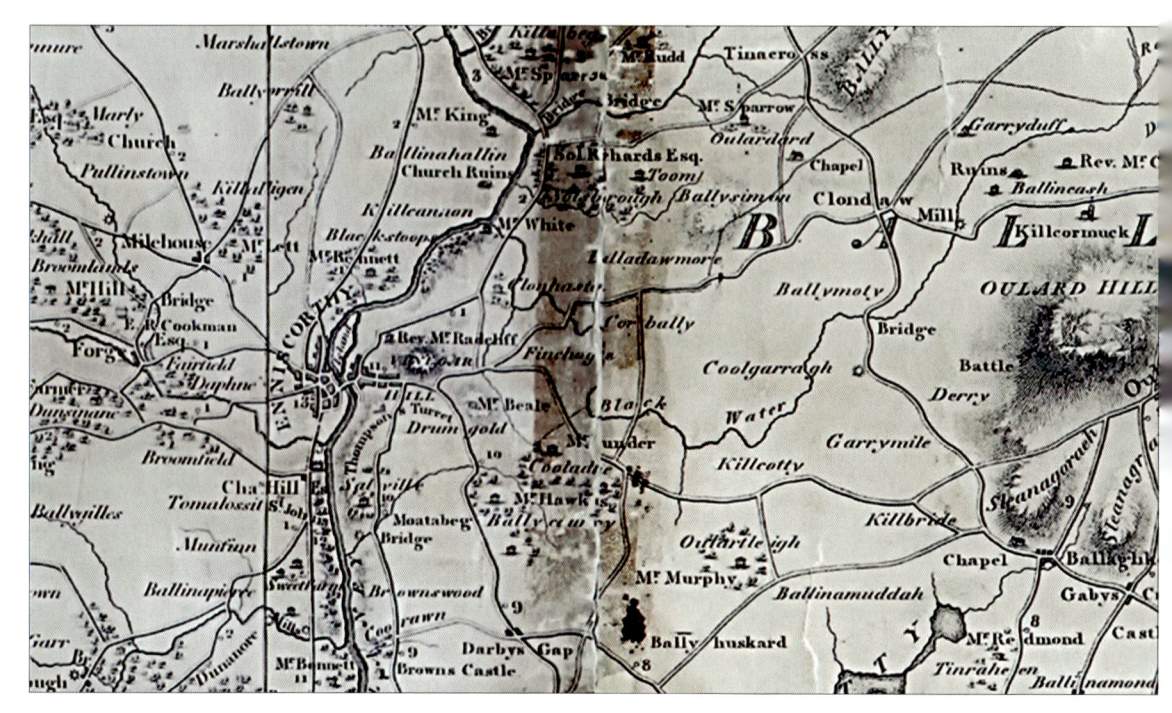

6.3 Valentine Gill map of 1811. Reproduced with permission of Wexford County Council Archive Service.

and south to Forth Mountain, thereby locating Wexford town as well, lying at the eastern end of that mountain. It overshadows the town of Enniscorthy to the west with views across to the Blackstairs and the routes to both New Ross and Carlow, while to the east is Oulart Hill, scene of the first major defeat of government forces during the rebellion in Wexford.

Strategically, then, Vinegar Hill could hardly be better chosen, providing visibility across almost the full extent of the operating area of the rebel forces.

THE BATTLE OF VINEGAR HILL: A GENERAL OVERVIEW

Before moving to discuss the battlefield along with the various contemporary accounts, it may be useful to give a general summary of what we now know of the course of the battle itself.

On 21 June 1798, a camp of some 20,000 insurgents on Vinegar Hill was surrounded and attacked by a force generally believed to be of some 13,000–15,000 government troops and possibly as many as 20,000. In command of these was General Gerard Lake, supported by no less than three other generals and sixteen general officers. Lake

The field of battle

had planned this as the final destruction of the rebel army, carefully manoeuvring his troops so that there could be no escape from the hill. A well-armed force, including both cavalry and infantry, with some thirty-four artillery pieces and a baggage train up to 7km long (see chapter 5), Lake's army was the most formidable to take the field in Ireland in a century. By contrast, the rebel camp included large numbers of non-combatants who had taken refuge on the hill. Those defending them and the hill were armed mainly with pikes, and had only two rounds for their cannon. The line of command on the hill is unclear, as the democratic principles of the rebellion applied even to that. However, the leaders included Anthony Perry, Miles Byrne and the charismatic Fr John Murphy of Boolavogue.

Lake was taking no chances. He gave the signal to advance with a gun at 4.00 a.m.. General Johnson seems to have already been engaging the rebels at this stage to the west of the town. When all contingents had moved to their assigned positions, artillery bombardment of the hill began, around 7.00 a.m. Lake had at his disposal a new exploding shell, used at Vinegar Hill for the first time. These were anti-personnel weapons, designed to explode in the air above the enemy or seconds after landing. This was shock-and-awe warfare of a kind never seen before in Ireland. Bombardment of the hill was combined with an infantry assault, and this deliberate, orderly attack continued for perhaps two hours (accounts differ). Contemporary accounts talk of the rebel defenders being slaughtered where they stood in their trenches. Meanwhile in the town, General Johnson had pushed the defenders, led by Barker and Kearns, back into the Market Square, where desperate house-to-house fighting continued throughout the morning. The rebels gradually yielded ground until they reached the bridge across the Slaney. Here they made a last stand. Despite overwhelming odds, they held the bridge – this was to prove crucial later.

On the hill, a multi-pronged attack was yielding results: Lieutenant General Dundas had made ground on the rebels' right flank, while Major Generals Loftus and Duff were pressing heavily on the centre and left. The rebel command began to contemplate a general retreat. They noticed a gap in the encircling forces to the south – a gap that was supposed to have been closed by the Hon. Major General Needham. Fortunately for the rebels, a change to the orders issued by Lake meant that Needham was delayed in taking up his position, leaving that crucial gap open and earning himself a place in history in the process as 'The Late General Needham' (see chapter 5). Sometime after 9.00 a.m. the rebels began to flood through 'Needham's Gap', protected to the west by their comrades in the town who still denied the bridge to the attacking crown forces there, and by an extraordinary rearguard action led by Fr Thomas Clinch. Once the main body of rebels had made good their escape, the defenders at the bridge made a successful retreat themselves. However, the rearguard led by Fr Clinch was overrun and Clinch himself was killed. All might yet still have been lost, for as the rebel force flooded back towards Wexford town, Major General

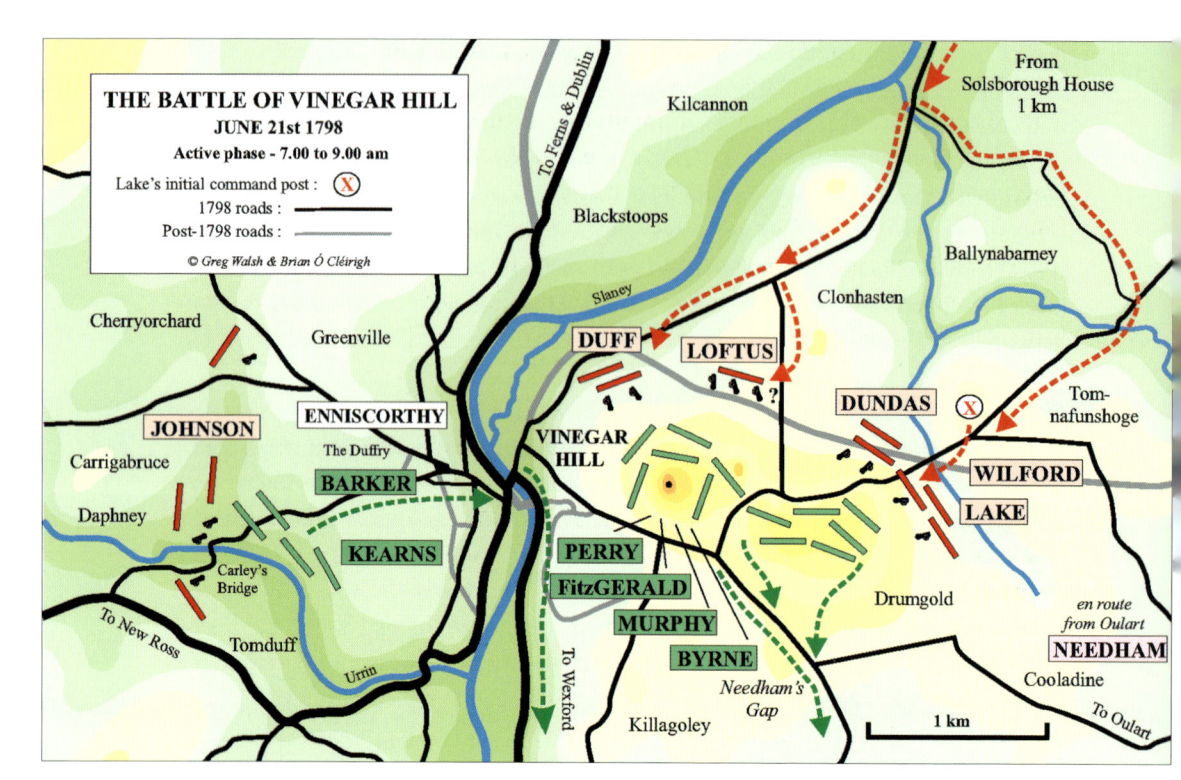

6.4 Plan of the Battle of Vinegar Hill. Map by Greg Walsh and Brian Ó Cléirigh.

Needham's cavalry finally came into sight and began a pursuit that could have inflicted terrible casualties had not the long-awaited relief force from Wexford under Edward Roche arrived on the scene. Roche and Needham engaged each other until eventually Needham withdrew. Some miles further south, the tattered remains of the rebel army limped into the temporary safety of Wexford town.

The defeat had been devastating but, remarkably, the rebel army had actually managed to escape from the hill relatively intact. This did not happen by chance. All the evidence, including the contemporary accounts from the government side, point to a surprisingly disciplined rebel defence and fighting retreat, holding their positions strongly even as they fell back. In fact, the French periodical *Le Bien Informé* of 8 July 1798, which had been covering the rebellion in Ireland from its inception, advised its readers not to 'believe news of a total defeat of the rebel forces at Vinegar Hill; it is quite possible that they have just moved camp to another hillside' (Dickson et al., 1993, p. 264). This, of course, is precisely what happened – the rebels did indeed regroup on Forth Mountain outside Wexford town – but to all intents and purposes the rebellion in Wexford was over.

THE FIELD OF BATTLE: ENNISCORTHY TOWN

Some easily identifiable structures of importance during the rebellion survive in the town. These include Enniscorthy Castle, the 'William Barker' Bridge, the Market House and St Mary's Church of Ireland church. A full architectural discussion of Enniscorthy town at the time of the rebellion can be found in chapter 7, but here we concentrate on the town as a battlefield, both at the Battle of Vinegar Hill on 21 June 1798, and at the Battle of Enniscorthy three weeks earlier on 28 May 1798 when it was first taken by the rebels.

Buildings and other structures

Although the most imposing of the various buildings surviving from the period, Enniscorthy Castle is actually the least significant in terms of its use by either side during the rebellion. This may be due to the fact that the castle appears to have been in somewhat of a ruined condition at this stage (Luckombe, 1783, p. 33). That said, it was secure enough to imprison suspected rebel sympathizers prior to the Battle of Enniscorthy on 28 May. In fact, Hay (1803, p. 93) comments that when the crown forces tried to execute these prisoners before abandoning the town they were unable to break through the locked castle door (the key holder having already fled).

The stone bridge in Enniscorthy featured extensively during both the Battle of Enniscorthy on 28 May 1798 and the Battle of Vinegar Hill on 21 June. The bridge, now renamed in honour of the rebel leader William Barker, has been modified quite extensively over the centuries (see chapter 7) and early illustrations show a much more steeply arched structure. However, although we have several contemporary descriptions of the fighting at the bridge during both battles, only one of the authors, John Jones, identifies a specific feature of the bridge itself, in this case the high walls on either side, which are presumably what he refers to as 'battlements', and which are visible in contemporary illustrations (fig. 6.5). Jones' account, which is of the defence of the bridge by the North Cork militia during the Battle of Enniscorthy, is as follows:

> Numbers of the rebels fell upon this occasion, by the fire of the North-Cork from the battlements of the bridge; and none of their shots took effect from their confusion, from the protection of the battlements, and from most of them levelling so high, that their shot went whistling over the heads of the North Cork. (Jones, 1834, p. 57)

The bridge would witness further fighting during the Battle of Vinegar Hill just three weeks later, this time while being defended by insurgent forces during General Johnson's attack on Enniscorthy town. British military annals recounting the activities of the Royal Irish Regiment of Dragoons identify strong points in Enniscorthy town where the insurgents prepared defences in advance of the battle, and one was the bridge:

> The insurgents were posted at this place in considerable force. They had fortified the bridge, the market-place, and other public buildings; and a most galling fire was kept up upon the King's troops from the houses and bye streets. (Phillips, 1801, ii, p. 230)

Musgrave also makes an interesting statement when recounting the final action by crown forces taking the bridge:

> The general [Johnson] then ordered the light infantry to charge over the bridge, and up the hill, which were occupied by a numerous body of rebels; but they having shewn an unwillingness to do so, he called on the county of Dublin regiment to perform that service, on which they gave three cheers, and led on by colonel Vesey and lord Blaney, in conjunction with the light infantry, forced the bridge, and marched up the steepest part of the hill, driving the rebels before them. (Musgrave, 1802, ii, p. 12)

The 'unwillingness' of the light infantry to charge over the bridge is telling, and indicates that it was fiercely defended by the insurgents.

One of the few rebel quotes relating to the defence of the bridge during the Battle of Vinegar Hill was that of a Wicklow rebel who related the following to Brother Luke Cullen in the 1840s:

> As we approached the bridge where the fighting was, Johnson's infantry was pressing forward under the protection of his artillery throwing shot and shells over them at us. Some of the brave fellows that preceded us had crossed the bridge. They staggered and reeled from the stream of musket balls that were pouring over the bridge and, as my informant says, although the men were falling like leaves in October, they still pressed forward, and our pikemen grappled with their muskets. At this moment we, the Wicklows, came to the bridge, Mr Wm. Byrne leading and crying: 'On! On! Forward boys! Forward!' Two of our Captains, Loftus and Kirwan, fell at the head of their companies at the foot of the bridge. The fire of nearly the whole of Johnson's infantry was at this moment directed on this spot, and yet we crossed the bridge. There was a bold and vigorous cheer in our rear, as about fifty of us passed over. And that cheer was responded to by a deafening one on Vinegar Hill. Our ammunition was now run out, and we had nothing to bring against a well-supplied infantry but our pikes, and in consequence thereof, we were obliged to give way. (Cullen, 1959, pp 26–7)

Other components of the rebellion landscape of the town survive today, albeit in reincarnated versions of their former selves. These structures include St Mary's Church of Ireland church, the Market House and the Courthouse. Unfortunately there are no

The field of battle

6.5 Enniscorthy *c*.1775, showing the castle and the bridge, which was hotly contested at both the Battle of Enniscorthy and the Battle of Vinegar Hill. From P. Sandby, *A collection of one hundred and fifty select views in England, Scotland and Ireland* (London, 1778). Private collection: Ronan O'Flaherty.

architectural descriptions of these buildings before the latter half of the nineteenth century but it is still possible to build a picture of the extent to which their appearance today is significantly different to that of 1798. Of these three buildings, the Market House (now home to Enniscorthy Municipal District Council), featured heavily in the Battle of Enniscorthy.

During the battle the Market House was garrisoned by a 'considerable guard' and also contained the arms and ammunition of the town's defenders (Musgrave, 1802, i, p. 350). It appears that through the course of the battle that the Market House may have been one of the last buildings to fall to the rebels and acted somewhat as a refuge to the retreating crown forces from the Duffry Gate direction, from where they made a last defence (Gordon, 1805, p. 112). The diary of Jane Barber may offer an insight as to the level of damage the Market House experienced during the battle. Barber recounts while being present in the building that in less than an hour, it, too, took to fire and all within it, armed men, helpless women and children, were forced to leave it and throw themselves into the midst of the rebels who now surrounded it in hundreds, or they would have been destroyed by the explosion of the gun-powder, which took place shortly after. (Beatty, 2001, p. 77)

Despite the fire, accounts by travelling authors visiting the town in the years shortly after the rebellion indicate that the Market House survived the insurrection reasonably intact (Urban, 1801, p. 977). It may well retain evidence of the battle in the form of bullet holes but if so these are likely to be concealed behind subsequent layers of render. Bullet holes can actually be seen on the façade of the building adjoining the Market House on the right, but again the render suggests that these are later than 1798 and they may in fact relate to brief fighting during the 1916 rising.

Unlike the Market House, neither St Mary's Church of Ireland church nor the Courthouse featured prominently during the Battle of Enniscorthy or the Battle of Vinegar Hill. Instead, these structures are more associated with some infamous acts carried out over the wider period of the rebellion itself. St Mary's Church, according to historical accounts, bore the brunt of sectarian attacks in the days following the Battle of Enniscorthy on 28 May:

> The rebels then proceeded to destroy the church of Enniscorthy, and having pulled down the organ, the pews, the reading desk, and the communion table, they carried them to the church door, where they burned them to ashes, together with all the bibles and prayer-books that were in the church. They then demolished the remainder of the inside part of the church leaving nothing but the roof and the bare walls. They also took down the bell and carried it to Vinegar-Hill camp, where they mounted it between two large beams, which were erected for that purpose. In case of surprise, the ringing of the bell was to give the alarm. (Anon., 1806, p. 76)

It is important to note that this account and similar contemporary records suggest that only the interior of the church was damaged during the rebellion.

The building commonly known today as the Courthouse is located on the site of a makeshift rebel hospital where one of the most infamous acts associated with the Battle of Vinegar Hill took place. The Courthouse (no longer serving that purpose) was originally built in 1819.[1] We have little indication as to the nature of the building that preceded it on this site but one would assume that it was substantial enough to draw the attention of the rebels and to render it suitable for use as a hospital capable of housing a large number of wounded. Historical accounts tend solely to examine

---

[1] Before that, the upper floor of the Market House was used for judicial purposes (*Penny Cyclopaedia*, 1843, p. 267).

the massacre that took place on the site and offer little information as to the fate of the building itself. Harwood (1844) offers one of the most extensive accounts of the event when he writes:

> The victorious British troops and their Hessian allies (for foreign mercenaries were hired on the occasion) actually burned a hospital with the patients in it. A large house in Enniscorthy, which the insurgent leaders had had fitted up for the reception of their sick and wounded, was totally consumed, with all its helpless, unresisting inmates, to the number, some say of more than thirty, others of nearly eighty. (Harwood, 1844, p. 193)

Hay (1803, p. 235) may offer us an insight to the extent of the fire as he recollects that the building continued burning until the morning of 22 June. If true, this would suggest that the building used as a hospital by the rebels was burning for almost 24 hours. It is therefore difficult to imagine any pre-insurrection fabric being incorporated into the courthouse that stands on the site today, but it cannot be entirely ruled out.

The surviving streetscape

During the battles of Enniscorthy and Vinegar Hill the following streets (listed here with their modern names) experienced intense fighting: Duffry Hill, Cathedral Street, Main Street, Market Square, Castle Street, Castle Hill, Abbey Square, Rafter Street, Court Street, St John's Street, Island Road and the quays on either side of the William Barker Bridge. Buildings along these streets would have played a significant part in the defence of the town, providing cover and vantage points for the defenders while firing on the town's assailants below. Furthermore, such buildings would have also been exposed to musket or cannon shot and those surviving today may retain such evidence behind their render.

Unfortunately, approximately 40 per cent of Enniscorthy is thought to have burned down during the 1798 rebellion and the rebuilding that followed throughout the nineteenth century and indeed the twentieth century has had a significant impact on the archaeological potential of even those areas within the town where we know intense fighting occurred. However, we should not forget the very real potential of the River Slaney itself, especially north and south of the William Barker Bridge, and of the 'Island' in the river, approximately 170m north of the bridge (fig. 6.6). During the Battle of Enniscorthy a number of eyewitness and subsequent historical accounts relate how the rebel forces tried to outflank their enemy by wading the River Slaney and attacking the crown forces via the Templeshannon side of Enniscorthy. All relate how these first attempts were driven back by heavy musket fire until the insurgents were forced to cross well out of musket range at Blackstoops approximately 1km north of the bridge as the crow flies:

> The assailants in a short time extending themselves around, and making dispositions to ford the river in several places, were galled from the bridge … At length, when the rebels, wading across the river, which was then low, both above and below the bridge, up to the middle in water, some to the neck, had entered the eastern part, called Templeshannon, and set some houses on fire. (Gordon, 1801, p. 93)

> The insurgents made an attempt to cross the river at the island above the bridge, from whence they were so galled as to oblige them to wade through the Slaney higher up at Blackstoops. (Hay, 1803, p. 92)

A number of authors clearly identify the 'Island' as being used by the rebel forces in an effort to cross the river and also pinpoint the crown force positions while repulsing the rebels during their attempted crossing, placing them on the bridge itself and in the vicinity of Glebe House:

> The rebels, defeated in the attempts which they made to cross the river on the north and west side of the town, made an effort to cross it, about a quarter of a mile above the bridge, where there is an island, in which they succeeded; but were soon repulsed by Captain Richards's corps, part of whom fired at them with carbines, from a place about one hundred yards above the glebe-house, and killed great numbers; at the same time Captain Snowe's corps severely annoyed them, from the bridge. (Anon., 1806, pp 69–70)

This anonymous account is clearly the source for the account in Musgrave (1802) as well:

> The enemy, defeated in the many attempts which they made on the north and west side of the town, made an effort to cross the river, about a quarter of a mile above the bridge, where there is an island, in which they succeeded; but were soon repulsed by captain Richards's corps, part of whom fired at them with carbines, from a place about one hundred yards above the glebe-house, and killed great numbers; at the same time they were severely galled by the North Cork on the bridge. (Musgrave, 1802, i, p. 352)

Jones also describes the scene:

> They [North Cork Militia] arrived in time to line the bridge, and to give a severe check to the rebel column, just then in the act of crossing the river, and a part of which had landed on an island in it. Numbers of the rebels fell upon this occasion, by the fire of the North-Cork from the battlements of the bridge. (Jones, 1800, p. 103)

The field of battle 117

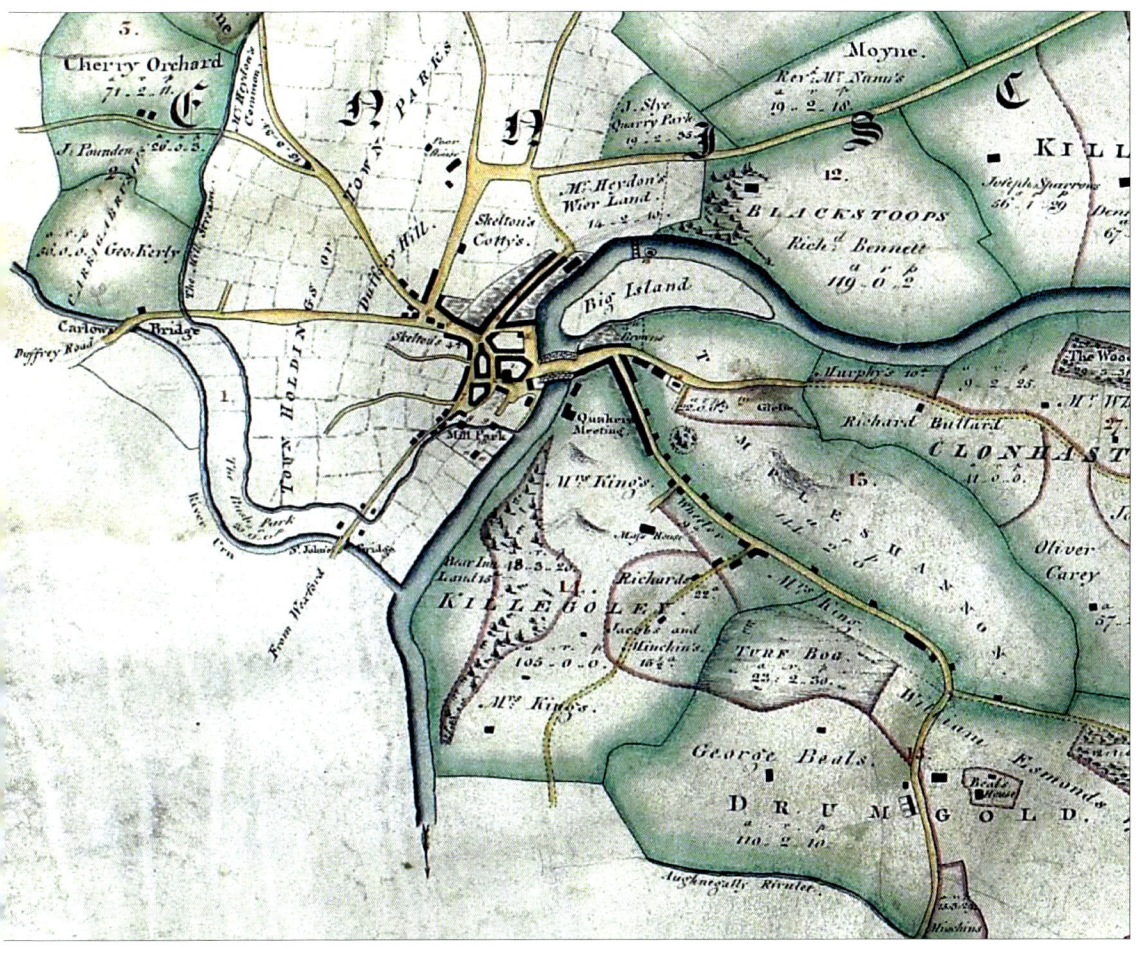

6.6 Detail from the Portsmouth estate map *c.*1822 showing the townscape of Enniscorthy and the Island that the rebels attempted to cross during the Battle of Enniscorthy. Courtesy of the earl of Portsmouth. Hampshire Record Office: 15M84/MP35.

The accounts suggest that casualties on the rebel side were extremely high and, indeed, Musgrave places the figure at some five hundred in all: 'The banks of the river, and the island in it were strewed with their dead bodies' (Musgrave, 1802, i, p. 354).

A limited underwater survey carried out in 2015 in the area around the bridge did not recover any finds from the battle, but it did suggest that these in all probability remained to be found in the lower levels of the riverbed (see chapter 9). Metal detection on the Island could also be very productive, given the recorded intensity of fire directed at this area as the rebels attempted to cross during the Battle of Enniscorthy, and the fact that – unlike the town – the Island has survived relatively untouched across the centuries, remaining entirely in agricultural use (grazing).

6.7 Vinegar Hill, probably late nineteenth century. Note how bare the landscape is without the scrub that covers the hill today. Robert French (Lawrence Collection), NLI L_CAB_07017. Courtesy of the National Library of Ireland.

THE FIELD OF BATTLE: VINEGAR HILL

Landscape of the hill

Vinegar Hill presents quite a different prospect today than it did two centuries ago. Now covered in scrub, heavy gorse and bracken, large areas of the hill are difficult to cross, but a late nineteenth-century photograph (fig. 6.7) shows the hill very much as it must have been in 1798 – a bare, extensively grazed landscape, at least on the slopes overshadowing the town. It is easy to imagine an encampment of some 20,000 people spread over the flanks of a hill like this, but how they were provisioned, supplied with water and shelter is another matter. This cannot have been an easy task and would have required some degree of centralized organization (see chapter 4).

The deep ditches that characterize the northern, eastern and southern flanks today were clearly present in 1798. Not only are they visible in the Ordnance Survey maps of the mid-nineteenth century (just forty years or so after the battle), but they are

The field of battle

6.8 Deep lane just below Vinegar Hill, probably one of the deep 'trenches' that rebels are described as occupying. Photo by Ronan O'Flaherty.

specifically mentioned in contemporary accounts of the battle. The frustration of rebel leader Miles Byrne, for example, is evident in his comments on arrival at Vinegar Hill the day before the battle:

> I had not seen Vinegar hill since the morning after the battle of Newtownbarry, the 2d of June, and I was surprised to find that scarcely anything had been done to make it formidable against the enemy; the vast fences and ditches which surrounded it on three sides, and which should have been levelled to the ground, for at least a cannon shot, or half a mile's distance, were all left untouched. The English forces, availing themselves of these fences, advanced from field to field, bringing with them their cannon, which they placed to great advantage behind and under the cover of the hedges and fences; whilst our men were exposed to a terrible fire from their artillery and small arms, without being able to drive them back from their strongholds in those fields. (Byrne, 1863, pp 169–72)

The survival of so many of these deep ditches today adds immeasurably to the value of Vinegar Hill as an almost intact battlefield. They are a key part of that landscape, in many cases marking lines of assault and defence, and very likely points of fierce fighting. Again, we have contemporary accounts describing just this, for example this

6.9 Electric Picnic 2018, where some 50,000 people were in attendance. During the Battle of Vinegar Hill, the combined number of rebel and crown personnel was about 35,000 across a similar landscape. Photo by An Garda Síochána, 2 Sept. 2018.

account from Archibald M'Laren in his *A minute description of the battles of Gorey, Arklow and Vinegar-Hill …*, published in 1798: 'The Croppies' musket men lined a ditch that ran along the foot of the hill, and kept up a very smart fire which did some damage to our troops' (M'Laren, 1798, p. 28). The ditches, field boundaries and lanes of Vinegar Hill deserve full protection in the same way as the surviving upstanding monuments, such as the Windmill or Beale's Barn (see below) do, and represent an essential part of our understanding of the battle. Ultimately, they also provide the basis for an incredibly rich tour of the battlefield, which has the potential to become an important tourist offering.

In terms of pure numbers involved, the Battle of Vinegar Hill represents the last great field engagement on Irish soil. Involving some 35,000 people, of whom about 30,000 were probably combatants of one sort or another, Vinegar Hill was double the scale of the much better known Battle of Culloden from some fifty years earlier and with a very similar level of casualties. An aerial photo of the Electric Picnic festival in 2018 (fig. 6.9) showing some 50,000 people spread across a not dissimilar landscape gives some idea of what the scene on Vinegar Hill must have been on the day of the battle. At the heart, on and around the hill itself, were some 20,000 people heavily compacted in particular areas, while around them again some 15,000 government troops were filing across the countryside to take up their positions and make their separate advances up the hill.

The battlefield encompasses a much greater area than just the hill – an area of over 10km^2, in fact, when measured from Johnson's encampment at Daphne Castle to Lake's at Solsborough, and not including the fighting retreat that continued for upwards of 10km south of Vinegar Hill itself. General Lake initially planned to completely surround the rebel position and in his letter to Lord Castlereagh of 21 June 1798 explained this division of troop movements along with their respective commanders:

> The relative importance of this very strong position with our operations, against Wexford, made it necessary to combine our attacks so as to insure success. A column, under major-generals Johnson and Eustace, was drawn from Ross, and began the attack upon the town of Enniscorthy, situated upon the right bank of the Slaney, close under Vinegar Hill, upon the right and rather in the rear of it. Lieutenant General Dundas commanded the centre column, supported by a column upon the right under major generals Sir James Duff and Loftus; a fourth column upon the left, was commanded by the honourable major general Needham. (Musgrave, 1802, ii, p. 439)

The historical accounts make clear the critical role that artillery played in securing victory for the crown forces, so much so that before issuing orders for his soldiers to advance on rebel positions, General Lake subjected the insurgent force to an artillery bombardment which may have lasted up to two hours (accounts vary). Gurley (1854) comments on the use of artillery at Vinegar Hill as follows:

> The thunder of the loyal artillery was answered by the insurgents with a terrible fire from their intrenchments. The rebel commanders knew that their fate, and the fate of their cause, hung on that battle; and they exhibited a martial courage and noble bearing worthy of a better cause. For an hour and three-quarters did the heavy ordnance of the besiegers vomit forth destruction upon their ranks. Grape-shot and balls rattled round them like a storm of hail, and every moment they saw their comrades sinking to the earth. (Gurley, 1854, p. 187)

The rebel perspective is provided by Miles Byrne, recalling the events many years later:

> His powerful artillery commenced a tremendous fire, which was for some time directed against the summit of the hill, considered our strong position and where it was thought our men were massed, ready to be brought into action. (Byrne, 1863, p. 170)

This comment by Byrne that the crown forces at first directed their fire towards the summit of Vinegar Hill is a useful pointer towards areas where the presence of cannon balls, grape shot or associated shrapnel might still survive, in the fields or green areas directly below the windmill. Furthermore the fact that Byrne describes bombardment of the summit lasting for 'some time' corroborates historical accounts as to the duration of the artillery offensive.

6.10 The windmill on Vinegar Hill – the iconic symbol of the rebellion in Wexford. Photo by Ronan O'Flaherty.

Vinegar Hill was the first battle in which the crown forces used explosive canister shot and this caused havoc among the rebel lines. An anonymous letter dated 1 August 1798 ('from a Gentleman in Ireland to Mr William Thompson') gives a good account of the use of these shells during the battle:

> At length the General resolved to try what effect a few boom-shells would have on them. About eighty or ninety of these deadly messengers were sent to the top of the hill, which were so faithful to their charge, that all except three or four, carried death in a variety of awful forms. (*Methodist Magazine*, Jan. 1799, p. 20)

The windmill

The windmill is the iconic image of Vinegar Hill, immediately recognizable, and presenting a dramatic interruption of the skyline then and today (fig. 6.10). However, the building itself played very little role at all in the battle, except to distract the artillery of the attackers who seemed to believe that it marked the heart of rebel resistance. Authors writing of the insurrection concur that the windmill was in a ruined condition during the summer of 1798. In fact, whether the building was ever fully completed, let alone put into operation, remains unclear (despite its depiction on the Taylor and Skinner Map of 1777 – see fig. 6.2). Reference to the function of the structure during the rebellion relates solely to its use as a prison by the rebels. Therefore contemporary historians tend to concentrate on the events in which the windmill played a part rather than on any discussion of features of the structure itself.

As a result, we must rely on more obscure references in order to gain a glimpse of what the windmill may have looked like during the rebellion. One such reference derives from Banim's mid-nineteenth-century fictional work *The croppy: a tale of the Irish rebellion of 1798* (1865). Reference to the windmill within this publication reads as follows:

> On the summit of the height stood a roofless, round building, originally intended for a windmill but never perfected … at the time of our story, this roofless round tower, about seven paces in diameter, and perhaps twenty five feet in height, was appropriated to a use very different from that for which it had been planned. It served, in fact, as a temporary prison for the unfortunate persons captured by the marauding garrison of Vinegar Hill (Banim, 1865, p. 287).

Although a fictional work, Banim had taken the time to actually visit Vinegar Hill while researching his subject and would have been in a position to accurately describe the windmill. Unlike the William Barker Bridge, the windmill on Vinegar Hill has undergone little change post rebellion. The only interventions appear to be those taken to prevent its further deterioration and, as a result, the windmill may yet reveal some of its story.[2]

---

[2] As part of the Longest Day Research Project a full photogrammetric survey of the windmill was carried out, creating a comprehensive record of all wall surfaces which can now be systematically examined stone by stone.

During the battle itself, the windmill – or rather the area around it – appears to have drawn the fire of the British artillery, as Miles Byrne noted (1863, p. 170). But the crown forces were mistaken in their belief in its importance: the rebel fighters were not sitting on the top of the hill in some Masada-like last stand, they were lined quite strategically around the hill, using the deep ditches and sunken ways as their entrenchments. Despite Miles Byrne's scathing attack on the failure of the defenders to clear these ditches in the weeks before the battle, it was to prove much harder than anyone thought to shift the rebels from these natural entrenchments. The contemporary accounts make the intensity of the fighting abundantly clear and it is arguable that without that initial massive artillery bombardment that left so many dead as they stood in those ditches, the battle itself must of necessity have become a much more prolonged and bloody affair.

Areas of intense fighting on the hill
The crown forces returns of wounded and killed at the Battle of Vinegar Hill combined with the historical record give us some indication of general areas of intense fighting. The heaviest casualties appear to have been experienced by those fighting under Dundas's command as he advanced on Vinegar Hill from an easterly direction. Eyewitness Archibald M'Laren points to some significant losses on the crown forces side during their infantry assault: 'The Croppies' musket men lined a ditch that ran along the foot of the hill, and kept up a very smart fire which did some damage to our troops' (M'Laren, 1798, p. 28). Musgrave also remarks on the rebel defence and describes how they fought a retreating action:

> At the same time, generals Lake, Dundas and Wilford, with colonel Campbell's light infantry, were advancing up the hill on the south-east side, and were firmly opposed by the rebels, who maintained a very brisk fire on them, retreating at the same time from one hedge to another, till they were driven over the hill. (Musgrave, 1802, ii, pp 6–7)

In response to the crown forces' advance, the rebels launched upwards of three pike charges. Miles Byrne records that

> a large column of chosen pikemen was formed, composed of the county of Wicklow men, Monaseed, Bally Ellis, Gory [sic] corps, etc., to attack the enemy's left flank and, if possible, to turn it and to bring our pikemen into the action …
> Several columns of our pikemen however, were instantly brought to attack the enemy's formidable position behind the fences in the fields, and it was in leading on one of those desperate charges, that the splendid Dan Kervin was killed, at the head of the brave county of Wicklow men. (Byrne, 1863, pp 171–2).

William Kerr, aide-de-camp to General Loftus, confirms Byrne's account while describing the rebels' reaction to the light infantry advancing on their right flank:

> On seeing Gen Dundas's light companies moving up towards their right the rebels began to file off in considerable numbers in order to line the hedges and ditches. They were gallantly attacked by the light infantry and stood their ground very well for about twenty minutes notwithstanding that a howitzer in front of Gen. Dundas's brigade was playing upon them the greater part of that time. (Bartlett, 1988–9, p. 82).

M'Laren records the rebels' pike charge and how the light infantry drove them back.

> A large party of them attempted to force their way on the left of the hill, but the Light Brigade under Colonel Campbell who occupied that post saluted them with a shower of hail stones something harder than boiled peas, drove them back. (M'Laren, 1798, p. 28)

Kerr continues to describe how the light infantry eventually began to advance up Vinegar Hill and the effect that the artillery played in ending any chance of a rebel counter-attack.

> We could plainly perceive from the road the attack of the light infantry upon the hill – the irregular fire which they kept up for about 20 minutes had a very beautiful effect. They gained ground upon the enemy gradually, but not completely until our guns as before mentioned had opened upon the enemy's centre and left. (Bartlett, 1988–9, pp 82–5)

An anonymous chronicler describes the rebel response once they were pushed off Vinegar Hill by the light infantry. What is telling here is the orderly nature of the retreat – the rebels are not streaming off Vinegar Hill in disarray, rather they have fallen back and, critically, re-formed their line:

> Finding they could hold out no longer they retreated from the top of the hill; which they hitherto considered impregnable, and took another position on the lower hill, on the east side … [They] took shelter behind the hedges, and again bid defiance to the king's troops. They maintained a heavy fire on the light brigade, commanded by Colonel Campbell, but nothing could withstand the valour and intrepidity of these troops, they rushed on them like furies – charging them in their entrenchments (Anon., 1806, pp 146–7).

Another anonymous chronicler describes the final stages of the battle where artillery once again played a significant part, as does M'Laren:

> The cannon were then drawn up, and as the rebels retreated down the hill, they fell like the mown grass. Nevertheless, many thousands of them escaped, though they were pursued for four hours, and the country was literally strewed with their carcasses. A Sergeant on whom I could depend, told me, he endeavoured to count the dead bodies, but they were too many'. (Anon., 1798, p. 4)

> In their retreat they were severely galled by the grape shot which flew from the field-pieces belonging to the Dunbartonshire Regiment. (M'Laren, 1798, p. 28)

WILL THE REAL 'GREEN HILL' PLEASE STAND UP?

A turning point in the battle was the early capture by General Loftus of a 'green hill', on the lower slopes of Vinegar Hill. The hill in question may have been an outpost for the rebel forces, whose main lines occupied the deep ditches marking the townland boundary below this. Only when Loftus had occupied the little hill and placed his guns there was its true strategic value realized: from his position he could very effectively 'enfilade' the rebel lines on either side, firing along their full length, and he did so to terrible effect.

But where exactly was this 'green hill' and can we identify it in the landscape today? Despite the various descriptions provided in the contemporary accounts, and even with the existence of contemporary maps purporting to show the location of the hill, it is still not possible to say with confidence where the all-important hill was. The contemporary accounts, and maps, are unfortunately not consistent and none of the candidates visited in the field fulfil all the requirements. There are, however, three strong candidates and these will be described later. However, first let us consider the contemporary descriptions of the hill and its capture. Musgrave (1802) describes the position taken up by Loftus as follows:

> When they had arrived at the beginning of the ascent to Vinegar-hill, General Loftus was detached by General Duff to occupy a green hill in a park enclosed with stone walls, which was on the side, and composed a part of Vinegar-hill. General Loftus surprised the rebels by the celerity of this movement because the hill was steep; and the ground which he occupied there was divided by stone walls; but by breaking open gaps, he had two guns carried over at first, and soon after four more, by having untackled them from the horses. From this position he was able to fire into the lower line of the enemy, rather on his left, with such effect that eighty-five of them were afterwards found in their trenches killed with grape-shot. General Loftus made his movement by a narrow road on the left, diverging from the main one, and then rapidly ascended the hill. (Musgrave, 1802, i, p. 477)

The field of battle

6.11a Junction of the old Ferns and Clonhasten roads, where General Loftus broke away from the main force and made his dash to capture the all-important 'green hill'. Base image © Google.

Gordon (1805) also makes reference to the area in which Loftus was positioned:

> At length after the soldiery had fully sated themselves in the cold blooded slaughter of all suspected & persons, General Johnson [actually Duff] led them to the ascent of Vinegar-Hill, when he detached General Loftus with three thousand men, to occupy a small deer-park which adjoined Vinegar-Hill. (Gordon, 1805, ii, pp 52–3).

Kerr describes the area:

> Gen. Loftus was fortunate enough to find a very advantageous [position?] for guns attached to us. It was a small rocky rising ground nearly in front of the enemy's centre which tho' low relatively [*sic*] to Vinegar Hill, was sufficiently

6.11b The outline of Vinegar Hill on the skyline, much as it would have appeared to General Loftus when he veered away from the main force to take 'the road to the fields'. Photo by Ronan O'Flaherty.

high to protect the cavalry which was shortly afterwards ordered to draw up behind it, had the enemy had presence of mind enough to direct their fire upon them …

I now received an order to move forward with the cavalry and to form behind the guns on the rocky eminence. In filing thro' a narrow lane for this purpose we were completely exposed to the enemy's fire had they taken advantage of the circumstance, but by this time their confusion had begun and they soon after gave way in all directions. (Bartlett, 1988–9, pp 82–3)

These three accounts provide a significant amount of information and corroborate each other in a number of respects. As regards the approach, Musgrave writes that General Loftus made his movement by a 'narrow road on the left, diverging from the main one'. This, we can be relatively confident, is the modern junction between the old Ferns and Clonhasten roads (fig. 6.11a), where Vinegar Hill suddenly makes its appearance on the skyline once you veer off the main road (fig. 6.11b). Maps provided

The field of battle

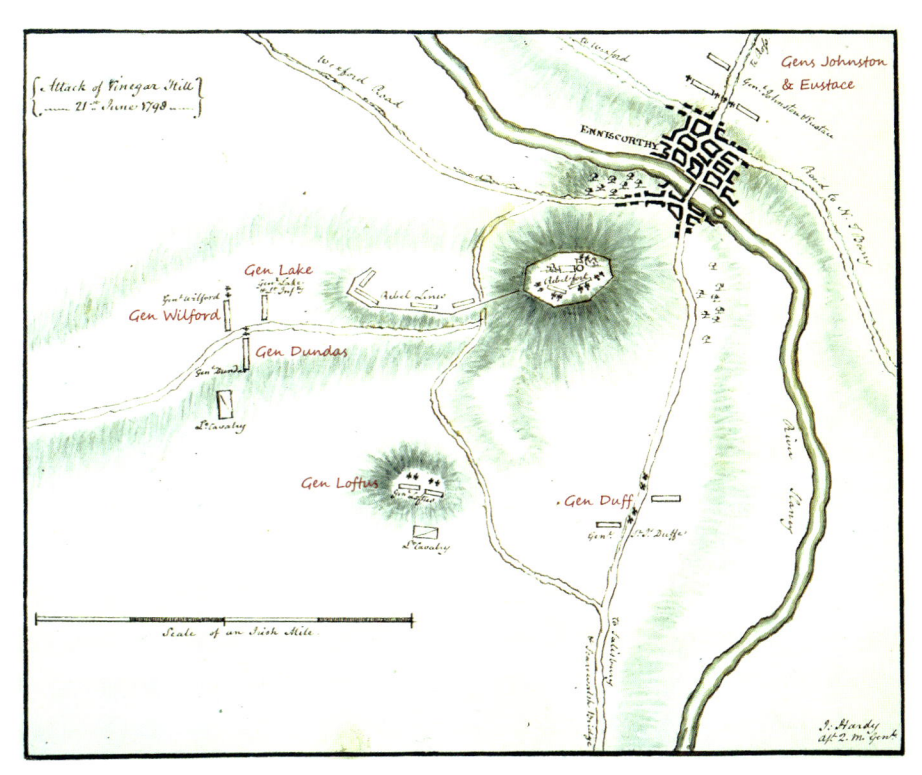

6.12a Sketch plan of the battle, by Hardy after McGurk 1798. Location of Loftus indicated to the left of the Clonhasten Road. PD HP (1798) 21. Courtesy of the National Library of Ireland. Names of crown commanders added in red.

by both Musgrave and McGurk (figs 6.12a and 6.12b) illustrate a fork in the road that matches up well with the modern road layout. We can be reasonably sure therefore that this is the point where Loftus detached himself with 3,000 men from the main force to make that rapid movement that resulted in the capture of the green hill. After that, however, things become decidedly less clear – nor can we rely entirely on the accuracy of the two maps, both of which leave out some important landscape feature.

The 'green hill' captured was apparently at the foot of Vinegar Hill and according to Musgrave was actually on the side of that hill and formed part of it. This is a highly significant statement, endorsed by Gordon, who similarly describes it as adjoining Vinegar Hill. According to Kerr, it was relatively low, compared to Vinegar Hill, but still high enough to shelter the cavalry who were drawn up behind it. Kerr also describes it as a small 'rocky' rising ground, and Musgrave says that Loftus had to break openings in stone walls around the hill to get his guns up. Musgrave also says that the rebels were taken by surprise at the speed of Loftus' movement as the hill was steep. It is also interesting to note that Loftus had to untackle the guns from

6.12b Red circle marks the location of Loftus to the right of the Clonhasten Road (shown here as the 'road to the fields'). Contemporary map (rotated view) by Alexander Taylor of the Royal Engineers. Reproduced with permission of Wexford County Council Archive Service.

their horse teams and manhandle them over the stone walls. Gordon may imply the existence of such walls when he describes it as a 'small deer-park'. The hill was also steep enough to allow the cavalry to form up behind it. It was approached by way of a narrow road or lane, which as Kerr points out left the column horribly exposed had the rebels used the opportunity to attack. This is probably the Clonhasten Road itself, along which the column had to move and which, at the time, was just a narrow lane, described as a 'road to the fields' on Musgrave's map. Had they been attacked, Loftus' men would have had nowhere to go, so this was indeed a daring manoeuvre. The feared rebel attack never came and the defenders seem not to have realized just what Loftus had planned.

The field of battle

6.12c Red circle marks location of Loftus to the right of the Clonhasten Road. Reproduced with permission of Wexford County Council Archive Service.

Unfortunately, the two maps (Musgrave's and McGurk's) locate Loftus' ultimate position, and therefore our green hill, in two different places: Musgrave positions Loftus' artillery to the right of the Clonhasten Road while McGurk depicts them to the left. It also should be noted that while Musgrave's battle plan shows Loftus occupying a hill on the right of the road, the illustration of the battle in the same volume (fig. 6.12c) shows Loftus very clearly on the left of that same road. Both locations, when considered in terms of the modern landscape, are viable as regards the contemporary descriptions, but neither provides a complete match. There are low hills in both areas, rising to 50m–60m above sea level but neither displays the steepness of the hill which is such an important feature in two of the three accounts above.

Our first candidate (figs 6.13a and 6.13b) for the green hill is a small rocky outcrop on the left (eastern) side of the Clonhasten Road as you travel from the modern junction with the old Ferns Road. McGurk's map shows Loftus occupying what seems to be just such an outcrop, which also recalls Kerr's description of a 'rocky eminence', and the depiction in Musgrave's illustration of the battle. In addition, the early Ordnance Survey maps show an area just north of this called 'the Rock Field', which recalls Kerr's reference to 'rocky rising ground', while the proximity to Greenmount House allows for the possibility of a 'deer-park' in the vicinity, as suggested by Gordon. The hill is a commanding site and one which any commander would have eyed with interest. There is plenty of space for the cavalry to line up below and it has a direct line of site to the windmill on Vinegar Hill itself, which we know was the focus of the crown

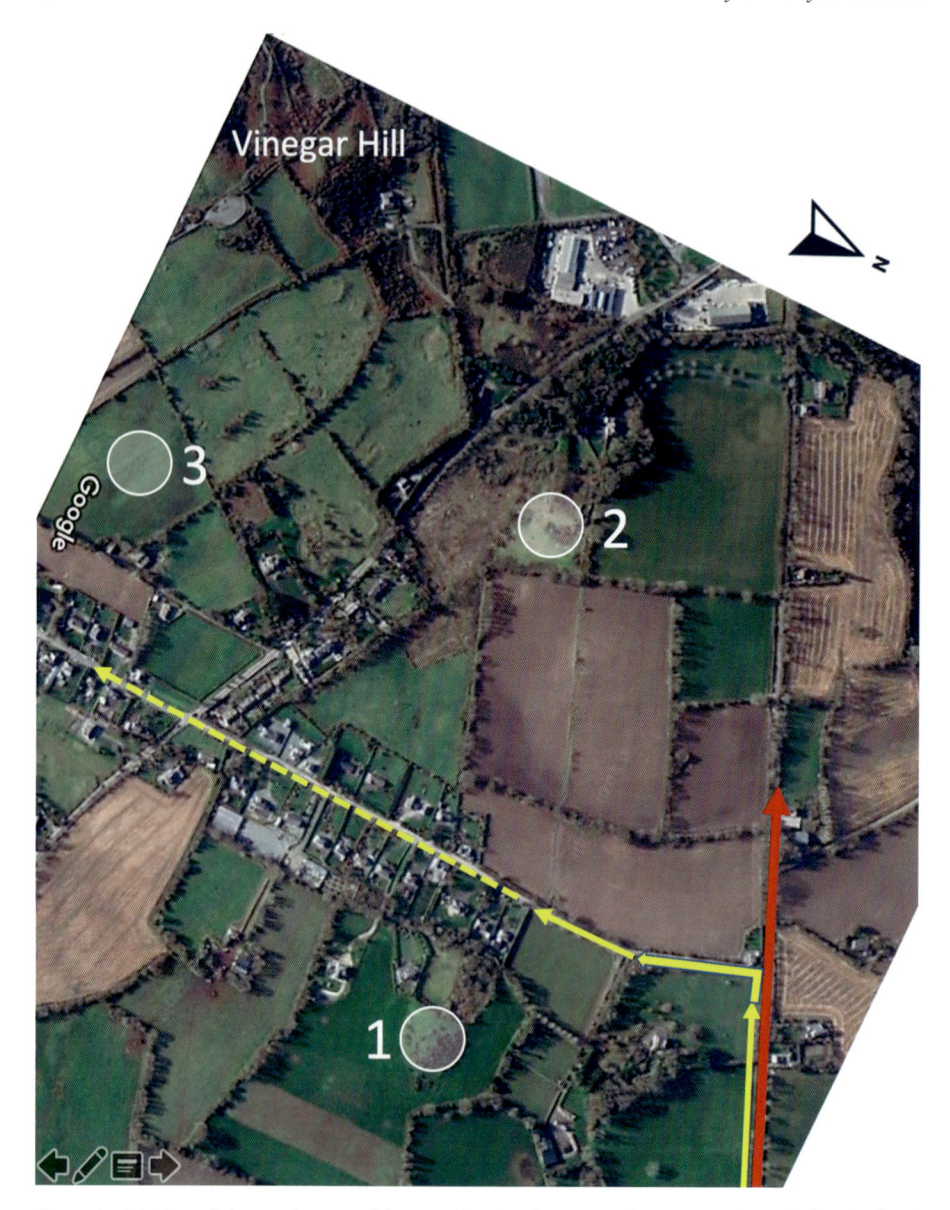

6.13a Aerial view of the modern road layout, showing location of junction where Loftus (yellow) detached from the main column (red) and the possible locations of the all-important 'green hill' (1–3) per the contemporary records. The dashed yellow line indicates the possible extent of his advance, per the Hardy-McGurk Map. Base image © Google.

attack. However, while this candidate ticks many of the boxes, it could in no way be regarded as composing a 'part of Vinegar-hill', as Musgrave asserts – it is simply too far away. Furthermore, a rapid movement *to the east* of the Clonhasten road actually

The field of battle 133

6.13b Our first candidate for the 'green hill' occupied by Loftus – looking north-east, with the view south-west to Vinegar Hill inset. This is clearly a rocky outcrop and undoubtedly the hill shown on two of the contemporary illustrations. However, it is possibly too far from the action to have the strategic impact described. Photos by Ronan O'Flaherty.

moves away from Vinegar Hill, and is unlikely to have surprised anybody (although it is quite possible that the rebels may have had an outpost there). In addition, it is hard to see how one could enfilade the rebel lines from this point as described, unless the outer line of the rebel defences was actually along the Clonhasten road itself, which does not appear to have been the case as Loftus had just travelled along this without coming under attack. Nor can the capture of this outcrop be conceived as the beginning of a joint assault on Vinegar Hill itself, by Loftus on one side and Lake, Dundas and Wilford on the other, which is clearly how Musgrave describes the action: 'The movement of the two columns was so well-timed that they met at the same moment on the top of the hill.' To do so, Loftus would have to cross back on his own path, having already placed himself further from Vinegar Hill by taking this rocky outcrop than he was initially when moving down the Clonhasten road. All that said, there is no doubt that this is in fact the location shown as occupied by Loftus on McGurk's map and in Musgrave's illustration of the battle, but its location simply does not make sense having regard to the written accounts: it is always possible that the contemporary illustrators may have been just as confused as we are about the detail and they may simply have drawn us the wrong hill. However, we certainly cannot rule it out, and even if this is not our 'green hill', we have at the very least pinpointed in

6.13c Vinegar Hill as viewed from the top of our second candidate for the 'green hill' occupied by Loftus. This hill is low but strategically placed. Evidence for fighting and for the presence of government troops in this area was found in 2020. Photo by Ronan O'Flaherty.

the modern landscape a landmark that is clearly depicted also in the contemporary illustrations.

The second candidate (fig. 6.13c) is much more persuasive as regards strategic value. The location is to the right of the Clonhasten road as Loftus travelled it and matches well with the location shown on Musgrave's map. While the land rises almost imperceptibly when approached from the road, it falls away more steeply on the Vinegar Hill side once you have crested the low hill itself. It could, plausibly, be regarded as being on the side of, and forming a part of, Vinegar Hill, as described by Musgrave, and is approached through fields that are still bounded by stone walls, again as Musgrave describes. The site was originally identified by the Irish Battlefields Project and included in their 2008 report on Vinegar Hill (Cronin et al., 2008). Tactically, its position is excellent: it provides a clear line of sight onto Vinegar Hill and critically would have allowed Loftus to enfilade the rebel lines to the left and possibly the right, assuming that they occupied the ditches marking the townland boundary in this area, as proposed by the authors of the 2008 report. It also positions him well for a direct assault on the hill. The one difficulty with this candidate is that it does not sit well with Musgrave's description of a hill steep enough that Loftus' rapid ascent to capture it took the rebels by surprise, or to shelter the cavalry in its lee, as Kerr states. Nor does it match Kerr's description of a 'rocky eminence', though his impression may possibly have been coloured by stones scattered around from the dismantled stone walls through which the guns had been dragged. It does fit reasonably well, however, with Gordon's description of the site as a small 'deer-park' or indeed Musgrave's comment that the hill was located in a 'park'. More importantly still, some compelling evidence for an attack at this very spot was recovered during an archaeological survey by Stafford McLoughlin Archaeology Ltd in 2020 at this site, in advance of a planned housing development. The results of this survey are discussed in detail in chapter 11 but some hard fighting is certainly indicated in precisely this area, along with the presence of government troops.

A re-evaluation of McGurk's map, using his own scale, provides a possible third candidate.[3] The scale suggests that Loftus travelled along the Clonhasten road for about half an 'Irish mile' from the Solsborough road junction, before occupying the green hill, which McGurk shows as lying to the left of the road as Loftus travelled it. Half an Irish mile is 3,360ft, just over half of one statute mile today. The map at fig. 6.13a shows (dashed yellow line) where Loftus would have reached had he marched the distance suggested and, if the scale applied to McGurk's map was accurate, the green hill he indicates must lie either to the east or the west of this point. Very interestingly, as you approach the half-mile mark along the road today, travelling from the junction as Loftus did, a striking 'green hill' does come suddenly into view, on the right (i.e. west) of the road (fig. 6.13d). It is in fact the lower flank of Vinegar Hill itself, very clearly on the side and composing part of the bigger hill, just as Musgrave describes. To approach it, Loftus would have wheeled right from the Clonhasten road across some stone-walled fields, through which he would have had to break a passage for his guns, which again fits the descriptions. Although relatively low, the hill is also very steep (the only one of our candidates that really fulfils that criterion) and any defenders would have been thrown into immediate disarray if Loftus did indeed ascend it as rapidly as is suggested. It would have been an audacious move, bringing Loftus suddenly into the heart of the rebel defences, like a fox into a chicken coop. Once in possession of this hill, Loftus would have held a commanding position, with his guns brought within terrifying range and in addition been able to fire down upon the lower rebel lines exactly as described – there is in fact a deep lane running across the hill just below this point that we had already identified as a likely 1798 defence (fig. 6.8). There is also ample space for the cavalry to draw up below, well protected in the lee of the hill from defenders higher up. Kerr comments that by the time he was moving forward with the cavalry into this position, the rebels' 'confusion had begun and they soon after gave way in all directions'. This would certainly back up an interpretation that Loftus' bold move brought him into much closer quarters with the

---

[3] The research team are indebted to Brian Ó Cléirigh and Greg Walsh for bringing this third candidate to light.

6.13d A view of our third candidate for the 'green hill' as it appears to the west of the Clonhasten Road, at the point where McGurk's map shows Loftus to have reached (but placing him on the opposite side of the road). Photo by Ronan O'Flaherty.

core rebel defences than is usually believed to be the case. Kerr's comment that in the assault that followed General Loftus asked him to 'level and open up the lane in our rear to the high road in order to make a freer passage for the guns in case they should be ordered that way' also fits in with the landscape around this third candidate for our green hill, as the lane in question does lead directly onto the high road for Vinegar Hill. The fact that Kerr also ran into General Lake 'just 50 yards on the hill above me' also seems to place him in the close vicinity of this part of the battlefield. If our third candidate is in fact the elusive 'green hill', then Loftus' sudden appearance here with 3,000 men would have been a game changer, just as Kerr describes, and he would have been in a position to continue his ascent to meet 'at the same moment on the top of the hill' with Lake's column.

There are a few problems with this candidate as our 'green hill' however. In the first place, it is not a 'rocky eminence', or at least it isn't such now. Secondly, it is harder to reconcile its position with what is on the contemporary maps although it does tie in very well with the scale provided on McGurk's map and makes strategic sense in the context of the simultaneous assaults by Duff and Lake on either flank.

So, instead of one green hill, we now have three. At this point in time it is impossible to say with certainty which of these is the 'real' green hill, and even the authors cannot agree on a preferred candidate. However, we do agree that it must be one of these three candidates. Only further fieldwork may answer this question. In that regard, the results of the predevelopment survey carried out by Stafford McLoughlin at our second candidate site in 2020 substantially strengthens the case for identifying this as the 'green hill' captured by Loftus – the finds show that there was clearly an attack here during the battle and the only crown commander in the area was Loftus.

A WIDER FIELD OF BATTLE: THE 'BIG HOUSES'

We now turn to the field of battle as it played out in the wider countryside. From the various contemporary accounts it is evident that many local 'Big Houses' played important roles during the rebellion. These houses were used by both sides in the rebellion, serving as operational headquarters for the crown forces and as outposts for the rebels. In addition, they were a hugely important source of provisions for the rebels through their stores of foodstuffs and livestock. The houses also yielded many items of plunder to both sides. Of these houses, we can identify a number in the Enniscorthy area that played direct roles during the rebellion including Solsborough House, Beale's House (specifically Beale's Barn), Daphne Castle and Glebe House. What we know also includes the movement of the various armed forces through and around these estates. This can be very useful in terms of placing the main protagonists in the days immediately before the Battle of Vinegar Hill in particular.

Daphne Castle

Many authors have placed General Johnson and his troops within the townland of Bloomfield on the eve of the Battle of Vinegar Hill. However the diary of Alicia Pounden very clearly places Johnson at Daphne Castle. Pounden writes:

> On the 20th of June, the Ross Road provided a most brilliant appearance; as far as the eye could extend from Daphne was crowded with troops of every description, cannon, ammunition, sumpter carts, and all things necessary for 4 or 5,000 men. When they arrived the Pioneers pulled down sufficient of the demesne wall to allow them to march in with all their artillery, cavalry, etc. … Daphne House being built in the Castle style, the two Gothic entrance gates were soon guarded by two of Hompuck's Hessians, who showed the greatest humanity to me and my children. (Beatty, 2001, pp 151–2)

Barbara Newtown Lett confirms the above account in her own diary while discussing a chance meeting with a soldier from the Donegal militia just before the battle:

> This soldier was a private from the Donegal Militia. We used every argument to induce him to accompany us to the town, but this he declined, saying he should join his regiment who were encamped at Daphne. (Beatty, 2001, p. 136).

Alicia Pounden, in her diary, also confirms that the insurgents previously housed their own forces at Daphne Castle, possibly using it as an outpost sometime between the Battles of Enniscorthy and Vinegar Hill. She draws some very unfavourable comparisons between the rebel army and the crown forces, commenting on the contrast the latter made with 'the dirty ragged creatures we had been accustomed to for the last three weeks'.

Solsborough House

Solsborough House, owned by Captain Solomon Richards, who was commander of the Enniscorthy yeoman cavalry at the Battle of Enniscorthy on 28 May 1798, is a key location occupied by the crown forces just before the Battle of Vinegar Hill. Although like many similar complexes, Solsborough House may have been used by rebel forces for stores or billets, accounts of that do not survive in the historical record. In relation to the Battle of Vinegar Hill the importance of Solsborough House lies in its association with the commander-in-chief General Lake and his encampment there on the eve of the battle. This is recorded by Musgrave:

> Lieutenant-generals Lake and Dundas, and major general Wilford, with their staff, and the first brigade of light infantry under the command of colonel Campbell, remained all the night of the twentieth of June upon their arms, at Solsborough. (Musgrave, 1802, i, p. 476)

Solsborough played a particular role in the delayed arrival of General Needham at his appointed position on the morning of the battle, which in turn created the eponymous 'Needham's Gap' through which the bulk of the rebel army ultimately made their escape. Arriving at Solsborough around 3.30 a.m., Needham found that his orders had been changed and that he was to assume his original position east and south of Vinegar Hill. However, the logistics of turning a 7km-long baggage train on the narrow roads leading to Solsborough and resuming an arcing march around the flanks of Vinegar Hill made it impossible that Needham could ever have reached his destination in time. This was demonstrated very clearly in a dedicated re-enactment on 3 September 2017, which is fully discussed in chapter 5.

Beale's Barn

George Beale's house at Drumgoold still survives as part of a modern farm complex very close to Vinegar Hill, and the house itself is still occupied. The original house was built by John Beale (1682–1742) and the site features on a number of maps and documents, with the landowner variously shown or listed as Beale, Beal, Bayle or Bale. On the later Ordnance Survey maps c.1840s the name has transformed into the more elegant sounding 'Bell Grove'. During the rebellion, insurgent forces used Mr Beale's house for billets and provisions, as evidenced by George Beale's claim for compensation after the rebellion for 'Houses burned, Furniture, Cattle, Corn' through which he was awarded the sum of £1,051 and 12 shillings. Historical accounts, however, generally associate George Beale's farm complex with the use of his barn as a prison by the rebels. Authors on the rebellion identify three locations within the vicinity of Vinegar Hill where the rebels held prisoners, these being a guard house at an unknown location in Enniscorthy, Beale's Barn at the foot of Vinegar Hill and the ruin of the windmill on the summit of the hill.

The field of battle 139

6.14 Beale's Barn, the notorious rebel prison at the foot of Vinegar Hill, as it appears today – still standing and very much intact. Photo by Jacqui Hynes.

> Different gangs of assassins were sent through the country in search of protestants; some of whom, on being taken, were immediately put to death, but the generality were brought prisoners to Vinegar-hill, and confined in a prison at the foot of the hill, or in the town. (Burdy, 1817, p. 520)

Mary Hall, giving evidence at the trial of William Fenlon on 12 September 1799, specifically names Beale's (Bayle's):

> Say, that, on the morning of 14th of June, in the rebellion, she sent her son with some tea to her husband, who was the night before a prisoner with the rebels in Mr Bayle's barn … (Gordon, 1801, appendix II, p. 369)

One of the aims of the Longest Day Research Project was to see if the location of 'Mr Beale's Barn' could be identified and if any remains of the building survived. The barn itself is not shown on any maps, although there were tantalizing references to a brewery on site, which was marked on the maps, and it was felt that the much-sought barn might have been near this. However, the simplest approach often proves the most effective and in this instance a conversation with the current owner led to the identification of a building that had been traditionally pointed out as the barn used during the rebellion. An examination by architectural historian Edmund Joyce revealed that this building was simply not old enough to have been used in 1798. However, in looking round the farm complex, another candidate quickly suggested itself and detailed examination by Mr Joyce indicates that it was indeed a barn and does indeed date from the time of the rebellion (see chapter 7). Given its proximity to Mr Beale's house (forming one side of the courtyard to the side of the house), there seems little doubt that this is in fact 'Mr Beale's Barn', the prison used by the insurgents. The barn (fig. 6.14) is completely intact, with a modern roof, and by any standards is a hugely significant addition to what we know of the battlefield landscape. Vinegar Hill is clearly visible from the barn, as is the windmill on its top, and it is a sobering thought to imagine the terror of those prisoners pulled from the barn as they realized their destination was Vinegar Hill, 'trial' and almost certain execution.

CONCLUDING REMARKS

What makes Vinegar Hill so important is that the battlefield landscape remains substantially intact. Through prudent purchasing and planning control by Wexford County Council, strong local pride, as well as the survival of traditional farming techniques around and on the hill, much of the landscape directly associated with the final stages of the battle has been preserved. This includes the deep ditches and lanes that are commented on so often by writers from both sides. Even the field structure seems substantially intact and would probably be recognisable to combatants if they could revisit the site today. Other than the spread of new housing developments, the main modern intervention is the construction of the R744 road, which bisects the northern field of battle and can be confusing to a reconstruction of troop movements until its late construction is appreciated. Within the town, the progress of the battle can be clearly traced and several key buildings/landmarks that played a role in both the Battle of Enniscorthy and the Battle of Vinegar Hill still survive. Beyond that again, in the wider battle, we can identify big houses that were occupied by one side or the other and played important roles in providing supplies and shelter, as well as supporting the command structure.

Vinegar Hill has already revealed itself as the richest of our battlefields in terms of finds recovered. This, combined with the extent to which its landscape has remained substantially intact, along with its enormous symbolic importance, makes Vinegar Hill utterly unique.

CHAPTER SEVEN

The architectural landscape of Enniscorthy in 1798

EDMUND JOYCE

INTRODUCTION

Enniscorthy is typical of many Irish towns that have developed over numerous centuries. The town, which evolved organically as a busy market town, is systematically interwoven with winding streets. Such town layouts with streets of irregular formation, characterized by buildings of varying proportions, indicate a town with foundations of pre-Georgian origin. The development of a town and its associated building types is influenced by local economic, social and cultural attitudes. In addition to this, site topography also plays a major role in the form and layout of buildings within a townscape. Enniscorthy with its steep inclines and stepping gables, radiating from a central nucleus encompassing the castle and the Market Square is typical in both form and function of a town that evolved on the back of ever-growing trade.

Demolition, site clearance and reconstruction have become a part of the modern age of construction. However, in centuries past, the lack of machinery meant that this was a greater undertaking. Most buildings, if of solid construction, were retained and modified to accommodate the requirements of their developer. No street or even individual building within an active town such as Enniscorthy has survived without accommodating some change. The purpose of this study is to examine the extant architectural fabric, written records, maps and old images in order to conjure an image of how the town of Enniscorthy and its environs looked in 1798.

According to Patrick and Maura Shaffery in *Buildings of Irish towns*, 'The great thrust of urban building began in the eighteenth century' (Shaffery, 1983, p. 14). This is certainly true at Enniscorthy where many buildings extant in the townscape have their roots in the eighteenth century. These buildings offer an architectural palimpsest, as many have been modified and adapted as fashions have evolved. During the late nineteenth century and into the early twentieth century it was common practice to embellish earlier buildings. The earlier mundane architectural anodynes were dressed with pronounced mouldings, often in cement – for example: banded window surrounds, imitation cornerstones etc. As might be expected, many buildings have had their fenestration changed, whether in Victorian times or later. It is usual for those commissioning such change not to follow conservation principles, but instead to replace with the conventional form and materials available at the time. This means that many buildings, although of great age, can take on the appearance of a building with a much later provenance. This is not peculiar to Enniscorthy – it can be seen right across the country.

TOPOGRAPHICAL ANALYSIS OF ENNISCORTHY

Eighteenth-century topographical views are the nearest thing the architectural historian can get to a contemporary photograph. The views often capture important details, but caution needs to be exercised, as in some instances those producing the drawings may have been generating views based on information and sketches prepared by others. Despite such shortfalls, the views provide important information, such as the locations of buildings, materials used and the forms that roofs, windows and chimneys took.

An insight into how Enniscorthy might have looked in 1798 is given in a late eighteenth-century engraving by Sparrows that depicts Enniscorthy Castle and Bridge (fig. 7.1). The engraving, created in 1793, after a drawing by the Revd Dr Wynne, was reproduced in Francis Grose's *The antiquities of Ireland*. The view captures a number of buildings on the climb between the bridge and the castle. As would be expected of buildings of this mid- to late Georgian period they are gabled and have steeply pitched roofs. The large stone edifice to the left of the bridge with its disorderly arrangement of windows, stone barge, pedimented door surround and eave-perched dormers is somewhat at odds with the order and symmetry generally associated with Georgian architecture. This informal façade arrangement can be explained by the fact that according to the 1729 and early nineteenth-century Portsmouth estate maps (the 'Munday' and 'Newton' maps respectively), this is the back of a group of buildings adjacent to the bridge whose gardens back onto the Slaney. It appears that this building is detached from the building to its left, and a small gable window can be seen in the neighbouring building, indicating the presence of an attic storey.

The building to the right of this stone range, and directly in line with the bridge, appears to be covered in thatch. The whiteness of its walls by contrast to its neighbour indicates that it may have been lime-washed. The building appears not to have its own gable chimney, and unless its occupants were sharing the gable chimney of the neighbouring building, it is likely that this building was a store or commercial premises rather than a dwelling. This group of buildings that fronted onto Slaney Place cannot be identified in modern-day Enniscorthy as it appears they were removed during

The architectural landscape of Enniscorthy in 1798

7.1 A 1793 view of 'Enniscorthy Castle and Bridge, Co. Wexford' (Grose, 1795). Private collection: Ronan O'Flaherty.

7.2 'Enniscorthy Castle, Co. Wexford.' By Francis Grose, 1792. Private collection: Ronan O'Flaherty.

the construction of the quay in order to improve access to the Slaney. The site, now occupied by the late nineteenth-century red-brick Allied Irish Banks building, is just out of frame to the left of this engraving.

Towering behind the low thatched building adjacent to the bridge appears to be the remains of a derelict building. The roofless structure appears to be supporting lush vegetation, suggesting that the building has been derelict for a number of years. Due to the change in level however, it is more likely that this apparently derelict building is a representation of the walls that enclose the castle garden. The castle itself is shown here without its nineteenth- and twentieth-century enlarged openings. It is, as would be expected of a castle built for defensive purposes, a monolithic stone structure with strong corners, the interior of which was lit by an array of lancet windows that increase in size as they ascend through the upper storeys. The remains of the tower in the corner of the garden that is visible over the bridge are still extant today, but they are confined undignifiedly behind the now empty Castle Nightclub premises.

Another engraving (fig. 7.2) of Enniscorthy Castle also published in Grose's *The antiquities of Ireland* depicts the castle from the perspective of the castle garden. This level garden on such a sloping site is an astonishing feat of engineering. The engraving also captures a thatched roof that appears to be covering a circular structure. This is most likely a garden folly rather than a habitable building.

One of the most informative topographical views of Enniscorthy prior to the 1798 rebellion is a *c*.1775 painting by Paul Sandby (fig. 7.3). The view represented is taken from a similar position to Sparrows' engraving of Enniscorthy Castle and Bridge. The painting by Sandby does, however, take in a greater perspective than Sparrows' riverside engraving and captures a view of the Abbey south of Slaney Place. The Belfry, with its ogee-profiled roof and the gable of the church (most likely the north transept) dominate the view downstream of the bridge. Jonathon Binns, in his account of Enniscorthy in his 1837 publication *The miseries and beauties of Ireland*, outlines how

> a tower, standing alone in an open space, is all that remains of the ancient church, which was destroyed at that period [of 1798]. The erection of a Market-house has been proposed, and a plan suggested, according to which the tower is to form part of the projected building. (Binns, 1837, ii, p. 244)

According to the architectural historian Peter Pearson (Pearson, 2010, p. 373) this tower collapsed in 1839. The abbey site as represented on the first edition of the Ordnance Survey map, surveyed in the late 1830s, is completely devoid of all structures. On this map the 'Ross Road' as it is labelled (later Mill Park Rd) is the closest road to the water's edge.[1] This area and that of Mill Park appear to be completely underdeveloped on the early nineteenth-century Portsmouth estate map copied by J. & W. Newton (n.d.). The

---

1 Ordnance Survey first-edition map, *c*.1840.

The architectural landscape of Enniscorthy in 1798 145

7.3 Enniscorthy, oil on canvas, by Paul Sandby, *c*.1775.

1729 Portsmouth estate map by William Munday shows a large residence, occupied by a man named Eames, in the area of Mill Park. This is presumably the same house as is referred to as Mill Park House on the Ordnance Survey first-edition map and as Manor Mills House on the early twentieth-century Ordnance Survey second-edition map. The 1729 Munday Map also illustrates a cluster of mills in this quarter, all of which appear to have been powered by a meandering mill-race. Better order was put on this mill race as the area of Mill Park evolved over the coming years.

The bridge in Sandby's painting, with its high arches, represents the bridge at its original height prior to the *c*.1840s widening and lowering. During this phase of development, the two quays were also built (Lewis, 1849, i, p. 590). The painting illustrates how Enniscorthy had failed to capitalize on its geographical proximity to the river prior to the development of the quays. It is clear that prime riverside land was occupied by houses with gardens enclosed by high walls. The edge of the river itself was bordered by a broad irregular sloping grassed bank. John Gorton writing of Enniscorthy in 1833 outlined how 'a quay is much wanted here' (Gorton, 1833, i, p. 739). A couple of small quays, each labelled 'key' and probably then in private

7.4 'Vinegar Hill from the Bridge of Enniscorthy', *Gentleman's Journal*, 1801. Private collection: Ronan O'Flaherty.

ownership, did exist on 1729 Munday Map. The development of these quays, although inconsiderable in scale, probably unveiled to the business people of Enniscorthy the potential that the Slaney held. The building of the quays and the lowering of the bridge would bring great power to Enniscorthy. Unrestrained trade could thrive south of the bridge and due to the reduced height of the arches supporting the bridge, Enniscorthy now held control on the size of vessel that could travel up river.

On the 1729 Munday Map many properties existed on the Templeshannon side of Enniscorthy. These buildings line the street directly aligned with the bridge. Development however does not appear to extend beyond the ruins of the old church. The church, which is represented, but not labelled, is flanked by a large property belonging to a Mr Gamble. His property includes a large garden orchard and grove. The road that heads towards Clonhasten did not exist at the time. It does appear on the early nineteenth-century map, but since it was just newly formed, there are very few buildings on it. The Shannon itself was richly populated with groups of terraced houses. In their infancy, before later developments, many of these houses were lower and would have had thatched roofs. James Fraser, in his observation of Enniscorthy in 1844, describes how 'in the centre of the town there are a number of respectable houses, but the suburbs consist of long lines of poor cabins' (Fraser, 1844, p. 116). This was certainly true in Templeshannon, where the short line of houses represented on the early nineteenth-century Newton Map was, by the time the Ordnance Survey first-edition map of 1838 was published, further extended along the then Wexford Road (almost as far as Drumgoold House). The terraced houses that lined the Shannon in 1798 are represented in a sketch of Vinegar Hill, published in 1801. Although the representation is somewhat naive, it does indicate that the houses were terraced and that a regular form was adopted in their construction (*Gentleman's Magazine*, 1801, lxxi, p. 977).

THE TOWN DURING THE BATTLE

Descriptions of St Mary's Church of Ireland church as it was in 1798 are few and far between. Most writers recollecting the events of 1798 concentrate on activities within and surrounding the church rather than describing the architectural composition of the church. George Cruickshank's retrospective illustration, 'The destruction of the church at Enniscorthy' (fig. 7.5), which was published in Maxwell's 1845 *History of the Irish rebellion in 1798*, cannot be taken as a factually accurate representation of the church as it was produced to illustrate and dramatize the contemporary accounts of the destruction and plunder rather than the veracity of the physical environment (Maxwell, 1845, p. 97). A contemporary account published in the *Weekly Journal* (no. 409, 1866, p. 207) indicates that the insurgents

7.5 Destruction of the church at Enniscorthy, engraved by George Cruickshank (Maxwell, 1845, p. 97). Courtesy of Wexford Public Library Service, Local Studies Collection.

> made bonfires of the organ, the pews, the communion-table and pulpit before the church door, and flung the Bibles and Prayers into the flames. They carried the church bell on beams to Vinegar Hill, as an alarm bell for the camp they were making there …

The 1729 Munday Map shows that St Mary's was concealed by a ribbon of buildings stretching up the street now known as Church Street and along the street where modern day Rafter Street meets Court Street. A short street (the top of modern day Friary Hill and a stretch which aligns with part of modern day Lower Church Street) returns in around to the side of the site of St Mary's; on the map, this road then tapers to the width of a lane to exit between two buildings onto the top of Castle Hill. This road configuration appears to correspond with the layout of the early nineteenth-century Newton Map, meaning this layout remained extant during the 1798 rebellion. The church, due to the constraints of the site, was probably a humble building. Nicky Furlong indicates that in the 1730s, its church minister 'petitioned parliament to fund a gallery to cater for its overflowing congregation of 700' (Furlong, 2003). It is not clear how old the church was but it is known that George Ogle MP presented a petition to parliament from the parishioners of the parish of Enniscorthy 'for aid towards rebuilding their parish church' following the damage caused in 1798. The project seemed considerable, as the Parliamentary Register shows they requested £700. Whether this was to fund a complete rebuilding or a major remodelling is not clear.

A letter dated 1807 to the editor of the *Antijacobean Review* and written from the perspective of William Champitt, a gentleman killed in the battle of Vinegar Hill, documents the events encompassing St Mary's during the rebellion:

> My father, mother, and brother, have successively filled the office of sexton in the church of Enniscorthy for upwards of forty years. In the cruel rebellion of 1798, the church of that town was made a total wreck; the bell, organ, bible, prayer-books, &c. were destroyed; the pulpit, pews, and chancel demolished; and forges for the fabrication of pikes for the rebel army erected in this ancient house of divine worship. Since that period, the Protestants of the parish have been compelled to resort to the Market-house to perform their devotion; and a small market bell has tolled to give notice of the time for assembling themselves together, which, from its size, is incapable of sounding out a solemn peal. It is only within these last six months that the church has been opened for divine service, and the rebuilding of it completed. (1807, xxvii, p. 515)

The letter acts as a solemn reminder of the sheer upheaval suffered by the town and its people in the aftermath of the battle. It also manages to put some sort of timeframe on at least one part of the reconstruction of the town.

Contemporary accounts of the destruction evoke images of a town and its people trapped in chaos. They show that the initial defeat of crown forces was quickened when the residents of the town set fire to their houses in order to smother the troops in smoke, subsequently moving them from their posts and putting their attack strategy into chaos (*The terrific register ...*, 1825, ii, p. 722). A band of troops that were protecting the town at the Duffry Gate were pushed 'down by degrees into the town, leaving the suburbs, composed of thatched houses, unprotected, which then were set fire to ...' (Anon., 1805, pp 76–7). Many buildings were destroyed beyond repair. 'By midnight [on May 26], four hundred and seventy-eight houses, taverns, store-sheds, and malt-houses had been reduced to ashes.' (*All the Year Round*, 17 (1867), p. 207). This destruction at Enniscorthy forewarned the occupants of Wexford, where, in anticipation of an attack, the residents were instructed to remove the thatched roofs to prevent the spread of fire through the town (*The terrific register ...*, 1825, ii, p. 722).

Fearing the destruction of their houses by fire, many families in the vicinity of Enniscorthy acted quickly and moved all portable goods of importance from their houses. In her recollection of the events of 1798, Jane Barber, daughter of Sam Barber of Clohass, described how

> we saw eleven distant blazes in the distance, every one, from its situation, marking out to us where the house and property of some neighbour, friend or relation was consuming. In immediate expectation of a similar fate, we instantly began to load our cars with whatever furniture and provisions were most portable, that at daybreak we might flee with them into Enniscorthy. (Jane Barber, *Recollections*)

The Barbers retrenched to Enniscorthy town, where they sheltered in the Willis' house, directly opposite the Market House. As the rebels advanced, the house in which the Barbers sheltered caught fire, destroying the few treasured possessions that they had saved previously, forcing them and others who were sheltering there out into the midst of the fighting. Options were limited, and the only obvious spot to take relative cover was inside the Market House, which was at that time occupied by the yeomanry. After regrouping and taking stock of the potential repercussions that their proximity to the fighting was likely to have, they fled in haste towards the river. In a state of desperation they attempted to remove themselves from the openness of the streets by knocking on the doors of several properties. Door after door refused their entry, until a man named Walsh, on recognizing Jane Barber's mother, allowed them to enter his house. Before the door could be closed behind them, they were followed by five or six 'pikemen', who instructed Walsh to 'to turn us out, or they would burn the house over our heads'. The family, after losing Sam, Jane's father, to a pikeman, returned to their farm at Clohass. On their return they found that the house and farmyard had been burnt to the ground; the side walls had fallen in and nothing was left standing, but one chimney and a small out house, from which the door had been torn. (Jane Barber, *Recollections*)

The Barbers waited until the following summer to build a new house.

For the older residents of Enniscorthy, the smouldering ruinous shells that appeared after the smoke cleared must have evoked memories of the major fire of 1731 in which forty-two dwelling houses in Enniscorthy were consumed (*Gentleman's Magazine*, 1831, i, p. 130). The use of thatch in an urban context proved unsatisfactory as it allowed fire to spread through terraces, consuming entire streets without restraint. Thatch, however, remained a popular choice in Enniscorthy as a roof covering for more humble dwellings. Photographs from the late nineteenth early twentieth centuries in the National Library of Ireland's collection of digitized photographs depict many houses, particularly those on the outskirts of town and in Templeshannon, with whitewashed walls and thatched roofs.

PREMISES EXTANT IN 1798

Identifying eighteenth-century fabric in a town that has accommodated so much change is difficult. Many buildings, if being re-roofed, would have adopted the traditions and forms of the time, i.e. in the early to mid-nineteenth century the protruding soffit at eaves level was introduced. This soffit, often constructed in flagstone or slate, greatly contrasts with the simple parapets or flush eaves typically associated with their eighteenth-century predecessors. Since conservation and reinstatement are concepts only adopted to any great measure in recent decades, when it came to replacing integral elements such as windows, if recently evolved technologies such as large plate-glass windows were in vogue, then that is what was put into use.

Many of the buildings that are extant today do harbour eighteenth-century and possibly even earlier fabric in their construction. The castle is a prime example of the tradition for upgrading rather than replacing. According to Philip Hore, writing in 1905, Enniscorthy Castle was built in the late sixteenth century on the ruins of an earlier castle. This earlier castle is likely to have taken the form of a fortified dwelling house. As subsequent improvements and extensions to buildings generally reflect the period in which they were created, identifying earlier structures clothed in later detail is the key to this study. Georgian pastiche has always been a popular choice for those developing buildings in later periods. However, there are usually subtle differences in detail that help establish their later provenance.

The big question is, if many of the buildings in Enniscorthy did survive 1798, where are they now? Although Enniscorthy has the appearance of an eighteenth-century town, it is for the most part a nineteenth-century composition. The town underwent a major redevelopment in the mid-nineteenth century. The 1837 *Report upon the proposed municipal boundary of the borough of Enniscorthy* by George Hotham identifies Enniscorthy as a town that 'has the appearance of prosperity' (Hotham, 1837, ix, p. 83).

Prior to this redevelopment Enniscorthy had operated as a market town, and goods were transported to and from it via the then rudimentary road network. The Portsmouth rental records from 1785 provide an inventory of the types of businesses operating at Enniscorthy just prior to the 1798 rebellion. At this time there were fifteen malt houses, three drying kilns, two distilleries, one brewery, five tan yards, a salt and lime works, a woollen manufactory, a bleach green and a timber yard (Walsh, 2010, p. 191).

As mentioned before, in 1837 the bridge was lowered and the quays were built. This sparked a major phase of building in the town. Commercial prosperity soon enveloped it. The river could now be used for the transport of goods. James Fraser observed in 1844 that

> Enniscorthy, which of late years has expanded considerably, carries on a very considerable retail trade, and at the weekly markets a great deal of grain and other agricultural produce are disposed of. The Slaney, which from Enniscorthy downwards, is a large tidal river, is navigable for barges of considerable tonnage, and by it, coal, timber, iron, limestone, manure, and other commodities, are brought up from Wexford; and by which also the agricultural produce for shipment is borne down to that port. To facilitate the trade by the Slaney, two quays have been built at a considerable expense, which sum was partly defrayed by the trustees of the Earl of Portsmouth, and partly by subscription. (Fraser, 1844, p. 200)

Enniscorthy was to expand beyond recognition. The large brownfield site that once accommodated the abbey provided a great location for those wanting to construct purpose-built warehouses within close proximity of the water. Large granaries soon began to populate both sides of the river. Archaic and domestic buildings that stood in the way of this development were simply removed. The town was experiencing a commercial boom and prime sites were in short supply. Many of the streets that had served Enniscorthy in earlier incarnations needed to be realigned and in some instances widened.

The Market Square, which appears on the 1729 Munday Map, experienced a dramatic overhaul in the mid-nineteenth century. This redevelopment took place around the then two-storey Market House, which had been built in the early nineteenth century to replace the Market House that was badly damaged in 1798. The two-storey Market

House of the early nineteenth century was later extended upwards with the addition of a third storey (National Inventory of Architectural Heritage, 2020). The mid-nineteenth-century phase of redevelopment was however not a measure to replace buildings damaged in 1798 but instead it was an exercise in commercial expansion. The town, which was thriving commercially, needed a smart, modern centre where trade could take place. As a result of this redevelopment many of the buildings throughout the town are of mid-nineteenth-century appearance. Some constitute parts of large blocks of mid-nineteenth-century origin, whereas others are sandwiched between earlier buildings and duly take on the form and scale of their neighbours. In this newly ordered town there was no place for purely domestic dwellings near the centre of town and, subsequently, residential streets were soon consumed by the ever spreading wave of commercial redevelopment. The market square itself was reshaped and increased in size. The buildings on the St Mary's side of Market Street (part of which is now Castle Street) were demolished and the building line pulled back in order to expand the square. These new premises (as their predecessors probably did) contained shop fronts on the ground floor and spacious living accommodation on the upper levels. Fortunately, the town's tradition of using building date stones was continued, and many of these buildings have date stones from the 1840s.

The town was greatly extended in the direction of the Duffry Gate in the early nineteenth century. The early nineteenth-century Portsmouth map shows little development beyond the area that later became known as the Pig Market. There is a line of terraced buildings on the opposite side of the current site of the Presentation Convent. These are not present in 1729 on the Munday Map. They do appear again on the Ordnance Survey first-edition map, but have incredibly small back gardens. These have disappeared by the time the 1920s Ordnance Survey map was published. It is likely, based on their density and scale, that these were thatched cottages.

The new shopfronts developed on this side of the Market Square took on a clearly defined order. The ground floors adopted arcades, a form typically associated with market buildings. This architectural feature, according to Peter Pearson, was 'popularized in Dublin, by the Wide Streets Commissioners in the late eighteenth century [and] shows a serious attempt at urban planning in Enniscorthy' (Pearson, 2010, p. 373). The newly developed town was soon open for business and a growing trade automatically spurred a population growth. This influx of workers had to be accommodated in this newly emerging power base. The structure of the old town was unable to accommodate increased numbers of dwellings. Sprawling ribbon-developments along the main arteries out of the town were an inefficient use of valuable land and were unsustainable. The answer was to augment the existing road structure with additional roads that would liberate any previously inaccessible sites and help alleviate any potential congestion from this spurt in growth. James Fraser, writing in 1844, states that

> as the river occupies the greater part of the valley, the principal part of the town reaches along the abrupt banks on either side; consequently, the streets are in many places inconveniently steep. This, however, as regards the ingress and egress to and from the town, has been remedied by level lines of roads, which have been lately formed in various directions. (Fraser, 1844, p. 200)

Premises such as Holohan's contain a great deal of eighteenth-century fabric. The overall form and layout is typical of a Georgian building. The sash windows that are present appear to be early nineteenth-century eight-over-eight sashes with simple curved sash horns. Window horns were only introduced in the very late eighteenth century and early nineteenth century and, as earlier window horns are less decorative than their later Victorian counterparts, those in Holohan's probably support the notion that they were inserted/replaced as a result of damage suffered in 1798. According to the Buildings of Ireland database, this building is *c*.1775. The pattress plates on the upper storeys are more typically associated with granary type buildings but were most likely added at a later date to prevent subsidence. It is not known whether or not this stabilization measure was introduced to offset a structural defect incurred during the 1798 rebellion. In terms of establishing the original use of this building, it has a lower ceiling height on the ground floor than in the upper storeys, indicating that, as would be expected, the ground floor was likely used as a commercial premises, with lofty living accommodation above (National Inventory of Architectural Heritage, 2020).

The introduction of the railway through Enniscorthy saw the destruction of many buildings that were likely to have been extant in 1798. An account in *Bradshaw's Railway Manual, Shareholders' Guide and Official Directory for 1867* indicates that the tunnel under the town of Enniscorthy had recently been finished (*Bradshaw's … 1867*, p. 85). Mary Street, which became a secondary road with the construction of Island Street (*c*.1830s), later became obsolete when intersected by the rail line. The two buildings that now form P.J. Kenny Cycle Repairs were built in 1790. Despite their proximity to the bridge and the centre of upheaval, their survival without any apparent damage can be explained by the fact that they were sheltered by a distillery building which was positioned on the opposite side of the street. This complex, the other side of which faced onto a then narrower Island Street, was demolished to make way for the railway. This mid-nineteenth-century intervention opened up the view from the two brick-built buildings to the river. The height difference between Island Street and Mary Street was also a by-product of the railway. The Island Road which sat at a lower level was bridged over the railway and since Mary Street was to become a cul-de-sac it was left at its original level. These nineteenth-century changes have resulted in a much altered setting for the eighteenth-century buildings in the vicinity.

With regards to streets that were not extant in 1798, Lymington Street, Mernagh Street, the Pig Market, Mill Park Road and Weafer Street (originally known as New

Street) were all nineteenth-century creations (first appearing on the nineteenth-century Newton Map), thus buildings along these streets are most likely to be nineteenth-century at the earliest. Fortunately for Enniscorthy, there is an unusually high number of building date stones present. These date stones, many of which are carved into dressed granite blocks, are very useful when establishing the histories of the buildings as, in most instances, either the name or the initials of the patron and the year it was built are extant (Pearson, 2010, pp 369–96).

According to the 1729 Munday Map, Irish Street seems to have been extensively developed at the time. The residents in each house are listed. Since Island Street did not exist at this point, the gardens of the houses on the Slaney side of the street ran down to the water's edge. Access to the water for those not residing on this side of the street appears to be limited to lanes such as Water Lane, which is sandwiched between a property leased by Pitman and another by Hughes. If the illustration is correct it indicates that although heavily developed, many of the properties on Irish Street are detached. Nicky Furlong (2003) estimates the population of Enniscorthy at this time, based on the number of properties illustrated, to be approximately 1,500. Many of the buildings in and around the centre of the town are of irregular form, which would most likely indicate that they had been extended on numerous occasions. This further strengthens the view that many of the buildings present in or around 1798, although Georgian in appearance, more than likely harboured earlier fabric in their construction. Pat Dargan, in his publication on Georgian town houses, writes that 'in contrast to the formal uniform house fronts, the rear elevations of the Georgian houses could be highly irregular' as they invariably incorporated extensions added by successive generations (2013, p. 49).

The large eighteenth-century buildings that flank the junction of the Shannon and the Clonhasten Road, apart from some muddling with the openings on the ground floor, have retained much of their original Georgian fabric. These buildings display an understated elegance and are typical of what to expect in eighteenth-century Enniscorthy. The large house, dated *c.*1775 by the National Inventory of Architectural Heritage, and now in use as offices, with a Tudor arched doorcase and opposite the hotel, is an essay in provincial Georgian style. The asymmetrical positioning of the door and the use of Tudor gothic embellishments in conjunction with neoclassical details creates a splendid composition that is unlikely to be duplicated elsewhere. These idiosyncrasies add to the character. The house in its original form is mostly eighteenth-century, although the window architraves, bracketed eaves and quoins are likely to be later than the original composition. The site was in use in 1729, indicating that the building, or at least the site, is likely to contain earlier fabric.

Since development in the Templeshannon area, apart from some development near the quay front, remained predominantly residential, much of the eighteenth-century and early nineteenth-century streetscape remains intact. The Society of Friends' Meeting

House, or at least the two-storey section closest to the river (*c.*1760), was extant in 1798. The site at this stage, though, was not so accessible or centrally located. It was at the end of a cul-de-sac accessed from a point near the bridge at Templeshannon. It was the mid-nineteenth century before the place was furnished with a through road.

Back across the river, the large building opposite and downhill of St Aidan's Cathedral is a prime example of an eighteenth-century building. It has a date stone indicating that it was built by J. Sparrow in 1793. Sadly, it has been the focus of several layers of so-called 'restoration', resulting in the loss of important earlier fabric; however, the overall form and classical proportions still remain. There are many buildings throughout the town that portray details synonymous with the late eighteenth early nineteenth century (National Inventory of Architectural Heritage, 2020).

On the outskirts of the town, there were country houses belonging to the minor gentry. Drumgoold and Clonhasten (or Clonhasten Manor) are the two most notable residences near Vinegar Hill. In 1798, Drumgoold House was in the possession of the Beale family, having being built by John Beale (1682–1742) (National Inventory of Architectural Heritage, 2020) from the north of Ireland on the site of an earlier house in the early eighteenth century (Scallan & Rowe, 2004, no. 438). The house, on the Ordnance Survey first-edition map (*c.*1840), is labelled 'Bell Grove House', whereas in 1798 it appears it was known as 'Bealegrove House'. According to Eithne Scallan and David Rowe, the site contains 'Beale's Barn', a structure that was used as a 'prison by both sides alternately'. Up until recently, the current owner believed Beale's Barn to be a two-storey building in one corner of the yard. A recent site visit, however, confirms that this building is early nineteenth-century in origin and was most probably built with compensation money administered as a result of the destruction caused to the complex. What the inspection did reveal was that the building to which this building adjoins is earlier in origin and predates 1798. Therefore, this building, which had a dovecote gable (now an internal party wall), is a strong contender for Beale's Barn, the infamous rebel prison where many unfortunates were held before being led away for trials and, in most cases, executions on Vinegar Hill. Drumgoold House itself was used by government forces as a hospital for officers (Scallan & Rowe, 2004, no. 438). The Ordnance Survey first-edition map (*c.*1840) depicts an 'Old Brewery' directly across the road from Drumgoold House, the name suggesting that it was extant in 1798. The land this brewery is on is shown in the possession of George Beale on the early nineteenth-century Newton Map.

Clonhasten House, in its current guise, is predominantly nineteenth-century. Scallan and Rowe (2004, no. 355) indicate that the house was built in 1783 by John White. The road directly behind the house, which progresses to Oulart, is a mid-nineteenth-century road, thus the only carriageway located between Clonhasten House and Vinegar Hill in 1798 was Vinegar Hill Lane.[2] The Glebe House, also

---

[2] Based on comparisons between printed maps of Enniscorthy and its environs.

known as Templeshannon Rectory or more recently as Knock Haven House, is an early nineteenth-century dwelling (National Inventory of Architectural Heritage, 2020). The original Glebe House of Enniscorthy was reduced to ashes in 1798. The Old Church Road did not exist in its current format in 1729, suggesting that if the glebe house that was burned in 1798 was on the site, it might not have been a very old building at the time. The Old Church Road is on the early nineteenth-century Portsmouth map, indicating that it was developed sometime between 1729 and the early nineteenth century. Evidence given in 1800 (*Speech*, p. 26) records the attack on the Glebe House, outlining how the rebels first burned it and then 'converted the out-offices into stores, for holding provisions and arms for the camp'. Letters from Charlotte Elizabeth published in 1838 confirm that the new Glebe House is on the site of the one attacked in 1798. She states that 'nearly at the foot of [Vinegar] hill stands the Glebe, rebuilt from its ruins' (1838, p. 70).

CONCLUSION

Despite redevelopment in the town, many buildings are of pre-1798 origin. These are true veterans, having survived the destruction that engulfed the town in 1798 and the later phases of redevelopment that swept through it. The often refined detail of such buildings is usually overshadowed by the richly ornamented buildings or features of later periods. These eighteenth-century buildings are dotted without pattern throughout the town. It is important that they are respected in Enniscorthy's architectural landscape. By examining the form and type of buildings extant in 1798 and multiplying this through the streets that existed at the time, one can imagine how this prosperous eighteenth-century town would have looked.

With major infrastructural additions and an increased building stock, Enniscorthy has become a much more complex arrangement to that which existed in 1798. The stepped streetscapes echo the form of an eighteenth-century town, but when viewed from above, the colonization of prime sites with modern buildings and an overdevelopment and expansion of existing buildings to consume the once spacious back gardens is in stark contrast with the once open spaces that originally populated the town. Synthetic materials that allow shallow pitched and flat roofs encourage people to develop spaces on ground level without compromising the windows at upper levels. This type of development does little to compliment earlier structures, as the original sense of form and function is subsequently blurred. Little attention to age-appropriate detail has been adopted by those developing their buildings in recent decades. Developers and those making so-called improvements need to remember that buildings are physically much bigger and have a much greater history than the people who own them at any time.

CHAPTER EIGHT

Investigating potential mass graves on Vinegar Hill

JAMES BONSALL & CIAN HOGAN

INTRODUCTION

Documentary and folkloric evidence suggests the presence of both mass graves and individual graves on Vinegar Hill, containing buried human remains deposited in the aftermath of the 1798 battle. The Vinegar Hill landscape is rarely ploughed and thus much of the 1798 battlefield has been preserved. Any mass-grave pits dating to the battle are likely to have survived well, with little (if any) plough damage to skeletal remains buried at depth. This paper identifies the potential for mass graves on the hill, guided by documentary accounts, followed by analyses of the geology, topography and cartographic sources, as well as a geophysical survey. This investigation identified a previously unrecorded quarry-pit backfilled with loose and moist soils that may potentially contain human remains. The implications of the results are discussed with reference to the outcomes of archaeological research at other mass-grave sites, including the potential for a forensic excavation.

Battlefield combat typically results in the deaths of large numbers of soldiers and non-combatant victims, such as camp followers. The Christian traditions for interring the dead often led to the rapid burial of the slain in mass pits (Nicklisch et al., 2017) rather than in individual graves, often with the subsequent removal of remains for re-interment in more formalized graves in consecrated ground. This process could take days or weeks. At the 1645 Battle of Alerheim, Germany, for instance, the dead were exposed to summer heat for six weeks prior to burial; decomposition was advanced and the corpses were highly vulnerable to faunal scavenging (Misterek, 2012), which potentially led to the spread of disease. At Vinegar Hill, witnesses reported seeing dozens of bodies lying unburied on the hilltop 'outside the [wind]mill' or 'along the hillside' after the battle (see chapter 2).

Curry and Foard's (2016) study of mass-grave sites found that they typically occur very close to the location of the battle. The mass graves are created either by digging or by using existing features in the landscape, to avoid dragging or transporting multiple bodies over large distances. Despite this, mass graves can be elusive, which is hardly surprising when the exact location of fighting – and therefore, areas of likely burial – are also often unknown, even for many supposedly 'well located' battlefields. Folkloric accounts of the location of mass pits are often misleading and documentary evidence may contain false leads, embellished language and poor geographical/topographical data (ibid.).

HUNTING THE DEAD

A combination of folkloric, geological, topographical and remote-sensing data was used in this project to identify potential mass-grave pits. O'Connor's detailed analysis of documentary sources identified instances of both individual graves and mass pits (see chapter 2). Three accounts mention that the slain were interred in 'a vast pit', 'shallow graves' or a 'deep trench' on the hillslope, with bodies carted to the graveside. The first was a letter by Anthony Sinnot to the editor of *Gentleman's Magazine*:

> At the declivity of the hill there is a vast pit, in which the bodies of the unfortunate men who were killed in this ruinous and fatal contest are deposited, to the number (as I was informed) of five hundred. (18 July 1801)

The second was in an account collected by Michael Banim from 'a respectable, well-clad peasant of advanced age', and used as a basis for *The croppy: a tale of 1798*, by John Banim and Michael Banim, first published in 1828:

> A deep trench was dug at the base of the eminence, the bodies were laid therein, and the earth and stones from above, tumbled down to fill the excavation. (1865, p. 432)

And the third was recorded by Donohoe (1998, p. 6):

> The old people ... would tell of cart loads of the fallen being buried in shallow graves in the small fields under the hill overlooking Enniscorthy. One account was of the Whiteness of the fields, with upturned bones, which remained for years after the rebellion ...

There are also numerous accounts of individual graves; the body of at least one person, William Reynells, was subsequently retrieved from a grave by his family for re-burial in Monart, Enniscorthy (see chapter 12). Charles Davis suffered premature burial, *viz.* he was buried alive in an individual shallow pit, and later brought home (alive). Hynes recorded an account from Raymond Quirke in 2018 of many soldiers buried in 'the Barley Field', subsequently built upon in the 1980s, on the south-west

Investigating potential mass graves on Vinegar Hill 159

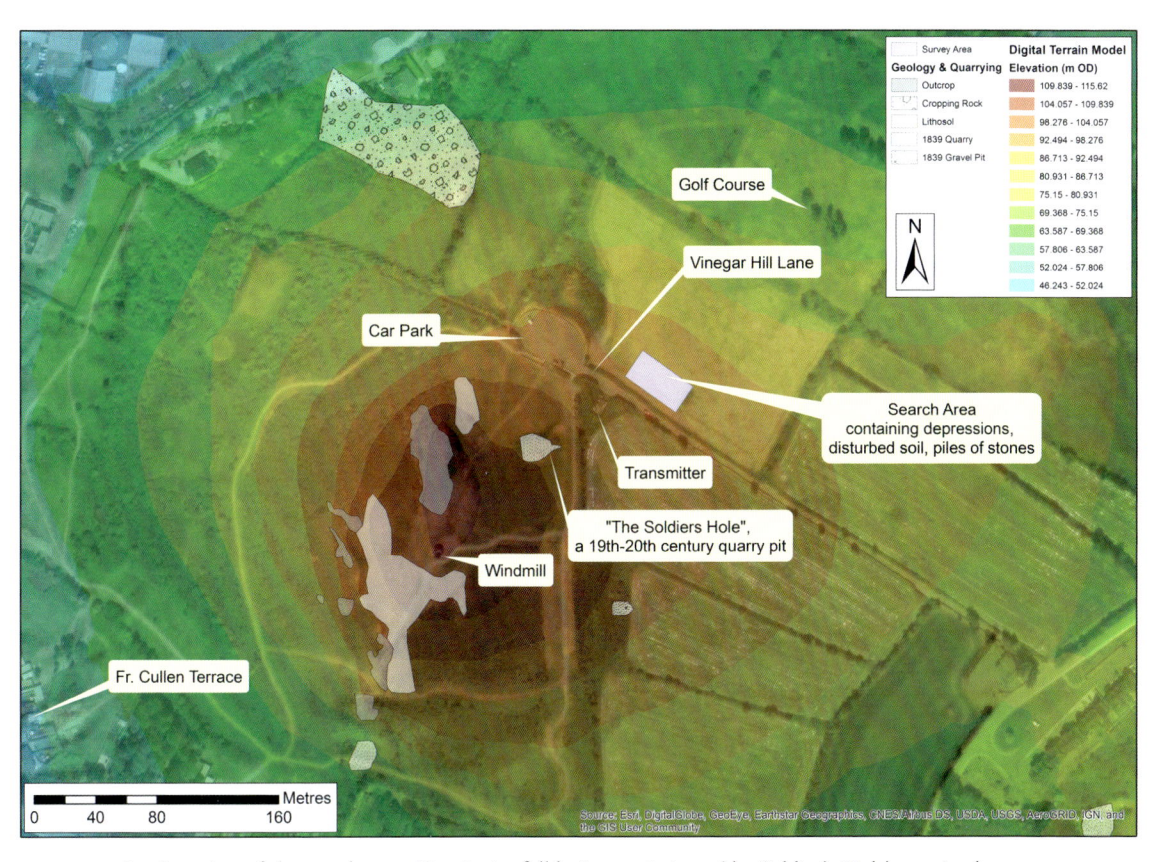

8.1 Location of the search area. Despite its folkloric associations, 'the Soldier's Hole' remained an open quarry into the twentieth century. Image by James Bonsall and Cian Hogan, based on data collected by Earthsound Archaeological Geophysics.

side of the hill (see chapter 12). Donohoe's account supports – and of course, may in turn be the inspiration for – Quirke's folklore. Donohoe's and Quirke's accounts also suggest that the shallow graves overlooked Enniscorthy, restricting those burials to the western side of the hill. Donohoe's description of the 'whiteness of the fields, with upturned bones' suggests that skeletal remains were exposed by agricultural activity. It would seem therefore that multiple burial sites are located in and around Vinegar Hill: there is probably no one single burial location.

To begin identifying possible mass-grave sites, the Vinegar Hill landscape (fig. 8.1) was assessed in detail, using the folklore as a starting point. 'Diggability', the ease with which a soil can be dug (Donnelly & Harrison, 2013), was assessed to limit the number of locations for potential mass graves, on the principle of least effort. Some areas of Vinegar Hill were quickly discounted as sites where a large trench or pit could be excavated given the poor diggability of the soil. This is particularly true around the top of the hill, which is dominated by exposed rock outcrops and lithosols (thin soil lenses above the underlying bedrock). Other areas were discounted due to modern disturbance or subsequent construction (e.g. Fr Cullen Terrace to the south-west, the golf course to the north), or vegetation (scrub, heather and gorse cover much of the hill, with particularly dense areas on the western slopes).

Open quarry pits are known in the vicinity and may have been re-used as grave pits removing the immediate need to hastily dig elsewhere. Seven isolated quarry and gravel pits mapped on the Ordnance Survey first-edition six-inch map (drawn 1839, published 1841) were dismissed by this study as burial locations as they remain open nowadays, containing little or no apparent in-fill (fig. 8.1). These include a deep pit near the summit of Vinegar Hill known locally as 'the Soldier's Hole', which remained in use as a quarry into the early twentieth century and was confidently discounted as a burial site.

Several depressions and piles of exposed and loose stones/boulders are visible in a field 15m north of Vinegar Hill Lane, in a series of aerial photographs dating from 1995, 2000, 2005, 2011 and 2017, and verified on the ground. These indicate soil disturbance, possibly related to a large excavation, and an adjacent deposit of stone. The nineteenth- and twentieth-century quarrying activity in the wider area could account for some of this material, but these topographical features do not coincide with any known or mapped quarry pits depicted on the historic Ordnance Survey maps.

After excluding certain areas as unlikely to hold mass graves, the field to the east of the modern car park was selected as a search area, focused on the disturbed soil and stone piles 15m north of Vinegar Hill Lane, described above. The search area was suitable for geophysical survey, with short pasture grass vegetation (amenable for survey) and its location on the battlefield (direct access offered by Vinegar Hill Lane for carts carrying the dead).

NON-INTRUSIVE TECHNIQUES TO ASSESS MASS-GRAVE PITS

The application of a high-resolution geophysical survey, blending the sub-disciplines of archaeology and forensics, was used to map the sub-surface properties of suspected pits in the search area at Vinegar Hill in 2016 and 2017. Human bones cannot be detected with geophysical methods, but the soil-fill of a mass-grave pit can be identified by mapping underlying contrasts in the earth's properties. A large pit can be mapped as a contrast in the electrical resistivity/conductivity of the soil, reflecting a change between the moisture content of the pit fill compared to the soils and geology surrounding it. The magnetic content of the pit could be extremely high if iron-bearing minerals are present. For instance, armour and weaponry will create a strong and sharp magnetic contrast. Other metals indicative of battlefield remains, particularly lead bullets or copper-alloy buttons on uniforms, can be identified by licensed metal detecting (see chapter 10). However, this may be negated by the possible stripping of useful/valuable materials from a corpse prior to burial and/or by the limited depth of penetration offered by metal detectors (commonly a few centimetres beneath the surface), which are unlikely to identify even large pieces of iron at a depth expected for a burial.

Electrical resistivity imaging (ERI) and ground-penetrating radar (GPR) have been used separately or in combination to identify and map Irish Famine mass graves, Lithuanian Holocaust execution trenches, and Spanish Civil War mass graves (Ruffell et al., 2009; Beck et al., 2018; McClymont et al., 2017; Rubio-Melendi et al., 2018) as well as clandestine cadaver simulation research (Cavalcanti et al., 2018). Geophysical techniques are also used to determine the absence of mass-grave pits and challenge long-held assumptions regarding 'known' grave sites. For example, magnetometry, metal detection and earth-resistance surveys at Towton, England, were used over sites suspected to be related to a 1461 battle that were subsequently proved to be archaeological features dating to the prehistoric, medieval and modern times (Sutherland & Schmidt, 2003).

The soils at Vinegar Hill were favourable for magnetometry, earth-resistance and electrical-resistivity-imaging surveys. GPR was unsuitable due to the presence of a transmitter on the south side of Vinegar Hill Lane, 30m away from the survey area. The transmitter would have introduced substantial electromagnetic interference and reduce the effectiveness of GPR partially or entirely.

Under Irish legislation – Section 2 (2) of the National Monuments (Amendment) Act, 1987 – any work that involves searching for archaeological objects or sites (including graves of any age or antiquity) requires a detection licence. As part of the application, the applicant must state the location and extent of the survey, and what techniques are to be used. Licence applications are processed by the National Monuments Service (NMS). If successful, consent is issued by the minister for culture, heritage and the Gaeltacht. Once a project is complete, copies of the final report are deposited with the NMS so that all archaeological geophysical survey reports can be consulted by members of the public. The geophysical surveys discussed below were carried out under detection licence 16R0204, issued by the NMS in 2016.

METHODOLOGY

Attempts by Landscape & Geophysical Services to identify potential pit(s) at Vinegar Hill in 2015 showed promise. However, the data, images and report were never published or made available for further assessment. Subsequently, a geophysical survey specification, designed by Rory O'Connor, involved assessing the suspected mass-grave pits 15m north of Vinegar Hill Lane in two phases. A magnetometer and earth-resistance meter were used in Phase 1 to create a 2D map of the suspected mass-grave pits. An ERI survey was used in Phase 2 to investigate their depth. Once identified, the ERI survey of the pits allowed for the calculation of their volume. The use of both magnetometry and earth-resistance surveys ensured that non-magnetic archaeological features of interest could be identified.

In December 2016, James Bonsall and Darren Regan (Earthsound Geophysics Ltd) carried out magnetometer (using dual Geoscan Research FM256s, acquired at 0.5m x 0.25m resolution) and earth-resistance (using a Geoscan Research RM15, twin-probe configuration acquired at 0.5m x 0.5m resolution) surveys over two days, completing the Phase 1 of the investigation, generating 2D 'plan view' datasets of the subsoil. A pile of exposed and loose stones/boulders was visible to the east of the survey area.

Phase 2 of the investigation was carried out in April 2017 by James Bonsall, Cian Hogan and Ciarán Davis (Earthsound Geophysics Ltd). ERI was used to further investigate the principal anomalies identified by Phase 1. The ERI survey (using an ABEM Terrameter LS 2 in Dipole-Dipole configuration, probe spacing 0.5m over a 32m profile) measured soil moisture. The ERI survey differed from the 2D earth-resistance survey by generating a 'section/elevation profile' through the soil and bedrock, obtaining important depth information and giving a good approximation of the profile of the sides, and slope, of the pits. Topographical data were collected along the line with an RTK GPS to determine the precise elevation of each profile, to an accuracy of 1cm. Together, the 2D earth-resistance and ERI profile data determine the true size, shape and depth of a subsurface target based on a resistivity model created from a data inversion (seventh iteration model, absolute error value of 0.57–0.94 per cent).

2016/17 GEOPHYSICAL SURVEY RESULTS

The magnetometer survey (fig. 8.2) revealed a number of anomalies. A small oval anomaly may represent a possible pit. While pits have many functions, one possibility is that this represents a single grave. Two areas of magnetic disturbance indicating deposits of ferrous (iron) material (each measuring approximately 4m x 8–9m) were detected along the edge of the survey area, beside Vinegar Hill Lane. A ferrous response is distinctive in magnetic data and typically indicates the presence of modern iron material, though their origin can also be archaeological. Rather than representing battlefield-related activities, these are likely to represent dumping of modern rubbish. A positive magnetic anomaly partially encircles the pile of stones located immediately to the east and may represent a narrow gully. This can now be discounted as a mass grave.

Investigating potential mass graves on Vinegar Hill 163

8.2 Magnetometry survey results.

The earth-resistance survey (fig. 8.3) provided more encouraging results. A broad area of low resistance located across the centre of the survey area is flanked to the south-east by a large area of high resistance. The low resistance anomaly is suggestive of disturbed soil, while the high resistance deposits may relate to near-surface geology or humanly transported and deposited stony material. The disturbed soil contains three distinct anomalies of extremely low resistance. Each of these responses represent discrete cut features, that is, excavations of the sediment that were subsequently back-filled with looser material, i.e. they represent three large pits cut into a broader area of disturbed soil. The absence of these pit-type anomalies in the magnetometer data suggests that the back-fill is non-magnetic (i.e. it does not contrast with the surrounding host soils) or that magnetic contrasts are buried at a depth greater than that investigated by the magnetometer (approximately 1m beneath the surface). These pit-type anomalies, identified as the 'northern pit', 'southern pit' and 'south-western pit', were selected for the Phase 2 ERI survey to determine their depth and profile.

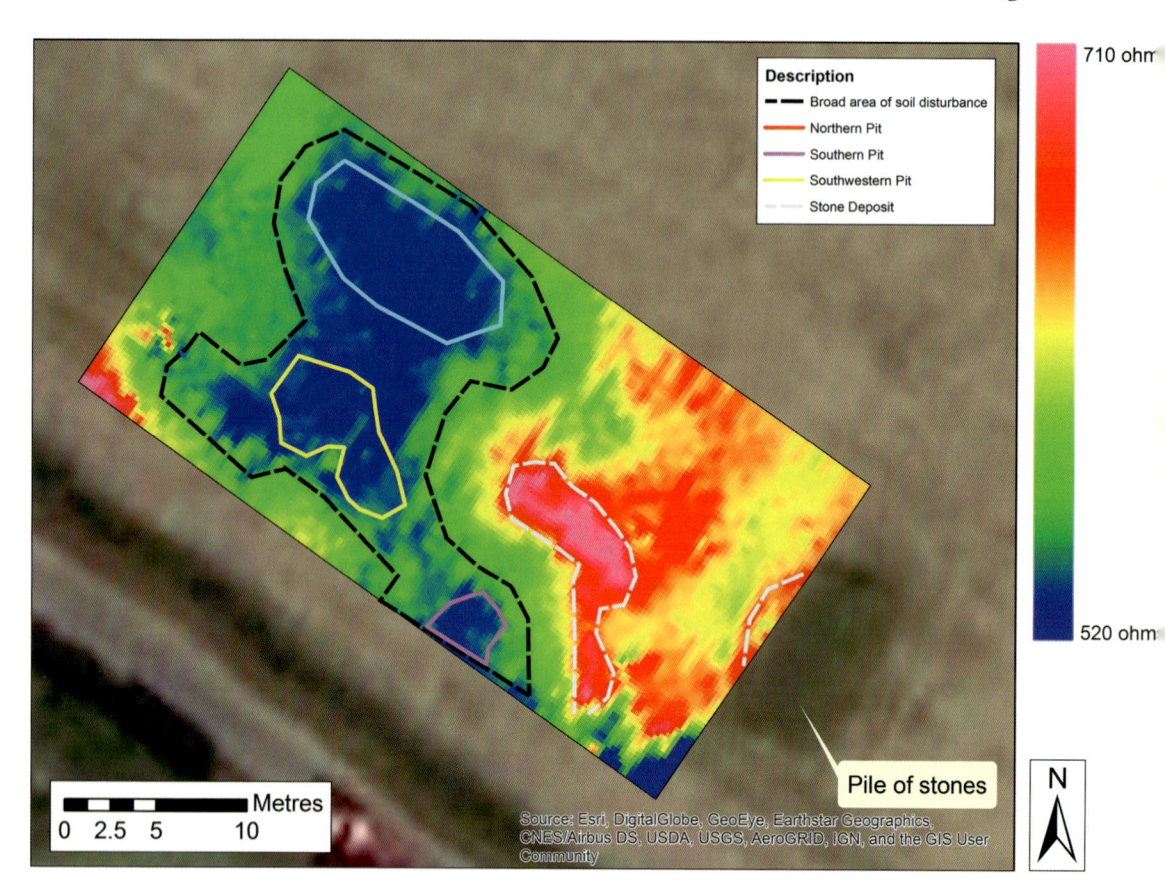

8.3 Earth resistance survey results.

Four ERI profiles assessed the long axis (and where possible, the short axis) of each pit-type anomaly (fig. 8.4). The surveys obtained depth information down to 8m below the surface on all four lines of data. The northern pit was mapped by two profiles as an area of very low resistivity measuring 12m x 7m and 2m deep, with steep (almost vertical) sides, a stepped cut to the south-east (downslope), and a flat base. To the north-west of this pit is a high resistance area corresponding with a localized rise in topography that represents the rubble fill of another pit. The south-western pit was examined by two ERI profiles which mapped it as comprising multiple small cuts or pits that together measure 7.7m x 4m and 1.2m deep. The pits are in close proximity (possibly intercutting one another) and some are shallow (4.2m wide, 0.6m deep). The final pit-type anomaly was located along the southern boundary of the field. Only a small portion of it could be assessed by two ERI profiles, one of which imaged the very edge of the southern pit as a shallow scoop. Responses obtained along the tapering edge of ERI profiles such as this should be treated with caution. However, the 2D earth-resistance survey provides a degree of confirmation and confidence in this

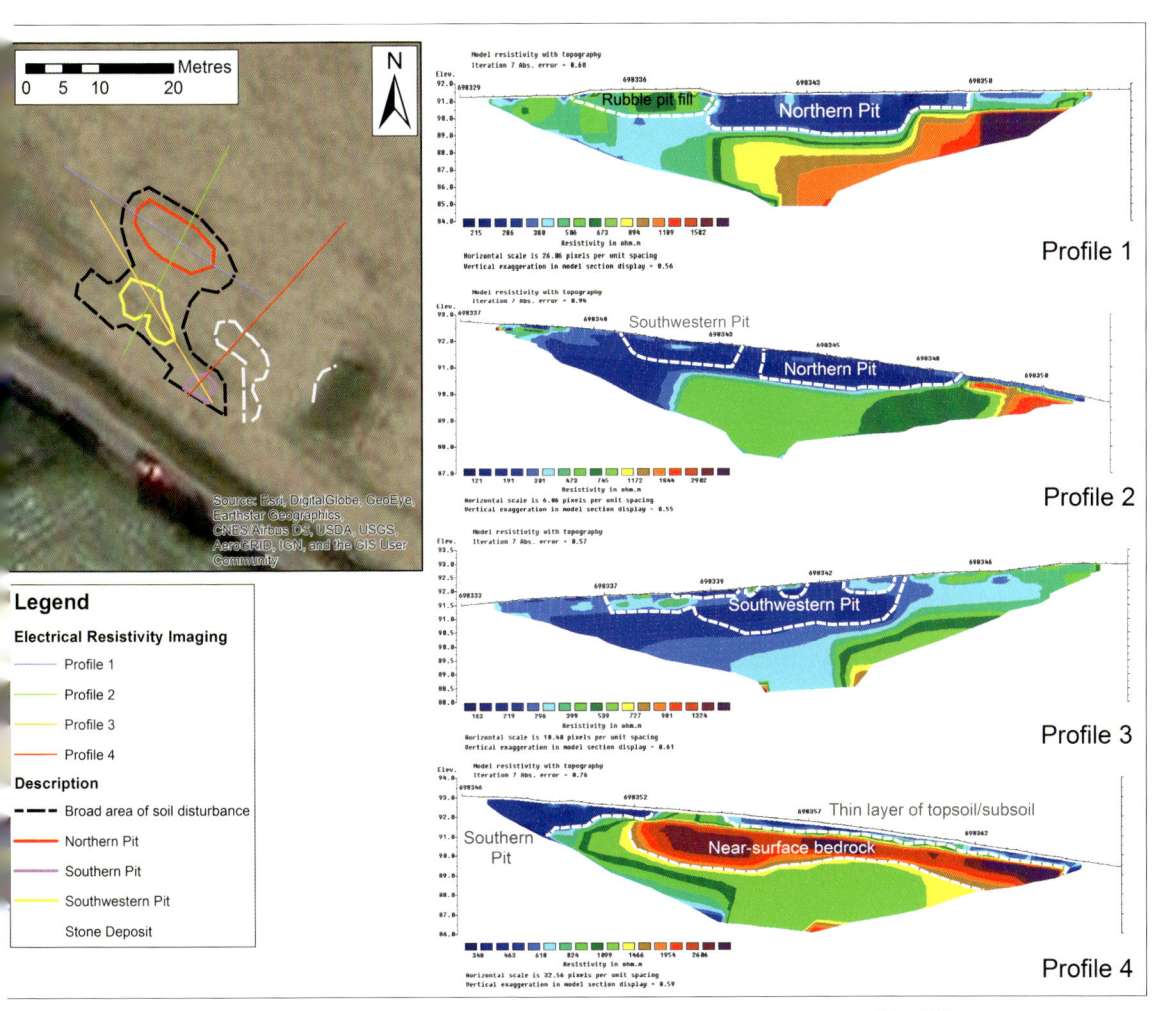

Investigating potential mass graves on Vinegar Hill

8.4 Electrical resistivity imaging (ERI) survey and interpretation. Inset: Location of the ERI survey profiles across the pits.

interpretation. The southern pit measured 3.8m x 3.0m and 0.5–1.0m deep. The ERI also mapped three zones of very high resistivity that correspond with stony material identified in the 2D earth-resistance data, representing the natural geology at a depth of 0.7–2m beneath the surface.

IMPLICATIONS OF THE GEOPHYSICAL SURVEY RESULTS

The 2D earth-resistance and ERI surveys mapped three large cut features which have been termed as the northern, south-western and southern pits. Their dimensions, shapes and approximate volumes have been calculated and their morphologies offer insights into their functions. To excavate the northern pit, approximately 168m^3 of soil and bedrock was removed. The longest axis of the northern pit could be extended to 17–20m length, if adjacent anomalies, suggestive of backfilled rubble in the same, or a smaller adjacent pit, are also included. Evidently a great deal of time was spent excavating the northern pit, differing from the rapidly dug and backfilled pits typically found as mass graves. The industrial morphology of the northern pit – its size, steep sides, step cut berms and flat base – all suggest that it was a pre-existing quarry pit that had been backfilled and subsequently re-purposed as a mass grave. The rubble backfill to the north-west and the pile of stones to the east could represent the remnants of quarry spoil that was not carted away down Vinegar Hill Lane to Enniscorthy. The southern and south-western pits may equally represent further quarry works such as pilot/trial holes, or shallow graves adjacent to the large northern pit. The widespread soil disturbance identified by the 2D earth-resistance survey may represent further pilot/trial holes for quarrying or the impact of general groundworks. The isolated pit identified in the magnetometer survey has an unknown function: it could represent yet another (small) grave, it may be connected to the quarry works or it may be something else.

Folkloric and cartographic evidence may shed light on the geophysical data (fig. 8.5). A very large pit of 168m^3 (the 'northern pit') was excavated on an unknown date 20m north of Vinegar Hill Lane. This was not unusual; seven other similarly sized quarry pits were mapped on the Ordnance Survey first-edition six-inch map within a 0.5km radius. The ERI data mapped the local geology 0.7–2m beneath the surface. Traditional spade-digging can excavate shallow pits in the topsoil and subsoil, however, the deeper excavations identified here would require more intensive (or explosive) industrial means to break the underlying near-surface rock. No editions of the Ordnance Survey maps include the northern pit or the shallower southern (5.7 to 11.4 m^3) and south-western (37m^3) pits that were discovered in the geophysical surveys. It is likely, therefore, that these pits were excavated and backfilled before the 1839 Ordnance Survey first-edition map was drawn. Key to understanding the northern pit is the nature of the backfill – a low resistance moisture-retaining deposit of loose soils or sediment that is consistent with the expected conductive layer response of decomposed remains observed at mass-grave pits (Cavalcanti et al., 2018; Rubio-Melendi et al., 2018) and which differ substantially from the high-resistance response of the adjacent rubble-fill. Magnetometry confirmed the backfilled pits do not contain substantial magnetic material in the upper 1m that might reflect a rapid in-filling of industrial quarry waste material, such as that seen at nearby Slaney Place, Enniscorthy (Stafford, 2006). It is quite possible that in 1798 the northern pit was a large exposed hollow of an active or disused quarry pit that was utilized as a convenient site to bury the slain or backfill loose soils. This northern pit potentially represents Sinnot's 'vast pit' at 'the declivity of the hill' that was used for burying the battle-slain. Use of such a feature as a makeshift burial ground is highly likely. Curry and Foard (2016) suggest that using existing hollows and ditches for graves would 'avoid the need to dig deeply',

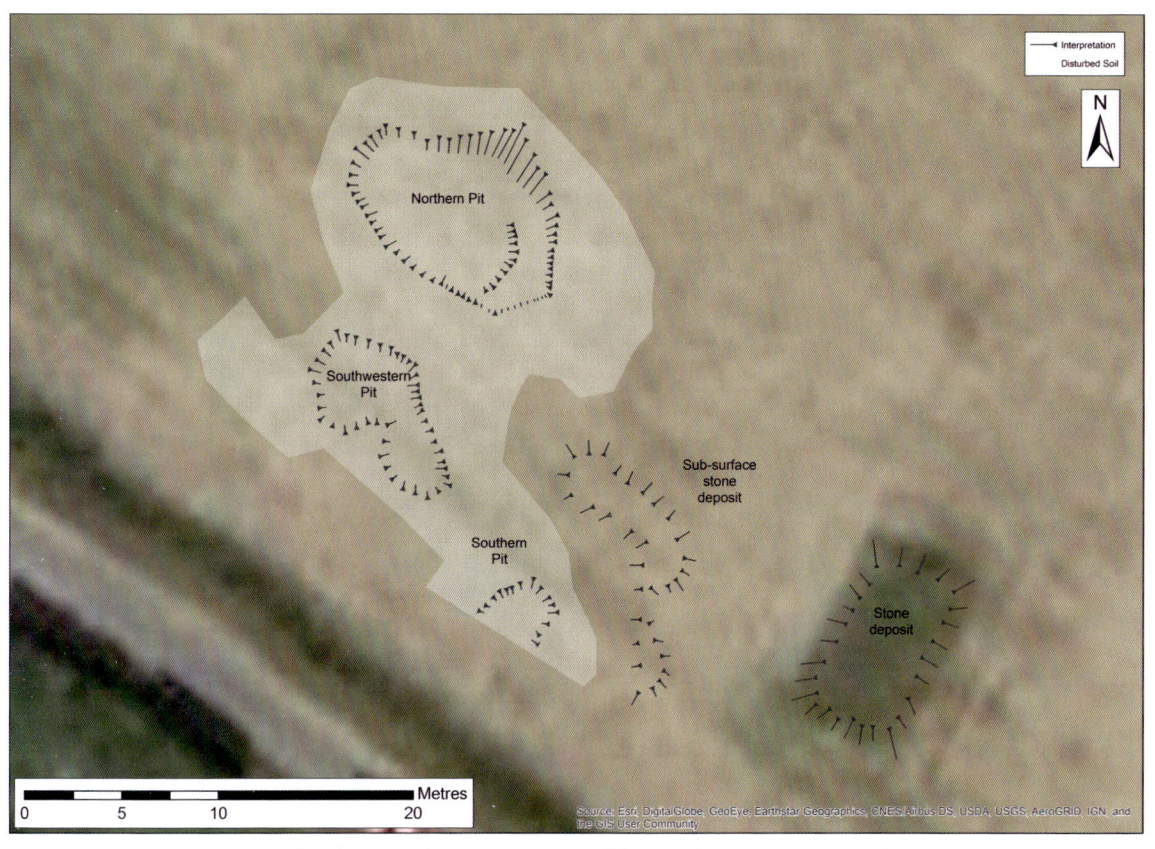

Investigating potential mass graves on Vinegar Hill

8.5 Interpretive model of the search area, comprised of the backfilled quarry pit (northern pit) and pilot/trial pits or shallow graves (southern and south-western pits), along with stone deposits and disturbed soils.

allowing the bodies to be buried 'quickly and conveniently as possible close to where they fell, but with a view to moving them later'. Similarly, the shallower southern and south-western pits may have been excavated either prior to 1798 as early trial holes for the quarry pit, or in the aftermath of the battle in 1798 to inter additional corpses next to the larger hollow. In either case, following the backfilling of all pits, no surface features remained for the Ordnance Survey cartographers to map forty-one years later.

The battlefield architecture (Carman & Carman, 2006) of Vinegar Hill has been enhanced by the geophysical research of 2016/17 that identified several previously unrecorded elements. A large quarry pit (the 'northern pit'), a rubble spread from a pilot/trial pit and associated disturbed-ground worked soils were present in the 1798 landscape, offering impassable obstacles for the armies to overcome, impeding visibility and movement, but also offering cover for protection. Did this quarry pit play a part in the battlefield action? Any further research that examines the landscape will need to consider these new elements of battlefield architecture.

WAKING THE DEAD: THE CASE FOR EXCAVATING MASS GRAVES

Our research suggests that quarry pits and shallow pits recently identified adjacent to Vinegar Hill Lane were used as mass graves. While these pits may have been used to inter slain soldiers, as hinted at in folk accounts, they may also contain nothing more than 'normal' backfilled low-resistance soils, unconnected to the battle.

There are two techniques by which the presence or absence of burials can be investigated. Firstly, a high-resolution analysis of soil in and around the pits could determine the presence of increased phosphorous using X-ray fluorescence (XRF). Any such increase localized exclusively to the pits would help confirm the presence of human or animal remains. The use of XRF, with either laboratory or portable instruments, would allow for a relatively non-intrusive or minimally intrusive assessment of the pits, requiring only small samples of topsoil or subsoil. This is a key consideration, as any further analysis of the pits is likely to require the second technique: intrusive excavation. This is ultimately a destructive process of 'preservation by record', which would remove all soils, finds and human remains from the grave for further study. Excavation of mass graves is a complex and sensitive subject (e.g. Renshaw, 2013; Shelbourn, 2015; Steele, 2008). Larsson (2013) highlighted important issues that require consideration, including ethical considerations about excavating burials; the high cost of such research; the benefits to tourism; and the restriction of development-led projects. These can also be extended to issues around storage in a museum and/or reburial.

The number of interred bodies would greatly affect the size and scope of any intrusive research. How many dead can be expected from the pits of the site discovered here? Curry and Foard (2016) have outlined the difficulty of estimating the number of dead, particularly as historical sources often inflate the number for propaganda or deflate it by favouring records of noble/high-born participants at the expense of greater numbers of low-born participants. The sizes of the pits identified by the geophysical survey at Vinegar Hill vary in volume from 5.7–11.4m^3 to 37m^3 and 168m^3. At the 1461 Battle of Towton, thirty-eight individuals were packed into a relatively shallow 6m^3 grave (Holst & Sutherland, 2014). A similar number (forty-seven individuals) were recovered from a much larger 48.3m^3 mass grave of the 1632 Battle of Lützen, Germany (Nicklisch et al., 2017). The largest pit at Vinegar Hill, the northern pit, is 3.5 times greater in volume than that at Lützen, meaning considerably higher numbers of remains might be expected from such a space.

Any intrusive excavation would require extensive forensic-level expertise, conservation, processing and analysis. If the recovery of human remains is envisaged, adequate funding and planning must be given to dedicated and expert forensic analyses. If such analyses occur, what could be learnt from the mass graves at Vinegar Hill? Recent comparative studies have indicated some of the potential outcomes. Significant insights into the lives of soldiers in the late eighteenth century can be expected generally, and levels of violence in warfare endured at the Battle of Vinegar Hill specifically. The demographics of a mass grave can be established to identify participants, both on a broad scale and a specific scale. Osteoarchaeologists working on skeletal evidence from a mass grave of the Battle of Lützen identified forty-seven men who were between 15 and 50 years of age at death, with the average age being 28 years (Nicklish et al., 2017). If the dead were clothed when interred, an analysis of surviving uniform buckles and buttons could be used to identify which regiment(s) were buried. Ancient DNA (aDNA) analysis can help identify hair and eye colour as well as ethnicity within regional models, which may be useful for distinguishing between combatants, particularly if foreign (non-Irish, non-British) auxiliaries participated in the battle. While the dead of Vinegar Hill may not be as uniquely identifiable as combat victims from the First World War or Spanish Civil War (Renshaw, 2013), the relatively short time-scale (less than 225 years since the battle) means that aDNA analysis may offer the opportunity to identify familial groups and descendants among present-day populations.

Cause of death can be established by forensic and archaeological analyses of the human remains and associated artefacts, giving insight into the nature of warfare, weaponry and trauma at Vinegar Hill. Gunshot wounds found in 57 per cent of individuals recovered from the Battle of Lützen mass grave were the main cause of death for 44.7 per cent of the deceased (Nicklisch et al., 2017), far outweighing blade injuries. Further, the osteoarchaeological data allowed researchers to convincingly narrate the battle, noting that the majority of the people interred were killed during a cavalry attack.

Bioarchaeology, the study of biological markers in human bone, can also shed light on the conditions endured by soldiers before the battle, as part of their daily and occupational routines. Thirty individuals recovered from the 1809 Battle of Aspern, Austria, revealed a wealth of bioarchaeological data for those serving in the military, including traces of vitamin C deficiency resulting in scurvy; osteoarthritis (joint inflammation) caused by long, hard marches carrying heavy loads; and the presence of pneumonia and other diseases that could have been spread throughout a military camp (Quade & Binder, 2018).

Burial practices can indicate important social and/or ritual customs observed by those interring the dead. The care, or lack thereof, given to interring the dead in single/multiple burials and mass graves may be reflected in the amount of effort that was put into the burial (Komar, 2008). O'Connor's assessment (in chapter 2) of contemporary accounts demonstrates a wide variety of care (single graves, the excavation of deep trenches) and neglect (premature burial, 'numerous pits crammed with dead bodies', 'dead bodies half buried', 'dozens' of bodies lying unburied and others thrown into the River Slaney). Such variety might be accounted for by who (victor/defeated/neutral) carried out the burials, their motivation and who was being buried. Careless treatment may indicate a negative or neutral attitude towards the deceased. Burial in accordance with religious beliefs is likely to have involved greater care than the hasty burial of decomposing remains to mitigate for bad odours and the spread of disease. The absence of carnivore bite marks on skeletal remains may confirm rapid burial, and conversely their presence could suggest the dead were exposed for a period of time after battle. Reconstruction data based on the Battle of Lützen mass-grave excavation (Nicklisch et al., 2017) showed that no care was taken to inter the dead in a systematic manner; rather, some were thrown into the grave from several sides at once, and an absence of finds led to the conclusion that the bodies were stripped of clothing, equipment and weaponry.

CONCLUSION

At the outset, this research aimed to accurately map what were initially believed to be depressions indicative of mass-grave pits excavated rapidly after the 1798 Battle of Vinegar Hill. The 2D earth-resistance survey and the ERI profiles mapped the presence of three large pits north of Vinegar Hill Lane. The geophysical data suggest that, post-battle, an existing landscape of hollows created by local industrial quarrying may have been utilized to bury the dead, supplemented by smaller, shallow spade-dug scoops in the topsoil. The number of dead interred within those hollows is conjectural, however, comparative studies from battles at Towton and Lützen suggest that even the smallest of the 'shallow scoops' at Vinegar Hill has the potential to contain the remains of at least forty individuals.

Further research on these mass-grave pits can be carried out, but importantly, all interested researchers must consider the key ethical question: is excavation necessary? Should the slain of Vinegar Hill be sensitively excavated, and if so, what will be the outcomes? A wealth of archaeological data will be assembled from any human remains buried on Vinegar Hill. However, local and national stakeholders will need wide-ranging discussions of what happens after an excavation: memorialization, possible repatriation, reburial or long-term storage of the dead must be considered for this nationally important site, before any decision is made to disturb the soil.

ACKNOWLEDGMENTS

The geophysical surveys were funded by Wexford County Council. The authors would like to thank their colleagues Darren Regan and Ciarán Davis at Earthsound Geophysics Ltd, for assistance with collecting the geophysical data.

CHAPTER NINE

The underwater surveys

NIALL BRADY & REX BANGERTER

The accounts of 1798 recall the bridge across the Slaney in Enniscorthy as the site of a strong defence by loyalist troops in May, and then by the rebels on 21 June, when it served as an important bulwark to stem the loyalist attack and protect the rebel retreat. The action, immortalized as part of the greater Battle of Vinegar Hill, has become part of a national identity, but how visible is such an important, dramatic and traumatic event in the material culture that survives? The question was to the fore during the first systematic study and survey of the river as it passes through Enniscorthy, carried out in 2015 at the request of the National 1798 Rebellion Centre and Wexford County Council. Archaeology is an incredibly illuminating approach employed to reveal the historic past, yet historians will inevitably find it a frustrating discipline because it rarely observes precise and particular moments in the distant past. Such is the case with the River Slaney and Enniscorthy at the surface level, yet the work that was completed has laid an important foundation for further and more detailed research and has indicated where the potential lies for the river gravels and the bridge to retain traces of the events of 1798. It has also presented a rich insight into how the river was central to the importance of the town, as it grew from its core area on the west bank. This essay charts some of these details.

THE RIVER SLANEY

The River Slaney rises in the western part of the Wicklow Mountains at Lugnaquilla and follows a 117km course before discharging into a narrow estuary at Wexford Harbour. The river runs south-east on its course to Enniscorthy town. The underlying bedrock changes between granite, slate, and shale and the river system is bounded by well-drained soils. The tidal influence reaches Enniscorthy Bridge, and this helps to explain why the town is located where it is, at the most inland point of navigable access to the sea.

There is little noticeable drop in bed levels as the river traverses its floodplain and on which the town is built. The river meanders through a landscape of hills on

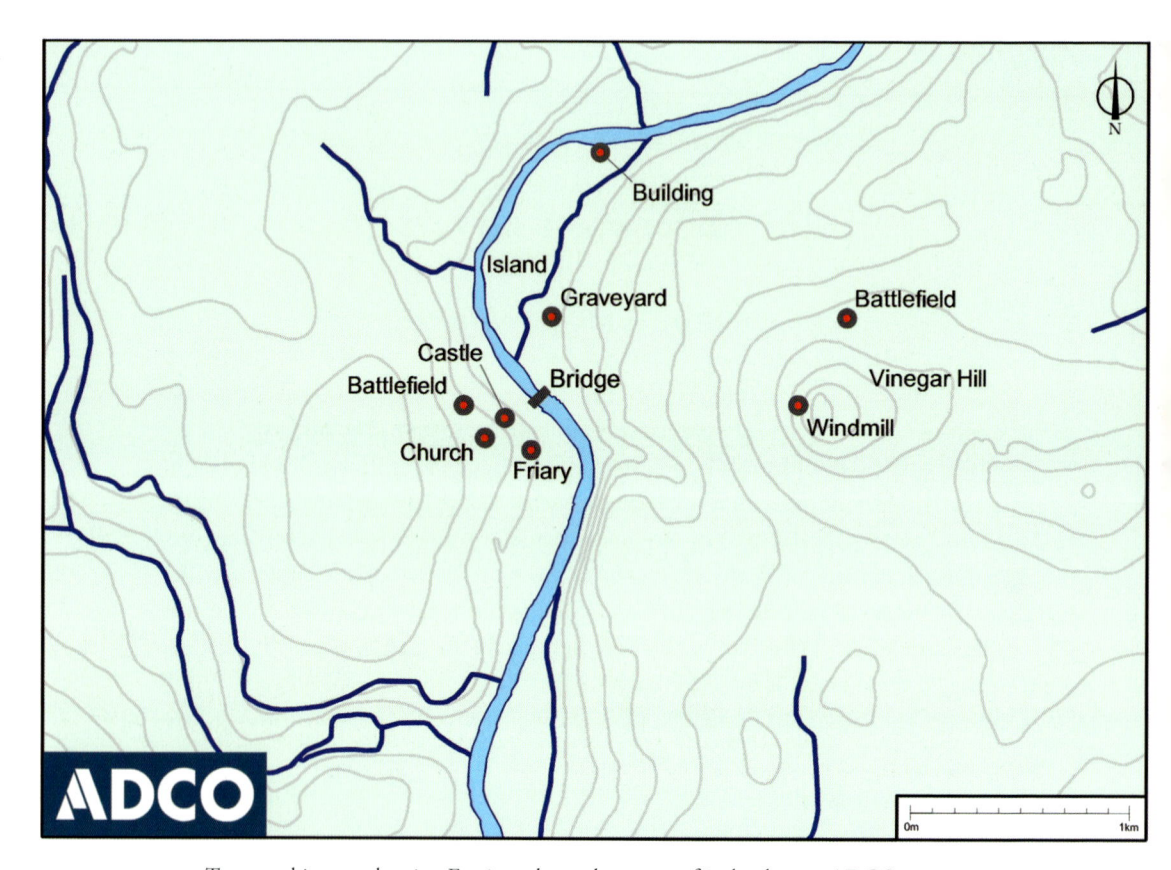

9.1 Topographic map showing Enniscorthy at the centre of its landscape. ADCO.

either side, which are focussed on the towering headland of the west bank, where the medieval castle stands, and that of Vinegar Hill off the east bank (fig. 9.1). The waters flow under Enniscorthy Bridge with force and reflect some artificial narrowing of the river channel over time (fig. 9.2). It can be traced by studying the metrically accurate Ordnance Survey (OS) maps, which demonstrate a reduction of some 16m in width upstream of the Enniscorthy Bridge between 1840 and 1903. The change can be attributed to the impact of the newly constructed railway bridge, which opened in 1872 and saw the construction of a series of six in-water bridge piers and the embanking of land off both riverbanks. With every direct impact, a river's flow reacts, and areas of hard structure serve to focus water-borne erosion and exert change. The process can be mapped since the 1840s, but it is a constant and can be appreciated as a dynamic that would have been at work on Enniscorthy Bridge in 1798 and indeed since this location was bridged centuries earlier.

The underwater surveys

9.2 View across the River Slaney in 2015, highlighting the dynamic water flow as it traverses Enniscorthy Bridge. ADCO.

The Island

The Battle of Enniscorthy took place in May 1798, when rebel forces attacked the town and took possession of it by overwhelming numbers. According to contemporary accounts, rebels attempted to cross the river above the bridge at the Island. The Island is a wide linear meadow formed in a bend of the main channel. It is quite flat and grass-covered. While it retains several dips across its extent, some of which may be drainage channels, it is essentially featureless. The clay nature of its fabric is exposed on the riverbank faces cut by the main channel on its west side, and by the narrow stream channel on its east side. There is one structure built on the Island close to its northern limit (fig. 9.3). The structure is not recorded on the Ordnance Survey first-edition map (1840) and is not registered on either the archaeological or the architectural heritage databases, but it does feature on later maps. It was identified during the walkover survey as a ruined building, consisting of one long wall orientated north-south and one end wall at right angles, constructed from poured concrete mixed with river gravel/stone. There are two substantial stone-built buttresses supporting the western long wall. It may have served as a livestock shed or barn but the buttresses seem out of place in a simple agricultural building. Subsequent survey has revealed that the

9.3 View across the north end of the Island, highlighting its ruined building today with its curiously robust abutments. ADCO.

standing elements are only part of a larger square-shaped foundation, suggesting the possibility that the building was a more substantial structure originally.

A narrow channel separates the Island from the slopes of Vinegar Hill. The landscape today is quite changed from that of 1798 (fig. 9.4). The building of the railway in the 1870s included construction of a long embankment to support the rail and its station, which has effectively buried the original ground surface, while the narrow channel has become a poorly drained shallow stream that is overgrown.

As it flows through Enniscorthy, the main channel of the Slaney is dynamic, with changes in riverbed topography, sediment deposition, riverbed erosion and localized scouring. Compact river cobbles with pockets of coarse gravel form a bed level that is predominantly flat upstream of the Railway Bridge, with steep-sided earthen riverbanks. Where the narrow channel returns to the main river at the south end of the Island, considerable deposition of graded gravel and sand deposits is evident. The water level decreases to approximately 0.30m here, and the shallowing is most likely because of the deposition of these discharged sediments.

The river enjoys a different topography between the Railway Bridge and Enniscorthy Bridge. The bed slopes at an angle of approximately 40° from the base of each bank before flattening out in the central area. Compact sub-rounded cobbles and graded gravels overlie coarse sand, with occasional larger sub-angular rocks present.

The underwater surveys

9.4 View looking from the Island towards Vinegar Hill obscured by the railway and its embankment that was built for its opening in 1872, and subsequent development. ADCO.

The waterway is at its narrowest at a point 40m upstream of Enniscorthy Bridge, where significant deposition of waterborne sediment is taking place along the north side of the river. A build-up of riverbed deposits is also evident across the section of riverbed immediately upstream of Enniscorthy Bridge, in which sections of bonded masonry lie, offering tantalizing possibilities as collapsed masonry from earlier bridge structures.

Underneath the bridge, the riverbed is largely covered by an artificial sill that gives an added protection to the bridge piers against erosion and scour. Much of the sill is eroded along its upstream side, revealing the riverbed below and exposing sections of rough-cut masonry/rubble stone, which provide further indicators of earlier bridge remains.

The riverbed drops away on the downstream side of the bridge, almost vertically for a distance of *c.*0.80m, revealing a bed of coarse sand that gives way to a line of angular rock immediately downstream of the sill. It is a high-energy environment, water flowing over the sill to form turbulent rapids and a series of scour-holes some 3m downstream of the bridge arches. A number of sandbars or spits extend from the bridge piers, where water velocity is limited by the structure.

As the river flows past the bridge, the channel widens and its formal quaysides, built in the nineteenth century, will have changed its appearance from that of 1798, perhaps formalizing or replacing existing arrangements to offload and replenish boats with cargo. The bridge marks the upstream tidal limit of the River Slaney and the present-day townscape masks its more ancient nature. Where shingle bars develop along the north side of the river channel today they may retain some historic resonance, but the pattern of flow and deposition further downstream, below Seamus Rafter Bridge, was changed irreversibly by active dredging of the channel in the late twentieth century.

EARLY DEVELOPMENT OF THE TOWN AND ITS RIVER FRONTAGE

The Down Survey for Wexford compiled between 1655 and 1659 depicts 'Iniscorthy towne' as a medium-sized enclosed settlement located on the west side of the River Slaney, north of where the Urinn River flows into the Slaney. The nature of the wider land holding suggests the strategic location of the town, positioned as it is in the angle of these two rivers. The barony (Scarawalsh) and parish (Shannough) maps repeat this observation, but do not indicate the presence of the walled or earthen enclosure that is included on the county map (fig. 9.5). What is clear however is the absence of any indication of a bridge or fording point across either river from the town. This is supported by examination of the corresponding parish map for Templeshannon and Ballaghgeene on the east side of the Slaney, which shows open land and 'unforfeited' land. The accompanying terrier describes the land in Templeshannon as having generally good soil up to the heath and furze, which we might understand as a reference to the side of Vinegar Hill. The terrier also notes that the river was a very good source for all types of fish, including salmon. The terrier for Templeshannon parish makes no mention of a bridge either. It describes the castle and church within the town, and notes that the wider landscape was known at the time for its provisioning of 'pipe staffs', which was its principal commodity. Renowned for its timber trade, it is no surprise to see mention of 'pipe staffs', which were cut from woodland and floated downstream to Enniscorthy where they would be loaded onto vessels, and a fee paid to the town at the castle. The pipe staffs were probably barrel staves (Ronan O'Flaherty, pers. comm., 2016). The detail reinforces the point that Enniscorthy marked the upper limit of river navigation at the time, as it was to here that the staffs were floated from upriver, and from here that they were loaded onto vessels for further transportation.

The absence of any depiction of a river crossing point or bridge structure in the seventeenth century contrasts with a source originating in 1581 that refers to the construction of a timber bridge at the town. The source is a works contract dated

The underwater surveys

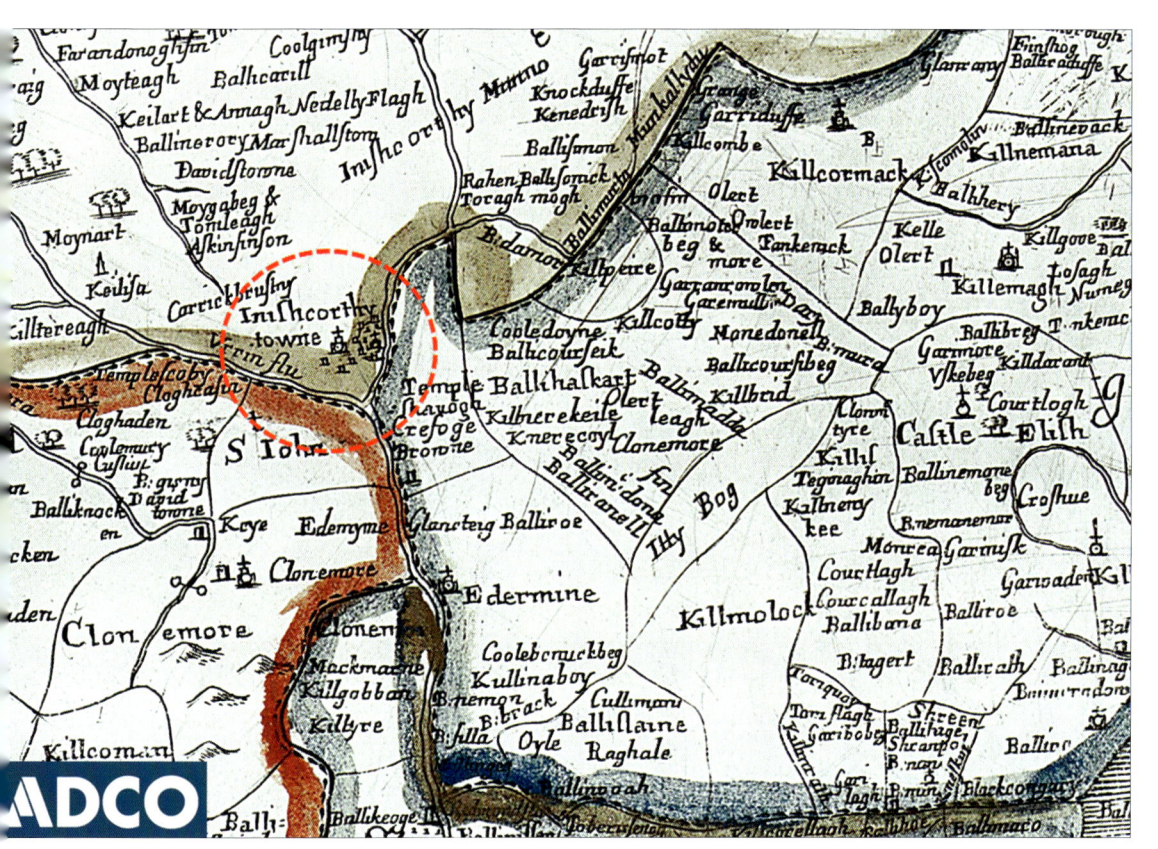

9.5 Down Survey, showing the town in 1654, with dashed line highlighting Enniscorthy. L. Brown Collection of Digital Historic Maps.

15 September 1581 between Lord Deputy Grey and Paule Finglas, a carpenter, to build a bridge across the Slaney (O'Keeffe & Simington, 1991, pp 178–80). The bridge was to be of timber construction with a 'castell of lyme and stone' in its middle portion. The bridge structure was to be made of good, sound and substantial timber and was to be 240ft long and 11ft wide within the rails. It was to be supported by fourteen arches, and each arch was to include three squared 'pillars', or timber posts, that measure 18 inches in diameter. Each post was to be shod in 2 stone-weight of iron. The timbers were to be braced in a certain manner, and the contract specified the nature of the bridge deck and parapets. The central stone tower was to be built on a new foundation. It was to measure 10ft wide and 10ft high, it was to be two-storeyed above the bridge surface, and it was to be defensible, with murder holes, presumably under the arch itself, and with drawbridges on either side to impede passage across the bridge if needed. Mr Finglas had eighteen months to build the structure, which was to be completed on 25 March 1583. The contract also set the cost at £350 and set a sequence of staged payments.

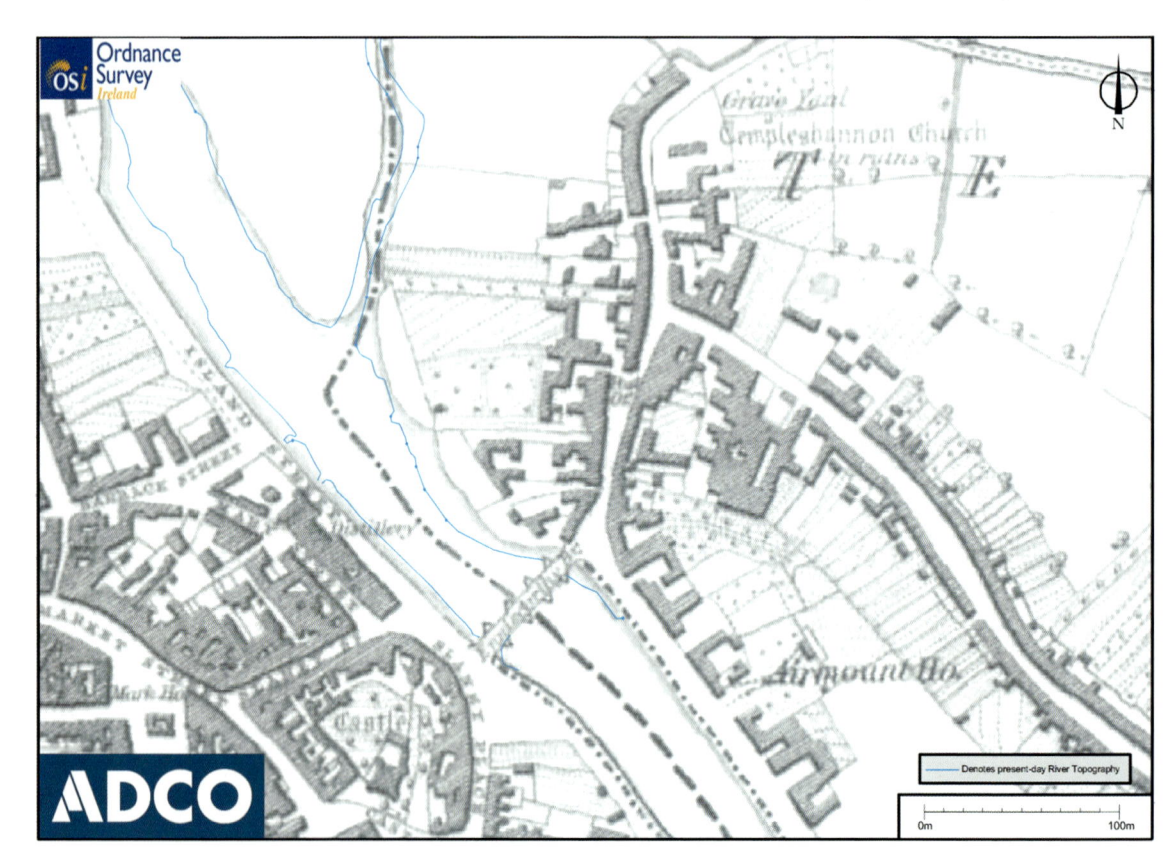

9.6 Detail from Ordnance Survey first-edition six-inch map sheet 20 highlighting the bridge in 1840, with overlay of modern river bank. © Ordnance Survey Ireland/Government of Ireland. Copyright permit MP 001021.

To put it into context, the present-day bridge is shorter but wider. It is some 216ft long and 30ft wide. The shorter distance can be explained in terms of infill along both riverbanks over time, while the greater width indicates that the footprint of such a sixteenth-century bridge would be absorbed fully by that of the present-day one.

There is no record of the 1581 bridge having been built. O'Keeffe and Simington's detailed consideration of the contract suggested that the bridge would have resulted in very closely spaced arches and that these would have fouled easily during flood events, giving many opportunities for such a bridge to collapse. They also highlight the requirement for the stone tower to be built on a 'new foundation' as a possible indication of replacing an existing structure. As they conclude, it is also possible that the bridge was destroyed in the wars of the 1640s, before the Down Survey was commissioned, explaining the absence of a bridge at that time. The Enniscorthy contract remains an important source; even if the bridge was never built, it shows clear intention to cross the river at this point, as one should expect given the presence of the growing town on the west bank.

The underwater surveys

Though not shown cartographically, the first stone bridge recorded across the Slaney in Enniscorthy was built in the last quarter of the seventeenth century. The present bridge dates to 1715 according to O'Keeffe & Simington (1991, p. 180), although a later date of 1775 is sometimes given by others. A bridge is indicated on Herman Moll's *New Map of Ireland*, 1714, where the bridge is implied by showing the road crossing the river at this point (O'Keeffe & Simington, 1991, p. 323).

It is not until the Ordnance Survey first-edition six-inch map of 1840 that detailed mapping exists, showing a bridge with piers that had pointed cutwaters (fig. 9.6). The map also shows the town's development concentrated on the west bank of the river, close to Enniscorthy Castle and along the roadway (Temple Street) leading north from Enniscorthy Bridge. By 1903, the river downstream of Enniscorthy Bridge is formally enquayed.

There are no known contemporary images showing the Battle of Enniscorthy or that of Vinegar Hill from the river. There is an historic print by Daniel Grose dated to 1793 that shows Enniscorthy Bridge from the downstream side (fig. 7.1). While the bridge today retains a slight central rise or camber, the early prints, perhaps somewhat romantically, suggest a more arched form or hump design. Six arches are depicted, as in the present-day bridge, and a central feature juts out from the bridge as a wall-like edifice rising from the bridge pier. It could be a central strengthening element. Given the building contract of 1581 requiring a central stone tower, it is also possible that such a feature could be the remnant of a pre-existing structure. The bridge's cutwaters are depicted as triangular in shape, rather than the rounded/semi-circular ones of today. These various features combine to tell the modern viewer that while today's bridge is considered to be of eighteenth-century date, it has been modified and upgraded over the years. Consequently, the stonework and façades that exist today are unlikely to be those that existed in 1798, even if the basic footprint remains the same. The print by Grose also shows the type of boat used on the river. The larger of the two boats shown is a cot, and most likely a Slaney Cot, which is a flat-bottomed craft ideally suited to the shallow river channel, drawing little in the way of draft and being relatively small in size (Tully, 2008, p. 588). Later maps and images continue to show this type of vessel.

1798 EVENTS AND THE RIVER

The events preceding June 1798 included the rebel attack on Enniscorthy in May, and accounts of this brief action record the bridge and the river as theatres of engagement. Captain William Snowe of the North Cork militia marched his troops from the bridge towards Market Square and made a futile attack on the rebels before withdrawing to the bridge. At the same time, a detachment of rebels crossed the river and were engaging the North Corks on the east side of the Slaney:

> At length, when the rebels, wading across the river, which was then low, both above and below the bridge, up to the middle in water, some to the neck, had entered the eastern part, called Templeshannon, and set some houses on fire … (Gordon, 1801, p. 93)

The action is also reported as a series of events where the rebels sought to cross the river but came under heavy fire.

> [The North Cork militia] … arrived in time to line the bridge, and to give a severe check to the rebel column, just then in the act of crossing the river, and a part of which had landed on an island in it. Numbers of the rebels fell on this occasion, by the fire of the North Cork from the battlements of the bridge; and none of their shot took effect from their confusion, from the protection of the battlements, and from most of them levelling so high, that their shot went whistling over the heads of the North Cork, whose shot was so incessant, that it was with the utmost difficulty it could be constrained even after the rebels had gone beyond its effect. (Jones, 1800, p. 103)

Undeterred, the rebels sought to cross to the north, using the Island as the point of transfer, but here they were repulsed. A further attempt, north again in Blackstoops was also stymied:

> The enemy, defeated in the many attempts which they made on the north and west side of the town, made an effort to cross the river, about a quarter of a mile above the bridge, where there is an island, in which they succeeded; but were soon repulsed by captain Richards's corps, part of whom fired at them with carbines, from a place about a hundred yards above the glebe-house, and killed great numbers; at the same time they were severely galled by the North Cork on the bridge … They attempted to cross the river higher up, out of reach of the fire of the North Cork. On this, captain Snowe detached lieutenant Prior, with a sergeant and sixteen men of his corps, to oppose them, which they did most effectually; for having taken post behind a hedge, they continued to kill great numbers of them, till their ammunition was expended …
>
> It was generally believed, that not less than five hundred of the rebels were killed or wounded. The banks of the river, and the island in it were strewed with their dead bodies. (Musgrave, 1802, p. 429)

The Battle of Enniscorthy lasted some three hours at its peak, after which the loyalist forces ran out of ammunition. They were flanked by rebels wading across the river. Despite having driven the rebels out of town, the loyalist forces were ordered to abandon the town and withdraw to Wexford. The place-names mentioned give a clear account of the topography of the engagement. In a river-scape unencumbered by formal quays up- and down-stream of the bridge, it is easy to imagine the rebel forces crossing the relatively low water and exposed shingle bars. However, they were easy targets for militia defending from the bridge. It seems only the sheer number of rebels ensured their success. The crossing north of the town was at the north end of the Island, and then further north again at a location in Blackstoops townland. The river remains deep in its main channel, but the north end of the Island provides some shallower ground. This crossing was also very exposed, and the rebels were again easy prey to being fired upon, this time from troops positioned on the rising ground above the flood plain north of the Glebe house in Templeshannon townland.

The opportunity to reverse the roles was presented in June, when the regrouped loyalist forces attacked the now rebel-held town and its forces stationed on Vinegar Hill. In this instance, the loyalist forces approached the hill from the east as well as attacking the town. The bridge becomes a significant defensive position, as the rebels retreat over the bridge from the town. The rebel leader, Barker, was seriously wounded here when his arm was blown off, while reinforcements from Wicklow led by Billy Byrne aided the rebel leader Kearns in his defence of the bridge. The bridge was held and there continued to be an active defence by Kearns as the rebels retreated from Vinegar Hill to Wexford town.

OBSERVATIONS

The archaeological assessment completed in 2015 extended along a 417m stretch of the Slaney and its banks, commencing at a point 280m upstream of Enniscorthy Bridge and terminating at a point 137m downstream of the bridge. For the present focus, comment is restricted to those observations associated with the Island and the bridge site.

The Island is an attractive location for archaeological prospection because it appears to be largely undeveloped. The presence of probable drainage channels across its width represents some degree of impact, while the larger meadow is periodically inundated during flood events. The previously unrecorded building at the north end of the Island is in a location that would have been close to where the rebel forces sought to cross onto the Island in 1798, if it were standing at that time. It is a curious structure that will repay further consideration in the future.

As it stands today, the bridge replaced an earlier structure. The new bridge was built sometime in the eighteenth century (there are conflicting views on the precise date) and remedial works in 1837 and in 1991 have widened the bridge on its downstream side. The nineteenth-century works formed part of the wider redevelopment of the waterway that was subsidized by the Estate of the Lord of Portsmouth and the grand jury.

a

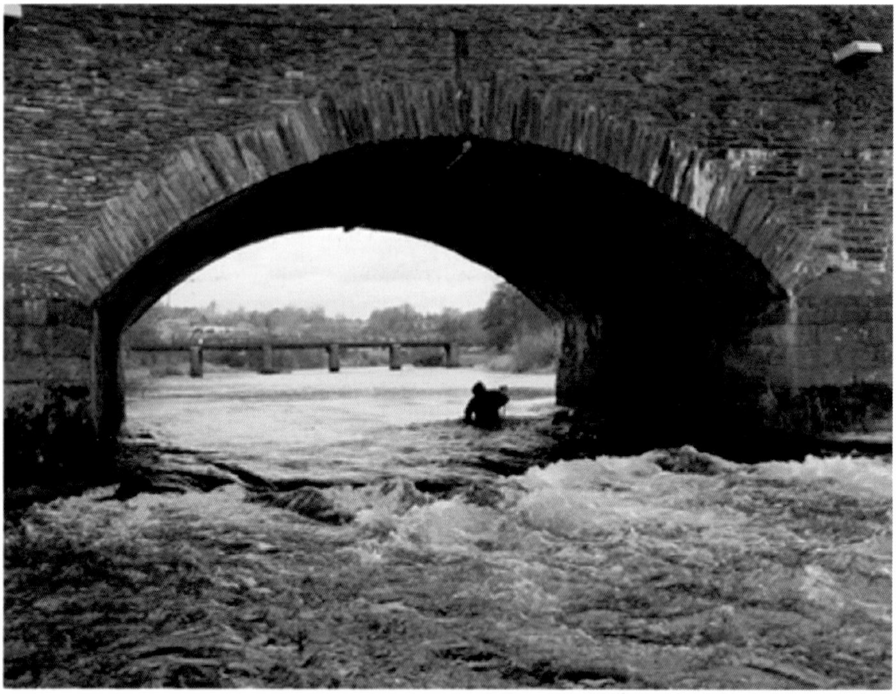

b

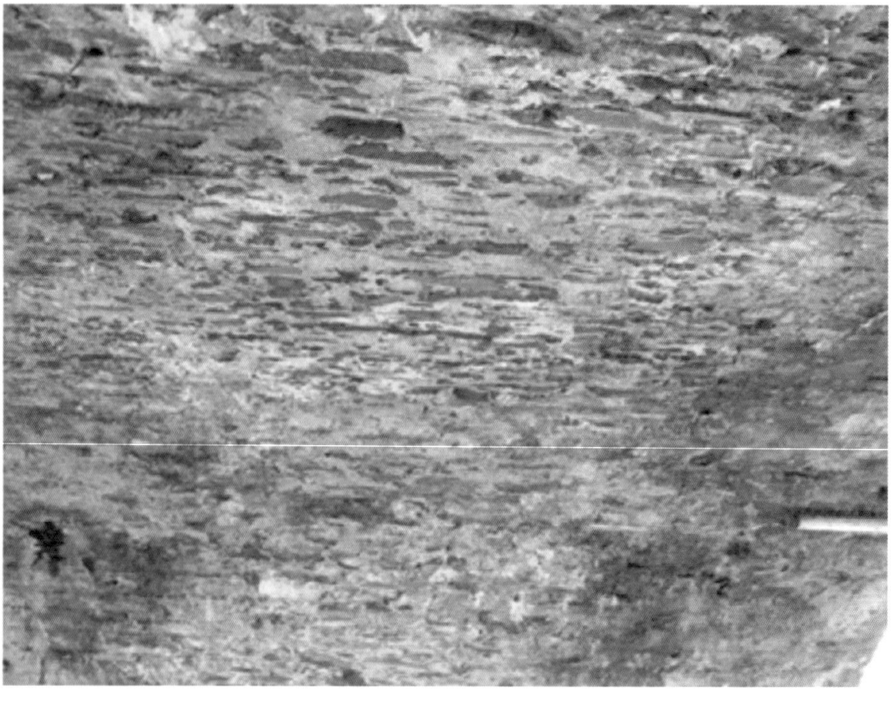

The underwater surveys

9.7 Different aspects of the bridge's stonework today: a) west-facing view of Enniscorthy Bridge (Arch 4) on its downstream side – note segmental arch spanning bridge piers; b) view of composition of the intrados (arch ceiling) within Arch 4; c) north-facing example shot of triangular cutwaters located on the upstream side of Enniscorthy Bridge (1m scale); d) example of rounded cutwater located on the downstream side of Enniscorthy Bridge (1m scale). ADCO.

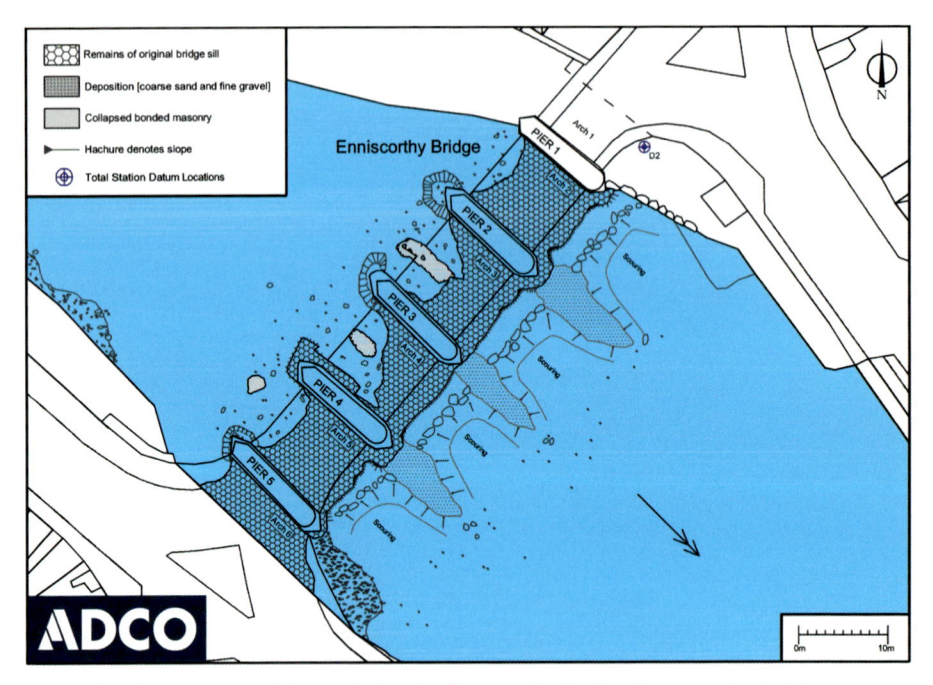

9.8 Archaeological survey of the riverbed under Enniscorthy Bridge, showing principal observations. ADCO.

Both upstream and downstream arches are segmental in form, each comprised of 80–90 semi-dressed arch-stones (*voussoirs*) of schist (fig. 9.7). Roughly coursed random rubble-stone has been used to form the bridge façade on both sides of the structure, and vertically set rough-cut stones adorn the bridge parapets. The *intrados* (arch-ceiling) of each archway comprises narrow, rough-cut, rectangular schist that is partially obscured by the residue of an overlying lime render. Five triangular cutwaters are present on the upstream side of the bridge. These extend from the upper surface of the bridge piers to a height of approximately 3.5m, obscuring much of the haunch and those arch-stones that form the lower part of each arch-ring. Each cutwater is finished with rendered pyramidal coping. The five downstream cutwaters are rounded, constructed of neatly cut granite blocks, and have rendered hemispherical tops above the waterline. While the general construction technique observed for the downstream side of the bridge matches that of the upstream, the presence of rounded cut-waters contrasts with the original build; the rounded forms represent changes that are probably associated with widening the bridge after 1840. The base of the downstream cutwaters retain a triangular plan.

Three blocks of masonry observed in the riverbed immediately underneath and upstream of Enniscorthy Bridge represent collapsed or discarded remnants of earlier

9.9 Underwater view of section of bonded masonry from the third section of collapsed masonry, identified under Arch 3, Section 8 (1m scale). ADCO.

bridge components and are the clearest testimony to the presence of a pre-existing bridge (fig. 9.8). One block is located 3.5m upstream of the standing bridge, at Arch 5, and measures 2m x 1.9m in visible extent. It is a heavily water-eroded block of limestone masonry bonded by hydraulic lime mortar. It was possibly from the façade or haunch area of a bridge. A second block of masonry is located beneath Arch 4, at the approximate mid-point between Pier 3 and Pier 4. It measures 3.5m in visible length and 1.8m in width. It is also a section of water-eroded limestone masonry bonded with a hydraulic lime mortar and displays characteristics consistent with that of a bridge pier. The third block is located beneath Arch 3, mid-way between standing bridge Pier 2 and Pier 3 (fig. 9.9). It is more exposed and measures 6.6m in length x 2m in width and is well defined along its south side. It is also thought to be part of a former bridge pier.

These earlier bridge elements are visible due to erosion of the more recent bridge sill and it is likely that similar remains survive under the sill as it extends beneath the other arches. Significant remains of the earlier bridge's structure undoubtedly lie embedded in the river deposits that remain concealed from view today.

A programme of non-disturbance metal-detection was carried out up- and downstream of the bridge site, in anticipation of recovering small finds that might be

9.10 Cast-iron bell-shaped object recovered from debris concentration upstream of Enniscorthy Bridge and considered to be a mud-anchor. ADCO.

associated with the events of 1798, such as musket shot and shrapnel. Unfortunately, such tantalizing items were not observed, largely because the detection was non-disturbance in nature and did not extend in depth. In general, the graded river gravels have excellent holding potential. Ferrous and non-ferrous metal hits were consistently registering as targets, and among the material identified on the riverbed's surface were holy medallions, modern coins, fishing weights and miscellaneous iron fragments. One Victorian penny (1850s) was recovered from a recess in the masonry of the bridge-sill, and a large number of modern coins were encountered upstream of the bridge, wedged in the gaps in the masonry of a piece of collapsed bridge structure. The bowl fragment from a pewter spoon was also located. Downstream of the bridge, the high water-flow velocity inhibits detailed survey and the areas where scouring is taking place are considered to be of limited potential.

A dump of nineteenth-century and early twentieth-century debris was observed along the west side of the river upstream of Enniscorthy Bridge. The objects include glassware, stoneware, mixed ceramics, clay pipes, red brick, a cobbler's anvil, an iron bell-shaped object and other miscellaneous forged iron pieces. Thirty-four intact glass bottles were among the assemblage, all dating from the mid- and late nineteenth-century. Most are beer bottles bearing the names of 'J.Donohoe Ltd, Enniscorthy' and 'C.H. Lett, Enniscorthy'. Four bottles with rounded bottoms (cucumber bottles) were also recovered, two marked 'C.H. Lett' and one 'Donohoe Ltd Star Mark'. These may originally have contained ginger beer. Three square-profile bottles marked 'Pattersons' and a single beer bottle marked 'Wexford' were recovered along with a glass ink pot and wine glass base. Ceramic material included a number of stoneware bottles and small 'mustard' type pots, fragments of spongeware, blackware, blue-and-white ware and red earthenware. These fragments were from vessels that include a teapot, cups, plates, platters, serving dishes and large bowls. A number of clay pipe fragments (bowl and stem pieces) were noted, and an intact pipe was recovered. Three of the bowls are of twentieth-century form and one is late nineteenth-century. Two are stamped 'Ben Nevis Cutty' and 'Patrick Byrne, Market Square, Enniscorthy'. The intact pipe is ornate, with the Maid of Erin Harp depicted on one side of the bowl and a loose sprig of shamrock on the other. This patriotic pipe dates between 1880 and 1910.

Only two intact forged iron pieces were recovered: a cobbler's anvil of twentieth-century date and a bell-shaped iron object of probable nineteenth-century date (fig. 9.10). The bell-shaped object measures 0.45m in length x 0.20m in width at base. A 5mm hole, lined with a brass ring, is located 1.5cm from its base. The hole is thought to have accommodated a draw string for the bell clapper. There is no bell clapper evident. Though bell-shaped, this object may have served as a mud-anchor.

CONCLUDING REMARKS

This archaeological assessment was the first methodical record of a section of the River Slaney as it flows through Enniscorthy town. Despite intensive inspection of the surface deposits, no material remains directly associated with 1798 were observed. The riverbed deposits, however, are very mobile and the surface stratum consists of river cobbles. It is a dynamic river environment. Comparable contexts were recorded in the River Nore at Kilkenny, where investigations conducted in advance of the River Nore Flood Alleviation Scheme revealed complex archaeological deposits and numerous archaeological objects embedded in the riverbed strata underlying a mobile and dynamic surface layer of cobbles (Brady, 2004). The same situation was identified further downstream on the Nore at Newtown Jerpoint (Bangerter, 2012). In both instances, deposits retaining rich archaeological remains were observed at the principal bridge sites in each settlement and, while many of the objects recovered are of modern and early modern date, significant remains of medieval date were also present. In Kilkenny, these included a series of grave slabs that had been taken from nearby graveyards and put into the river, perhaps as measures to stabilize the eroding bridge piers, or as an action of iconoclasm during the Reformation, when such objects were routinely defaced and discarded.[1]

There is every reason to expect that significant remains lie buried at some depth below the surface stratum in Enniscorthy. The siting of the town on the west bank presupposes activity and engagement with the river channel since the town was founded and probably for a considerable period before then. The presence of substantial blocks of masonry relating to a previous bridge structure/s underneath Enniscorthy Bridge complements this observation and offers positive proof of it.

The bridge itself is effectively the same structure that stood in 1798 but it has been widened and subject to remedial works since then, so that the late eighteenth-century fabric is concealed within its core and is not obviously evident on the present-day façades. To access earlier material and material directly related to 1798, it is necessary to excavate a series of trenches into the riverbed, and it is likely that such trenches would need to exceed 1m in depth. Such work would delve below the surface levels and expose the *in situ* deposits. The 2015 survey has indicated where such work would perhaps yield the greatest archaeological insight.

ACKNOWLEDGMENTS

The authors extend warm thanks to Jacqui Sidney and to Rory O'Connor, manager of the National 1798 Rebellion Centre, to Ronan O'Flaherty of Crane Bag Consulting,

---

[1] One of the gravestones, a fourteenth-century effigial slab, now forms part of the permanent exhibition in St Mary's Church, repurposed as Kilkenny's Medieval Mile Museum.

and to the other members of the Vinegar Hill Battlefield Archaeological Study Steering Group. Thanks also to Catherine Kavanagh, GIS Project Leader at Wexford County Council, for her assistance in the provision of the OSI mapping tiles. Claudia Theune of the University of Vienna provided insight in our quest to understand the bell-shaped metal object, and we are most grateful to Samuel Connell of Foothill College, and Chad Gifford of Columbia University, who introduced Niall to Jacqui and Ronan in 2014, when the potential river survey was first discussed. Since the 2015 survey, ADCO has returned to the Slaney to conduct further assessment of the river and its features as part of the environmental-impact assessment report for the flood-defence scheme; these works are still in process but initial findings support the anticipations indicated in this essay. We wish to thank Niamh Roche, Kevin Stephens and Neshul Samachetty of Mott MacDonald Consulting Engineers for the scheme, Larry MacHale of Wexford County Council and Ivor McElveen, heritage engineer, for their support and interest. The archaeological team in 2015 included Derek Copeland, Jimmy Lenehan, Dan Lenehan, Brian MacAllister and Feargal Morrissey.

CHAPTER TEN

Picking up the pieces: the archaeological survey of Vinegar Hill

DAMIAN SHIELS & JAMES BONSALL

BATTLEFIELD ARCHAEOLOGY

The most effective tool in the archaeological armoury for investigating Ireland's battlefields is the systematic licensed metal-detection survey. The metal detection undertaken as part of the Longest Day Research Project represents the largest and most successful such survey yet attempted in the Republic of Ireland. The fieldwork was carried out in 2017 and uncovered significant quantities of artefacts deposited in and around Vinegar Hill on 21 June 1798, definitively demonstrating the value of such approaches to the archaeological investigation of Irish battlefields.

The archaeological investigation of battlefields owes it origins to the work of Dr Douglas Scott on the 1876 battlefield of Little Bighorn, Montana, USA, the site of what is sometimes referred to as 'Custer's Last Stand'. In the early 1980s, Scott and his team began an archaeological detection survey on the battlefield, carefully analysing their finds and scientifically mapping the exact findspots (Scott & Fox, 1987). This allowed the team to build up a picture not only of the battle's development, but also of the experiences of certain individuals. Since that time, a range of projects – particularly in the United States and Europe – have repeatedly reinforced the value of battlefield archaeology, and the importance of employing specialized archaeological strategies on such sites. Such techniques have now revealed unique data from a wide array of engagements, ranging from the first-century AD Varus battlefield in Germany (Wilbers-Rost, 2001) to the industrial-scale confrontations of the twentieth-century world wars. The growth of battlefield archaeology and the wider field of conflict archaeology has in turn led to the establishment of a number of postgraduate programmes dedicated to its study – most notably in Britain, home to the Centre for Battlefield Archaeology at the University of Glasgow – as well as the *Journal of Conflict Archaeology*, which is published by Taylor & Francis. There are multiple annual conferences, but the most significant conference on the international calendar is Fields of Conflict, which occurs every two years, and was held in Ireland in 2016.

Although battlefield archaeology is now well established internationally, the techniques developed as part of this sub-discipline are not widely practised by archaeologists in Ireland. This is not to say that battlefield investigations have not been carried out; a number of small-scale research-led projects have revealed their usefulness in an Irish context. This includes the work of Paul Logue and James O'Neill at the 1598 battlefield of the Yellow Ford, Co. Armagh (O'Neill & Logue, 2010), that of the UCD School of Archaeology at the 1690 battlefield of the Boyne, Co. Meath (Brady et al., 2007), and that of Damian Shiels and Paul O'Keeffe at the site of the 1601 siege and battlefield of Kinsale, Co. Cork (Shiels, 2008), to name but a few. However, none have come close to approaching the scale or scope of the Longest Day Research Project at Vinegar Hill.

IRISH BATTLEFIELDS PROJECT

Although the majority of invasive archaeological battlefield investigations in Ireland have been of a limited nature, there has been a wider nationwide historical and archaeological assessment of Irish battlefields. Entitled the 'Irish Battlefields Project', it was established in 2007 by the then Department of the Environment, Heritage and Local Government. It sought to detail the archaeological and historical particulars of every battlefield in the Republic of Ireland between the eighth and eighteenth centuries that met criteria established by an expert advisory panel. Among the reports produced was an assessment of Vinegar Hill, the first archaeological appraisal to be undertaken at the battle site (Cronin, Fitzsimons & Shiels, 2008). This analysis identified Vinegar Hill as a site of high archaeological potential. What was particularly noticeable during the site analysis was the extent to which today's landscape – on and about the hill – is representative of what existed in 1798, making it one of the most important physical battlefield landscapes on the island.

The main aim of the Battlefields Project was to identify a number of key locations associated with Irish battlefields in order to create a map that could serve as a management tool for this historic landscape. It did this through analysis of primary sources, which confirmed that significant portions of the battlefield at Vinegar Hill look much the same today as they did in 1798. Of particular note were the fields in Templeshannon townland, dominated by high, thick clay banks that survive particularly well on the north-eastern slope of Vinegar Hill. The Ordnance Survey mapped this terrain in 1838–9, only forty years after the battle, and it seems likely that the field systems had not significantly altered over that time. Indeed, comparative analysis of the modern and 1830s boundaries indicates that the vast majority remain the same. When this information is combined with contemporary accounts that earthen banks were being used as defensive positions by the United Irishmen, we can draw the conclusion that

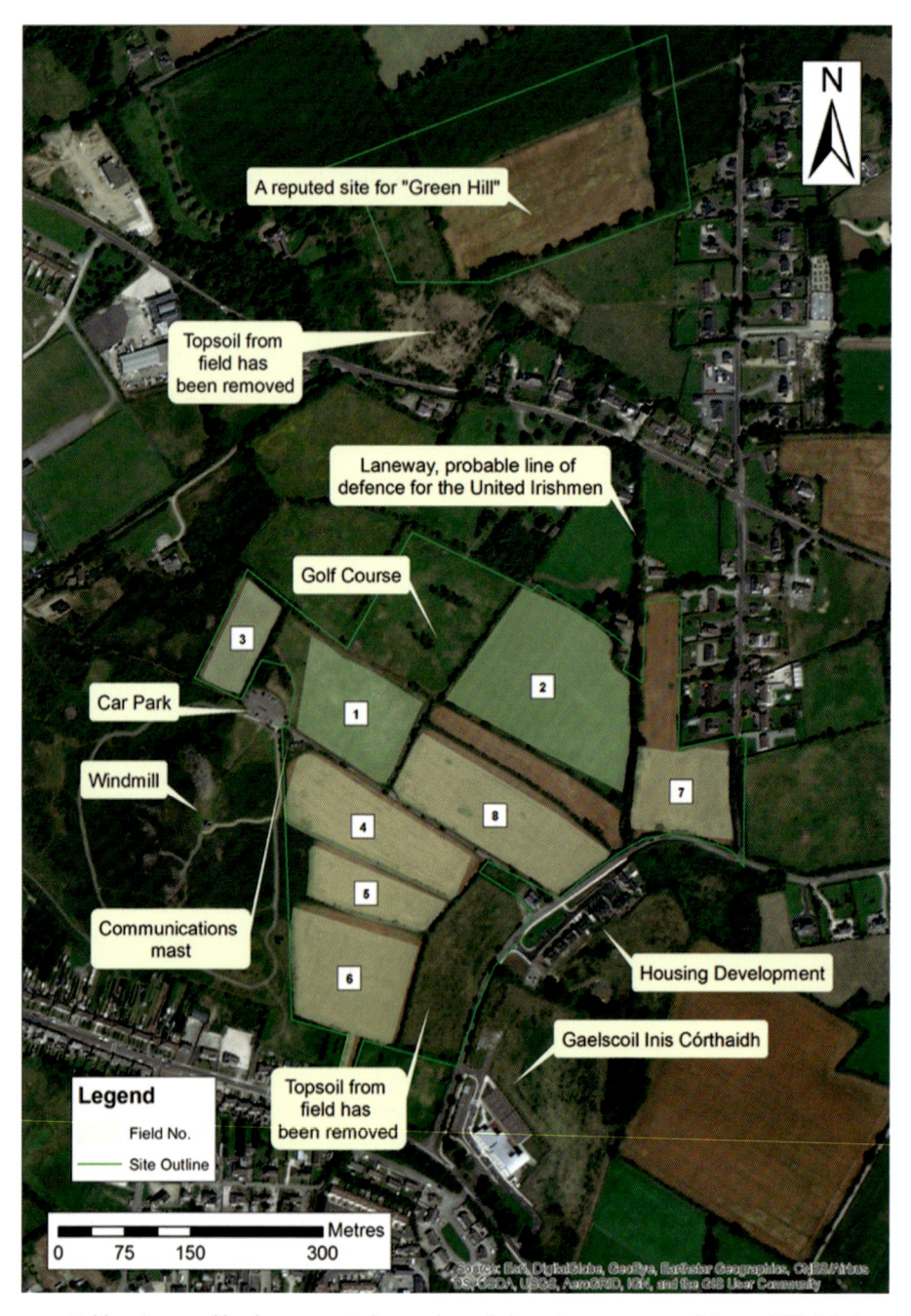

10.1 Fields 1–8 assessed by the systematic licenced metal-detection survey across Vinegar Hill. Modern encroachments on the battlefield are marked, as are some elements of the battlefield architecture. Across two large areas, the topsoil was removed on an industrial scale: these were likely to have contained some battle-related finds, which are now lost. Image by James Bonsall and Damian Shiels.

Picking up the pieces: the archaeological survey of Vinegar Hill 193

much of the field layout we see today is in fact an intrinsic part of the battlefield landscape. This in turn provides us with a window into how the United Irishmen sought to defend the hill, and how the government troops attempted to attack it.

It seems likely that the United Irishmen made use of the largest bank in the area – the Templeshannon townland boundary – as their outer line of defence. Such a position also conforms with the original location that the Irish Battlefields Project put forward for the 'green hill' in Clonhasten townland (Candidate 2 of those considered in chapter 6). This was the government artillery position that was the key to breaking the rebel defensive line as it brought enfilading fire to bear on their position, i.e. the government forces were able to fire down along the length of the rebel line. Treating the surviving field boundaries as remnants of the 1798 battlefield also changes our perspective on other elements of the landscape we see today. For example, contemporary depictions illustrate that General Loftus advanced his men over ground that contained a series of stone walls, and there are a number that can still be seen across Vinegar Hill (fig. 10.1). Similarly, lanes and roadways marked on the Ordnance Survey first-edition map are almost certainly intrinsically linked to the battle, having been used then (as now) for access to and egress from the hill.

The Irish Battlefields Project report on Vinegar Hill identified the landscape survivals, but it was only intended as an initial step. A more wide-ranging and intensive analysis was required to add further details to our knowledge of how the fighting developed on 21 June 1798. The archaeological fieldwork undertaken in 2017 as part of the Longest Day Research Project provided an opportunity to test the potential ascribed to the site, to see if it was merited. Vinegar Hill did not disappoint.

WHAT WERE WE LOOKING FOR?

The primary aim of our survey was to identify and plot metal objects that had been deposited either during the United Irish occupation of Vinegar Hill, or during the battle itself. Metal objects were sought as they survive for a greater length of time in the topsoil than organic items (such as wood or bone). During the three-week encampment of the United Irish forces on Vinegar Hill, many thousands of objects would have been dropped, discarded or lost, trodden into the soil by innumerable feet. These can range from lost coins and buttons that came loose, to pieces of broken equipment. Here the importance of an archaeological approach is again evident, as the precise distribution pattern of this material sometimes makes it possible to discern how an encampment was laid out or functioned.

The largest number of objects on Vinegar Hill associated with 1798 may well relate to the fighting. The nature of combat, particularly in the age of gunpowder, can lead to large volumes of material being discarded as an army and their camp followers rushed to and fro through the landscape, often under considerable stress. The key object on any battlefield from the age of gunpowder is the lead bullet, which was fired and dropped in its thousands on 21 June 1798. Lead bullets are also among the most likely artefacts to survive in the topsoil. These projectiles can reveal incredible detail about how an engagement developed, but only if their precise locations are recorded and they are subjected to detailed specialist analysis. For example, examining the size and type of bullets recovered can identify the use of different firearms. In 1797 the British army adopted the India-pattern Brown Bess musket, a weapon that had a calibre (internal diameter of the gun barrel) of 0.75in (Blackmore, 1969); bullets of a specific size related to that calibre were fired from it, and can be identified as such. Units equipped with less modern weapons likely fired bullets of a different size, as did those armed with different gun types, such as cavalry. Similarly, it might be expected that the United Irishmen employed a range of different weapon types, reflecting the guns they had captured during the campaign, from pistols to muskets to fowling pieces. As a result, bullet distribution can sometimes indicate who was doing the firing, and what type of troops they were. Examination of the bullets themselves can often tell us if the projectiles were fired or simply dropped, and sometimes provide information on both the distance they may have travelled and what they might have struck. When all this data is precisely plotted using archaeological techniques, highly detailed patterns emerge of how a firefight developed and progressed.

Lead bullets were not the only projectiles used at Vinegar Hill. Indeed, the key weapon employed by the government forces that day was their artillery. Weapons such as 6-pounders and howitzers (the latter often referred to in the contemporary accounts as 'mortars') were among those that sought to bombard the United Irish position into submission. We know that the 6-pounders used were likely either Congreve's light 6-pounders of 4ft 6in barrel-length, or the Belford and Blomefield light 6-pounder of 5ft. The howitzers had a bore of 5.5 inches, and those at Vinegar Hill were likely either the light or heavy brass version. These weapons could fire shells over obstacles such as thick field boundaries, with their fuses set to explode over their targets. Many of the contemporary accounts also record the use of 'grapeshot' by British 6-pounders, which is likely a reference to either 'canister' or 'case shot.' This type of ammunition consisted of a canister filled with spherical balls and was generally fired against bodies of troops at close range, having the impact of a giant shotgun blast. The different types of artillery projectiles are again identifiable archaeologically and can reveal significant detail when their precise findspot is known. For example, canister or case-shot tended not to be used unless within 500 yards of the target, so identification of these fragments can help us to pinpoint potential locations for government artillery that supported the advance.

Aside from projectiles, many other items are lost during the heat of battle, such as clothing and weapon parts. Many of the United Irishmen would have been equipped with pikes, and there would also have been large numbers of swords, bayonets and other pieces of equipment on the field. Occasionally, distribution patterns of such material can be indicative of close-quarters or even hand-to-hand combat, when parts of weapons fractured and broke under impact. Being aware of the precise locations of material such as this enables us to locate key flashpoints, areas where the outcome of the battle was decided.

THE APPROACH

As outlined above, battlefield archaeology is a specialized sub-discipline, one that employs scientific approaches that can reveal information often missed through conventional archaeological investigation such as monitoring and test trenching. While much of the previous archaeological work in and around Vinegar Hill has been conventional in nature, some battlefield artefacts have been recovered. By far the most significant was that carried out near the summit of the hill by Stafford-McLoughlin Archaeology Ltd in 2014 (see chapter 11). Undertaken on behalf of Wexford County Council, the work involved archaeological monitoring, under excavation licence 14E0098, during the upgrading of the paths around the hill. Metal detection of spoil revealed a series of artefacts that directly related to the events of 1798, including four musket balls, scraps of lead, buttons and a coin. This work provided further indication that material relating to the fighting survived at Vinegar Hill, increasing the potential for positive results.

The Longest Day Research Project built upon the earlier research and engaged with active surveys across the battlefield. The key technique employed during the survey was systematic licensed metal detection. Metal detection for archaeological objects or deposits is illegal in the Republic of Ireland without a license issued by the appropriate national authorities, something only supplied once a detailed archaeological method statement has been submitted, reviewed and approved. A core tenet of this legal position is that all archaeological finds in Ireland are considered the collective property of the people of the state. Illegal metal detection has been a major problem on Irish battlefield sites, as it is an activity that destroys immeasurable amounts of information about the events in question. Battlefield archaeology relies on systematic, gridded metal-detection surveys to ensure even coverage, the assignation of precise Global Positioning System (GPS) co-ordinates for findspots to exactly record and plot their location, and the detailed analysis of all material recovered by specialists to reveal information about these objects. These three elements are absent in illegal detection, which destroys any opportunity the public have of discovering what this remarkable material might reveal. Another important distinction is that archaeological metal detection never pursues archaeological objects below the topsoil horizon. Below this level, it is likely that archaeological features relating to 1798 events survive intact, be they traces of camp rubbish pits, fireplaces, or even mass graves. Such features are often destroyed by 'blind' metal detection, where detectorists dig through archaeological layers, irreparably damaging an extremely fragile resource object in pursuit of an object below.

The survey team on the ground at Vinegar Hill consisted of five archaeological detectorists and one dedicated archaeological surveyor, whose job it was to record each find as it was recovered using a GPS, a high-resolution piece of equipment that employs satellites to plot artefact locations with sub-centimetre accuracy. Knowing the exact findspot is of key importance, as it can reveal details of where people fought, or even stood, during a battle. It can provide information on the location of defensive positions, the whereabouts of opposing firing lines, and even the siting of artillery pieces. In order to physically conduct the survey, every field under investigation was gridded into transects using small flags. These were set out at 5m intervals, with each archaeologist detecting up and down a line of flags until the whole field was covered. This was done so we could be confident that we had covered an area in a uniform and systematic fashion, vital if we were to trust our results.

The eight fields the project targeted for the licensed survey were in Templeshannon townland. Our aim was to determine if battle-related objects survived, and if so, how they could better help us understand the battlefield landscape and the events as they unfolded during the engagement. The timing of the work was dictated by land availability, and so was carried out in two one-week blocks, the first in May 2017 and the second in August 2017. During this time a total of 14 hectares were subjected to licensed survey, which although a small proportion of the whole battlefield, nonetheless revealed extremely exciting results.

The majority of our area of investigation was presumed to be within the confines of the United Irishmen camp on Vinegar Hill. It also encompassed the assumed location of the advance of the government column led by General Dundas (accompanied by General Lake) on the day of battle. It is known that this column swept towards the United Irishmen in the general proximity of a low ridgeline that runs east from the summit of Vinegar Hill, forming a saddle between it and the high ground in Drumgoold to the east-south-east. In one description of the fighting here, it was noted that 'the insurgents made a number of efforts to break this ever-tightening circle by charging the advancing crown forces, particularly on the positions of Lake and Dundas' (Musgrave, 1995, p. 446), which indicates that there were heavy clashes in this area. One of these charges was repulsed by Dundas' men, and a counter-charge led by Colonel Wandesford saw the government troops gain a foothold on the ridge, from where they were able to consolidate their position and push on towards the summit (Cronin, Fitzsimons & Shiels, 2008).

THE RESULTS

The metal detection occurred over two distinct phases. The Phase 1 Survey took place between 8 and 12 May 2017, and was restricted to those fields in the Templeshannon survey area that were not under crop. These three fields, to the north, north-north-east and north-east of the Vinegar Hill summit were thought to be part of the United Irishmen's encampment and the scene of fighting between government troops and the hill's defenders. The survey here was undertaken at 2.5m transect intervals, allowing for *c*.80 per cent coverage of this portion of the study area.

All three fields were under pasture at the time of the survey. Field 1 (1.28ha) is located immediately below the public car park at Vinegar Hill, to the north-north-east of the summit, where potential sub-surface cut features were identified by Earthsound Archaeological Geophysics' survey (see chapter 8). Field 2 (2.61ha) is located northeast of the summit and is bounded to the east by an old north-south laneway, which is thought to be contemporary with the battle. This feature, when combined with the steep terrain that is the dominant feature of this field, is thought to represent a probable line of defence for the United Irishmen holding the hill. Field 3 (0.53ha) is located to the north of the summit and given its location must have seen considerable activity both during the encampment and at the time of the fighting.

Fields 1–3 produced a total of 154 artefacts (fig. 10.2). The survey here encountered significant challenges, most notably interference with the metal-detection equipment caused by the Vinegar Hill communications mast. Given the sustained use of the area by the public, large quantities of discarded modern metal – particularly aluminium cans – also hampered recovery efforts, particularly in fields 1 and 3. Despite this, several finds likely relate to 1798 camp-activity, including buttons, coins and a key. This activity was most notable in field 2, which was also the field furthest from the summit car park. Although such finds firmly place 1798 activity in the area, only one bullet was recovered during the Phase 1 works. It had been fired and was impacted, and was recovered from the high ground in Field 2. It likely represents incoming fire from government forces on the day of the battle.

Despite providing evidence for the encampment, the discovery of only one firmly battle-related object suggests that Field 2 may not have been a zone of intensive fighting. Fields 1 and 3 undoubtedly played a role as part of both the encampment and during the fighting, but they produced significantly less material than Field 2. There is potential that camp and battlefield finds in these fields are simply deeper than elsewhere, masking their signal, but unfortunately there is also a strong likelihood that illegal metal detection has had an impact. It is known from local sources that illegal detection has taken place on these fields, which are rarely ploughed. Prolonged illegal detection over an unploughed field (even a few hours a year over several years), where objects remain relatively stationary in the soil horizon can effectively remove

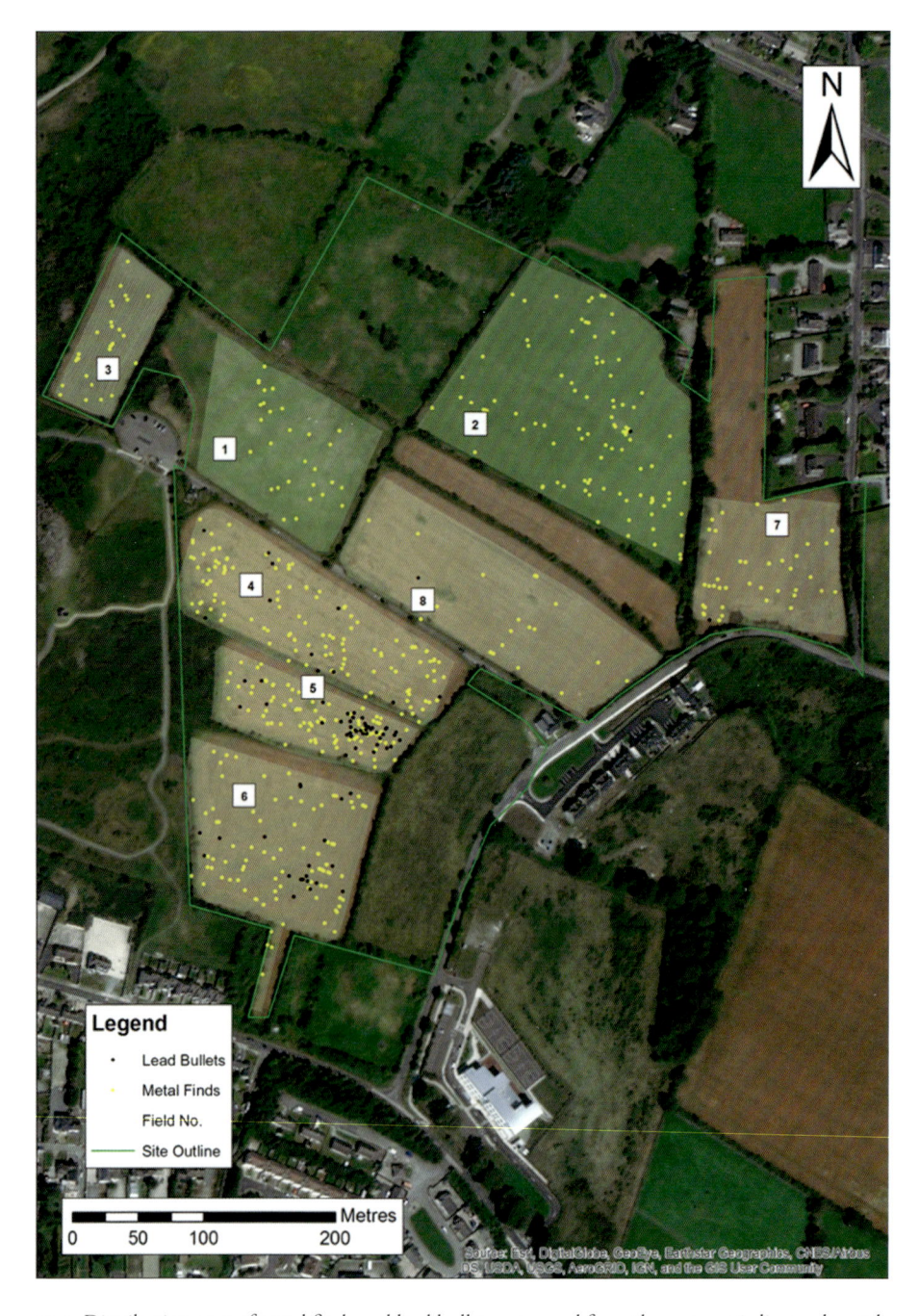

10.2 Distribution map of metal finds and lead bullets recovered from the systematic licensed metal-detection survey across Vinegar Hill. Infrequent finds recovered from Field 8 may imply that it had been illegally looted by unlicensed metal-detector activity in the past. Image by James Bonsall and Damian Shiels.

Picking up the pieces: the archaeological survey of Vinegar Hill

the upper layer of artefacts from the soil. This potential highlights how fragile an archaeological resource battlefields are, and how easily significant information can be lost. Further work may well reveal that substantial 1798 material does survive at depth, and there is no doubt that the landscape of these fields remains an intrinsic feature of the battlefield.

One find from Field 1 also provides a cautionary tale about how we utilize battlefields today. A 1798-era military button was uncovered here, a significant find that generated much excitement. However, further examination revealed that it also contained fragments of textile and red thread, material that would not have survived the passage of two centuries in the topsoil. This indicated that it was a re-enactor's button, which had fallen from a coat in recent years during one of the events to mark the anniversary of the fighting. Modern re-enactment apparel has become so accurate that after a few years in the soil it can become almost indistinguishable from original material deposited in 1798. This leads to potential contamination of the archaeological record, and highlights the importance of restricting living history events to locations that do not form part of the core battlefield area.

The Phase 2 survey took place between 21 and 25 August 2017 (fig. 10.2). It was made up of five fields in Templeshannon (fields 4–8) that had been under crop at the time of the previous work. The fact that the fields had been recently harvested considerably benefited the detection process. Four of the fields (fields 4, 5, 6 and 8) lie to the east of the Vinegar Hill summit, leading towards the saddle between the hill and the high ground in Drumgoold townland. Field 4 (1.48ha) is bounded to the north by the laneway that takes visitors to the summit car park, and was surveyed at 2.5m transect intervals. Field 8 (1.75ha) is located on the opposite side of the laneway and connects with Field 1 to the west. Due to time constraints, this was surveyed at 5m intervals. Field 5 (0.75ha) lies south of Field 4 towards Enniscorthy and was also surveyed at 2.5m intervals, with Field 6 (1.56ha) positioned to the south of Field 5. Field 6 was surveyed at a mix of 2.5m and 5m intervals. Field 7 (1.00ha) lay on the opposite side of the laneway adjacent to Field 2, and was investigated to determine if this lane saw any significant action on the day of the battle. It was surveyed at 5m intervals.

Field 7 produced a total of forty-one finds, the majority of which post-date the battle. However, one bullet that had been fired was recovered in the south-west corner of the field, and is almost certainly of 1798 date. Field 7 was thought to have been a potential attack route for government troops, assaulting the laneway and Field 2 beyond, thought to be defensive features utilized by the United Irishmen. The presence of two bullets in this zone (one in Field 2 and one in Field 7) does not suggest heavy fighting, but is more indicative of activity such as skirmishing.

Fields 4, 5, 6 and 8 dominate the eastern approach, through the saddle of high ground, towards Vinegar Hill. Field 8, located to the north of the car park laneway, revealed twenty-one artefacts. This was an extremely low artefact rate, and similar

10.3 Lead bullets fired from a musket (*left*) and pistol (*right*), collected from Vinegar Hill during the systematic licensed metal-detection survey. Recording the calibre of lead bullets helps map movement of different combatants across the battlefield. Image: Michael Cahill.

to the other fields on this (northern) side of the laneway; it is probable that illegal detection has taken its toll. One of the finds was a lead bullet that represented 1798 activity, again suggesting that the fighting in this field (which was certainly part of the encampment) was not intensive.

The picture to the south of the laneway is entirely different, and it was in Fields 4, 5 and 6 that the Battle of Vinegar Hill was brought to life via the archaeological evidence recovered (fig. 10.3). This part of the battlefield was clearly the scene of significant action on 21 June 1798, and the archaeological material recovered here is the most extensive assemblage of battlefield artefacts yet recovered on any such site in the Republic of Ireland. This evidence began to emerge in Field 4, where the transects produced 130 objects. Of these, a large number were related to the engagement. Included among them were at least twelve lead bullets, some of which bore clear evidence of firing and impaction. In addition, a large iron object, possibly representing a piece of mortar shell, was recovered, as was a potential sword fragment. Aside from the projectiles and weapons, Field 4 produced a range of other artefacts including eight buttons, twenty coins and a number of buckles, some of which are likely of 1798 origin.

Moving further south to Field 5, the pattern of evidence intensified still further. Here at least forty-one lead bullets were identified, including large concentrations towards the field's eastern edge. Some of these bullets appear to have been dropped during the action, while others had been severely impacted, suggesting they had struck the earth at relatively close range. Field 5 also produced a piece of suspected sandshot, evidence of close-range artillery support. Among the other material were at least eighteen coins, eight buttons and numerous buckles and badges. Field 6 continued the trend.

Picking up the pieces: the archaeological survey of Vinegar Hill 201

Among the 106 finds recorded here were at least 20 lead bullets, many bearing signs of impaction. Aside from the ubiquitous coins, buttons and buckles, there were also a number of fragments of weapon furniture from the battle, including the 'hammer' from a flintlock musket's firing mechanism, and the 'pan' from a flintlock pistol. The recovery of these items, and the recording of their precise findspots, promises to add significantly to our knowledge of the Battle of Vinegar Hill.

WHAT DOES IT MEAN?

The tremendous results from the archaeological survey, particularly the material retrieved in Fields 4, 5 and 6, represent the most significant battlefield assemblage yet recovered in the Republic of Ireland. But what does the survey tell us about both the 1798 battlefield and today's landscape? At the time of writing, work is ongoing on the conservation and detailed specialist analysis of the archaeological material, so any conclusions drawn at this stage can only be regarded as preliminary. However, it is possible to make a number of observations at this stage, starting with the battle itself.

The survey suggests that the government column under Dundas and Lake did not attack across the laneway that bisects Fields 2 and 7, though it remains probable that this line did represent a major element of the United Irishmen's defensive position. It may be that the government forces regarded the position as too strong, and instead placed some skirmishers here to occupy the line as they moved to flank it to the south. As is suggested by some of the contemporary mapping, Dundas and Lake appear to have swept over the high ground into Drumgoold townland, forming for their attack in the saddle between there and Vinegar Hill and advancing from south-east to north-west towards the summit. The archaeological evidence supports heavy fighting from east to west in this location, as the government force advanced and was periodically faced with United Irish efforts to repulse them. Interestingly, the material recovered by Stafford McLoughlin in 2014, immediately to the west of Fields 4, 5 and 6, is likely also part of this event, with both investigations demonstrating that there was significant action on this side of the hill.

That the contemporary landscape played a major role in the battle is further reinforced by the artefact distribution. The avoidance of the aforementioned laneway between Fields 2 and 7 is evidenced by the infrequent nature of the material recovered here. In this instance, it is the relative lack of material that is significant, an absence that paradoxically may be indicative of the formidable strength of this portion of the Vinegar Hill defensive line. Similarly, the lack of bullets in Field 8 (to the north of the small road that leads to the summit car park) is in stark contrast to the abundance of evidence for fighting in Fields 4, 5 and 6 (to the south). The most obvious interpretation for this distribution is that the government forces under Dundas and

Lake used this small road to the hill's summit as a guide on which to align their right flank, confirming this route's contemporaneity with the battle. This was a particularly important discovery, given that this road still serves as the main vehicular access point for Vinegar Hill. It was the fields to the south of it, through which Dundas and Lake drove their main advance, that were the scene of the most intensive actions on this side of the hill – fields where many of the people present in 1798 fought and died.

What of the artefact types recovered? The precise locationary evidence recorded for each of them allows for a detailed interpretation of their distribution, which forms a key component of the ongoing post-excavation process. It is apparent that there are a number of distinct clusters of bullets, some of which likely represent the firing lines of the opposing sides. The distribution reinforces the importance of the contemporary field boundaries, positions from which Dundas and Lake had to drive the defenders as they moved up the hill. A number of highly impacted bullets were recovered throughout the area, suggestive of exchanges of fire at extremely close range (fig. 10.4). Some represent incoming fire from attacking government troops, with the bullets slamming into the rising ground approaching the hill's summit, only yards from where they were first discharged. Such is the concentration of projectiles in Fields 4, 5 and 6 that some even appear to represent a potential static firing line of government troops in this vicinity. Quite a number of these bullets are unfired, potentially dropped by nervous troops as they fumbled to reload in the heat of the action. Intriguingly, specialist analysis has confirmed that artillery was also being employed in a close-support anti-personnel role here (Cahill, 2018). A small metal ball in Field 5 was part of a charge of canister known as sand shot. It was fired by a piece that had followed on the heels of the infantry as Dundas and Lake moved relentlessly towards the summit. The gun would have been deployed in close proximity to the findspot, in the very midst of the fighting, and its impact on the massed ranks of United Irish defenders standing in these fields would have been devastating. The artefacts also suggest that the United Irishmen launched at least one determined counter-attack in this area. The intensity of this clash is demonstrated by fragments of broken weapon furniture from a pistol and musket, likely lost during close-quarters action.

The projectiles of war were not all that was recovered in this archaeologically rich sector of the battlefield. Though analysis is ongoing, an initial assessment of the other finds indicates an abundance of other artefacts from 1798, particularly in Fields 5 and 6. These include a number of George III coins and privately produced commercial coinage, struck in the 1790s to meet a shortfall in the official currency. These were either dropped and lost or came from the pockets of fallen individuals during the fighting. A number of the buttons recovered here also owe their origins to 21 June 1798. One gilt example bears the inscription 'South Cork', and was presumably part of the uniform of a member of the South Cork militia. Further specialist investigation promises to add to what we know about this contemporary material. It seems certain

Picking up the pieces: the archaeological survey of Vinegar Hill 203

10.4 Some of the lead bullets collected from Vinegar Hill during the systematic licensed metal-detection survey, exhibiting various rates of impaction. Heavily impacted bullets indicate firing at close range. Bullets that exhibit no impact were probably dropped. Mapping the precise location of every bullet allows us to trace elements of the battle. Image: Michael Cahill.

that at least a portion of the everyday items recovered were left behind by the men, women and children who were camped across this landscape in the days leading up the government assault.

The recorded, contextualized archaeological recovery of this material has provided us with one of the most intimate and visceral portraits we have for an Irish battlefield. Yet, as highlighted above, the invaluable information that the survey provided on the surviving 1798 landscape features is arguably of equal significance. That these field boundaries and laneways had not previously been recognized as integral elements of the story of the battle demonstrates the importance of projects like the Longest Day. They also serve as reminder of the risks that this historic landscape continues to face.

The 2008 Irish Battlefields Project's look into Vinegar Hill identified a number of threats to the battlefield (Cronin, Fitzsimons & Shiels 2008), particularly the significant developments taking place in the vicinity of one of the candidates for the all-important 'green hill' and the periphery of Vinegar Hill itself. For example, it was known that a large section of the battlefield had been severely damaged in the 1990s by the construction of a golf course. The 2017 fieldwork further increased our understanding of these threats, and unfortunately identified a number of additional locations where archaeology relating to the battle has almost certainly been lost. To the immediate east of Fields 4, 5 and 6 a recent housing development has destroyed part of the battlefield, apparently with no significant archaeological work carried out. It seems probable that this field, facing onto the roadway, was the site of a defensive position of the United Irishmen. The archaeological work has highlighted the key importance of the high ground in Drumgoold for our understanding of the events of 21 June 1798. Unfortunately much of saddle has been severely impacted by a combination of housing and school development, both of which have seen extensive landscaping works take place. Although the subject of some archaeological investigation, the failure to employ systematic battlefield archaeology techniques has almost certainly led to the destruction of information relating to the engagement. As the survey demonstrated, the amount of information that can be gleaned from battlefields when systematic licensed archaeological techniques are applied is considerable. We know that illegal detection on the hill has taken place, but unfortunately we cannot know what damage has been done to the archaeological record as a result. The continued vigilance of the local population in preventing such activity in the future is key to the battlefield's survival.

Despite the renewed awareness that the survey has created for what has been lost, there are tremendous positives to be taken in that so much of the 1798 battlefield landscape has survived intact. The archaeology indicates that the laneways and field boundaries we can walk along today were key strategic locations during the battle. When we walk along them or beside them, we are interacting directly with upstanding features that crucially influenced events as they unfolded on that fateful day. Awareness of their importance is a major asset in terms of both the future management and interpretation of the Vinegar Hill battlefield.

CONCLUSION

The licensed battlefield archaeological survey undertaken as part of the Longest Day Research Project is the most extensive carried out in the Republic of Ireland, yet only a tiny fraction of the 1798 battlefield has been explored. Archaeological battlefield surveys of this nature often take many years to complete, and the two-week licensed survey should be regarded as a pilot study. Still, its results greatly exceeded expectations, demonstrating not only that significant battlefield material remains in place, but that it forms part of a wider battlefield landscape of fields, hedgerows, walls, roads and laneways that is remarkably well preserved. Further detailed examination of the fields investigated during this survey will undoubtedly uncover more of the battle's secrets. The future should also see efforts to expand the work to other parts of the hill and onto the critical high ground in Drumgoold townland. The vision of Wexford County Council in conducting this unique research is to be commended, and the results are just reward for that foresight. The Longest Day Research Project will undoubtedly serve as an exemplar for the investigation of other such sites around the country. It has revealed new opportunities for the management and interpretation of the site, and allowed us to visualize – in a way never before possible – the realities of that summer day over 200 years ago, when United Irishmen and government troops fought, struggled and died in that murderous contest on the slopes of Vinegar Hill.

CHAPTER ELEVEN

Archaeological monitoring and licensed surveys at Vinegar Hill and Clonhasten

CATHERINE McLOUGHLIN, EMMET STAFFORD & COLM MORIARTY

INTRODUCTION

In 2014 and 2020 Stafford McLoughlin Archaeology undertook programmes of archaeological mitigation related to development works on Vinegar Hill and in the adjoining townland of Clonhasten. Both projects were development-led in nature, and unconnected with the Longest Day Research Project, but nevertheless yielded results that are important to the understanding of the overall story of the Battle of Vinegar Hill. In 2014 licensed archaeological monitoring was undertaken around the summit of Vinegar Hill due to the upgrading of existing path networks. In 2020 a licensed archaeological survey was carried out in advance of residential development works in the townland of Clonhasten, to the north-east of the summit of the hill. Both programmes of work uncovered a number of artefacts directly related to the battle, such as musket shot, coins and buttons. Both campaigns of work were undertaken under archaeological licence to the then Department of Culture, Heritage and Gaeltacht.

VINEGAR HILL ARCHAEOLOGICAL MONITORING

Archaeological monitoring of groundworks on Vinegar Hill was undertaken at the request of Wexford County Council in 2014. The monitoring was necessary as the council was then upgrading an existing network of paths and trails around the hill. Vinegar Hill, as the location of one of the pivotal battles of the United Irishmen's rebellion of 1798, is a sensitive historical site and all construction works at or near the hill are subject to archaeological planning conditions. As part of the programme of monitoring, licensed metal-detecting of the soil removed during path construction was carried out, and a number of artefacts such as musket balls, lead strips, buttons and a single copper-alloy thimble were recovered (fig. 11.1).

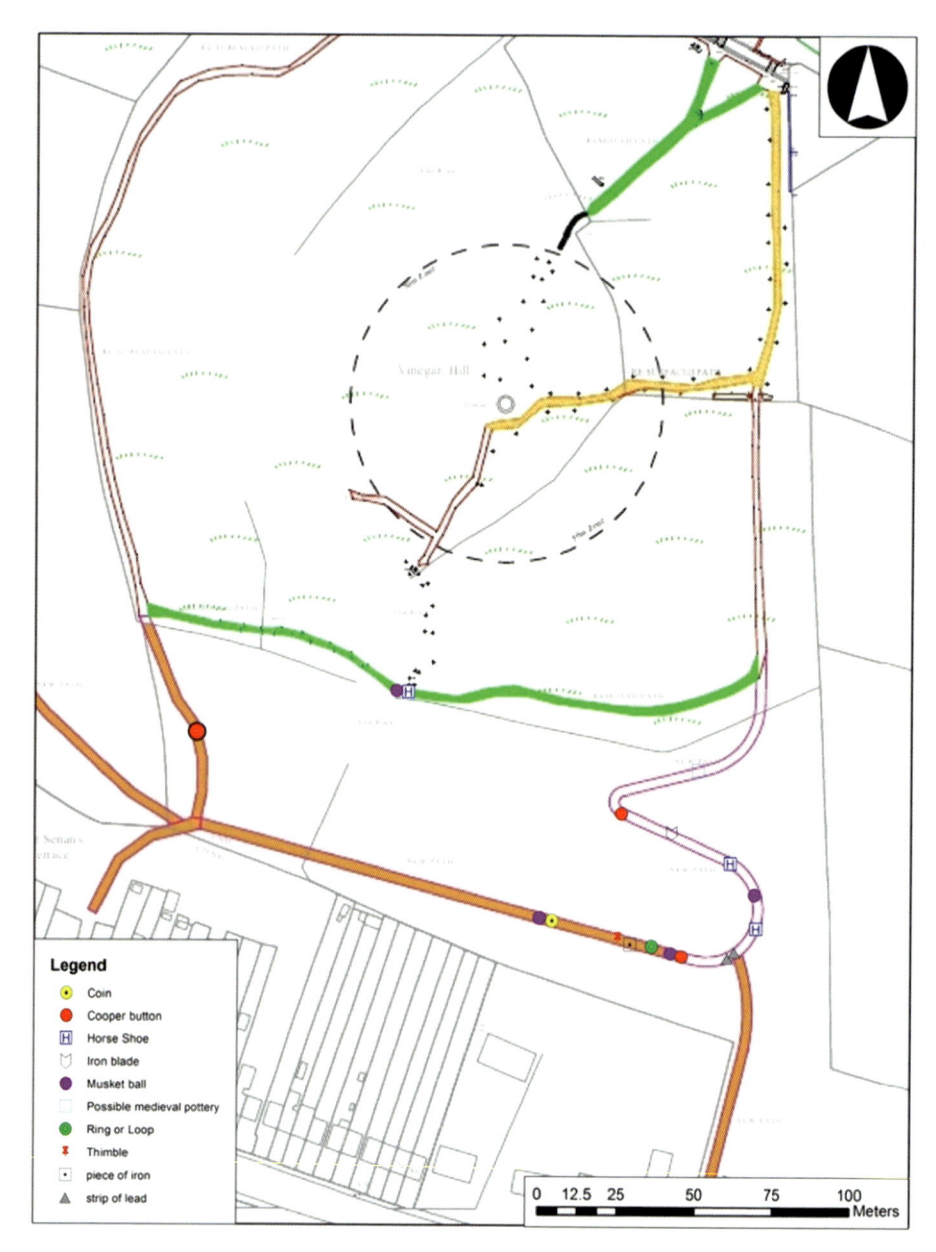

11.1 Locations of findspots of archaeological artefacts recovered during metal-detecting of stripped topsoil during the Vinegar Hill monitoring. © Stafford McLoughlin Archaeology.

Archaeological monitoring investigations are undertaken under state-issued licence and the works at Vinegar Hill were conducted under licence numbers 14E0098 and 14R0029. The works took place at various dates in 2014 during the upgrading of the

11.2 Topsoil stripping of main pathway to summit of Vinegar Hill, looking west (western section). © Stafford McLoughlin Archaeology.

existing path network (McLoughlin, 2015). The monitored groundworks consisted of the excavation of new pathways and the upgrading of existing ones as well as the installation of kerbing, seating and gate piers around the hill. The excavations were carried out by a mini-digger fitted with a toothless bucket. No archaeological features were identified during the monitoring works but a selection of archaeological artefacts were recovered, most notably four musket balls associated with the 1798 battle. Topsoil removed from the newly created paths was used to cover over the unsafe elements of the existing pathways. Some areas of excavation had been previously disturbed during the installation of the original narrower pathways around the hill. One such area was the existing pathway in the vicinity of the Coláiste Bríde school, where twentieth-century demolition material was encountered during the monitoring process.

Main section of the new pedestrian pathway

One of the main areas of topsoil stripping for the new pathway network was located in an area of relatively undisturbed green-field (fig. 11.2). A shallow trench was opened that was approximately 1.6m wide. The depth of soil stripped before the path was

11.3 Musket balls recovered from pathways. © Stafford McLoughlin Archaeology.

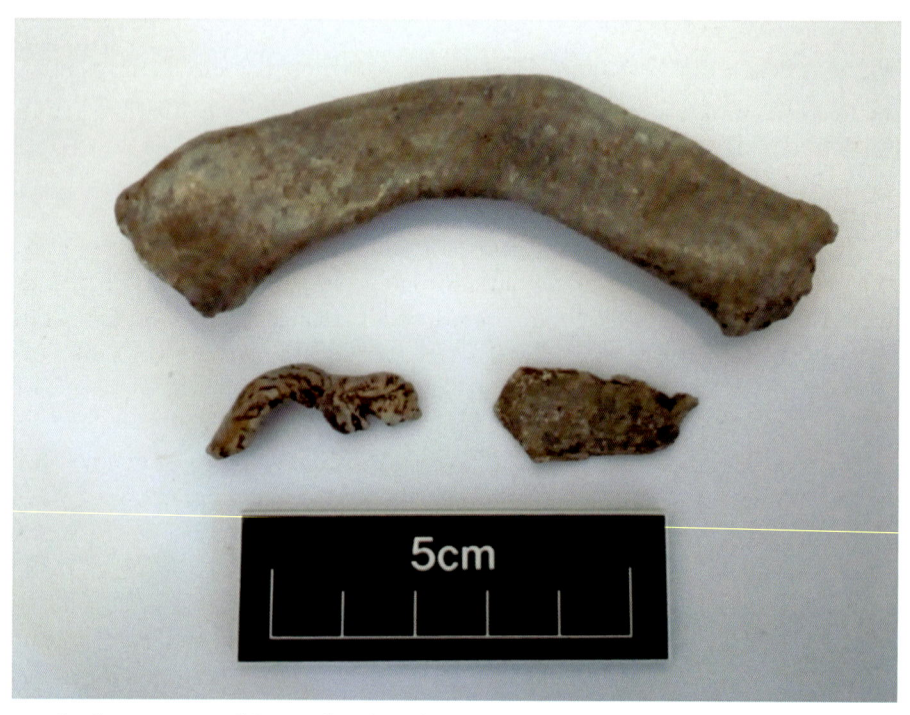

11.4 Lead strips recovered from archaeological monitoring. © Stafford McLoughlin Archaeology.

11.5 Copper alloy objects recovered including a thimble, buttons and a George II or III coin dating to the eighteenth century. © Stafford McLoughlin Archaeology.

laid measured between 0.1m and 0.2m. This topsoil contained iron nails, nineteenth- and twentieth-century pottery fragments, occasional horseshoes and shards of glass. These artefacts may have resulted from nineteenth-century manuring of the land, as there were also the faint suggestions of north-south orientated cultivation furrows in the area. The topsoil deposit overlay light greyish-brown silty clay plough-soil. The stripped pathway was metal detected, as was the soil removed from the excavated trench.

As the main pathway moved higher up onto the southern slope of Vinegar Hill, the depth of topsoil removed generally varied between 0.15 and 0.2m, but in places where the pathway cut into the hill-slope the depth measured up to 0.4m and revealed a stony orange brown subsoil. The soil removed was generally a brown silty clay topsoil that was relatively sterile of archaeological material. Metal-detecting revealed a number of objects of archaeological interest, especially in the south-east corner of the hill. These artefacts included three musket balls (figs 11.3–11.5). An area of wooden steps giving access to the top of the hill from the west was also removed during this work. This activity was monitored and metal-detected and a single, impacted, musket ball was identified in this area.

Opening of additional pathway

An additional pathway ran roughly parallel and to the south of the main pedestrian path. The works in this area involved flattening and removing heavy vegetation with the mini-digger and scraping the surface of the ground with the digger bucket. The path was *c.*1.6m wide and the maximum depth of topsoil excavated was *c.*0.1m. The soil removed was mainly dark silty clay that contained large quantities of modern rubbish including plastic, broken glass and beer cans. However, at its very south-eastern end, as the path started to rise up the side of Vinegar Hill a less disturbed topsoil layer was encountered. A sherd of possible medieval pottery was recovered from this layer indicating that, whatever its association with the 1798 battle, Vinegar Hill has been a site of human settlement since at least the foundation of Enniscorthy.

Trench for stone kerbing

New stone kerbing was added to a pre-existing pathway that leads from the windmill tower on top of Vinegar Hill to the car park. The pathway was also upgraded, but this did not require any ground disturbance. To facilitate the insertion of the kerbing a narrow trench, *c.*0.3m deep by 0.4m wide, was excavated along either side of the pre-existing pathway. The topsoil removed was black/brown peaty clay and bedrock was encountered in a number of locations, especially close to the very top of the hill. The area was metal detected before the stripping began and the stripped topsoil was also inspected. Very few objects were recovered apart from a few modern beer-bottle caps, foil from cigarette packets and aluminium-can ring-pulls. In addition, two twentieth-century coins were found beside the windmill. No objects or features of archaeological interest were identified in this area.

Artefacts and finds-retrieval strategy

The soil from the topsoil-stripping process was scanned by metal detector. When the soil was metal-detected it had been slightly moved from its primary position, ready to be taken away by a small site dumper. During this process any artefacts that were seen to be nineteenth century or older were retrieved from the soil. Modern finds were discarded at this point. Artefacts that appeared to have an association with the Battle of Vinegar Hill had their positions recorded both manually and by hand-held GPS. Other artefacts such as nails and horseshoes had their relative positions recorded. A sub-sample of identified pottery was removed from the soil. The fragmentary nature of the recovered pottery suggests that it is likely to have been deposited through an historic manuring process (where animal manure and domestic rubbish was carted from nearby farmyards to pastures on Vinegar Hill). Where appropriate, the artefacts have been cleaned and conserved and registered according to National Museum of Ireland guidelines. An X-ray was taken of the objects not selected for conservation, which included a mixture of horseshoes, nails and other iron objects, some of which are likely to be modern.

LICENSED ARCHAEOLOGICAL SURVEY AT CLONHASTEN IN 2020

A residential development site in the townland of Clonhasten, *c.*500m to the north-north-east of the summit of Vinegar Hill, was subject to licensed archaeological survey in 2020 as part of a grant of planning permission for the development of housing at the site (licence numbers 20E0025 and 20R0011; McLoughlin 2020; figs 11.6 and 11.7).

11.6 View of Clonhasten development site from the car park at Vinegar Hill. © Stafford McLoughlin Archaeology.

11.7 Location of the Clonhasten survey area in relation to the location of Vinegar Hill. Base map © Google Earth.

11.8 Fields surveyed at Clonhasten and general location of the lead shot and militaria uncovered during the survey (possible location of the 'green hill'). Base map © Google Earth.

At the time of writing the post-excavation process for this site is ongoing. It is however clear that this survey has yielded positive results and has given new information regarding the battle and the potential location of the 'green hill', the location of which is a subject of speculation by O'Flaherty and O'Connor as well as Shiels and Bonsall in this volume (see chapters 5 and 10).

Methodology

The development site at Clonhasten had previously been subject to archaeological testing in 2007 and the site was partially topsoil-stripped by 2008. The townland of Clonhasten, located in the immediate vicinity of Vinegar Hill, was flagged as having potential for battlefield-related archaeology in the report on Vinegar Hill completed as part of the Irish Battlefields Project (Cronin et al., 2008). Following a new planning application for residential development at the site it was recommended that a licensed archaeological survey be carried out.

The development site was divided into three fields (fig. 11.8) and initially six target areas were chosen for a sample licensed metal-detector survey. The sample survey yielded positive results and the archaeological licence was extended to accommodate a wider survey area. Survey and excavation was undertaken in spaced transects at a distance of 1m, 2.5m or 5m depending on the results of the initial surveys. The work was undertaken by a three-person archaeological team with a dedicated surveyor to plot all the finds via GPS.

Results

A total of 176 positive targets were identified within the development site. These targets were each given a unique number and excavated. The excavated items included fifty-two iron objects (mostly nail-shaped objects, a couple of horseshoes and several pieces of heavy iron), two pieces of probable broken pike heads, six lead shot, thirty-nine small circular copper alloy objects (coins, buttons and discs), twenty-four copper alloy objects (other than circular) such as small buckles, uniform badges and other pieces, as well as several pieces of lead. The majority of the lead shot came from one area in the north-east of Field 2.

A total of six pieces of lead shot were found in the cluster of artefacts in this area. Three of the pieces were impacted musket balls, one was an unfired musket ball and one was an unfired pistol ball. In addition a number of items of interest such as a cap badge and coins were uncovered in this area.

Discussion

The artefacts recovered from the survey at Clonhasten are clearly related to the Battle of Vinegar Hill. The concentration of artefacts in the north-eastern portion of Field 2 suggests that this area was the location of one of General Loftus' guns and may be the 'green hill' noted in the accounts of the battle. Sir Richard's Musgrave's account of the battle relates the following:

> General Loftus was detached by General Duff to occupy a green hill in a park enclosed by stone walls, which was on the side, and composed a part of Vinegar Hill. General Loftus surprised the rebels by the celerity of this movement because the hill was steep, and the ground which he occupied there was divided by stone walls, but by breaking open gaps he had two guns carried over at first, and soon after four more by having untackled them from the horses. From this position he was able to fire into the lower line of the enemy, rather on his left … (Musgrave, 1802, i, p. 477)

The location of the artefacts identified through our survey fits with Musgrave's description of Loftus' movements. The ground to the north of the findspot slopes steeply down to the old Ferns to Enniscorthy road and from that location the area could appear to be a 'green hill' at the foot of Vinegar Hill itself. The field boundaries in the survey area are stone walls topped by now mature trees. In 1798 this tree cover may have been largely absent.

The artefacts recovered include several impacted musket balls (fig. 11.9). This means that those musket balls had been fired and had hit a hard target and become deformed. This implies that the musket balls were shot from the rebel lines at the south towards Loftus' advancing guns. In addition pieces of militaria such as a uniform badge were

11.9 Lead shot recovered from Field 2 during the survey at Clonhasten. Both impacted and non-impacted musket shot, and pistol shot, were recovered. © Stafford McLoughlin Archaeology.

11.10 Selection of militaria recovered from the Clonhasten survey. © Stafford McLoughlin Archaeology.

found at this location, indicating a high level of uniformed activity in the immediate area (fig. 11.10).

One of the musket balls from our Vinegar Hill survey is also impact-damaged and likely fired by the advancing crown forces toward the rebels on top of the hill. It was recovered adjacent to a rocky outcrop on the southern part of the summit and may have hit that rocky outcrop and fallen straight into the soil. Several lead strips were also uncovered on the hill and it is likely that these had been scavenged by individual rebels and were intended to be used in the making of musket balls. A decorated lead mount was identified, along with several copper-alloy buttons, some of which were decorated. These items may have fallen off clothes and uniforms during the battle, or when the dead and injured were taken from the hill.

Although it is a relatively small sample (four from the Vinegar Hill monitoring project and five from the Clonhasten survey), all of the musket balls recovered measure between 16mm (0.63 inches) and 18mm (0.71 inches) in diameter. This consistency suggests a near-uniform use of issued (to the crown forces) and seized (by rebel forces) Brown Bess muskets on both sides. The Brown Bess musket, which was the standard British military flintlock weapon of the late eighteenth century and early nineteenth century, had a calibre of 0.75in. A suitable musket ball for the Brown Bess had to be smaller than the actual calibre of the barrel, which was often fouled, like a dirty chimney, by the residue of previous firings. The musket ball was held in place by a wad of paper which was rammed down the barrel of the musket to prepare it for firing (Holmes, 2002, pp 194–200). These musket balls could be easily cast, by soldiers on either side, from melted lead scavenged from pipes, roofs and water tanks encountered en route to the battlefield. For the rebel forces a reliable source of gunpowder would have been far harder to source than the lead to make additional musket balls. The Brown Bess musket had an effective range equivalent to a modern shotgun and unless fired in massed volleys could not be relied upon to hit a target at anything in excess of 100m, making the rebel forces very vulnerable to the longer range fire of the cannons hauled up the 'green hill' by General Loftus' forces. The pistol ball recovered from the Clonhasten site measured 12mm (0.47 inches) in diameter. The pistol ball does not appear to have been fired and is likely to have belonged to an officer armed with a personal sidearm of perhaps 0.50 calibre. Unlike the enlisted soldiers, with their Brown Bess muskets, officers were not issued with a standard pattern or calibre pistol and were instead expected to purchase their own private weapons (ibid., p. 208). The un-impacted musket balls recovered from both sites are likely to have been dropped shot and could have belonged to either the rebels or to the advancing crown forces as they advanced on Vinegar Hill and forced the rebel retreat back off the hill.

Metal-detecting surveys such as that undertaken at Clonhasten can produce an array of artefacts, dating both to before and after a specific event such as the 1798 battle. One such item recovered from Clonhasten was a very worn William III

11.11 Two of the coins recovered from Clonhasten. On the left a very worn William III halfpenny dating to 1696 and on the right, a George II halfpenny dating to 1736. © Stafford McLoughlin Archaeology.

half-penny dating to 1696 (fig. 11.11). Rather than being a stray find it is possible that this century-old item was associated with the Battle of Vinegar Hill. Evidence from other battlefields in Britain suggests that such well-thumbed coins may have been carried by the soldiers as charms (Professor Tony Pollard, pers. comm.). Such an interpretation would place a very human face on the analysis of this historic battle, allowing one to picture an individual soldier nervously rubbing his favoured good-luck charm as the firing commenced. Given the political significance of William III (William of Orange) in Ireland, such a good-luck charm would undoubtedly have belonged to a member of the crown forces.

CONCLUSIONS

Archaeological monitoring of groundworks at Vinegar Hill uncovered a number of artefacts directly related to the Battle of Vinegar Hill, most notably four musket balls, one of which was damaged from impact. The artefacts were generally located in the south-eastern extent of the area topsoil stripped for the new pathways.

While this appears to suggest a focus of activity on the south-eastern side of the hill these results must be interpreted with some degree of caution. The area of archaeological monitoring on Vinegar Hill was relatively modest and the artefacts were recovered from the southern slopes of the hill, which appear to have been less cultivated in the post-1798 period than the flatter western side of the archaeologically monitored area. On the western side there was a faint indication of cultivation ridges and frequent finds of nineteenth- and twentieth-century glass, nails, horseshoes, pottery, etc., which suggests there was more extensive historic cultivation and manuring in this area. Cultivation and manuring will have resulted in the movement of artefacts throughout the soil and perhaps resulted in the loss of evidence related to the battle.

The archaeological survey of the Clonhasten development site, which was more extensive than the works undertaken on Vinegar Hill, produced results that may be considered more definitive. On the Clonhasten site a line of contact has been established with a series of impacted musket shot indicating the position of one or more of Loftus' guns as they broke through the field boundaries in this area and made their move towards Vinegar Hill. The survey has also been able to suggest this site as a potential location of the 'green hill' mentioned in historic accounts of the battle.

The artefacts recovered both in Clonhasten and at Vinegar Hill include militaria, musket balls and more mundane personal items such as a thimble and a good luck charm. These recovered items of material culture inform an understanding of the activities of the period preceding the battle itself. Clothes might be mended at one rebel camp fire while roofing lead scavenged from a nearby house was recast to make musket balls at another. The next day, in the artillery firing line of the crown forces, an individual soldier handled his good luck charm while contemplating the battle to come. Incoming musket balls fired from the forward rebel lines may have startled that soldier into dropping his well rubbed coin and knocked the cap badge from his comrade's head. All of those items lay in the ground for two centuries until recovered as part of the archaeological analysis of the Vinegar Hill landscape.

The results from the archaeological monitoring on Vinegar Hill and the pre-development survey at Clonhasten confirm the importance of archaeological involvement in the planning and development system. Both projects have recovered artefacts and produced data which aids our developing understanding of the Battle of Vinegar Hill. In particular the identification of a possible site of the 'green hill', supported by retrieved artefactual evidence, indicates the importance of applying professional archaeological techniques to historic battlefield sites.

ACKNOWLEDGMENTS

We wish to thank the editors for asking us to contribute to this volume. Although our surveys were not directly related to the Longest Day Research Project, it is important that the results of development-led archaeological surveys are added to the outputs of adjacent and related research projects. We would also like to thank Wexford County Council and the private developer of the Clonhasten site for funding the works described above and for their enthusiasm for the publication of this information.

CHAPTER TWELVE

Oral histories of the 1798 rebellion in Enniscorthy and surrounding areas

JACQUI HYNES

> I watched him die under the blood red sky
> Near the foot of Vinegar Hill
> And as he died the old man cried
> And time it just stood still.
> —from a poem recorded locally in 1997

INTRODUCTION

The oral histories, or folk traditions, of the 1798 rebellion contribute significantly to our understanding of the course of events, participants, and the aftermath of the rebellion in Enniscorthy and the surrounding areas, while simultaneously offering an insight into the psyche of a mid-twentieth-century community[1] and the longevity, or lack thereof, of these traditions in the present.

Writing about the events of 1798, Beiner (2006, p. 139) comments that 'historians who choose to ignore folklore sources limit their choice of sources for local participation in the rebellion.' Frequently, stories from the oral history echo accounts recorded in the historical record. Additionally, and significantly, it offers accounts of local heroes not generally preserved in the historical record; locations of interest (through field, site or place-names); the human cost of the rebellion; and individual acts (both positive and negative) undertaken by both sides. The stories also include many internationally recognized folk motifs such as a river running red with blood, or animals used to guard buried treasure. Consequently, these accounts also fit within a wider international context of stories recorded in the folk tradition.

As is to be expected, some narratives occasionally allude to influences from written accounts. One source of information, particularly for stories recorded in the National

---

[1] Most stories noted in this chapter were recorded between 1937 and 1938.

Folklore Collection, was *A popular history of the insurrection of 1798* by Revd Patrick F. Kavanagh (first published as *The Wexford rebellion* in 1870), which also inspired the rewriting of traditional Mummers' rhymes to incorporate the pantheon of 1798 heroes set out in that volume (Beiner, 2006, p. 141). Kavanagh's book portrayed the rebellion as a Catholic insurrection, downplaying the role of the United Irishmen as a suspect and even corrupt secret society (Beiner, 2006, p. 251). In latter years printed sources have been superseded by online repositories such as Wikipedia. Songs and poems of the period were also a method of transmitting knowledge and awareness of the course of the rebellion to a wider audience. As a child in school, from the parish of the song composer P.J. McCall, our classes were taught 'Boolavogue' and 'Kelly the Boy from Killanne'. The songs and poems outlined in this chapter commemorate both the 1798 rebellion and the Fenian rising of 1867 (where the commitment of the rebels of 1798 was invoked). The language used in these songs and poems often indicates empathy for a particular 'side' on the part of the composer or informant.

SOURCES OF INFORMATION

The narratives used in this chapter come from a variety of sources, including stories contained in the National Folklore Collection (housed at UCD, and partially online); stories and songs recorded as part of a Co. Wexford folklore collection initiative (1996–8); and folklore collection projects undertaken by the Vinegar Hill Battlefield research team in Enniscorthy primary schools and with members of the public (2015–17). The main corpus of information comes from the manuscripts of the National Folklore Collection, which is collated in two collections – the Main Manuscript (IFC) and the Schools' Folklore (IFC S) collections.[2]

The Schools' Folklore Scheme was undertaken in 1937 by the Irish Folklore Commission, in collaboration with the Department of Education, and was an innovative scheme whereby school children collected and documented folklore and local history. The topics of research were broad and diverse, and included stories about historical individuals, historical traditions, events, songs and poems – from which many of these accounts are derived. The Main Manuscript Collection comprises detailed transcripts of interviews conducted by folklore collectors from the 1930s to the present. There is less information pertaining to the 1798 rebellion in Co. Wexford in this than in the Schools Collection – only 21 accounts, in comparison to 190.

The Schools initiative coincided with the 140th anniversary commemorations of the rebellion in Co. Wexford, so one could anticipate a significant body of material

---

[2] The references in this chapter use the terms IFC and IFC S. IFC refers to accounts from the National Folklore Collection Main Manuscript Collection and IFC S relates to the National Folklore Collection Schools' Collection. The volume number, and page numbers are then noted with information on the school, informant and collector (where recorded).

from this source. According to www.duchas.ie (an initiative to digitize the National Folklore Collection of Ireland), there are over eight hundred recorded accounts from the Schools' Folklore Scheme pertaining to the 1798 rebellion, with stories from each of the twenty-six counties in the Republic of Ireland. More accounts were collected in Wexford than in any other county.

The final sources of information for this chapter are derived from projects supported by Wexford County Council. The first, a folklore reminiscence project undertaken between 1996 and 1998, was tasked with recording a variety of folk traditions of Co. Wexford. The second corpus of material came from recordings of folk traditions of the 1798 rebellion in Enniscorthy and the surrounding areas, undertaken as part of this research project (2013–15). The latter comprised two elements – firstly, to assist pupils from schools in Enniscorthy (St Mary's National School, Parnell Road, and Meánscoil Gharman, Brownswood) to record stories of the 1798 rebellion in Enniscorthy and its environs. This was particularly symbolic, as the children of St Mary's National School had contributed to the Schools' Folklore Scheme of 1937, and this created a tangible link between 1937 and 2017. The research team also spoke with particular local landowners, held 'open days' inviting members of the public to contribute their stories, and used online and print media to invite contributions from around the world to further our knowledge. While the volume of information from these sources is smaller, it is invaluable in serving to confirm information recorded previously, or highlight the changing, and possibly dwindling, nature of storytelling and tradition preservation in Ireland.

THE BATTLES OF ENNISCORTHY AND VINEGAR HILL[3]

> During the insurrection in 1798 the town was the scene of many of the principal events then enacted … The town and castle were attacked and taken possession of by the insurgents, the high hill over-looking the town on the opposite side of the river, known as Vinegar Hill, being made their principal encampment, which they occupied until 21st June, on which date a combined attack by the troops under General Lake was made on the town and hill, both being taken, the insurgents retreating to Wexford. (IFC S 878: 54–5)

From accounts of battles recorded in the National Folklore Collection, we observe that many only detail the 'major' battles of the rebellion, such as New Ross, Enniscorthy or Arklow, essentially those that were either of great success or major defeat to the rebels.

---

[3] This chapter has preserved the spellings of words as recorded (particularly the use of yeo and yoe). Where the entry has a title, it is given in *italics* at the start of the narrative. Only accounts that make reference to Vinegar Hill, Enniscorthy, or its immediate environs are included.

There are accounts relating to both battles in Enniscorthy. The first, widely referred to as the 'Battle of Enniscorthy', took place on Monday, 28 May 1798, while the second battle, the 'Battle of Vinegar Hill', took place on Thursday, 21 June 1798. They had contrasting outcomes for the United Irishmen and crown forces.

Surprisingly, only one account of the Battle of Enniscorthy and five accounts of the Battle of Vinegar Hill are recorded in the Schools' Folklore Scheme, with only two from Enniscorthy schools. The reason for this is a puzzle. Was it because there were no stories of the battle? Surely that was not the case. Was it because the teacher had no interest in the rebellion? Not so, as there are a variety of accounts of the rebellion from schools in Enniscorthy, recorded from people living in the town. Possibly the teachers tried to gather as diverse a range of stories as possible, and show the breadth of narratives regarding the rebellion, and although minimal, they serve to re-inforce the historical record, highlight the language of recounting rebellion, and bring to mind the divisively stark nature of conflict.

The research team also gathered a previously unpublished story pertaining to the battle, recalled by the historian Brian Ó Cléirigh. While undertaking research on behalf of Comóradh '98 (the organizing committee for bicentenary commemorations in Wexford), Ó Cléirigh was informed by Mr Brian Jordan, a landowner at the foot of Vinegar Hill, of a tradition that a field on their land was used by General Lake as his command-post and as the location for his artillery. Mr Jordan heard this from his own father, who in turn had been told the story by the previous owners of the farm. Mr Jordan was able to bring the research team to the actual spot on his farm, which does indeed offer commanding views over the landscape. We know from the contemporary maps that General Lake was indeed in this area but these maps are frustratingly short on detail. To have his presence here preserved in the folk memory, and what is quite likely the actual location of his command post identified as well, shows the value of exploring the oral tradition.

The aftermath of the battle is recorded in two final accounts, one referring to the arrival of the rebel leader General Edward Roche with reinforcements of Shelmalier men from Wexford, who then engage General Francis Needham at Darby's Gap (later sometimes called 'Needham's Gap').

The only account of the Battle of Enniscorthy recalls its most legendary phase. This account, as with others, simplifies the battle as involving 'the Irish' with the inference being 'against' the British. This simplification is understandable, but of course we know in reality the situation was much more complex.

> Another great battle during the '98 insurrection was the attack on Enniscorthy. The town was well fortified, but the Irish saw a way of getting in. They went into a field where there were many bullocks. These they drove out on the road. They stuck their pikes in the bullocks making them run at a very quick pace.

> The bullocks fearing the pikes charged at the fortification, breaking it open. This enabled the Irish to pass through. (IFC S 893: 263)

In relation to the Battle of Vinegar Hill, a concise account notes that of the battles fought in Ireland long ago 'this one was the worst':

> A lot of battles were fought in Ireland long ago. Some of them were, the Battle of Benburb, the Battle of the Boyne, the Siege of Limerick and the Insurrection of seventeen and ninety eight. This one was the worst of them all. One of the battles was fought on Vinegar Hill. One bright, sunny morning when the people were all encamped on Vinegar Hill a shout from one of the guards was heard saying that the enemy was coming. Soon a fierce battle was in force and a lot of Yeomen were killed, but a lot of Rebels were killed also. The Rebel army was decreasing when one of the men came to Father Murphy, who was the leader of the Rebels, and told him it would be better to retreat. Father Murphy said it would be a good idea and they escaped through a gap known as Needham's gap. (IFC S 893: 264)

Nicholas Furlong (1991, p. 130) also notes that Fr John Murphy, along with Edward Fitzgerald and Anthony Perry, was charged with directing events on Vinegar Hill during the battle.

Another narrative, reminding us that the children of 1937 were a mere five generations removed from the events, gives an unsettling account of a child witness to the battle:

> My grandfather's great grandfather fought at many battles in '98 and especially at Vinegar Hill. During the battle of Vinegar Hill my great grandfather was very young and he and another crowd of young chaps gathered together and went to Beckett's Bog a place not far from Vinegar Hill to watch the fight and a few cowardly yeomen that escaped from the battle ran them across the bog shooting at them and when they were getting over the ditch Hatchels water Dog jumped up on my great grandfather's back to pull him back but while he was on his back one of the yeomen fired but hit the dog instead of the man. (IFC S 884: 44–5)

This must surely be an eyewitness account passed down from generation to generation through the oral tradition and reminds us that children were also witnesses and victims of this rebellion. Stories like this, which are so rare, add important detail to our overall knowledge of the battle.

A third account illustrates how the use of particular phrases and descriptions can simplify events to set one group against another (in this case 'English' against 'Irish').

This narrative also refers to the River Slaney running red with blood in the aftermath of the battle. This motif is recorded by Thompson (1949, p. 1238) as motif F1084.1 (deep streams of blood flow during battle), and is also found in descriptions for the battles of New Ross and Hacketstown.

The aftermath of the battle (IFC S 893: 264–5) is recorded in two final accounts. The first refers to the arrival of General Edward Roche and General Edward Fitzgerald with reinforcements of Shelmalier men from Wexford, who then engaged General Needham at Darby's Gap (later to be known as 'Needham's Gap'):

> They [General Roche, General Fitzgerald] were on their way to Enniscorthy, with 3000 men and had reached Ballymurn when news came that the insurgents had been defeated at Vinegar Hill. (IFC S 885: 197)

The second deals with the return home of a group of Wicklowmen, who were shot by a group of their 'own religion'. It is not clear, however, whether the men were shot by accident or intentionally.

> The Tinahely yeomen was commanded by one of the big Byrnes of Coolalug. They were called the 'True Blues', and Coates of Tankerley had another corps of yeomen. Byrnes were mostly Catholics. After the battle of Vinegar Hill the last stand of the rebels Coates & Byrne was returning home with their men. Coates came upon two brothers by the name of Laceys with a pike a piece in their hands, retreating from the fight too. 'Go home boys', says Coates, 'all is over. Yous need not be afraid to meet anyone for Byrne a man of your own religion is coming after me.' When Byrne came up he shot the two of them. (IFC S 909: 140)

LEADERS AND PARTICIPANTS

Fr John Murphy

Of the rebel leaders, only one is mentioned as being present at Vinegar Hill – Fr John Murphy. His involvement in the 1798 rebellion raised him from little-known curate to national hero. He is recalled as a man of his word, brave, fearless and loyal, undertaking his role as leader in a subtle but effective manner. The volume of material about him from the folk tradition is matched only by that for John Kelly of Killanne (Wexford) and Michael Dwyer (Wicklow). The first account gives details of the battles he participated in:

> On May 31st the rebel forces were divided into two sections the Southern army and the Northern Army. From that on Father John fought throughout the campaign with the Northern army, which fought at Tubberneering, Arklow,

Carnew, etc. At the battle of Vinegar Hill on June 21st he took a prominent part. (IFC S 901: 120)

Another account, from his own parish of Ferns, curiously uses phrases identical to the account above. These two accounts, from schools quite a distance from each other, and on opposite sides of Enniscorthy, must surely show the folk tradition being influenced by some as yet unknown written source:

> Father John Murphy, Leader of the Wexford Insurgents in '98 – On May 31st the rebel forces were divided into two sections, the Southern army and the Northern army. Father John fought with the Northern army at Tubberneering, Arklow, Carnew etc. He marched from Vinegar Hill to Carlow and when he was coming back to Ferns the yeomen took him and they whipped him and they hung him and then they burnt his body. When his sister Mrs Walsh of Effernogue heard of his death she went to Carlow and tradition says she took the ashes of his body and buried it at the back of the church here in Ferns. (IFC S 896: 41–2)

A third account, from Co. Carlow, mentions that he sustained a wound at the Battle of Vinegar Hill:

> We have it on the authority of General Cloney, that Father John's expedition from Wexford the previous day but was forced to remain behind between Wexford and Sleedagh as he was suffering from a wound received at the battle of Vinegar Hill that day. (IFC S: 904: 269–70)

We know from historical accounts that Fr Murphy did pass through Sleedagh, in southern Wexford, on his retreat from Vinegar Hill, prior to proceeding to Co. Carlow, but there is no mention of an injury sustained at Vinegar Hill.

John Kelly

Another 'famous' rebel leader was 'Kelly the Boy from Killanne'. Although not present at either battle in Enniscorthy, there is reference to his march through the town prior to the battles, recruiting men along the way.

> The hour came when John Kelly had a fine force of men under his command, fully armed with pikes, and as they marched from Killanne the numbers increased until Enniscorthy was reached. (IFC S 900: 136–7)

Generals Edward Roche and Edward Fitzgerald

Much has been written about Edward Roche and Edward Fitzgerald, prominent leaders of the United Irishmen in Wexford. However, they receive only scant mention in the folk tradition, which mentioned only where they were from and that General Roche arrived from Wexford to support the rebels on Vinegar Hill, but was too late for the battle. He and his Shelmalier men, however, did provide support to the retreating rebels, engaging General Needham at 'Darby's Gap':

> Local insurgents were led by General Roche, Garrylough and General Fitzgerald, New Park, who were relatives. Both generals fought at Oulart Hill, which is situated seven miles from Screen. (IFC S 885: 197)

General participants

The folk tradition is an invaluable source of information about those 'ordinary' men and women who participated in the rebellion in Co. Wexford. Stories of their involvement, which otherwise would have been lost to us, have been passed down from generation to generation. These accounts, though minimal, also give other information about the battles, including participants' routes, incidents along the way and return home (alive or dead). We note from the folk tradition that families or groups from particular areas also participated in the battles, with many being involved in more than one, and sometimes on opposing sides. One can only imagine how they must have felt before, during and after the battles. Did they regret their decision to participate and wish to return to their homes and families? Were they spurred on by initial victories, or determined to seek success after defeat? While we note the language and terminology used in these accounts, it is worth considering if this is language the participants themselves would have used. Did they describe smaller events in the rebellion as battles? Did they use the terms 'Irish' or 'British'? How would they have described the Battle of Vinegar Hill itself?

Thomas Canning

> There lived in Rathquile Adamstown Co. Wexford, a man named Thomas Canning. His house was on the top of Rathquille hill in a field, now occupied by Myles Noctor Rathquile Adamstown Co. Wexford. In the rebellion of '98 he left his home and family and went and joined the Irish forces on Vinegar Hill; and from that he marched to Ross. He fought bravely in all the battles around and he came home safe and lived to see his children and grand-children grow up. He died in the year 1848. (IFC S 902: 21)

John Cox

There are two accounts recorded of his participation in the rebellion. The first notes that, along with participating in the Battle of Vinegar Hill, he, and another man named Parle, also took part in the Battle of Horetown. He was a very accurate shot at that battle and wounded one of the officers of Sir John Moore. The informant says:

> I heard old people say that they heard that Parle said that he saw the buttons flying off the soldier's coats while Cox was firing. (IFC 54: 152–3)

The second account tells that:

> Johnny Cox was my grandfather's name. He was through all the rebellion of '98. He was in the battle of Vinegar Hill, and at Ross. And in the battle of Horetown he wounded one of the principal officers. He was a great shot. In the song 'The Boys of Wexford' 'a young man from our ranks, a cannon he let go …' it was he was supposed to have fired that cannon, 'and strapped it into Lord Mountjoy, a tyrant he laid low'. (IFC 107: 171)

An account from the local parish journal notes that Cox was only nineteen years old at the time. It says he also fought at the battle of Ross, where it is traditionally recorded he had three men continuously loading muskets for him. He returned to Duncormick after the rebellion, with his trusty gun, and lived until 1860. The author Richard Roche (1979, pp 12–13) notes that Cox is buried in the old graveyard above Duncormick village, where a stone marks his grave near the church door, and

> that his grandchildren, especially Mary and Clim remembered the old survivor of '98 and retold many times the stories of his deeds and daring.

Billy McDonald

> Billy McDonald went with the Dorans Glenglass to Vinegar Hill. Whyte thinks that only a few went from Killanne to this battle. They went by Ricks Bridge through Killougharam and Monart into Enniscorthy, the night before the battle. They rode three abreast. They travelled during the night. On their way Billy noticed his horse limped. In the morning he saw where a bullet skinned the fetlock joint. (IFC S 901: 2 & 5)

Stafford from Littlegraigue

> This man was the 1st South Wexford man to answer the call of Fr. Murphy in '98. He went to Boolavogue and fought through all the battles. He came home without a scratch after the war was over and lived to be a very old age. (IFC S 871: 22)

The Harpar Brothers

> My grandfather's name was Harpar and with his brother fought in the Rising of 1798. After the victory at Oulart the Rebel forces took Enniscorthy. The two brothers were in Pye Lane watching the yeos at the top. A man passed up and

they asked him not to pretend that there were only the two down the lane. A short time afterwards a shot rang out and one brother was killed and the other wounded. The Yeos stripped the latter thinking he was dead. He remained where he fell 'till darkness set in. Then he crawled to a neighbour's house, where he remained in bed unconscious for three weeks. When he recovered the fight was over. (IFC S 880: 433)

Pye Lane, now known as 'Spout Lane', is still in existence. It is a small lane, opposite St Aidan's Cathedral, and links Main Street and Fairview Terrace, which in turn leads to Parnell Road.

Joseph Warren Snr and Joseph Warren Jnr, Enniscorthy, Templeshannon.

Old Joe Warren and his son Joe, fought at Vinegar Hill and at Ross. They were fortunate in coming through without a wound. When they returned after the war they could find no trace of the family. The house was open, and the old faithful dog welcomed them and led them to where the family with many others, were hiding – in an old rath – 'The Killaggs'. (IFC S 871: 24)

Hugh Keegan, and his two brothers

Born Askahegh, Clonegal, a mason by trade; fought at the battles of Bunclody, New Ross, Vinegar Hill, and Ballyellis. Was known through Wexford as 'The six-foot man with the ten-foot pike'. Was captured after the battle of Ross, and confined in Duncannon fort. He escaped by jumping over the strong surrounding wall into the sea & swimming. The place is still known as 'Keegan's Leap'. Michael Keegan, Hugh's brother; pitchcapped by the infamous De Renzy, captain of the Yeomen in Clonegal area; in his agony jumped into the river Derry which runs through the village of Clonegal, and was shot by the brutal yeos. Another brother was hanged by De Renzy in the archway at Clonegal – still known as the 'Hanging archway'. (IFC S 911: 84)

Jasper O'Connor and Thomas Cullen

The account for Thomas Cullen is particularly interesting, as it refers to a specific location within Enniscorthy town for the death of a named individual. It notes that he died at the castle wall, but there is, unfortunately, no indication of the date or circumstances of his death.

Two Local Heroes who fought in the Rebellion
(1) Jasper O'Connor grand father to Marian O'Connor …
(2) Thomas Cullen Ballyvaldon killed at the 'Castle wall' Enniscorthy

> Jaspar O'Connor was 70 years of age at the Rebellion. He came home in tatters riding a white pony and 'jumped the pig house' to show I suppose he was not downhearted. He died 13 years later and his grave is in Ballyvaldon graveyard. Thomas Cullen was brought home by his brother 'on a horse'. (IFC S 886: 122–3)

The account for Thomas Cullen goes on to record the inscription on his gravestone (see appendix 15).

'Babes in the Wood'

The name 'Babes in the Wood' is one that has survived in the folk memory to the present day. It refers to the group of rebels who held out in the woods to the west of Enniscorthy for some time after the rebellion had ended.

> After the battle of Vinegar Hill (June 21st '98) the Insurgents proceeded to Wexford. On the following day Fr John Murphy led the largest section of the Insurgents into counties Carlow and Kilkenny. These returned defeated through Scollagh Gap on June 26. Some of them went to Killoughram Wood where they held out for months. The wood at the time stretched over several sq. mls. [square miles]. These men were called 'The Babes' in the wood. The British forces used every endeavour to exterminate them and as a last resort were compelled to fire sections of the wood. (IFC S 893: 35)

Also:

> The Rebels in Killoughrim Forest – My grandad told my mum that the rebels hid in Killoughrim forest. My mum's family lived in Killoughrim house right beside the forest. The house had lead lined shutters to protect it from bullets. It also has an escape tunnel leading from the cellar to the forest. The rebels in the forest numbered around three hundred. They were known as the 'Babes in the Woods'. Fr Murphy hid with them after the battle of Vinegar Hill. (LDRP, Gethings)

Families from the Kilmuckridge area

A final account recalls some of the families from the Kilmuckridge area who participated in the Battle of Enniscorthy:

> The O'Briens of Tinnaberna, the O'Connors of Ballinamona, and Raymond FitzSimms of Christnastow all fought at Oulart Hill & Enniscorthy. (IFC S 887: 53)

Members of the crown forces

Members of the crown forces, particularly officers of rank, are generally only mentioned as participants in folklore accounts. Three, however, garner particular reference – General Francis Needham, a yeoman named Reynolds and an officer named Hunter Gowan. Needham is recalled in the place-name 'Needham's Gap' (see also under 'Landmarks, features and place-names'), and Gowan, while not at Vinegar Hill, is mentioned in great detail in the folk tradition as being particularly brutal. He is recalled in the story of an engagement between his ghost and a local man (see also under 'Ghostly encounters', below). A number of accounts tell the story of the yeoman Reynolds, who died on Vinegar Hill and was buried on or near his home in Monart (see 'Final Resting Places', below).

THE ROLE OF THE BLACKSMITH

The folk tradition is invaluable in recalling the work of the most significant contributor to the arming of the rebels – the blacksmith. It was he who manufactured pikes, whose forges were inspected for evidence of weapons production and who was often pitchcapped to reveal his knowledge of the rebellion. There are only two accounts of blacksmiths relating to Enniscorthy or Vinegar Hill, one where there is active participation in the battle and the other about a blacksmith from Co. Wicklow who makes his way to Enniscorthy and joins the rebels.

The first account tells the story of a blacksmith and his two sons who went with their pikes to participate in the Battle of Vinegar Hill. The second son had a very dramatic experience en route:

> Long ago a man who had three sons lived at Wexford. At this time there was a fight at Vinegar Hill. The Irish were fighting against the English. The smith used to make pikes for the Irish. One day the smith and one of his sons made two pikes and went to the hill to fight. When they were gone the other son got another pike and followed them. When he was half way up he saw soldiers coming after him. He thought they were Irish soldiers and waited for them. The officer told him to go in the field until he would see was he able to fight, and he told one of his own soldiers to go and fight him. The two of them went in. The son stuck his pike in the soldier's coat and pulled him off his horse but the officer told him to spare the soldier's life and he did. (IFC S 647: 273)

The second account, recalled by Rory Murphy (Sidney, 1997, cassette recording), tells of a blacksmith named James Connors from Co. Wicklow, who, when released on bail, fled to Enniscorthy and joined the insurgents there. He observed that Connor's grand-nephew, Isaac Brennan, aged 85, was still living in Bunclody in 1997, and that the binding stone from Connors' forge forms a centrepiece in the garden in Market Square there. Interestingly, this story is recorded in greater detail by Kavanagh, who notes that Connors escaped not once but twice, including this second occasion, when he broke the conditions of his bail by joining the rebel army (1918, pp 310–11). It is unknown whether Murphy was told this story by Brennan himself, or was aware of it from Kavanagh, but if it was the latter, it would illustrate how written accounts can influence the oral tradition. About Connors' escape, Kavanagh recalls:

> He was informed on by a neighbour of his own for making pikes, was arrested, with thirty-nine other young men of the district, and lodged in the darkest and most noisome cellar of the castle of Carnew …
>
> Mr Blaney, Umeragar, gave £200 bail for Connors to let him out for one hour to see his wife, who was ill. When he got him outside the gate, he told him not to go home but to try to escape, that he was going to be shot in an hour. He started for Enniscorthy, hotly pursued by a parcel of the yeos.
>
> He took to the river after crossing the bridge, and baffled his pursuers in Ballinahallin wood, got into Enniscorthy, joined the Insurgent army, fought through most of the campaign, returned home when all was over, and lived for many a year in his old home at Tombrane.

WOMEN OF THE REBELLION

The contribution of 'everyday' women to the events of the rebellion finds unparalleled recognition in the oral tradition. This is a crucial source of information as to how Enniscorthy and its environs continued to function during the rebellion, as these women kept the homes and farms operational, travelled through dangerous territory to feed or collect the bodies of loved ones, and were sometimes forced to take a life if it meant the preservation of their own. It also illustrates the reality that women could not afford to adopt a passive role in these events. Many accounts of this nature are recorded in the folk traditions of Co. Wexford, but only four make specific reference to Enniscorthy or Vinegar Hill (Sidney, 1999).

The first account tells the story of Mr Carty's wife, who forgot to give a secret sign to her husband that the crown forces were in their house. This story, frequently recorded in the folk tradition, also illustrates how many people, particularly men, had to resort to living away from home during this time:

> In the year 1798 Mr Carty lived in a house near Enniscorthy. In the night himself and his wife used to be afraid to stop at home for fear of the English soldiers. They used to go out in the deep trenches at night time and stay there until the morning. If the English soldiers went in the house the woman would put a

brush in the window to show her husband that the soldiers were there. One day she forgot to put the brush in the window and the man came in and the soldiers killed him. (IFC S 880: 95–6)

A second account relates to a couple who fought at Vinegar Hill. It too is particularly interesting as it recalls how they fought in two of the most intense battles of the rebellion, while leaving their children in the care of a relative at home. One wonders what motivated both parents to participate in the rebellion? Perhaps this was a more regular occurance than we think?

> James Cadogan and his wife Nellie. Both fought at Ross and Vinegar Hill. When James went to the fight his wife followed him with a pike and fought side by side with him. She often loaded his gun for him while he used the pike. She was a strong brave woman and it was reported she killed a Hessian near Old Ross on her way to Vinegar Hill. They left their children in charge of the grandmother while away at the war. They both survived and lived to be a fine old age. (IFC S 871: 25)

Madge Dixon

One woman, mentioned at great length in the folk tradition, is Madge Dixon. She appears also in the historical literature and is fascinating because of how she is represented so differently in each tradition. The historical tradition has her at the side of her husband Thomas Dixon during his involvement in the rebellion. These accounts are emphatic in their descriptions of Thomas as brutal in his treatment of loyalist prisoners and how he incited fear, hatred and vengefulness among his followers. Taylor (1800, p. 206) goes so far as to suggest 'his wife, if possible, was more sanguinary than himself'.

In stark contrast, the folk tradition portrays Madge as the most renowned Wexford woman of 1798, depicted in an heroic light, with more recorded accounts of her than any other woman. Some of these accounts bear similarities to those told of the famous Wicklow rebel Michael Dwyer, as both seem to have possessed the ability to disguise and conceal themselves when the need arose. She is also the woman spoken of in the song 'The boys of Wexford':

> In comes the captain's daughter, the captain of the yeos,
> Saying, 'Brave United man, we'll ne 'er again be foes,
> A thousand pounds I'll give you, and fly from home with thee,
> And dress myself in man's attire, and fight for libertie!' (IFC 107: 171)

The folk tradition, along with this song, recount the fact that she grew up in a yeoman household, but rejected her father's allegiances and fought, with her husband, for the rebels.

There is but passing reference to Madge at Vinegar Hill, but in their entirety the accounts are extremely insightful and illustrate the deeply conflicted depictions of her between the oral and historical traditions. These contradictory stories and accounts reflect the opinions of different authors and different perspectives. The positive depiction in the oral tradition could be a counter-balance to the actions of her husband, Thomas, who was responsible for atrocities in Wexford, prior to and after the Battle of Vinegar Hill, or a romanticized view of a woman who rejects her family and joins a band of rebels to fight for a noble cause. Stories also show paralells to Gráinne Mhaol (Grace O'Malley) or Betsy Gray (Co. Antrim in 1798), similar folk heroines who lead men into battle. Or do historical accounts depict a cruel and brutal woman seeking revenge for acts committed against her by a 'redcoat'?

The first account, written by a child in Castlebridge, where her family came from, recalls her participation in the Battle of Vinegar Hill, noting her rank as general:

> This General Madge Dixon fought side by side with her husband at the battle of Vinegar Hill. When the Rising was over and the Rebels disappeared, she was in hiding in a place called Light Water below Wexford and her baby was born there … She reached France where her husband Captain Thomas Dixon was both went to New York, where they are both buried. (IFC S 884: 47–9)

Interestingly, this account records that her baby was born while she was waiting to flee Wexford. This is of particular interest, as it refers to the point also made by local historian Nicky Furlong (1996), that she was with child during the rebellion:

> Thomas Dixon, sea captain, master, merchant in a dominant position in the grain port of Castlebridge in Wexford harbour, was married to Margaret Roche, a sister of General Edward Roche. The Roches, a highly respected family, had been evicted and their lands granted to a Cromwellian officer, Le Hunte. In the period of the 1798 outbreak, Margaret Dixon, Thomas Dixon's wife, recorded as a very handsome woman, was raped by a redcoat …

A second account, also from Castlebridge, again references Vinegar Hill, but mentions their burial in a different country:

> She was married to Captain Thomas Dixon and fought side by side with him at Vinegar Hill. Some time after the Rebellion they both sailed to Rome where they are buried. (IFC S 884: 59)

Daniel Gahan (1995, p. 256) also refers to their final resting place, citing 'popular legend':

Ironically, Captain Thomas Dixon's whereabouts was completely unknown. Popular legend would later have it that he made his escape to America and lived there peacefully for the rest of his life. Thus the one southern rebel 'leader' who deserved severe punishment had vanished without a trace.

Madge is one of only a handful of women mentioned as actively participating in the Battle of Vinegar Hill. Some of these accounts are given further plausability as they are recorded by people from her area, and the sources of some of these stories can be traced back to those who also fought at Vinegar Hill, e.g. 'My grandfather's great grandfather fought at many battles in '98 and especially at Vinegar Hill' (IFC 884: 44).

LANDMARKS, FEATURES AND PLACE-NAMES

Accounts of place-names, landmarks and features, preserved to this day in the oral tradition provide an invaluable insight into the course of events of the rebellion. There are six landmarks recorded to date in the oral tradition of this period in Enniscorthy or the surrounding areas, namely 'the Bloody Bridge', 'Babes' Glen', 'the Barley Field', 'the Cannon Bank', 'Needham's Gap', and 'the Soldier's Hole'. Interestingly 'the Soldier's Hole' is recorded at two different locations, one on Vinegar Hill itself, and the second near Edermine, to the south of the town. Some of the longer records from the folklore collections can be found at appendix 15.

'The Bloody Bridge'
The most recorded place-name in Enniscorthy related to the rebellion is 'the Bloody Bridge', with six accounts. Located on Milehouse Road, to the west of the town, the stone bridge was removed in the 1970s. It was said that handprints were to be seen on a particular stone, but the location of that stone is now unknown.[4] Some accounts claim the location got its name from the ambush of a priest on his way to attend a hoax sick call. Another account suggests the priest was killed by the bullet of a renegade Catholic, after successfully stopping bullets from other yeomen (another internationally recognized motif[5]), while others make no mention of clerical involvement. A further account recalls a similar version of the story, save the method of inflicting the fatal blow. The story also continues with the additional appearance of a ghostly white horse, and manifestations of hoofprints and blood flowing when it rains (IFC S 894: 70). The appearance of a white horse is also prevalent in the mythological and Christian traditions from earliest times, used for their exceptional abilities and intuition, or for carrying the hero figure into triumph over a negative force.

[4] Information by Seamus Corrigan, Ross Road, Enniscorthy, 4 Jan. 2018. [5] Motif G229.4.2 (catches bullets and sends them back) from Stith Thompson Motif Index.

Two of the accounts name the priest as 'Father Redmond'. There were four clergymen with this surname officiating in Co. Wexford in 1798: Fr Edward Redmond, Ferns; Fr John Redmond, Ballyoughter; Fr Michael Redmond, Castlebridge; and Fr Nicholas Redmond from Ballygarrett. From the historical record, we know that none are a match for this story. There is, however, reference to a Fr Patrick Cogley, parish priest of Monageer in 1798 (north-east of Enniscorthy). According to Whelan (1997, pp 166–7):

> He took no part whatsover in the rebellion but in October 1799, he was accosted while going on a sick call and beaten over the head with a large stone by two local Protestants, whom he knew well but was afraid to prosecute. Subsequently, he was forced to flee to Wexford town, when various plots were formed against him. Only on application to the magistrates in Enniscorthy, and on restoration of his gun in December 1799, did he return to his parochial duties.

Could this Fr Cogley be our priest at the Bloody Bridge?

'Babes' Glen'
There is an account of treasure buried prior to the rebellion at a place called the 'Babes Glen', so called after the rebels who remained at large after the rising was suppressed, in Killoughrim wood. As in other narratives, the depositor kills another, who then has responsibility for guarding the treasure. Following the well-known format, people attempt to recover the treasure, only to be chased by an otherworld entity, and for there to be repercussions to their actions.

'The Barley Field'
In an unpublished interview with Raymond Quirke in 2018 as part of this research project:

> The Barley field got its name from the 1798 battle. It is the closest flat piece of land on the town side of the hill. Legend has it that many were buried here after the battle and barley grew from the seeds in the pockets of the dead. Fr Cullen Terrace and The Barley Field are built on the field now. Padraig Pearse gave a speech in the Barley Field just before the 1916 rising. The stone he stood on was in the rear garden of No. 17 Fr Cullen Terrace. I don't know if any bodies were found in the 1950s when Fr Cullens was built. The Barley Field name is well known to all in the area. It was beside the Nun's field and Mickey's field, and originally connected to Vinegar Hill Lane. There was a playground built in the Barley field in the 1970s, but it was allowed to fall into disuse, so the houses were built there in the mid-1980s. Nothing was found when these Barley Field houses were built.

The connection with Seamus Heaney's famous 'Requiem for the croppies' is evident.

'The Cannon Banks'

This feature, a semi-circular spur within a stone-faced ditch, is located on a ditch leading from the middle gate lodge of Solomon Richards' estate, and is quite a conundrum. There is a wooden marker to the feature, saying '1798 Cannon Bank', and the suggestion is that cannonballs were fired from here at Vinegar Hill – which is quite impossible given the distance to the hill (some 3.5km as the crow flies). Could it be a defensive feature thrown up while the crown forces were camped at arms there over the previous days? Possibly, but we remain unsure of its exact purpose. Mary Hendrick, whose family presently live at Solsborough, offered the following information in 2018 as part of this research project:

> The Cannon Bank is on our family farm. Colonel Lake and his men were based here during the 1798 rebellion. The cannon bank is a mound and was used to fire on Vinegar Hill. It has a good view of Vinegar Hill. All soldiers camped on the front lawn. The Richards family owned Solsborough at the time. Their ancestor Colonel Richards was given the property after Cromwell's conquest. He was the Governor of Wexford, and was a prominent member of the British Army. He is buried in Westminster Abbey. The cannons used there in 1798 are to be found in Newfoundland.

'Needham's Gap'

This location is where General Francis Needham was intercepted by the rebels coming from Wexford to re-inforce those retreating from Vinegar Hill. The place is still known by that name today, and even has a commemorative stone at the crossroads. The place is referred to on maps of the period as Darby's Gap, but is still widely known as 'Needham's Gap' or 'Gap Cross'.

'The Soldier's Hole'

Two stories, recorded from different schools, tell of a box of gold hidden or treasure being hidden in the same place, located in the River Boro to the south-west of Enniscorthy. Curiously, one account suggests the gold belonged to a member of the crown forces, and the other, to a rebel. There are also a number of international motifs contained in these stories, including B576.2 (animals guard treasure), D449.2 (corpse transformed to serpent), E291 (ghosts protect treasure), N511.1 (buried treasure) and G354.1.1 (serpent demon guards treasure). Both accounts can be read in appendix 15. Two further accounts, both from the Presentation Convent school, refer to a similar site, but either do not specifically refer to 1798, or only refer to soldiers being thrown into the hole. It is, however, most likely that these are two further accounts relating to this site.

It is interesting to note the existence of a townland in this locality named Dunanore or Dún an Óir (the fort of the gold). O'Crualaoich and Mac Giolla Chomhghaill (2016, pp 844–5) document that this location has over time been referred to as

Dononore, Dunanore or Donnemoire – derivatives of an Dún Mór (the Big Fort). The name Dún an Óir is first recorded in 1840, which poses a tantalizing question as to whether a story of treasure buried during the 1798 rebellion could have been transposed to another location, resulting in a subtle alteration to the pronunciation of a place-name, and a significant alternation to its meaning.

There is, however, a second location called the 'Soldier's Hole', which is recorded as such to the present day on Vinegar Hill. Locals identify a quarried-out area beneath the summit of the hill (on the car-park side) as the location of this feature. There is no specific reference to it being rebellion-related, but it is possible that this place-name recalls a mass grave on the hill – one possible mass grave was discovered by the research team in an adjoining field and the tradition may have transferred to this obvious depression nearby.

Other locations
A number of other locations appear in the folklore tradition in connection with the battles of Enniscorthy and Vinegar Hill. These include Enniscorthy Castle, Daphne Castle, Ballinahallen Wood, the Scollough Gap and Riverchapel.

Enniscorthy Castle
The folk narrative recalls the use of Enniscorthy Castle as a prison during the rebellion:

> When the Irish were being cruelly persecuted by the English soldiers the castle of Enniscorthy was used as a prison by the English. (IFC S 894: 27)

This account is confirmed in the historical tradition, where Jane Barber, in her first-hand account of the rebellion in the town, notes that in advance of the battle of Enniscorthy:

> a guard of yeomen was placed over the Market House, where there was a great store of arms and ammunition, and where a few prisoners were confined; some more mounted guard over the castle, where some dangerous rebels were lodged … (Beatty, 2001, p. 76)

Also, O'Kelly (1842, p. 122) notes:

> The numbers of the insurgents were so overwhelming, that the military became alarmed, and at length overpowered. It was proposed to Captain Snowe, to put the prisoners in the castle to death; this sanguinary advice would not be listened to by that officer; and this so exasperated the Orange yeomen, that they undertook of themselves to carry their threat into execution; they proceeded to perform their bloody intentions, but providentially for the prisoners, the door

or entrance could not be burst open, and no key was to be had, in consequence of the gaoler having, in the general alarm, set out with others who were flying, for Wexford.

Daphne Castle[6]

There is a castle near my home. It is surrounded by trees and the Urrin river flows past it. It was burnt after the rebellion of 1798 but the people were not burnt. (IFC S 893: 206–7)

Ballinahallen Wood

Many of the '98 insurgents camped in the woods and caves for safety. One of their principal hiding places was Ballinahallen Wood. It is situated about two miles from Enniscorthy, and three from Ferns. (IFC S 894: 16)

Scollough Gap

This Scollough Gap, pronounced locally 'Scullock Gap' is situated about three miles in a south-easterly direction from Rathanna School, and divides that section of the Blackstairs mountains, known as the Mount Leinster range from the Blackstairs Mountains proper. It is also on the boundary line between Co. Carlow and Co. Wexford. The Insurgent army arrived in Scollough Gap on the evening of the 22nd June, the day following the battle of Vinegar Hill in which all of them had taken part. They had on this day marched from Sleedagh in the Barony of Bargy, a distance of 45 miles, passing through Killane, the birthplace of 'dauntless Kelly'. (IFC S 904: 265)

Riverchapel

Next we come to Riverchapel which means the 'church on the river'. This was burned in '98. Many Irishmen took shelter in the ruins of the old church when they were flying in haste from Vinegar Hill and Oulart. (IFC S 888: 16)

FINAL RESTING PLACES

The folk tradition also recalls the final resting places of an unknown number of those who died in the battles of Vinegar Hill or Enniscorthy. These include St Senan's graveyard in Enniscorthy town, the Corrig graveyard to the south-south-west of the town and Reynold's grave to the west.

---

6 Home of Lieutenant Joshua Pounden of the Enniscorthy yeoman infantry (brother of Captain John Pounden), situated to the west of Enniscorthy.

12.1 View of Vinegar Hill from Corrig graveyard. Photo by Jacqui Hynes.

St Senan's Graveyard

> The oldest graveyard is that of St Senan. This one is situated in Templeshannon. In it stands the ruin of Saint Senan's Church. There are three burying places inside the walls of the ruin. Around it are the graves of hundreds of Enniscorthy folk. Among them are the graves of soldiers who fought in 1798. A pattern is held in this graveyard every year. (IFC S 893: 214)

The Corrig/Carrig Graveyard

> The Corrig Graveyard is a notable spot in Enniscorthy. The road leading to this graveyard is known as St John's Road … The greatest man that is laid to rest in it is Henry Hatton. On the tombstone is the following inscription 'Here lieth the body of Henry Hatton who was basely murdered by the rebels in 1798 on Vinegar Hill merchant of Enniscorthy.' (IFC S 893: 216)

Also:

> The Corrig graveyard is important because of the graves of the men of 1798 and of other soldiers and men who took part in battles for the freedom of Ireland. In this graveyard a patron is held each year … (IFC S 293: 217)

A third account, which uses the Gaelic version of the place-name (*carraig* meaning rock), is also recorded, and both names are to the present day used and recognized.

> The Carraig: About one and three quarter miles outside Enniscorthy on the right hand side of the Ringwood this old grave yard is situated. All its space is now filled … In the middle of the grave yard a tomb-stone lies flat on the ground in memory of someone who was killed on Vinegar Hill during the 1798 rebellion. (IFC S 893: 178–9)

Monart – Reynells/Rennells/Reynolds grave

There are many accounts (see appendix 15 for full records) pertaining to a man named 'Reynolds', who was either a yeoman officer or joined the yeomanry on the morning of the Battle of Vinegar Hill. What is agreed is that he died on Vinegar Hill, and was buried on his land, or neighbouring land. The most verifiable account refers to him being buried inside a ditch, a few yards from the road, with a tombstone. Another account gives the name as 'Reynold Grannells' and says that a rough stone monument was raised near his grave. There is an onomastical curiosity about the name in this case: Grannell, predominantly a Wexford surname, is derived from MacRaghnaill (the son of Reginald) and is anglicized to Reynolds. This rough stone monument mentioned is untraceable at present but apparently carried the inscription:

> Reynold Grannells
> Shot and piked on Vinegar Hill
> Dead and buried and alive still

Another, similar account, giving the name as 'John Reynolds', says that a bright light was often to be seen at the grave at night, while one couple passing by even saw the ghostly apparition of a pike rising above the ditch! A final account, also naming the man as Reynolds, claims his wife went to reclaim his body, something not unheard of in the folk tradition, but also a particularly dangerous venture.

A man called Reynolds was indeed killed on Vinegar Hill, according to the witness statement of Mary Hall, at the trial of Nicholas Walsh, dated 24 April 1800 (Sweetman, 2013, p. 537):

12.2 Tomb of Stephen William Reynells. Photo by Jacqui Hynes.

> My husband was kept in that guard house, where I saw him repeatedly, every day, till the 11th of June. On the morning of that day, the prisoner came to the guard house in Enniscorthy, where I was then. He asked what reason the prisoners in the guard house were not killed and said if they were not put to death before the next day he would kill the guard themselves. He seemed to have the full command. That evening the prisoners (amongst whom, was my husband) to the amount of 24 (I think) were brought up to Mr Bail's Barn, which lies under Vinegar Hill and was used as a prison. The next day, Mr Hunt, Mr Reynolds, Mr Robinson, one, Simson, a weaver and another man were taken out of the Barn and murdered.

As it happens, in the townland of Monart East, there is a tomb with the inscription:

> Reynells. Here lyeth the body of Stephen William Reynells aged 48, who was inhumanely murdered by the rebels on Vinegar Hill, June the 12th 1798

This tomb is also noted by Cantwell (1992, pp 50–1) citing Dickson (1955). Dickson, spelling the surname 'Reynolds', notes that he was the brother-in-law of Matthew Keogh (governor of Wexford) and his body was brought home by his widow and buried at Monart in the corner of a field beside the road. Cantwell notes that his widow, Catherine, died in 1833 at the age of 91. She was buried in St John's, Corrig. This must surely be the 'Mr Reynolds' who Mary Hall testified had been murdered. The name, location and date correspond. However, is this also the Reynolds or Reynold Grannells from the folk tradition? That is more difficult to say, and certainly in this case the inscription recalled in the folk tradition does not match the inscription on the tomb ascribed to Stephen Reynells.

Enniscorthy: location unidentified
This story tells of a man from Wexford town who was buried in Enniscorthy during the rebellion. His story undoubtedly mirrors others, in that their final burial place is either away from their locality or unknown. It also reminds us of the immense risks involved in seeking out the remains of loved ones to ensure their burial in a more appropriate location.

> A man named Richard Kyan who was living in Selskar (Wexford) was being pursued by some English soldiers in '98. The soldiers had wounded him and he was going to a place where twenty Rebels were hiding. He arrived there exhausted and gasped out the warning. The men escaped but he refused to go with them. He remained behind to cover up their tracks. He kept the Yeos under fire for ten minutes with an old gun. After ten minutes he was captured and shot. When the English had gone some Irish women buried his body in Enniscorthy. (IFC S 880: 424)

Kilcashel, Co. Wicklow
A final account recalls three members of one family buried in Kilcashel graveyard, Annacurra, Co. Wicklow.

> There are many 1798 stones. One large tombstone contains the names of three Kirwans – one hanged in 1798 on Vinegar Hill, another shot as a rebel, and a third deported and died in France … (IFC S 888: 185)

It is interesting that this narrative states that one was hanged on Vinegar Hill. There are few accounts, if any, of rebels being hanged on Vinegar Hill. The fate of the final brother also reflects the reality for many rebels – that of deportation. It is certain that France was not his initial destination for deportation, but he obviously joined other rebels who made their way to France over time.

GHOSTLY ENCOUNTERS

There are two accounts from the folk tradition of encounters between the living and dead. The first paints a vivid and illustrative picture of an epic contest between 'Jack the Cooper' and the ghost of Hunter Gowan (IFC S 891: 21–3). Gowan, a local magistrate, and captain of the notorious yeoman cavalry group 'the Black Mob', lived at Mount Nebo (near Craanford, north Wexford), and is recorded as having committed some of the worst atrocities of this time. According to Turner (2017), he survived the rebellion and died in 1824 at the age of 97.

There are many stories of Gowan and his mob in the folk tradition. This story, preserved in the Schools Folklore Scheme, must have been fully recorded by an adult, given its comprehensive description. It also includes a number of mythological images, including those of a red-eyed animal spitting fire; using holy water to invoke protection against supernatural beings; issuing a challenge and invoking the support of dead heroes and ancestors; reference to Old Nick (the Devil), and the disappearance of both horse and rider in a ball of flame. The full account is in appendix 15.

ARTEFACTS AND SIGNS OF BATTLE

Accounts of artefacts or signs of battle are an important aspect in facilitating our understanding of the progression of the battles, and these accounts, although minimal, supplement our archaeological knowledge. Our research team undertook public information sessions during 2016 and 2017, and received information about musket balls in the garden of a house in Templeshannon, cannonballs found during the construction of a house in the Rectory Heights area during the 1960s and cannonballs located in the area between Milehouse Road and The Still. The Schools Folklore Scheme also refers to a number of artefacts dispersed around the town:

> The yoes ammunition were muskets and guns and one of those muskets is still to be seen at Nick Rossiters Ardcavan his great grand-father captured it at the battle of Vinegar Hill. (IFC 884: 46)

A further account mentions a drinking trough used by the 'Babes in the Wood' at Killaughrim:

> The Babe's trough. Up to 40 years ago a large granite stone shaped like a trough was to be seen in this wood. It was finally broken up and the stones used in building a cottage nearby. It was used for holding water for those Insurgents who took shelter in the wood after '98. Locally it is believed also that the Wicklowmen who came into Wexford hid in this wood. (IFC S 893: 35)

Three accounts from the Presentation Convent School, Enniscorthy, are very interesting for the fact that they appear to refer to the same location for the mark of a cannon ball. From the description of a ringwood, chapel and graveyard, we can hypothesize that they are talking about a house in the vicinity of The Carraig graveyard. However, given its distance from Vinegar Hill, it is unlikely that the cannonball came from there. The final account also talks about a family from the Milehouse area having a cannon ball, which is possible, as we know that cannon balls were found in that area:

> He chose a house for himself by the bank of the Slaney. Four or five steps lead up to this house. In one of these steps is a round hole made by a cannon ball fired by the Rebels from Vinegar Hill. This house is encircled by a wood called Ringwood in which there was a little chapel with a graveyard attached. (IFC S 894: 67–8)

Also:

> There is a round hole, the mark of a cannon ball, in the steps of Kavanagh's House. It is said that during the battle of '98 a cannon ball was shot from Vinegar Hill and flew across the Slaney through the steps. The hole is still to be seen. (IFC S 894: 26)

Finally:

> We have a cannon ball at home which was fired from Vinegar Hill in 1798. It was found in a field not far from our house. (IFC S 894: 12)

SONGS AND POEMS

The songs and poems composed about the 1798 rebellion provide a valuable insight into the course of events during that time. From the collections of the Irish Folklore Commission, twenty-four songs or poems have so far come to light, of which only four have particular reference to the rebellion in Enniscorthy or Vinegar Hill. A further poem is also an attempt to fuel nationalist feeling, and calls on a Fr Dwyer and the Fenians to band together and avenge the fallen rebels of 1798. Only the verses of songs and poems with references to Vinegar Hill or Enniscorthy have been reproduced here. There are of course many more written about this period.

According to Munnelly (1988, pp 160–71) the second half of the nineteenth-century was 'poetically a romantic age in Ireland' when patriotism combined with romanticism led to the composition of many songs and recitations about the '98 period. The 1840s saw the birth of the Young Ireland movement, and romantic nationalists were acutely aware of the power of song in conveying their message to all levels of public opinion.

This was also the period of the 140th and 150th celebrations, which were focal points for groups to recall events, sing old patriotic songs and compose new ones.

The 1860s saw the Fenian rising and a national revival of Gaelic literature and culture, while the centenary celebrations of 1898 provided further opportunities for the composition of songs remembering the events of the rebellion. This was also the time P.J. McCall composed his famous songs of the rebellion, 'Boolavogue' and 'Kelly the Boy from Killanne'. Popular topics for songs and poems included the struggle between the 'heroic' croppy and 'despised' yeoman, the valiant fight for freedom, or laments for those who died or lost opportunities for victory.

'Boolavogue'
No account of the Battle of Vinegar Hill is complete without reference to the most famous song of the rebellion in Wexford. 'Boolavogue' charts the course of the battles in Wexford, and culminates with a rousing final verse. It is well known, particularly the first and last verses, and to this day is played and sung at all commemorative events and many sporting events. It is surely the anthem of the Wexford rebellion:

> At Vinegar Hill, o'er the pleasant Slaney,
> Our heroes vainly stood back to back.
> And the yeos at Tullow took Father Murphy
> And burned his body upon the rack.
> God grant you glory, brave Father Murphy,
> And open Heaven to all your men.
> For the cause that called you may call tomorrow
> In another fight for the green again.

'The boys of Wexford'
A further 'famous' song of the rebellion is 'The boys of Wexford', composed by Robert Dwyer Joyce. Performed when President John F. Kennedy visited New Ross in June 1963, it has been sung by Irish traditional groups including the Clancy Brothers and the Wolfe Tones. James Joyce even mentions 'The boys of Wexford' in his novel *Ulysses* (1922, p. 230) and it also appears in Flann O'Brien's comic novel *An béal bocht*. As mentioned already, this is also the song that appears to mention Madge Dixon, and could be considered the 'anthem' of the Wexford GAA teams, who traditionally visit Vinegar Hill before significant matches. Liam Dunne (2017), a member of the 1996 All-Ireland-winning Wexford hurling team, recalls how Liam Griffin, the manager, 'brought us back down the centuries to Vinegar Hill':

> The passionate way he spoke about Wexford brought tears to our eyes. It got worse when he spoke about our families and neighbours and ancestors and all the battles they'd had to fight over the years. And the fact they had risen, almost

alone, in 1798 to give their blood in the cause of freedom. As [Martin] Storey [captain of the team] remembers it, the players had no indication of what Griffin was planning to do that day. There were even suspicions that the bus was broken down when they initially pulled in. As the players returned to the bus filled with emotion, the captain felt the significance of Griffin's message sinking in. When we were getting back in on the bus, you realized that this was a big thing. It's not going back up again and coming back again.

From the folk tradition we note the following account, which recalls an interesting alteration to a verse of this song:

> There is a difference in that widely known ballad 'The boys of Wexford' – when the song was composed first this is how one of the verses went:
>
> We bravely fought and conquered at Ross and Wexford town,
> But if we fell at Vinegar Hill 'twas drink that brought us down
>
> As time went on this was changed and now notes:
>
> We bravely fought and conquered at Ross and Wexford town,
> Three Bullet Gate for years to come will tell of our renown. (IFC 437: 196–7)

What is unusual about this account is that there seems to be no other obvious mention from other sources (historical, literary or oral) of rebels being drunk on Vinegar Hill. This is in contrast to the Battle of New Ross, where intoxication certainly contributed to the rebel loss.

A second account of the same song, recorded in its entirety, also refers to Vinegar Hill, but without attributing the loss in any way to alcohol. However, its wider impact across the rebellion is noted:

> My curse upon all drinking! It made our hearts full sore;
> For bravery won each battle, but drink lost ever more;
> And if, for want of leaders, we lost at Vinegar Hill,
> We're ready for another fight, and love our country still! (IFC 107 :171)

'I had a dream the other day'

This poem, recorded in 1997 (Sidney, cassette recording), most likely for the impending bicentenary commemorations, tells of an old man whose son has joined the rebels, roaming a lonely strand for the last 200 years looking for him. As the author looks into his eyes, he too is transported back to 1798, and sees the man's son as he fights in various battles throughout the county. One verse goes as follows:

I saw him last as night had passed on a hill outside the town
And as the cannons roared the redcoats soared and cut that gallant young man down
I watched him die under the blood red sky near the foot of Vinegar Hill
And as he died the old man cried and time it just stood still.

'O'Rourke the blacksmith'
As mentioned, blacksmiths played a most significant role in the 1798 rebellion. Therefore, it is unsurprising that their role is immortalized in song and poem. Of this eighteen-line poem, lines one to four and thirteen and fourteen are noted here.

O'Rourke the blacksmith forged a pike
And better neir was made
'Twas eight feet long in handle
And six inch wide in blade …
And we'll march through Enniscorthy
By the dawning of the day. (IFC S 881: 341)

'The boys of the flail'
This poem, by an unknown author, is an epic with nine verses of twelve lines each – an account of a grandfather telling his four grandchildren of his involvement in the rebellion. The verse of particular interest to Enniscorthy references the Duffry men. The Duffry, and its gate, is at the 'top of the town', on its western side. A flail is a wooden agricultural implement used to thresh wheat.

Then Duffry men forward, the yeomen
Shall never say you turned tail
They'll be crushed by the giants and the heroes
Who for weapons are wielding the flail. (IFC S 891: 26–31)

'Father Dwyer'
This final poem was written the year after the Fenian rising of 1867. It refers to the lack of ammunition among those on Vinegar Hill – an historically accurate observation – mentioned in the verse reproduced below.

The following was composed by the late Richard Cooper Killabeg about 1868:

Their orange flag we will pull down, our glorious band will play
We will let those cursed Saxons see, they will not have their way.
For God he will assist us, for sworn blood to spill
We will have guns and ammunition boys, not like on Vinegar Hill (IFC S 896: 246)

CONCLUSION

The diversity of folk traditions recorded in this chapter is in large part a reflection of the invaluable repository of information contained in the Irish Folklore Commission's work of the late 1930s. Through the folk tradition, including songs and poems, we learn more of the actions of the leaders, the names of 'local heroes', and the significant roles of women and blacksmiths – all of which are often absent from the historical record. The accounts from the National Folklore Collection also shine a light on events that are less well known, but no less important. We can also map place-names and trace where artefacts relating to the battles have been located.

The accounts also give a wonderful insight into the psyche of a people during a Gaelic and nationalist revival. The stories of ghostly apparitions, buried treasure and serpent-headed custodians are entertaining and were undoubtedly told with impressive performance to frighten or amuse. They also reflect the significance of the events of the 1798 rebellion to the population, and their desire to remember these by taking the opportunity to update, adapt or intertwine 'older' myths or stories with these events.

The research team's own attempts to gather oral history pertaining to the rebellion yielded a small corpus of material in comparison to the National Folklore Collection. This causes us to reflect on our own present awareness, knowledge or interest in the rebellion. The informants of 1937 had direct awareness of those who fought in the rebellion of 1798, as illustrated in the following:

> James Whyte Killanne aged 95 yrs. gave me the following about John Kelly 'the Boy from Killanne.' Billy McDonald who fought in the Rebellion 1798 was an uncle to Whyte. Whyte remembers to hear McDonald speak of Kelly and tell of the rebellion. (IFC S 901: 2 & 5)

This begs the question – who now shares the stories of the men and women who participated in the 1798 rebellion? Who will talk about the places they fought and died? And who will sing or recite the songs and poems about them? And who, if anyone, will listen?

CHAPTER THIRTEEN

From Vinegar Hill to Knightstown Bog: the last march of the Wexford pikemen

CIARÁN McDONNELL

INTRODUCTION

The Wexford rebel army had been decisively defeated at Vinegar Hill, but thanks to Needham's failure to close the trap, and a stout rearguard action led by Fr Thomas Clinch, it had been able to escape relatively intact. In fact the Wexfordmen would continue to fight on for another twenty-three days before they were finally defeated in a bog in north Co. Meath. How and why did they end up there, far from their homes? This final chapter will examine the reasons why the rebel army left Wexford and the hardships they endured as they marched through Leinster.

RETREAT THROUGH WEXFORD AND WICKLOW

In the aftermath of the defeat at Vinegar Hill the rebel army retreated towards Wexford town, camping on the night of 22 June at Sleedagh south of the town (Doyle, 2011, p. 21). In the following days they marched north-west (about 5,000 strong and under the leadership of Fr John Murphy), attacking a number of towns in Kilkenny including Goresbridge and Castlecomer. This was not simply an army of pikemen; many women followed the men, cooking and cleaning (Byrne, 1863, p. 210). The government forces struggled to locate and keep up with the rebel army as it marched north into Laois, but local support for the rebellion was less than what the rebels hoped for, and the Wexfordmen decided to wheel east back towards their home county (Pakenham, 1972, p. 309). They suffered a further blow to their morale when Fr Murphy, having lost contact with his men due to a thick fog, was apprehended by the authorities, tried and brutally executed at Tullow.

For just over a week (26 June to 5 July) the rebel army (or more precisely a number of armies) marched around Wexford, where they experienced tactical successes and defeats but these did not affect the overall strategic situation. Notably, whenever the rebels attempted to take buildings with strong stone walls (such as at Hacketstown or Carnew) they were defeated (Pakenham, 1972, p. 310). Their lack of artillery was critical. The Reverend James Gordon observed after Hacketstown: 'We must admit that the garrison could not possibly have maintained its post if the assailants had been furnished with cannon' (Gordon, 1803, p. 206). Rebel morale was boosted briefly by a significant victory over the Ancient Britons cavalry regiment at Ballyellis on 30 June, where the rebels ambushed the regiment as it marched along a road. As Miles Byrne, one of the rebel leaders, observed, 'it made the "prestige" or illusion vanish, respecting the pre-eminence or superiority of the English cavalry' (Byrne, 1863, p. 268). Eventually General Duff brought the rebels to battle on 5 July at Ballygullen near Craanford; the rebels fought well and both sides inflicted heavy casualties on each other before the rebels withdrew when they learned that General Needham was approaching with reinforcements (Doyle, 2011, p. 24). This was the last battle to take place on Wexford soil. The army marched north into Wicklow, where they met with the local Wicklow rebels under the command of Joseph Holt at Whelp Rock on the Black Hill, overlooking the lake at Poulaphouca (O'Donnell, 2015, p. 429).

For the next three days the rebel commanders debated and argued over their next move. The lack of an overall commander, or rather the problem of too many competing commanders – including Esmond Kane (Kyan), Anthony Perry, Fr Mogue Kearns and Joseph Holt – meant that they could not decide on one definitive strategy. Holt argued for a swift attack towards Arklow, from where Dublin could be threatened. This was countered by Kearns' plan to march west into Kildare and link up with the rebel army there, under the command of United Irishman William Aylmer. While Holt's plan was relatively sound, the same cannot be said for Kearns', as it relied very much on the support of the Kildare rebels and it also would leave the rebels exposed in open countryside, where, as Byrne observed, 'the enemy's cavalry enjoyed every possible advantage' (Byrne, 1863, p. 303). The terrain of the Wexford and Wicklow hills favoured an army of insurgents, unlike the plains of Kildare. Eventually a vote was held and Kearns narrowly won. The Wexfordmen would march into Kildare.

MARCH THROUGH KILDARE

On 9 July the Wexford army under Kearns marched west through Blessington and out into Kildare; the following day they came to Timahoe Bog, where Aylmer had his camp. Aylmer had around 15,000 men under his command but in his eyes the rebellion was already over (Doyle, 2011, p. 33). He had won a number of battles at Kilcock and Maynooth but he had suffered a significant defeat at Ovidstown near Kilcock on 19 June, two days before the battle at Vinegar Hill (O'Donnell, 1998b, p. 278). When the Wexfordmen arrived he was in the middle of negotiating a precarious truce and surrender, in return for safe passage home for his men (Pakenham, 1972, p. 315). The last thing he needed was a new army of rebels arriving in his district, trying to stir life into the embers of insurrection (O'Donnell, 2015, p. 429). After a day of deliberation Aylmer and his men declined the appeal and the 'fierce Wexfordians' pressed on (Gordon, 1803, p. 213). While some attributed this to the apathy of the Kildaremen, a realistic assessment of the situation at this point shows that little could be gained from fighting on and Aylmer knew it. Part of the Wexford army, led by Edward Fitzgerald (another pragmatist), remained in Timahoe and sought terms alongside Aylmer (Pakenham, 1972, p. 316). The remainder would push north, but it is impossible to determine if this was part of a determined strategy to link with the rebels of Ulster, convince the rebels in Meath to take up arms once more, or simply to remain on the move, avoiding the government columns that were pursuing them.

ENTERING MEATH, BATTLE AT LEINSTER BRIDGE

Later on the 11 July the Wexford army marched north-west towards Clonard, where there was a strategic crossing of the Boyne at Leinster Bridge, on the main coach road from Dublin to Mullingar (fig. 13.1). The bridge was a toll bridge and therefore had a strong gate, and there were a number of stone buildings nearby, including the house occupied by John Tyrell and his family. One of his kinsmen was Thomas Tyrell, high sheriff of Kildare, and Thomas had decided to move in and strengthen the buildings by closing up the lower windows and constructing a small tower within the courtyard of the farmstead and toll house (Doyle, 2011, p. 38). These might have been rudimentary fortifications but to the lightly armed rebels the position would prove deadly. When the Tyrells and their fellow loyalists learned of the rebel approach they hastily barred the windows and sent for aid to nearby Kinnegad.

The rebel army probably numbered 2,000–2,500 men, while the defenders numbered about forty, including eighteen soldiers. Tyrell placed his best marksmen in the small tower and the rest sheltered behind the fortifications (Doyle, 2011, p. 39). The rebels attacked but suffered greatly from the weight of firepower from the building, in particular from the men in the tower. Eventually the attackers broke into the lower floor of the tower (fig. 13.2) and 'as the ladder had been drawn up by the defenders of the upper storey the rebels, by climbing on each other's shoulders, attempted to force through the trapway – but everyone who tried it perished' (Maxwell, 1871, p. 178). Frustrated, they set fire to the tower, killing two of the marksmen, while the other four jumped to safety. The fighting had lasted about six hours when soldiers were sighted coming from Kinnegad (O'Donnell, 1998b, p. 278). Their arrival coincided with the rebels' decision to retreat.

The defenders had suffered lightly (three dead yeomen) but the same could not be said for the rebels who lost about sixty men (O'Donnell, 1998b, p. 278). Harassed by

13.1 Location of the old bridge over the Boyne at Leinster Bridge, Clonard. The modern bridge is in the background. Photo by Ciarán McDonnell.

13.2 Depiction of the attack on the tower at Clonard by George Cruickshank (Maxwell, 1845). Courtesy of Wexford Public Library Service, Local Studies Collection.

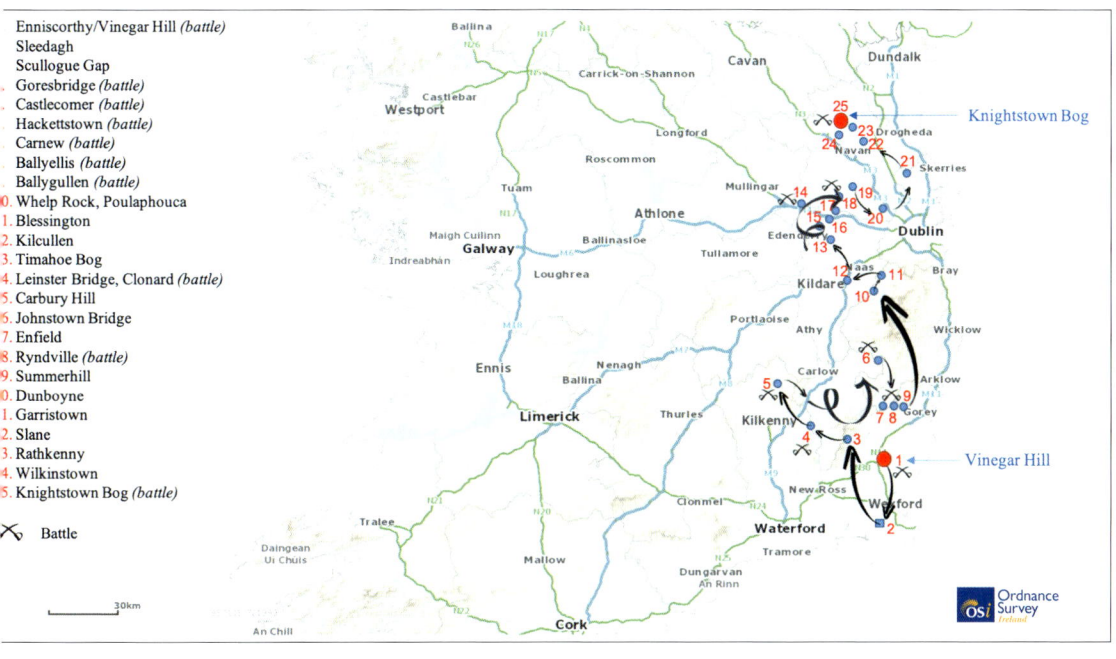

From Vinegar Hill to Knightstown Bog: the last march of the Wexford pikemen 253

Enniscorthy/Vinegar Hill *(battle)*
Sleedagh
Scullogue Gap
. Goresbridge *(battle)*
. Castlecomer *(battle)*
. Hackettstown *(battle)*
. Carnew *(battle)*
. Ballyellis *(battle)*
. Ballygullen *(battle)*
10. Whelp Rock, Poulaphouca
11. Blessington
12. Kilcullen
13. Timahoe Bog
14. Leinster Bridge, Clonard *(battle)*
15. Carbury Hill
16. Johnstown Bridge
17. Enfield
18. Ryndville *(battle)*
19. Summerhill
20. Dunboyne
21. Garristown
22. Slane
23. Rathkenny
24. Wilkinstown
25. Knightstown Bog *(battle)*
✗ Battle

13.3 Map of the approximate route taken by the rebel army. Map drawn by Morogh O'Flaherty. Base map © Ordnance Survey Ireland/Government of Ireland. Copyright permit MP 001021.

mounted yeomanry, the rebels withdrew back into Kildare, camping that night on the hill at Carbury (O'Donnell, 2015, p. 430). On the morning of the 12th July most of the Wicklow men, under Holt's command, decided to leave the army and return to Wicklow, no doubt disheartened by the lacklustre results of the foray into Kildare. This was quite a blow for the rebel army as they not only lost experienced men but also the good leadership of Holt (Doyle, 2011, p. 49). The army of mostly Wexfordmen marched north, this time towards the bridge at Johnstown where they crossed into Meath.

EARLIER 1798 ACTIVITIES IN MEATH

The inhabitants of Meath, like those of Kildare, had already experienced the turmoil of insurrection in the earlier months of the summer. Early in the rebellion the United Irishmen of Meath had fought a short but sharp battle on the hill of Tara. This location was chosen by the rebels not only due to the strategic views it offered but also due to its symbolic value for Irish sovereignty (Pakenham, 1972, p. 181). On 26 May a force of Scottish fencibles and local yeomanry (roughly 300 men) approached Tara and attacked the rebel army of approximately 5,000 men. The poorly equipped rebels charged down the hill, abandoning the prehistoric earthworks that had offered some degree of shelter and ran into the teeth of trained musketry fire, supported by a field gun (McDonnell, 2017, p. 339). This cannon was used to great effect, in particular as the government forces counter-attacked up the hill and finally drove off the rebels (Steen, 1991, p. 26). Few prisoners were taken and local tradition has it that around 300 or 400 dead rebels were buried in a mass grave dug into the Forrad (one of the ancient mounds of Tara) and marked by the relocation of the ancient Lia Fáil, the Stone of Destiny (O'Donnell, 2015, p. 425). The local yeomanry, including Catholic yeomen recruited by Lord Fingall of the nearby Kileen Castle, led the pursuit of the scattered Meathmen. This decisive defeat had put an end to the rebellion in Meath, and the Wexfordmen were unlikely to find much support for continued fighting when they arrived in the county (McDonnell, 2017, p. 343).

PURSUIT

Having entered Meath, Kearns' army passed through Enfield (then called Innfield) and made their way towards Summerhill. It was near here at Knockderrig (now known as Ryndville) that the army halted to face a government force under the command of Lt Col. Gough, marching south from Trim. Gough was an able commander and his force attacked rapidly, catching the Wexfordmen off guard and scattering many of them (O'Donnell, 1998b, p. 280). They were not defeated however; as Gough (1798) himself explained in a letter, 'the closeness of the country prevented the cavalry pursuing'. The rebels regrouped and continued marching north and west, through Longwood and on to Dunboyne, where they camped on the night of 12 July.

As had happened in Wexford itself, the government forces were beginning to close in on the rebel army (Doyle, 2011, p. 51). The defeat earlier that day had badly shaken the men and any stragglers or outlying groups were easy targets for the pursuing soldiers, and for the yeomanry cavalry in particular. The yeomanry are usually remembered as ill-disciplined and, as Lord Lieutenant and Commander-in-Chief Charles Cornwallis himself admitted, the leaders 'in rapine and plunder' (Ross, 1859, p. 371). They did have two major advantages however: they knew their local area intimately and they were determined to defend it and their fellow loyalists. Many of them were members of the Protestant gentry and middle classes, well-used to fox-hunting and handling horses over rough terrain. Armed with pistols, carbines and the deadly 1796-pattern light-cavalry sabre (fig. 13.4), the yeomanry cavalry were rightly feared by the rebels. The Meath militia, a more evenly mixed force of Protestant officers and Catholic rank and file, were at this time deployed in Wexford (McDonnell, 2019, p. 174).

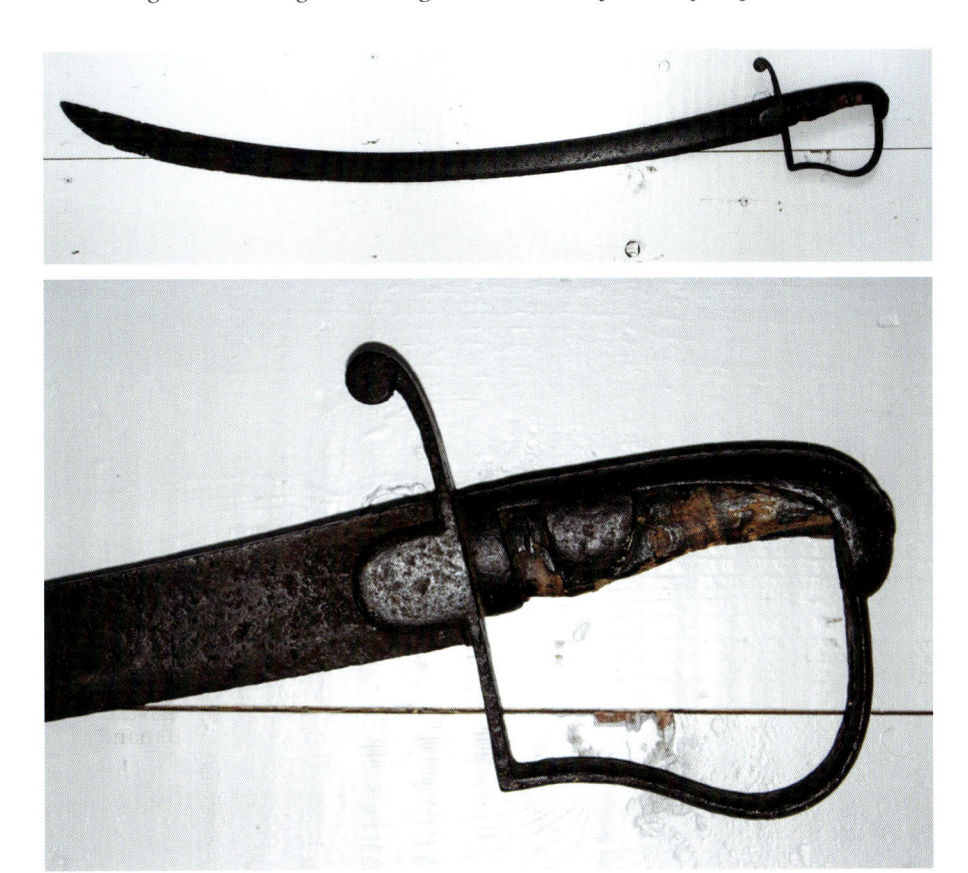

From Vinegar Hill to Knightstown Bog: the last march of the Wexford pikemen

13.4 a) 1796-pattern British light-cavalry sabre with b) close-up of hilt. Discovered in the thatch of a cottage in Meath. Photo by Ciarán McDonnell.

LAST STAND AT KNIGHTSTOWN BOG

On the morning of the 13 July the rebel army moved out, heading north once more. Government forces were closing in from all sides. They crossed the Boyne in the vicinity of Slane, closely pursued by a number of military columns, under the command of generals Myers, Meyrick and Wemyss. It is possible that at this point there was not one main rebel army but a series of smaller forces marching in roughly the same direction (Doyle, 2011, p. 54). A number of confused skirmishes occurred in the countryside on the Meath and Louth border as the government forces sought to pin down the rebels. Doyle estimates that by this stage the rebels numbered about 1,000, of whom 400 were mounted (Doyle, 2011, p. 54). The following morning the rebels moved onto Rathkenny, once again closely pursued by soldiers. The vanguard

13.5 Bogland at Knightstown. It was in or around this area the rebel army was finally caught. Photo by Ciarán McDonnell.

of the government forces, the Durham cavalry, skirmished with the rearguard of the rebels, before the main force (a mix of local yeomanry, Scottish and English regiments) made contact with the rebels at Knightstown Bog (fig. 13.5), just off the road north of Wilkinstown, on the main road that ran from Navan up to Nobber (O'Donnell, 1998b, p. 282).

The rebels, who had marched over 400 miles since leaving Wexford, formed up to face the government forces. As had happened at Vinegar Hill, the Wexfordmen suffered greatly under artillery bombardment (O'Donnell, 2015, p. 431). What firearms they had were by this time no doubt short of gunpowder and ammunition. Determined pike charges might have carried the day in the early engagements of the rebellion, but the élan had been ground out of the rebels after weeks of pursuit, harassment and hunger. Wemyss (1798), in a letter the following day, described how 'the Highlanders got into the bog and killed all that were in it'. The government forces had the rebels at their mercy and at around midday the Wexford army finally disintegrated, the men scattering in all directions as they sought to escape the vengeful soldiers.

FLIGHT

The rebels took flight in small groups and as individuals, often abandoning their weapons in their haste to make it to safety and to blend in with the locals. As Doyle observes, there is no mention of powder or shot in the reports of captured weapons,

13.6 A croppy grave in Co. Meath. Photo by Ciarán McDonnell.

showing how low the Wexfordmen would have been in these supplies (Doyle, 2011, p. 56). Byrne had lamented this constant shortage of ammunition; he believed the rebels could have held out in the mountains until the French arrival in the west in August, if they had been properly armed (Byrne, 1863, p. 283).

13.7 The 1798 memorial at Mountainstown. Photo by Ciarán McDonnell.

Perry and Kearns made their escape together but were apprehended near Clonbullogue in Offaly (then King's Co.). They were both executed near Edenderry on 21 July (O'Donnell, 2015, p. 431). The rest of the rebels made their way from Knightstown in small groups or as individuals but their situation was grim, pursued by the determined soldiers and vengeful and at times bloodthirsty yeomanry. Many were executed where they were caught, their graves later marked by whitewashed crosses (fig. 13.6). These 'croppy graves' still exist in Meath, albeit often in an overgrown state. Later that day one of the larger groups (said to be around 350 cavalry) was apprehended and defeated at the village of Ballyboughal, just across the border in Dublin (Doyle, 2011, p. 56).

Some rebels were more fortunate. The Schools Folklore Project of the 1930s record how some Wexfordmen were sheltered by the locals until they were able to return home (IFC S 714: 235). Others stayed in Meath, marrying local girls (Doyle, 2011, p. 108). It was not just the common folk that came to their aid; it was said that local magistrate and yeoman John Pollock of nearby Mountainstown House gave shelter to rebels crossing his land (Doyle, 2011, p. 110). The Pollock family still live at Mountainstown, and in 1998 erected a monument on the estate to the rebels (fig. 13.7).

The Folklore Project also records some colourful tales of the '98 rebellion in Meath, including a Catholic priest with the rebels who could catch bullets (IFC S 771: 272). Other local tales tell how a Father Thomas Murphy (sometimes mistakenly conflated with Father John Murphy of the Wexford rebels, who had been killed on 2 July) was brutally attacked and killed by three yeomen at Drakestown Bridge after the battle, and his blood was allegedly still to be seen in 1938 (IFC S 708: 7). This bridge was marked with a crudely incised '1798' and in 1998 a new plaque to the murdered priest was unveiled (Doyle, 2011, p. 60). It was said that Fr Murphy was buried in a place called Raffin and in later years a man from Kells supposedly dug up the grave, in the hope of finding the priest's valuables, 'and for his pains only got the head of a pike and the head of a spear' (IFC S 703: 130–1). The croppy graves of the county are often assumed to mark the final resting places of Meath rebels but many, especially those in the north part of the county, also mark those of the Wexfordmen (McDonnell, 2017, p. 344). In 1998, at the bicentennial of the rebellion, many of these memorials were restored and new ones added; it is possible to trace the journey of the Wexford and Wicklow pikemen through Meath via these memorials and the various field names such as 'Croppy Field' or 'Cnoc an áir' ('Hill of Slaughter') (Mullen, 2013, pp 235–9). Thanks to the visionary efforts of the Schools Folklore Project the oral memory of the rebels was recorded in 1938 for posterity by people who had heard the tales from their grandparents, whom Doyle fittingly refers to as 'the last of the storytellers' (Doyle, 2013, p. 223).

The army had endured great hardships ever since leaving their home county (and indeed before that): hunger, exhaustion and the ever-present danger of attack. The flight that began on the slopes of Vinegar Hill ended in the bogland of north Meath. The rebel army had suffered from lack of supplies, lack of support and, most crucially, a lack of a coherent and realistic strategy. Slowly disintegrating, it is nevertheless remarkable that the pikemen held together for as long as they did and marched as far as they did. These exploits might not be as well-known as the fierce fighting in Wexford and Wicklow during that long hot summer, but they at least remind us that for many in Leinster the 1798 rebellion did not end at Vinegar Hill on the longest day of the year.

Appendices

1(a)	Details of garrison in Enniscorthy	262
1(b)	Numbers killed and wounded in defence of Enniscorthy on 28 May 1798	263
2	Extracts of Jane Barber's diary	264
3	Extracts of Barbara Lett's diary	273
4	Extracts of Alicia Pounden's diary	275
5	Details of trials of those court martialled for participation in the rebellion of 1798	277
6	Numbers of government troops in Ireland, 1796–9	280
7	General Needham's force at the Battle of Arklow	281
8	Government troops (field army) for the Battle of Vinegar Hill	282
9	General orders for the Battle of Vinegar Hill	284
10	Eyewitness account of William Kerr of the Midlothian fencible regiment	286
11	Government casualties at the Battle of Vinegar Hill	289
12	Extract from Letter of 21 June 1798 from Lake to Castlereagh	291
13	Ranges for guns used by government forces	293
14	Daily rates of pay for the British army at the time of the rebellion	294
15	Extracts from folk narratives	295

APPENDIX 1(a)

Details of garrison in Enniscorthy

(Musgrave, 1802, pp 429–30)

	Captains	Subalterns	Serjeants	Drummers	Rank and file
North Cork militia					
Capt. Snowe's company	1	1	3	2	56
Capt. De Courcy's company	0	1	2	1	24
Total of North Cork	1	2	5	3	80
Enniscorthy infantry					
Capt. Pounden	1	2	2	1	50
Supplementary	0	1	3	0	57
Scarawalsh infantry					
Capt. Cornock	1	2	3	1	60
Enniscorthy cavalry					
Capt. Richards	1	2	2	1	50
Total	**4**	**9**	**15**	**6**	**297**

Officers' names
North Cork: Captain Snowe, Lieutenant Bowen, Ensign Harman
Enniscorthy infantry: Captain Pounden, Lieutenants Drury and Hunt
Supplementary: Lieutenant Pounden
Scarawalsh infantry: Captain Cornock, Lieutenants Carden and Rudd
Lieutenant Spring on half-pay, and formerly lieutenant of the 63rd Regiment, joined the troops as a volunteer

APPENDIX 1(b)

Numbers killed and wounded in defence of Enniscorthy on 28 May 1798

(after Musgrave, 1802, p. 437)

	Killed			Wounded	
	Officers	Serjeants	Privates	Officers	Privates
North Cork militia	0	1	3	0	3
Scarawalsh infantry	1	2	17	1	3
Enniscorthy infantry	1	0	6	0	4
Supplementary infantry	1	0	30	0	0
Enniscorthy cavalry	0	0	11	0	6
Total	**3**	**3 (1 drum)**	**67**	**1**	**16**

'The rebels killed in cold blood most of those who had been wounded. Captain John Pounden,[1] who commanded the supplementary yeomen, lieutenant Hunt of the Enniscorthy infantry, and lieutenant Carden of the Scarawalsh infantry, were killed … Of the garrison eighty-eight were killed and wounded; and deducting seven of the North Cork, there remain eighty-one loyal protestants who bled that day in defence of the constitution in church and state … It was generally believed, that not less than five hundred of the rebels were killed or wounded.'

[1] Husband of Alicia Pounden, extracts of whose diary are recorded in appendix 4.

APPENDIX TWO

Extracts of Jane Barber's diary

(Beatty, 2001, pp 70–89)

Recalling the immediate days and nights prior to the Battle of Enniscorthy, Jane Barber writes:

> We passed the entire night [of Saturday 26/Sunday 27 May 1798] doing this [hiding property and provisions], the poor children, hungry and sleepy, ate and lay down in the nearest corner, for we had already packed the beds on the cars. At the break of day, we milked the cows about the field, for we could not make use of the milk, and if we had left them unmilked, their udders would have become sore. After several unforeseen yet necessary delays, we set off for Enniscorthy about ten o'clock on Whit Sunday morning, just about the same hour we expected to have gone to its church.
>
> I carried the infant and my mother, yet weak from a bad confinement, leaned on my father's arm. The other children followed us and led on of the horses, but Martin remained behind with his mother in the little cottage my father had built for them, and when we next saw him he was an armed rebel, for he joined them on the ensuing day. Yet, from his subsequent conduct to us, I cannot think that he was ever guilty of the same cruelties committed by many of his comrades.
>
> When we entered Enniscorthy, we went to the house of a relation named Willis, who willingly received us, but when we entered, there was hardly room for us to sit down, it was so full of the Protestant inhabitants of the neighbourhood, who had fled into the town for protection… My father, on seeing us safe in the house, immediately went and enrolled himself amongst the supplementary Yeomanry and was provided with a musket and crossbelts to wear over his coloured clothes…
>
> I now began for the first time to see some of the miseries that threatened us, and thus passed a few uneasy hours over us, when it suddenly occurred to me that the cows would be injured if they were not milked again, and the servant-girl and I set out about six in the evening, and without meeting anything to injure us, reached Clovass in safety. We found all as we had left it, with the poor cows standing lowing to be milked. We each brought away a large pitcher and on the road home met several Roman Catholic neighbours with whom we had been on the most friendly terms; we spoke to them as usual, but they looked in our faces as though they had never seen us before and passed on… (pp 73–5)
>
> The milk was most gratefully received as well by our own children and by the other poor little creatures sheltered in that crowded house. We prayed and endeavoured

> to rest on the bare boards (for our beds were filled with wounded Yeomen), but, though worn out in mind and body, it was little rest I took that Sunday night with the moans of a wounded men in the very room with us and the heat and closeness of the air, so different from our pleasant, airy, little bed-chamber.
>
> At the dawn I arose, and after inquiring in vain through the house for the maid-servant (who I afterwards heard had stolen off in the night to join her relations in the rebel camp), my father, seeing me anxious again about our cows, said he would go with me, for he hoped there would be no immediate want of him in the town. We went accordingly to the little farm and found that, as yet, all was safe, the cows waiting for us and the poor poultry and pigs looking to us for the food we had not to give them. (p. 75)

In relation to the Battle of Enniscorthy, she recalls in detail the preparations, course and aftermath of the battle. Of the build-up to the battle she recalls:

> I obeyed him and we hastened back to Enniscorthy, where we arrived about nine in the forenoon. As we advanced towards it, we heard the drums beating to arms, and on entering, we heard that the enemy were closing in on all sides of it in a vast force. We saw our friends and neighbours hurrying through the streets to the different posts assigned to them; the North Cork Militia were placed on the bridge of the Slaney, which ran on the east side of the town; our infantry, amongst whom were the supplementary yeomen, were placed at the Duffry Gate, at the opposite extremity of the town toward the west. A guard of yeomen was placed over the Market House, where there was a great store of arms and ammunition, and where a few prisoners were confined; some were mounted guard over the castle, where some dangerous rebels were lodged, and in the midst of this confusion, my father, after leaving me with my mother, put on his belts, took up his musket, and joined my brother (whom he had never seen all this time) at the Duffry Gate, the post assigned to them.
>
> In the course of this morning, Willis, in whose house we were sheltered, put his wife and two infants on a horse, and mounting another, fled with them to Wexford. He never mentioned to us his intentions, nor could we blame him, for a calamity such as that in which we were all involved would have made the most generous man selfish. He was a friendly man, but he could not save us all so, as was most natural, he took with him that were dear to him. (p. 76)

In relation to the fighting at the Duffry Gate, Barber recalls:

> At eleven in the forenoon, the videttes brought word from the Duffry Gate that the rebels were advancing to the town from the northwest in a column that filled the road and was a mile in length; they were calculated by some of our garrison, who had served abroad to exceed six thousand in number. They soon closed with our Enniscorthy yeomen, and the shots and shouting fell sharply on our ears. I was at first greatly terrified, and the children hid their faces in my lap, but in a short time

I became accustomed to the noise and could speak to my mother, endeavouring to give her some comfort, but she seemed stupefied and could say nothing in answer, except to lament feebly that her son, William, was in the midst of such danger.

She seemed not to comprehend that my father was equally exposed, more especially as he, seeing that the disaffected inhabitants of the town had now begun to set it on fire in several places, twice or thrice, on the enemy being partially repulsed, had quitted his post to run down and see were we yet safe and to tell us that his William was behaving like a brave man and a soldier. He then, on hearing the advancing shouts of the rebels, would rush back to the fight…

The fearful firing had now continued three hours, when the King's men fell back into the town, for our little garrison was now reduced to less than two hundred; and though they did not fall unrevenged – for more than five hundred of the rebels were slain – yet so numerous were these last that they never felt the loss.

The North Corks were now forced to provide for their own safety, and I have heard it said that they neglected to sound a retreat which, if done, would have enabled many more of the Enniscorthy men to have escaped in time. As it was, some few dispersed over the field and gained Duncannon Fort in safety, amongst whom was my brother, and the rest, with whom was my father, slowly retreated through the town, now blazing in many places. They fought in the burning streets, and though so few in number, more than once repulsed the enemy, who, crowded into a narrow space, impeded each other by their own numbers; then this handful of brave men would retreat again from the hundreds that still pressed on them, till at last they gained the Market-house, disputing every inch of the ground. (pp 76–7)

She describes the scene in the Market Square as they flee from burning house to burning house, witnessing scenes of pure horror:

The house which sheltered us stood exactly opposite to this building, and though none within it dared venture to the windows, yet we knew from the increased uproar that destruction had now come near us. At last the house caught fire over us and we all rushed out from the flames into the midst of the fight. I don't know what became of the wounded men within it, but if they were consumed, it was a more merciful death than they would have met from the rebels.

We fled across the square to the Market-house, leaving all that we had so anxiously saved the day before to be burned, without bestowing one thought upon it, and I, who had never seen a dead body, had now to step over many corpses of the rebels, who had fallen by the fire of our men in the Market-house, whilst whichever way I cast my eyes, dozens more lay strewed around. The doors were hastily unbarred and we were admitted, and once more I clung around my father, and then, stupefied with fear, we sunk down amongst barrels of gunpowder, arms, provisions and furniture piled up in heaps together. (p. 77)

Amongst those who defended the Market-house was Grimes, the miller, who was one of the most eager to admit us into the already overcrowded place, and who, through the loopholes in the doors and walls, was one of the most active in defending it. But, in less than an hour, it, too, took to fire, and all within it, armed men, helpless women and infant children, were forced to leave it and throw themselves into the midst of the rebels who now surrounded it in hundreds, or they would have been destroyed by the explosion of the gunpowder, which took place shortly after.

As we were on the point of rushing out of the building, Grimes, determined on a desperate attempt for our safety, stretched his hand out of the half-open door and seized the pikes of two of the enemy who had fallen close to it, then turning to my father, he said, 'Act as I do, Sam; lay down that musket, and take this pike; tear one of those little green frocks of your children to put on the pike for a banner, and perhaps you and they may be spared'. But my father replied, 'Never! I will never quit the King's cause nor my musket while I have life!'

Grimes then stuck his pike into a large flitch of bacon, and bidding us to follow, he marched out of the burning Market-house, as though he were joining the rebels and triumphantly carrying provisions to him. My father, shouldering his musket, followed him. I came closely after him, carrying my little brother of four years old; the two little girls clung to my skirts, and my mother with the infant came after me. As we stepped from the door, my father turned round to me and said, 'Jane, dear child, take care of your mother and the children!' They were the last words I ever heard him speak.

As we left the Market-house, a fine infant of four years old, the son of Joseph Fitzgerald, a near neighbour of ours, a child whom I had a hundred times nursed on my knees, came out beside me. Unfortunately, one of the rebels, who had a particular hatred to its father, knew the child, and explaining, 'That's an orange brat', pushed him down, as I thought, on his back. The child gave a faint cry, and I was stooping down to raise him when I saw the pike drawn back, covered with its blood. A shiver for an instant shook its limbs -it was dead! I had strength given me to suppress a shriek, and I hid my face in my little brother's bosom, whilst the two other little creatures, without uttering a single cry, only pressed closer to me: my mother, whose eyes were never removed from my father, fortunately never saw it. (pp 77–8)

She describes the death of her father, and their subsequent search for a safe hiding place as follows:

We were allowed to pass over the square without being injured, and we still were following Grimes towards the river when I noticed one pikeman following us closely and at last pushing between my father and me … Concealed in a chimney at the corner of a lane we were now about entering, there was a yeoman, who, it was said, fired more than a hundred shots that day and made everyone tell. He, at this moment, took aim at a pikeman within a few paces of us, who staggered a few steps and fell dead behind me, exactly across my mother's feet. She dropped in a dead faint beside the corpse; I turned to raise her and to take the young infant from the ground on which it had slid out of her arms. I thus lost sight of my father and of the fearful pikeman that was following him and never saw him alive again. But Providence thus spared me the sight of his murder by the very man that had drawn his first nourishment from the same breast with him. He followed him into Barrack Lane and piked him at the door of Mr Sparrow's brewery; a man named Byrne, in charge of the place, saw him commit the act, and saw him, too, with his leather-cutter's knife, disfigure his face, after emptying his pockets and stripping him of the new coat and hat he had on.

In a few minutes after I had lost sight of my father, my mother came to herself. She arose and we both, unconscious of our loss, went with the children towards the river, thinking we might perhaps rejoin him. My mother was quite bewildered and unable even to speak to me, much less to advise me, and I, although born so near the town, had seldom been in it, but to church or to market, and was quite ignorant where to seek for shelter. We asked at many doors would they admit us, but we were constantly driven away and sometimes even with threats and curses. At last we came by chance to the house of one Walsh, a baker, who knew my mother and spoke kindly to us; he opened his door, but we hardly had time to enter, when five or six pikemen followed and ordered him to turn us out or they would burn the house over our heads. He dismissed us unwillingly and put a little open book into the hands of one of the children. When we had gone a few steps I saw it was a Romish prayerbook, which he seemed to have purposely opened at a picture of the Crucifixion; but whether he meant that this was to be a token to insure our lives or that it was to prepare us for the fate that was to await us, I cannot tell; I only recollect that I desired the child to lay it down, that we might not deny our religion in our last moments.

We now followed some other desolate beings, like ourselves, who led us into the garden of one Barker, who had borne a high command that day amongst the rebels. His family did not seem as though they noticed us, and we sat down with many more on the earth under the bushes. All were women and children, and I have since heard that thirty-two new-made widows passed the night in that garden. Many of these new their loss, yet fear had so completely conquered grief that not one dared to weep aloud; the children were as silent as their mothers, and whenever a footstep was heard to pass along, we all hid our faces against the earth. The moon shone brightly that night, and at one time I saw a man led into the garden … but Barker, who was then in the house, was so humane as not to put him to death amongst us, but ordered him off to Vinegar Hill. (pp 78–80)

Jane then explains how she went to retrieve the body of her father, while at the same time trying to guard her siblings and protect her mother, who was oblivious to the unfolding tragedy around her:

We went about a quarter of a mile to Barrack Lane, where, lying in the midst of five or six other bodies, with two pikemen looking on, I saw and knew my father. He lay on his back, with his hand across his back and one knee raised; his shirt was steeped in blood; the lower part of his face disfigured with the gashes of the ruffians knife, and his mouth filled purposely with dirt of the street. Beside him lay a large mastiff, which followed us from Clovass, which had licked all the blood off his face. This creature, though he was heard the ensuing night howling piteously round the ruins of our cottage, was never seen afterwards by anyone.

I can now describe what then nearly killed me to look upon. I felt a suffocation come over me; I thought, as I looked at him, I could have given my mother, my brother, and all, even my own life, to have him brought back. I fell on my knees and, whilst kissing his forehead, broke out into loud cries, when one of the rebels gave me such a blow with the handle of his pike in my side as laid me breathless for a moment beside my father and must have broken my ribs, but, for a very strong bodice I wore. He was going to repeat the blow, but then his comrade levelled his pike at him, crying with an oath, 'If you strike her again, I will thrust this through your body! Because the child is frightened, are you to beat her? I now knew him to be one Jack O'Brien, who but the preceding week had purchased some cloth from my father at a fair to which I had gone with him. He spoke with kindness to me, and he and Molly Martin brought me back to the garden where I had left my mother, advising me not to tell her what I had seen lest she should perish with terror and sorrow. (pp 81–2)

She then describes her attempts to get back home, only to be ordered by a group of rebels to proceed, with other prisoners, to Vinegar Hill. She also describes the scenes that greeted them there.

We remained without food all that day, but we wanted none, and towards evening, Barker's family turned us all out of the garden, telling us it was not safe for us to remain there any longer. I now thought of taking my mother home, for as she was quite stupefied and had never spoken all day, she was quite incapable of advising with me, so I was left entirely to myself and had to lead her after me like one of the children, but just as we reached the outskirts of the town and were slowly walking along the river, a party of rebels on the opposite bank ordered us back into the town again, threatening at the same time to fire on us. We then tried to quit it by another outlet, when we were surrounded by a large party of pikemen and marched off with many more prisoners, whom they had previously taken, to Vinegar Hill …

They seemed to have a few tents made of blankets, but the greater number were in the open air. I could see that some were cooking at large fires, whilst others lay scattered about, sleeping on the ground. It was about sunset when we were taken to the hill, where the men who were our fellow-prisoners were separated from us and driven like sheep higher up the hill; whilst we and many more women and children were ordered to sit down in a kind of dry ditch or trench about half-way up it. We had not been long here when we were accosted by a female neighbour named Mary Donnelly; she was a Roman Catholic and had come that day to join her husband on the hill. She wept over us and sat down close to my mother, who, knowing that her presence was a protection, would cower down beside her when she heard the slightest noise. And the entire of that night we heard fearful sounds above us, as the men who were brought with us to the hill were massacred one by one. We could hear plainly the cries of the murdered and the shouts of the executioners. Towards dawn, I saw in the bright moonlight what terrified me more than any sight I had yet beheld; I saw a tall white figure rushing down the hill directly towards us; as it drew nearer I saw it was a naked man, and I felt my heart die within me, for I though he was no living being. He passed so close to me that I could see the dark streams of blood running down his sides. In a few seconds, the uproar above showed that he was missed, and his pursuers also passed close to us. One saw me looking up and asked had I seen any one run past, but I was given courage to deny it. This – as I afterwards heard – was a singularly fine young man, not quite twenty, named Horneck, the son of an estated gentleman in the neighbourhood. He had been piked and stripped, but recovering, had fled thus from the hill. He waded in the Slaney and ran six miles to the ruins of his father's house, where his pursuers reached him and completed their work of destruction. (pp 82–3)

The traumatized state of her mother is highlighted in the following account:

On Wednesday, about eleven in the forenoon, owing to the intercession of Mary Donnelly, we were allowed to leave the Hill. When we had gone about a furlong, I cast my eyes on my mother and was shocked at missing the infant from her arms. I cried, 'O Mother, where is the child?' 'What child?' she said, 'Oh, I believe I left it in a trench in which we sat'. I went back and found the poor little creature asleep on the ground, my mother being so crazed with grief and fear that she had forgotten it. (p. 83)

She describes the sight of their house and factory when they returned home:

Murphy again gave my mother his arm and towards dusk we, at last, reached the home we had so long wished for and found but a heap of ashes. The house and haggard had been burnt to the ground; the side walls had fallen in, and nothing was left standing but one chimney and a small outhouse, from which the door had been torn. Our factory, with all our wheels, looms, presses and machines, was burned; all our wool and cloth which we had concealed in the corners carried off; our young cattle, pigs and horses (all but one) were driven to Vinegar Hill: all our hay and corn burned down, and yet we stood looking on all this destruction in utter silence as if we could not comprehend that it was ourselves on whom it had fallen. (p. 84)

Also their desperate search for food, under the support of their uncle:

All the provisions in the house had been given to the different parties of rebels, but we milked all the cows, both my uncle's and our own (for the four milch cows had been left) and made curds, which, for two days, was our only nourishment. On the third day poor Martin came to see us and gave us two sacks of barley-meal, which he and his comrades had, of course, plundered from some other distressed creatures, but which want forced us gratefully to accept. In a day or two after he came a second time with some tea and sugar, and I almost wept with joy at receiving it, for my mother was unable to take any nourishment, and the infant was perishing for the want at her breast. I have often thought their lives were prolonged by this supply, but my aunt and myself scrupulously refrained from touching it, not that we thought it sinful, but to make it last longer. In a day or two more, my uncle found that two of our pigs, which had been driven off, had returned home, and he killed them, which gave us a great supply of food. In about a fortnight the greater number of those creatures he had sheltered departed to what homes and friends were left to them, but still, for many weeks, we and several as desolate were almost dependant on him. (p. 85)

She describes their attempts to find their father's body,

On Friday, my aunt said to me, 'I shall tell your mother of your father's death, for it is better she should be in the most violent grief than in her present state'. She did so, and I cannot now bear to think of the manner in which my mother heard it, yet, in the midst of her anguish for his loss, the thoughts of his lying unburied seemed to give her most pain. My aunt, who was a woman of great strength, both of power and mind, and who loved my father as though he had been her own brother, proposed that I should accompany her the next day (Saturday) to the town, with a little car, to seek for the body, and we agreed to lay it in one of those pits in which we were accustomed to burying our potatoes, but which were now empty and open. We went accordingly and met no molestation, but on reaching the place, the body was nowhere to be seen. No other corpse was in sight, yet the smell of putridity was so strong that my aunt fainted. I got her home again, and there we saw Martin, who had just brought the meal, and who told my mother that he had himself laid his master's body in a gravel-pit and covered it over; that I know was but a pretence to pacify my mother.

For some weeks afterwards we searched that gravel pit in vain, and I was afterwards told that the body of my father and all the others had been thrown into the Slaney, which ran close beside, but a few hours we had gone to seek for it. (pp 85–6)

Barber also offers a description of the locality in the aftermath of the rebellion:

The rebel power now begun to decline, and we lived some weeks in dread, both of them and of the struggling parties of military sent in pursuit of them. From the first class we were protected by the female beggar and by Martin's mother, who still lived with us, and neither of whom were ever afterwards deserted by our two families; but the last either not knowing that we were suffering loyalists, or not caring, often behaved with great insolence. The smaller the party was, the more we were in dread of them; and more than once, myself and a few more young girls,

> fearing to pass the night in the house, slept in the centre of a large holly bush at some distance from it. But after the rebels were repulsed from Newtownbarry and after the battle of Vinegar Hill, where they were totally routed, a regular camp was formed within a field's length of my uncle's house. We were then protected, for the soldiers were under better discipline, and we found an excellent market for our milk and butter, which enabled us to purchase a few indispensable articles of furniture and clothing, and to fit up the outhouse for the dwellinghouse. Lord Tyrone, too, who commanded these men, sent every day a baker's cart to distribute bread to the families of the suffering loyalists, and we frequently got two loaves each day from it.
>
> On Vinegar Hill, being carried by assault, he sent to my mother desiring her to look if there was any of her furniture amongst the immense quantity of plunder that was on it; she went to thank him, but said she need not look, for all her's was burned in Enniscorthy. He smiled and called her a simple woman, and then asked her what she wanted most, for he would give it to her. She said if he could spare a feather-bed, she would be forever grateful, and he immediately ordered two of the best to be given to her. I shall not forget the joy we felt at being once more enabled to sleep in comfort for, 'till then, we had only loose straw thrown on the ground to sleep on. The latter end of July, a field of our barley, which had escaped the trampling, ripened; Mr Grimes, the miller, who had saved both his life and property, gave us back all our oats ready ground; our new potatoes were fit for use, and we never afterwards knew what want was. We did not, however, build a house till the next summer, and the blackened ruins of our little factory which (as he that managed it was gone) we never rebuilt, are yet to be seen. (pp 86–7)

She also describes seeing her brother after the rebellion, and how altered he was, both physically and emotionally.

> It was just six weeks from the beginning of our troubles that, as I was passing near the ruins of our house, I was startled at hearing within it the deep sobs and supressed cries of some person in sorrow. I ventured to look in and found they proceeded from a man who was sitting on a low part of the fallen wall, with his head resting on his knees. When he heard my steps he arose, and I saw my brother, but if it had not been for the strong likeness he yet bore to my father, I should never have known him. From a fair, ruddy, robust boy, he had become a tall, haggard, sunburned man, so thin that his waist might have been spanned; and yet he was not seventeen, and this change had been wrought in him by the hardship and want in the space of little more than two months, for it was just so long since we had last met. He immediately turned when he saw me and fled from me at his utmost speed. In three days, however, he returned to us again, more composed and able to meet my poor mother with at least the appearance of calmness. He afterwards got occasional leave of absence to assist in farming business, but he never was able to settle entirely with us till the winter was past. (p. 88)

APPENDIX THREE

Extracts of Barbara Lett's diary
(Beatty, 2001, pp 117–44)

Barbara Lett, like Jane Barber, left her home for the safety of Enniscorthy on 26 May. She recalls meeting Mr and Mrs Hayden, the rector of Ferns and his wife, but

> a monster named Bigan, a butcher, rushed upon Mr Hayden and dispatched him with many wounds from the pike, in [the] presence of Susan Lett who with bitter sorrow recounted this awful tragedy. His remains lay on the steps of Mr Lett's hall door until devoured by pigs.[1]

Barbara also recalls how she could not bring herself to look upon 'the mangled remains of Mr John Pounden' (Alicia Pounden's husband). She was told that he was 'in a state of nudity, surrounded by his murderers who were yelling fearfully and exulting in the barbarous act', but also said she 'should not omit to mention the kind and humane conduct of Father Doyle [James Doyle, parish priest of Davidstown] who obligingly said he was ready to perform any office that might contribute to our safety'.

Like Jane Barber she was involved in supporting her father, who had been arrested and taken to Wexford. She had sought permission to attend to him, but on Tuesday, 19 June she was summoned to return to her husband and children and leave her father for the last time. She notes how she arrived at Enniscorthy

> about 8 o'clock in the evening. On Castle Hill I met a fellow-sufferer whose life was spared because he played the violin & amused his enemies with party tunes. It was Henry Minchen, whose brother was shot before his face, and he was compelled to play every tune they demanded. I met him holding his violin in his hand and walking without shoes; our hearts were too full to give utterance to words; we gazed on each other and burst into tears. They were tears of bitter, heart-rending sorrow. Poor Henry would have rather played his dear brother's funeral requiem than play Party tunes demanded by the enemy. Every feeling was sacraficed [sic] to self-preservation at that time. We dare not express sorrow for our dearest friend. I walked on to Mrs Warren's, whose house escaped.

---

[1] It is interesting to note from this chapter that a man by the name of Nicholas Walsh was charged but found not guilty of murdering Revd Hayden (given as 'Heydon' in the trials), when Barbara Lett identifies another individual.

She describes the Battle of Vinegar Hill and mentions the possible location of General Johnson's guns, and also links with the cartographer of a map of the area from the period.

> Next morning the booming of cannon awoke us to a sense of our situation of heartfelt gratitude to the Almighty for the prospect of deliverance to our desolated country. Cannon was placed on Cherry Orchard Rock, and such deliberate aim was taken from Vinegar Hill that the Royal Cannon was dismounted. Val Gill[2] was the engineer that conducted the rebel guns. They had four cannon playing on our army, but a powerful force soon put them to flight. How fondly did I anticipate my next meeting with my father upon the explosion of every cannon. When I saw the tree of liberty fall on Vinegar hill, how did my heart dilate with pleasare [sic]; how different, I thought, shall our next meeting be to our last farewell.

There is mention of her protector, 'Williams', whose identity is unclear, but it is known that he was a Catholic and brother of George Williams, who is mentioned in her account. She says that:

> Williams every day attended the camp on Vinegar Hill and returned at night to his family, shocked and shuddering at the scenes of wholesale murders which he daily witnessed; innocent, unoffending persons for whom he could not utter a word that might obtain mercy or pardon.

---

2 A surveyor, whose well-known map of Co. Wexford was published in 1812. A loyalist in 1798, he was compelled under duress by the rebel army to position the rebel cannons against the English army. In 1799 he gave testimony against Thomas Cloney, who was accused of the murder of John Gill, his brother, on Vinegar Hill.

APPENDIX FOUR

Extracts of Alicia Pounden's diary
(Beatty, 2001, pp 145–52)

Alicia Pounden recalls how on the morning of the battle of Enniscorthy,

> I was blessed with a sight of my beloved husband, who came to hurry me and my little infants to Enniscorthy, thinking we should be more safe there. I can never forget what I felt at leaving my sweet home. I told darling John we were like Adam and Eve driven out of Paradise … My dearest John was amongst the first who fell and after about 3 hours engagement, the town was surrendered, the ammunition being all expended.

She escaped Enniscorthy after the battle, accompanied by her five children and their maids and waited until the Thursday aboard a ship in Wexford harbour for word that it was safe to return to her home. She then made her way initially to her husband's uncle's house before returning to her own house at Daphne even though 'the house and offices were full of rebels, but I was glad to get in on any terms, as I always endeavoured to submit without repining to the Will of the Almighty'.

She also describes the Battle of Vinegar Hill from the perspective of her location at Daphne Demense on the western extremities of the town.

> On the 20th of June, the Ross Road provided a most brilliant appearance; as far as the eye could extend from Daphne was crowded with troops of every description, cannon, ammunition, sumpter carts, and all things necessary for 4 or 5000 men. When they arrived the Pioneers pulled down sufficient of the demense wall to allow them to march in with all their artillery, cavalry, etc. From the situation of the lawn nothing could exceed the magnificent appearance of such an array, when they formed into the most exact order on the ground, and at the same time such a contrast to the dirty ragged creatures we had been accustomed to for the last three weeks.
>
> By the way, when the rebels were going to fight the battle of Vinegar Hill, they left two sheep roasting in the court at Daphne for their refreshment after the battle, but the Hessians came and ate them instead … til the following day, when two armies of 4000 each marched from opposite directions, so that on 21st June they all surrounded Vinegar Hill, and had the opportunity of killing every one of them. But Humanity triumphed and the orders were issued 'to disperse but not kill'. There was an opening left to them, and not more than 2000 were slain in the Battle.

When the army marched off the next day, it was impossible to describe the desolate appearance of everything around. The numbers of men, Horses, cannon that had been on the Lawn for two days completely burned up the grass; then the Demesne wall thrown down in several places, but above all the complete absence of every person except a couple of female servants, rendered it utterly cheerless, and as Wexford was not out of the Rebel Possession, I went with my family to my Mother's [house], where I remained about six months, during which time I added another son to my Stock, who from the agitations and perils I endured, was afflicted with severe fits.

Your Uncle [Colonel Joshua Pounden] came for me, and I with my two eldest children accompanied him to his house in Dublin, where his attention and that of his wife was most kindly extended towards us.

And I have been most wonderfully enabled to bear the various trials to which I have been exposed. I mention these few circumstances of my life to shew that with a firm reliance on Divine Providence, we are enabled to bear, what the very idea of would be worse than death, assuredly believing that all things work together for our good, and that had I remained in the uninterrupted state of happiness, I might have been too much attached to this world to wish for a better.[1]

---

[1] Alicia notes of her marriage to John Pounden: 'I am sometimes inclined to think it was a dream, but it was a delightful reality which lasted 12 years, the first four of which I had no children, but during the last 8 years, had one child each year, two of whom died at 3 months.'

APPENDIX FIVE

Details of trials of those court martialled for participation in the rebellion of 1798, where there are direct references to Enniscorthy or Vinegar Hill

William Barker was charged with the murder of Benjamin Stacey, being a leader, general, colonel or captain of rebels, and of having been enrolled in a yeomanry troop under the act passed in the 37th year of the king or deserted for the same. A number of witnesses testified for and against him. These included Elizabeth Stacey, William Evans, Elizabeth Plumber, Valentine Gill, Archibald Jacob, Dr John Potter, Peter Carton, Mrs Anne Petten, General Francis Grose, Mr Bennett, Edward St Leger. He was found not guilty. The court also found that he acted in the rebel army by compulsion and used whatever influence he possessed to save and protect many loyal subjects, according to Jane Barber's diary. (Sweetman, 2013, pp 4–22)

James Beahan was tried and convicted of assisting and abetting the murders of George Piper, Thomas Piper, William Piper and William Kean on or about 31 May 1798 during the rebellion in the vicinity of the windmill on Vinegar Hill. (Sweetman, 2013, pp 23–4)

James Brien was charged but found not guilty of the murder of John Stillman on a street in Enniscorthy. (Sweetman, 2013, pp 30–3)

John Bryan was charged with the murder of Nathaniel Croshee during the rebellion and with acting as a colonel, major or captain in the rebel army during the rebellion. He was found guilty of the charges and sentenced to death. (Sweetman, 2013, pp 35–65)

Patrick Bulger was charged with aiding, assisting and abetting the murder of Thos. Cavanagh at Vinegar Hill at the beginning of June 1798, during the rebellion. Findings missing from record. (Sweetman, 2013, pp 66–7)

James Burket was charged with assisting and abetting the murder of James Minchin at or near Vinegar Hill, about the beginning of June 1798, during the rebellion. He was found guilty and sentenced to death. (Sweetman, 2013, pp 68–9)

Laurence Butler was charged with aiding, abetting and assisting with murder of George Grimes, on or about the 29 May 1798, and also having acted as a rebel captain during the rebellion. No outcome recorded. (Sweetman, 2013, pp 77–81)

Thomas Cloney was first charged with being a general, colonel, major or captain in the rebel army during the late rebellion. Secondly, he was charged with being present at the murder of John Gill, on Vinegar Hill, on 29 May 1798. He was found guilty and sentenced to death. Lord Cornwallis reduced the sentence to two years in exile. He lived in England for the duration of his exile and returned to Ireland in February 1803, taking up residence in Graiguenamanagh. He died there on 20 February 1850 at the age of 76. (Sweetman, 2013, pp 106–40)

James D'Arcy accused of aiding, abetting and being a principal person concerned in the murders of Patrick Connors, James Rigley, John Plunkett and other loyalists on Vinegar Hill on 30 May 1798. 'The court are of the opinion that he is guilty of the crime laid to his charge and do therefore sentence him to suffer death by hanging at the spot on which the murder was committed and at such time as his Majesty shall appoint.' (Sweetman, 2013, pp 164–6)

John Devereux Jnr stood charged with high treason, and with being deeply implicated and concerned in the rebellion. His sentence was transportation for life. (Sweetman, 2013, pp 167–220)

Walter Devereux was sent to trial accused of being a leader of rebellion and concerned in the murder of different persons that were made prisoners by rebels who acted under his authority. He was sentenced to death. The sentence was confirmed, and the prisoner's body ordered to be dissected. (Sweetman, 2013, pp 221–35)

John Doyle was charged with aiding, assisting and abetting the murder of a person unknown in the street of Enniscorthy on or about the 31 May during the rebellion. He was unanimously sentenced to death. (Sweetman, 2013, pp 237–8)

Patrick Doyle was charged with aiding and abetting the murder of Henry Edwards on or about 29 May 1798. He was unanimously found guilty and sentenced to death. However, 'as the prisoner seemed to have acted in some instances with humanity, and as it does not appear that he was present at the murder of Henry Edwards, the court beg leave to recommend that the sentence be mitigated to transportation for life.' (Sweetman, 2013, pp 239–42)

Christopher Druhan was confined for having in his possession arms, not being duly qualified to carry same, and for forcibly and feloniously taking and carrying away Ann James, Hannah James, Elizabeth Sheal, Hannah Sheal and Rachael Murphy against their consent. He was found guilty and sentenced to death. (Sweetman, 2013, pp 243–4)

Patrick Elliot was charged with aiding, assisting and abetting the murder of Walter Green, on or about 28 May 1798, at Enniscorthy, during the rebellion. He was sentenced to death. (Sweetman, 2013, pp 251–4)

Andrew Farrel faced charges pertaining to the murder of individuals on Vinegar Hill. No sentence given. (Sweetman, 2013, pp 257–65)

Cornelius Grogan no charge given but was known as a significant leader of the rebels. One of the witnesses at his trial was asked about levels of damage to houses and violence to inhabitants of Enniscorthy. Grogan was found guilty and executed on Wexford Bridge on 28 June 1798. (Sweetman, 2013, pp 274–372)

APPENDIX FIVE *Details of trials of those court martialled*

Thomas Hatter was charged with being a rebel, having concealed arms and firing a gun. He was found guilty and sentenced to death. (Sweetman, 2013, pp 379–82)

Philip Hay, captain of the 3rd Regiment of Foot or 'Buffs', was charged with appearing in arms and being in rebellion against His Majesty. The court found that the charges against him were proven, but that he had been compelled to act as he had. Therefore, the court 'honourably' acquitted him. Hay continued as an officer in the British army and fought in the Peninsular War and at Waterloo. During his career as a soldier, he successfully survived two further court martials and eventually rose to the office of lieutenant general. (Sweetman, 2013, pp 404–31)

Michael Kehoe was charged with aiding, assisting and abetting the murder of Roger Percival on or about the 29 May 1798, during the rebellion. 'The court found him guilty of the crime laid to his charge and do therefore sentence him to suffer death. But the court take the liberty of recommending that sentence be mitigated to transportation for life.' (Sweetman, 2013, pp 457–8)

John Lacy was charged with treason and rebellion and with having conspired with certain other persons to murder Margaret Deacon. He was found guilty and sentenced to death. (Sweetman, 2013, pp 459–61)

Patrick MacDonald was charged with aiding and abetting the murder of John Ayres during the rebellion in June 1798. No charge was given as the case was adjourned to allow the prisoner time to produce his evidence. (Sweetman, 2013, pp 468–9)

James McDaniel was charged with having assisted in the carrying away of Michael Decon to Vinegar Hill, where he was murdered by the rebels. He was found guilty and sentenced to be transported for life, 'but in consideration of many circumstances which have appeared before the court in favour of the prisoner, they do earnestly recommend him to his Excellency the Lord Lieutenant as a fit object for mercy'. (Sweetman, 2013, p. 470)

James Murphy was charged with being enrolled in the Shelmalier yeoman cavalry, deserting and joining the rebels. He was unanimously found guilty and ordered to be transported for life. (Sweetman, 2013, pp 479–89)

Miles Power was accused of the murder of Bryan Neal at Vinegar Hill, on or about 30 May 1798. No decision noted. (Sweetman, 2013, 514–20)

John Walsh was charged with aiding and abetting the wilful murder of John Keating, late of Knockrow, in the county of Carlow. He was found guilty of having aided and assisted in the carrying off of John Keating to Vinegar Hill, where it appears, he was murdered. The court sentenced him to be transported for life, but upon payment of bail on his behalf, he was bound to keep the peace for seven years. (Sweetman, 2013, pp 534–6)

Nicholas Walsh was charged with the murders of John White, Samuel Barber, Lieutenant Hunt, Thomas Hall, Revd S. Heydon and several loyalists. Also, with acting as a rebel captain. He was found guilty of the murder of all the men save Revd S. Heydon and sentenced to be taken to Vinegar Hill, put to death and have his head severed from his body, affixed to a pole and put up in the castle of Enniscorthy. Lord Cornwallis confirmed the sentence save the treatment of the severed head. (Sweetman, 2013, pp 537–43)

APPENDIX SIX

Numbers of government troops in Ireland, 1796–9

(Bartlett & Jeffery, 1997, p. 249)

Type	January 1796	January 1797	January 1798	January 1799
Cavalry	2,296	3,640	3,957	4,151
Fencible cavalry	508	664	1,820	3,139
Infantry	1,480	1,699	1,812	5,572
Fencible infantry	10,210	9,085	10,788	13,516
Militia	17,162	18,188	22,358	32,583
Yeomanry	0	0	36,854	43,221
Total	**31,656**	**33,276**	**77,589**	**102,182**
Total less yeomanry	**31,656**	**33,276**	**40,735**	**58,961**

APPENDIX SEVEN

General Needham's force at the Battle of Arklow
(Musgrave, i, 1802, plate viii)

TABLE CREATED BY CHRIS ROBINSON & JACQUI HYNES

General Needham's column (as per 9th June 1798)

Division	Unit	Colonels	Field officers	Captains	Subalterns	Staff	Quarter masters	Serjeants	Drummer & trumpeters	Rank & file	Total
Col. Sir W.W. Wynne's division	4th (Royal Irish Dragoons Guards)			2	2			3		21	28
	5th (Royal Irish Dragoons)				1					18	19
	Ancient British fencible light dragoons	1	2	1	5	2	4	7	4	81	107
Lt. Col. Cope's division	Armagh militia		1		7			3	3	107	121
	Tyrone militia (light company)			1	1			3	1	42	48
	North Cork militia				1			1	1	28	31
	Suffolk fencibles (light company)			1	1			1	3	31	37
	Cavan militia	1	1	4	9	4		14	7	312	353
Col. Maxwell Barry's division	Antrim militia		1	1	6	2		9	2	201	222
	Londonderry militia (grenadier company)			1	1			4		66	72
	Durham fencible division	1	2	4	15	4		27	15	245	313
	Dumbarton fencible infantry			1	6	1		10	5	105	128
		3	7	16	55	13	4	82	41	1257	1478

Yeomanry corps		Mounted					Dismounted				
		Captain	Subalterns	Serjeants	Trumpeters	Rank & File	Subalterns	Serjeants	Drummer	Rank & file	
Captain – Lord Wicklow	North Arklow	2	2	3	1	40		1		25	
Captain Atkins	South Wicklow	1	2	4	1	43	1	1		15	
Captain – Earl Mountnorris	Camolin	1	2	2		57	1			24	
Captain Beauman	Coolgreany	1	2	4	1	43					
Captain Knox	Castleton	1	2	4		41				9	
		6	10	17	3	224	2	2		73	337
											1815

APPENDIX EIGHT

Government troops (field army) for the Battle of Vinegar Hill

Cavalry (Smith & Haythornthwaite, 2002, plate 23)
4th – Royal Irish Dragoon Guards	Dark blue facings
5th – Princess Charlotte of Wales Dragoon Guards	Pale Green facings
7th – Princess Royal	Black facings
9th Light Dragoons (Irish Regiment)	Pale buff facings on dark blue coats

Infantry (Smith & Haythornthwaite, 2002, plates 37 and 38)

Foot Guards
1st Regiment (Grenadier)	Royal blue facings
2nd Regiment (Coldstream)	Royal blue facings
3rd Regiment	Royal blue facings

Regiments of foot
2nd – The Queen's Royal Regiment	Blue facing
13th (First Somerset) Regiment of foot	Philemont yellow facings
24th (2nd Warwickshire) Regiment of foot	Green facings
30th (Cambridgeshire) Regiment of foot	Pale yellow facings
65th (Second Yorkshire North Riding) Regiment of foot	White facings
89th Regiment (an Irish regiment)	Black facings
100th (Highland) Regiment of foot[1]	Yellow facings and government set kilt with yellow over stripe (became known as the Gordon tartan)

Rifles
60th (Royal American) Regiment of foot, 5th Battalion	Red facings on green jacket

Fencibles
Loyal Durham Regiment of fencible infantry	Buff / pale yellow or green facings
Dumbarton fencibles	Black facings, Highland dress or trews
Suffolk fencibles	Unknown to research team at present
Ancient Britons fencibles (light dragoons)	Unknown to research team at present
Midlothian fencibles (light dragoons)	Unknown to research team at present
New Romney fencible cavalry (Duke of York's Own)	Red facings on blue jacket

[1] In October 1798 it changed its title to 92nd (Highland) Regiment of foot, also known as the Gordon Highlanders.

APPENDIX EIGHT *Government troops (field army) present at the Battle of Vinegar Hill*

Militia (Smith & Haythornthwaite, 2002, plate 52)

2nd – Tyrone militia	Royal blue facings
3rd – North Mayo militia	Pale yellow/straw facings
4th – Kildare militia	Black facings
6th – Westmeath militia	Egg yolk yellow facings
7th – Antrim militia	Pale yellow/straw facings
8th – Armagh militia	White facings
9th – Downshire militia[2]	Royal blue facings
10th – Leitrim militia	Buff facings
11th – Galway militia	Pale yellow/straw facings
13th – Limerick City militia	Buff facings
15th – The Prince of Wales Longford militia	Royal blue facings
16th – Londonderry militia	Egg yolk yellow facings
17th – Royal Meath militia	Royal blue facings
18th – Cavan militia	Black facings
19th – King's County (Offaly) militia	Royal blue facings
20th – Kilkenny militia	Yellow facings
21st – County Limerick militia	Royal blue facings
22nd – Sligo militia	Pea green facings
26th – Clare militia	Egg-yolk yellow facings
27th – Cork City militia	Royal blue facings
29th – Fermanagh militia	Pale yellow/straw facings
31st – Roscommon militia	Black facings
32nd – South Cork militia	White facings
33rd – Waterford militia	Pale yellow facings
34th – North Cork militia	Egg-yolk yellow facings
35th – Dublin County militia	White facings
36th – Dunnegal militia (Donegal)	Black facings
37th – Wicklow militia	Egg-yolk yellow facings
38th – Wexford militia	Pale yellow/straw facings

Mercenary Units

Hompesch Huzzars cavalry	Red facings on green jackets

Artillery (Smith & Haythornthwaite, 2002, plate 38)

Royal Horse Artillery	Red facings on blue light dragoon jacket.
Royal Irish Artillery	Red facings on dark blue, long-tailed jacket

---

2 Became North and South Down after 1800.

APPENDIX NINE

General orders for the Battle of Vinegar Hill
(Maxwell, 1866, pp 139–40)

G.O.
General Dundas will move on the 17th to Hacketstown, and issue orders to General Loftus at Tullow, to unite his force with him on the 18th at Carnew.

General Needham, to move at three o'clock A.M., on the 19th, to Gorey; General Dundas sending a strong patrole under General Loftus from Carnew, at six o'clock on the same morning to Grove's-Bridge, four or five miles on the road to Gorey, to support General Needham, in case he should meet resistance at Limerick-hill or Gorey; and also to communicate General Needham's situation to General Dundas.

General Johnson, on the 19th, at four A.M., to move to Old Ross, and unite with General Moore in driving the rebels from Carrickbyrne-hill. He will then take a position near Old Ross, and patrole the country towards the Black-stair mountains, in conjunction with Sir James Duff. This movement will require a concerted arrangement between General Johnson and Sir James Duff. The patroles to return to their respective corps on the same day.

Sir Charles Asgill, on the 18th, to occupy Gore's-bridge, Borris and Graigenamana, and remain in those positions until the 20th, when at three P.M. he will return, unless he shall have received order to the contrary.

Lieutenant-General Dundas, on the 20th, will march to Ballycarney-bridge, keeping the eastern bank of the Slaney, to Scarawalsh-bridge, so as to arrive there at noon.

Sir James Duff will also move on the 20th, by the west side of the Slaney to Scarawalsh-bridge, where he will arrive at twelve o'clock.

General Needham, on the 20th, to move from Gorey to Oulart, and be there at twelve o'clock.

General Loftus from Grove's-bridge, will move on the 20th, by Camolin and Ferns, and unite with General Dundas at Scarawalsh-bridge at twelve o'clock.

General Moore will land on the 18th at Ballyhack-ferry, and on the 19th, will move at three o'clock A.M. to Foulkes's-mill, and unite with General Johnson in driving the rebels from Carrickbyrne-hill. He will there take up a position for night, thus securing the escape of the rebels between that and Clonmines.

General Johnson, on the 20th, will move with his column to Ballymacus-bridge, to unite in the attack on Enniscorthy, if necessary, or prevent the escape of the rebels in that direction.

Should the rebels have evacuated Enniscorthy and Vinegar-hill, the columns under General Dundas and Sir James Duff will take up their position that day in front of Enniscorthy; and General Johnson will at the same time receive orders to take a position on the great road from Enniscorthy to Taghmon.

In this case, General Moore on the 20th, will move from Foulkes's-mill, and take post at Taghmon, still securing the country between Taghmon and Clonmines.

But should the enemy maintain their position at Enniscorthy, the attack will be made on the 21st at daylight, by the columns under General Dundas and Sir James Duff, with General Needham's moving from Oulart.

The general forward movement and investment of Wexford will take place on the 21st – when the several columns shall be so united, as to receive such directions as circumstances may point out.

Orders are to be sent to the naval commanders to station their gunboats and armed vessels in Wexford harbour early in the morning of the 21st, to co-operate in such manner as may be necessary for the attack of the town; – while the gun-boats from Waterford will be directed to support General Moore and the corps at Clonmines on the 19th.

APPENDIX TEN

Eyewitness account of William Kerr, 6th marquess of Lothian, commander of the Midlothian fencible regiment
(*JWHS*, 1988–9, pp 82–5)

We consequently moved forward and arrived at our position for the night about 10 o'clock. Gen. Lake and his staff slept at the house of Capt. Richards (Solsboro) and the army slept on their arms.

At this time we were about two miles from Vinegar Hill. Between 3 and 4 o'clock in the morning of the 21st the drums beat to arms. It was near six before the different brigades were put into motion. Our army was divided into two columns, the one under Gen. Dundas, the other under Sir James Duff to whose Brigade that of Gen. Loftus was added. The plan of attack as we found afterwards was as follows: Gen. Lake was to attack the enemy's right with the light companies of Gen. Dundas's brigade; Gen. Loftus was to attack the centre; and Sir James Duff their left. Gen. Johnston who had arrived the night before and had taken a position above Enniscorthy, was to attack on the rear of their left, and Gen. Needham, who we understand had orders to march from Gorey to Olart [*sic*] so as to intercept them in their retreat to Wexford, was to come in upon their rear and to the right of it. This last column by some mistake did not come up in time or the enemy must have been totally cut off.

On seeing Gen. Dundas's light companies moving up towards their right the rebels began to file off in considerable numbers in order to line the hedges and ditches. They were gallantly attacked by the light infantry and stood their ground very well for about twenty minutes notwithstanding that a howitzer was in front of Gen. Dundas's brigade was playing upon them the greater part of that time. The battalion guns of Sir James Duff and Gen. Loftus's columns now began to open their fire on their left and centre with grapeshot with the most formidable effect. There were no less than two six-pounders or howitzers bearing upon them from this quarter at the same time. Gen. Loftus was fortunate enough to find a very advantageous [position?] for the four guns attached to us. It was a small, rocky rising ground nearly in front of the enemy's centre which tho' low relatively [*sic*] to Vinegar Hill, was sufficiently high to protect the cavalry which was shortly afterwards ordered to draw up behind it, had the enemy had presence of mind enough to direct their fire upon them [sense?]

There were eight guns belonging to Sir James Duff's brigade which were firing upon them a little to our right, and before this time Gen. Johnston had attacked the town of Enniscorthy in the rear of their right. Before we had left our ground in the morning, my squadron being as usual much divided, I offered my services to Gen. Loftus again as an aide-de-camp which he accepted and immediately sent me back to hurry on the South Cork regt. Upon coming up to it I found that it had been detained by an accident: one of their currick guns had stuck in a gateway [and] one of the horses was lying in the ditch beside it. This circumstance, however, did not create much delay in the progress of the column which was shortly afterwards halted in order, as I supposed, to give time to Gen. Lake to turn the right of the enemy. Our column was again put in motion when I received an order from Gen. Loftus who had made forward, that the whole of the cavalry belonging to Sir James Duff and his brigade were to fall into the rear of the infantry. Accordingly after passing thro' Capt. Richardson's parkgate, the cavalry formed to let the infantry pass – thus, Col. Thurles with a small squadron of the 4th Dragoon Guards were on the right, about 50 of the 5th Dragoons commanded by Capt. Ledwell – the squadron of my regiment – and lastly a troop of yeomanry. We could plainly perceive from the road the attack of the light infantry upon the hill – the irregular fire which they kept up for about 20 minutes had a very beautiful effect. They gained ground upon the enemy gradually, but not completely until our guns as before mentioned had opened upon the enemy's centre and left. I now received an order to move forward with the cavalry and to form behind the guns on the rocky eminence. In filing thro' a narrow lane for this purpose we were completely exposed to the enemy's fire had they taken advantage of the circumstance, but by this time their confusion had begun and they soon after gave way in all directions. The whole of the cavalry formed, when conceiving the present to be a favourable opportunity for putting it into action [sic], I made up to Gen. Loftus to inform him that we formed as directed and to inquire what further orders he had for us.

He desired me to return to take charge of the four guns, to dismount ten or a dozen dragoons, to level and open up the lane in our rear to the high road in order to make a freer passage for the guns in case they should be ordered that way, and likewise to send a serjant and four or five men with himself by whom he would communicate to me any orders he might have for the cavalry. I immediately made back and detached Serjeant Johnston and five Dragoons who followed the General up the hill, and I desired Capt. Thurles to dismount ten or twelve of the 4th to enlarge and repair two or three bad passes in the lane, who replied that they had no tools.

As however, it being the General's orders, it was done to the best of their ability. In the meantime the troop of Yeomanry had, without any orders moved forward about 100 yards which as soon as I perceived [it] I ordered them back to their ground. Col. Thurles, Major Dwar and myself rode on a little to the front to observe what was going on [on] the hill.

About this time, the South Cork regt was marching up the lane on our right from its former position on the road where it had been halted. Somebody observed that they were hallowing or making signals on the hill, but we could observe none such and I [?asked], Col. Thurles and Major Dewar if they considered any such signals as sufficient authority for us to advance and quit our position, who answered in the negative.

Almost immediately afterwards we could distinguish Major Elrington, Brigade-Major to Gen. Loftus beckoning with his hat. I was uncertain whether this beckoning was intended for us or for the South Cork which had just passed us. However, I detached Major Dewar with the right half squadron to ascend the hill and had scarcely done so when one of my orderly Dragoons who had accompanied the General, arrived with orders for the whole of the cavalry to move forward. We did so accordingly, but I took it upon myself to leave Capt. Ledwell with his troop of the 5th in charge of the guns. We came up with the right half squadron but he had not proceeded far when it was reported to me that a Yeoman had come from the General with a message, which as I did not rightly understand it and as the man was pointed out to me going up the hill again, I galloped after him without halting the column. He told me it was no particular message but that he had overheard Gen. Wilford say that the cavalry was to go the left or somewhere in that direction. After wishing him in hell for his officiousness I joined the troops and we had scarcely turned the hill to the south when we were halted by an aide de camp of Sir James Duff's.

Being somewhat surprised at being halted on the road by which the enemy had taken his flight, I made up to Gen. Lake whom I discovered at that time not above 50 yards on the hill above me, to find out what was going on. I told him we had been ordered to halt to which he assented and after conversing with him for a minute I addressed myself to Gen. Loftus who was about 20 yards behind him, and told him that I had taken upon myself to leave Capt. Ledwell with the four battalion guns; he answered that in so doing I had only anticipated his intention. I left Cornet Barr with him by whom he said he would transmit to me any further orders there might be and on joining the squadron I found they had begun to file off towards their rear by order of an aide de camp of Sir James Duff who said the squadron was to go down a lane, which he pointed out, into a field below. We proceeded, but I hallowed out to Major Dewar to ride up to Gen. Lake whom I had just left with an order to stand fast where we were, to know what we were to do. In a few minutes he returned with orders that we were to form in and said field fronting the South Cork which was halted in advance. The rebels were by this time completely defeated and had been followed for a considerable distance upon the road upon which we had been first halted by a squadron of my regiment under the command of Sir James Foules, and some of the Hompesch regt. which had been with Gen. Johnston's brigade. From Gen. Johnston's position in the rear of the enemy, he had detached his cavalry after the enemy almost immediately after they had broke; but Sir James Foulis has since informed me that there was no possibility of pursuing them with effect from the very enclosed nature of the country.

We encamped this night on Vinegar Hill and the neighbourhood, and next morning proceeded towards Wexford and encamped at night near the town of which Gen. Moore had taken possession the preceding day.

APPENDIX ELEVEN

Government casualties at the Battle of Vinegar Hill

A dispatch entitled 'Affairs of Ireland', written by G. Hewit, adjutant general, and published in *Universal* magazine (1798, pp 66–8), records the government casualties from the Battle of Vinegar Hill:

> Whitehall, June 30, 1798
> A Dispatch of which the following is a copy, has been received by his Excellency the lord-lieutenant of Ireland, by his grace the duke of Portland, his majesty's principal secretary of state for the home department.
>
> Dublin Castle, June 25th
> My Lord, I have the honour of enclosing to your grace, the copy of a letter received this day by lord Castlereagh, from major-general sir Charles Asgill, and a return of the killed, wounded, and missing by the attack on Vinegar-hill, and the town of Enniscorthy. I have the honour to be, &c CORNWALLIS. His grace the Duke of Portland, &c………
>
> Return of the killed, wounded, and missing, on the 21st of June, in the Attack of Vinegar-hill, and the Town of Enniscorthy.
>
> **Lieutenant general Dundas' Corps**
> Major general Sir James Duff's brigade (89th Regiment) – 1 rank and file killed.
>
> **General Needham's brigade**
> 7th Dragoon Guards – 1 captain wounded.
>
> **Rank Wilford's brigade**
> 9th dragoons – 1 rank and file killed.
> Dunlavin yeoman cavalry – 1 rank and file wounded.
> First battalion of light infantry – 1 subaltern killed, 1 sergeant wounded, 2 rank and file killed, 18 ditto wounded, 3 ditto missing.
> Sligo militia – 1 field officer wounded, 2 rank and file killed, 3 ditto wounded.
> Suffolk fencibles – 2 rank and file wounded.
> Colonel King of the Sligo corps, wounded.
> Captain Dunn, of 7th dragoon guards, wounded.
> Lieutenant S. Sands, of the Longford corps, killed.

Major general Johnson's corps
Royal British artillery, 1 rank and file wounded.
Mid Lothian, 1 subaltern wounded, 1 rank and file wounded.
Hompesch's hussars, 2 rank and file wounded.
Fifth battalion, 60th regiment, 1 captain wounded, 1 sergeant missing, 5 rank and file killed, 5 ditto wounded.
Fourth battalion, 1 subaltern killed, 1 ditto wounded, 1 sergeant killed, 3 rank and file killed, 22 ditto wounded, 1 ditto missing.
Royal Meath regiment, 1 sergeant killed.
Roscommon ditto, 1 rank and file wounded, 1 ditto missing.
Dublin county ditto, 1 field officer wounded, 2 rank and file killed, 6 ditto wounded.
Lieut. Baines, of 13th foot, attached to 4th battalion killed.
Major Vesey, of Dublin county regiment, wounded.
Capt. Schneider, of 5th battalion, 60th regiment, wounded.
Lieut. Barker, of the Kildare, attached to the 4th battalion, wounded.
Lieut. Hill, of the Mid-Lothian, wounded.
Total, 2 field officers wounded, 2 captains wounded, 2 subalterns killed, 2 ditto wounded, 2 serjeants killed, 1 ditto wounded, 1 ditto missing, 16 rank and file killed, 62 ditto wounded, 5 ditto missing.

APPENDIX TWELVE

Extract from letter of 21 June 1798 from Lake to Castlereagh
(Musgrave, ii, pp 439–40, no. xxi)

Dublin Castle, 22nd June, 1798.
My Lord, I have the honour to acquaint your lordship, for his excellency the lord lieutenant's information, that the rebel camp, upon Vinegar-hill, was attacked this morning at seven o'clock, and carried in about an hour and a half. The relative importance of this very strong position with our operations against Wexford, made it necessary to combine our attacks so as to ensure success. A column, under major-generals Johnson and Eustace was drawn from Ross, and began the attack upon the town of Enniscorthy, situate upon the right bank of the Slaney, close under Vinegar-Hill upon the right, and rather in the rear of it.

Lieutenant general Dundas commanded the centre column, supported by a column upon the right under major generals Sir James Duff and Loftus; a fourth column upon the left was commanded by the honourable major-general Needham. To the determined spirit with which these columns were conducted, and the great gallantry of the troops, we are indebted for the short resistance of the rebels, who maintained their ground obstinately for the time above mentioned; but on perceiving the danger of being surrounded, they fled with great precipitation. Their loss is not yet ascertained, but it must be very considerable. The loss on our part is not great, the particulars of which I shall report as soon as possible. In the meantime, I am sorry to say, that lieutenant Sandys of the Longford regiment is killed; and that colonel King, of the Sligo, was wounded in gallantly leading his regiment. Lord Blayney, and colonel Vesey of the county of Dublin regiment, are also wounded but I am happy to add, that the wounds of these three officers are very slight.

I cannot too highly express my obligations, particularly to lieutenant-general Dundas, and the general officers, on this occasion, for the abilities and ardour so strongly manifested by them; and to the officers of every rank, and the private men, for a prompt, brave and effectual execution of their orders.

To colonel Campbell, with his light battalion, I am much indebted for their very spirited attack; and great praise is due to the Earl of Ancram and lord Roden, for their gallant charge with their regiments, at the moment the cavalry was wanted to complete the success of the day.

It is with great gratitude I also beg leave to mention the able assistance I received from major-generals Hewitt and Cradock, and from colonel Handfield, on this, as I do on all occasions; and should be extremely wanting to myself, as well as to lord Glentworth, lieutenant-colonel Blyth, and lieutenant-colonel Read, (who did me the honour to volunteer their service, and accompany me from Dublin), were I to omit expressing the high sense I entertain of their active and useful aid to me this morning. I also beg leave to mention, in the same warm terms, my aid-de-camp, captain Nicholson.

To the rapid and well-directed fire of the royal artillery, and the gallantry of their officers and men, for which they have ever been distinguished, I consider myself this day highly indebted; and I am happy in expressing my obligations to captain Bloomfield, commanding the British, and captain Crawford, commanding the Irish royal artillery, with the officers and men under their command.

I have, &c.
(Signed) G. LAKE.

PS. I have just learned that lieutenant-colonel Cole is slightly wounded. Enclosed is a return of the ordnance taken on Vinegar-hill, in which are included three taken from us on the fourth of June.

Return of ordnance taken from the rebels on Vinegar-hill 21 June 1798
3 Six-pounders, brass.
1 Three-pounder.
7 One-pounders.
15 ½ inch howitzer.
14 ½ inch howitzer.
13 Total.

Rounds of ammunition.
17 Six-pounders.
30 One pounders.
11 5 ½ Inch howitzers.

Note. A cart, with a vast variety of balls of different diameters, had been thrown down the hill after the action, and immense quantities of lead and leaden balls delivered over to the Dunbarton fencibles.

(Signed) ROBERT CRAWFORD, captain R.I.A.

APPENDIX THIRTEEN

Ranges for guns used by government forces

Gun type	Maximum (metres)	Effective (metres)	Firing canister (metres)
3-pounder	1,000	320–400	275 approx.
6-pounder	1,100–1,350	550–640	320–60
9-pounder*	1,550	725–825	410
Light 12-pounder	1,550	725–825	600
5½-inch howitzer	1,550	640	460

* 9-pounders were not used at Vinegar Hill, but are noted here for illustrative purposes.

APPENDIX FOURTEEN

Daily rates of pay for the British army in 1800
(Haythornthwaite, 1994, p. 269)

	Cavalry	Infantry	Militia
Colonel	32s. 10d.	22s. 6d.	22s. 6d.
Major	23s.	14s. 1d.	14s. 1d.
Captain	14s. 7d.	9s. 5d.	9s. 5d.
Lieutenant	9s.	4s. 8d.	4s. 8d.
Ensign		3s. 8d.	3s. 8d.
Cornet	8s.		3s. 8d.
Paymaster	15s.	15s.	15s.
Quartermaster		4s. 8d.	4s. 8d.
Surgeon	11s. 4d.	9s. 5d.	9s. 5d.
Assistant surgeon	5s.	5s.	5s.
Sergeant	2s. 11d.	1s. 7d.	1s. 7d.
Corporal	2s. 5d.	1s. 3d.	1s. 3d.
Trumpeter	2s. 4d.		
Fifer/drummer		1s. 2d.	
Private	2s.	1s.	1s.

APPENDIX FIFTEEN

Extracts from folk narratives

Grave of Thomas Cullen
Inscription on gravestone of Thomas Cullen, Ballyvaldon Graveyard, as recorded through the Schools Collection:

> Let patriots stop awhile and pause
> For his country's freedom and Erin's cause
> He died a victim to oppression's rage
> Freedom his banner Liberty his badge
>
> Orderly united for fight designed
> To conquer or die was well reigned
> Oulart, Enniscorthy, the fact can tell
> Alas, at the Castle Wall this hero fell
> Now in the mortal arm of his Father's care
> His soul immortal, his brother's ardent prayer
> No more anon, but this much I'll say
> His brother pinned is not far away (IFC S 886:122–3)

The Bloody Bridge, Enniscorthy

> <u>Stories of '98</u> – One night a priest was going on a sick call. It was a false call planned by the yeomen to enable them to kill the priest. This was in Enniscorthy. At this time there were no motor-cars. They used to ride on horseback. As the priest was crossing over a bridge, about a mile outside Enniscorthy, two men jumped out from behind the wall and held up the priest with guns. When the priest got off his horse, he hit one of the men with his horse-whip across the face. The mark of the whip is said to be on his descendants. The other caught the priest and threw him against the wall and ran his bayonet through his heart. The blood began to drop on the bridge and you can see the point of it there to the present day. (IFC S 880: 434)

> There is a bridge about one mile from Enniscorthy which is called the Bloody Bridge. Father Redmond another leader of '98 was surrounded by Yeomen at this bridge. He stood by the bridge and caught the bullets in his hand and fired them back at the yeomen. He said that no man but a man of his own faith could kill him. A catholic renegade who was with the troopers stepped forward and fired at him. The priest, wrapping a handkerchief around his neck placed his two elbows on the bridge. The

drops of blood falling from his neck fell on the bridge. To this day it is known as the Bloody Bridge. (IFC S 893: 256–7)

During the '98 rebellion the tragedy which gives Bloody Bridge its name occurred. A few miles from this [Duffry Gate, Enniscorthy] there lived three men and a girl. The girl was a Catholic. The three men conspired to kill a priest but the girl whom they thought was asleep overheard their plans. They induced the priest to leave his home late at night by sending him word to go on a sick call. He got his white horse and on his way to the patient's house he had to pass by Bloody Bridge. As he was passing it someone hit him on the head with an iron bar. He fell dead. When it is raining the blood can still be seen on the stones. The print of the horses hoofs can also be seen. It is said that the white horse can be seen after midnight guarding the bridge where his master was killed. (IFC S 894: 69–70)

<u>Historical Tradition</u> – About half way between Enniscorthy and Mile House is a bridge known as Bloody Bridge. During the '98 rebellion some insurgents marching from the town encountered a force of yoemen at this bridge. A fierce struggle ensued and many lives were lost on both sides and it is said that the blood can still be seen on the stones if thoroughly examined. Hence the name.

About a mile or so on the Enniscorthy side of the Mile House is a bridge called Bloody Bridge. A priest passing along that way on a sick call was captured by the yoemen. Just as he was nearing the bridge the yoemen placed a thick rope across the road with the result that the priest was thrown from his horse and broke his neck in the fall. (IFC S 894: 11–12)

Bloody Bridge – This is situated a quarter of a mile from Enniscorthy. In the year 1798 there was a great many people killed on a bridge and so it is called the Bloody Bridge. (IFC S 893: 177)

Jack the Cooper and the ghost of Hunter Gowan

Jack the Cooper, the best fighting man in Wexford on his way home one dark night from Enniscorthy encountered the ghostly horseman who was none other than the infamous Hunter Gowan himself, the notorious priest-hunter and rebel-killer of 1798. The Cooper arriving at the old disused graveyard opposite Lett's gate, suddenly observed the red nostrils of what seemed to be the shape of a horse spitting fire. Halting the auld ass Jack reached for the flail he purchased that day in Enniscorthy and taking off his coat demanded in a firm voice as he approached the apparition an explanation of their presence on such holy ground. There being no answer the Cooper withdrew from his pocket a bottle of holy water which he sprinkled over horse and rider and then challenged him like this.

> I have waited many years to encounter you Mr Hunter Gowan, and I stand here as a direct descendant of Father John our ancestor's gallant leader and saintly saggart who had they had a dog's chance in 1798, would have knocked the devil out of ye, ye dirty pack of brutal hell hounds, the scruff of the earth, collected from every element of debasement and dishonour. Not a hundred yards from

where you stand tradition tells us that you in the month of June 1798, hanged no less than 18 young men from a gibbet. You erected it by this graveyard wall and I suppose ould Nick permits you an occasional night off to remind you of your frolics, you filthy ould baste.

At that moment the Cooper observed the horse becoming restive and he heard a sound as if a sword was being drawn. He at once swung the flail landing a merciless blow directly on the rider's head and shoulders the sound of which might be heard for miles. From the wall to Lett's entrance every inch of the distance was contested, the whiz of the Cooper's weapon singing through the air, left and right mighty blows were administered and Gowan spurring on his charger to greater efforts. He parried and cut and feigned advanced and retired with the object of breaking through the Cooper's defence, but with little effect. Jack's winning card was to fight in the open and his strategy throughout the battle was not to permit himself to be drawn into the woodlands.

Once there, the flail would be of little use, consequently the battle continued on the roadway until the Cooper with unerring aim, let fly the bottle at the rider, and in an instant a roar of rumbling thunder broke over the immediate battleground and like a huge ball of fire the horse and rider instantly disappeared. (IFC S 891: 21–3)

Ghosts of rebels killed at Vinegar Hill

<u>Connection with Wexford</u> – Paul Kinsella's great great grandmother lived in the house at present occupied by the widow of Geoff Brennan. Her husband fought with the rebels at Vinegar Hill in 1798, and was shot there. She worried a great deal after his death, and as a result she completely lost her sight. Her son was a carpenter, and was married. He and his wife, and mother came to live to 'Mary Bradley's', a house which formerly stood on Kinsella's land, near the river. He was a journeyman carpenter, and was often away from home. One night he was away as usual, and his wife and mother-in-law were sleeping together. At the dead of night, the blind woman heard the door opening, and the sound of many voices. She recognized her husband's voice, and the voices of others who were killed with him at Vinegar Hill. They talked for a time, and suddenly there was a commotion as if they had been alarmed, and they all took their departure through the back window. The younger woman also heard the noise, and was very much frightened. When her husband arrived shortly afterwards, she was afraid to open the door for him, and the blind mother had to grope her way and let her son in. She said that there was no need to be alarmed, as they all came and went in good humour. (IFC S 865: 348–9)

Hidden Treasure

<u>Hidden Treasure</u> – A treasure is hidden in the centre of a wood about six miles north of Enniscorthy. This place is called Kil-Aughrim. The spot where the treasure is hidden is called the 'Babes Glen'. It was hidden there by a wealthy young man named Howlan before the rebellion of 1798. One night he put all his possessions

which consisted of bars of silver and gold into a coach and brought them to the 'Babes Glen' and buried them there. He then cut the coachman's head off and buried him with the treasure. Howlan buried his wealth because his life was in danger and he was a Yeoman also and was afraid the rebels would burn his house.

One night three men thought they would try and unearth the treasure. A farmer named Roche gave them picks and shovels to dig. (He himself was there also). It happened that one of them struck the chest. Suddenly a strange thing happened. They heard a noise louder than thunder. They looked around in amazement. Thundering up the little path was a carriage drawn by a pair of headless horses and a headless coachman driving it. The men ran for their lives.

The headless man followed Roche to his house. Roche ran upstairs and locked himself in his bedroom. The headless man shook the door so much that the end wall of Roche's house fell next day. (IFC S 893: 250–1)

There is a river named the Boro about 5 miles south of this school. In this river there is a hole which is called the 'Soldier's Hole'. There is a wood over that river. In 1798 there was a band of English soldiers in it and they had a box of gold with them. A crowd of men gathered together and ran them out of the wood. These soldiers threw the box of gold into this hole. They told a man to mind it and he said he would mind it for all time. Then the men who were chasing the soldiers shot the man and then he was changed into an eel with a man's head on him and he lived in the water. When there would be great silence he would come out of the water and graze the grass around him. Often times men used to try to get the box of gold out of the hole. They used to get a long rope and one man would go down in the water and put the rope around the box of gold and the other men would draw the box of gold to the top of the water but when it would come to the top of the water the eel would appear and cut the rope with his mouth so that every time they tried to get the gold they failed. (IFC S 893: 4–5)

Hidden Treasure – On the Boro the tributary of the Slaney there is a deep hole. This hole is known in the locality as 'the soldier's hole'. This was the camping place for the soldiers in 1798. There was a small bridge spanning the water. One night a man was run from his home because he was a 'rebel'. This man had gold in a trunk in his possession. When he was routed he grabbed the gold and made for the bridge. He was in the centre of the bridge when he was shot by the soldiers. He fell into the water gold and all. It is said that when the man hit the bottom he changed into a serpent. A diver attempted to recover the gold but the serpent would not let him go near it. (IFC S 893: 250)

Reynolds Grave

Historical Tradition – In the townland of Monart near Enniscorthy, there dwelt an officer of the English Yoemanary called Reynold Grannells. When the Yeomen had taken Enniscorthy from the Insurgents, like all Yeomen settlers in the County Wexford this man was allotted a portion of the land and dwelling house. The

Insurgents later regained their strength and made some fierce attacks on the yeomen. In one of these attacks Reynold Grannells was shot and piked on Vinegar Hill. His dying request was that he would be buried facing the lawn of his own dwelling. The place where he is buried can be seen from the roadway because there is a rough stone monument, such as a field post, marking the spot. The inscription on it can be read. It runs as follows:

> Reynold Grannells
> Shot and piked on Vinegar Hill
> Dead and buried and alive still. (IFC S 894: 65–6)

<u>John Reynold's Grave</u> – John Reynolds was a protestant who joined the yoes in '98. He was piked at the battle of Vinegar Hill. His grave is in a corner of Deacon's field in the townsland of Monart, Enniscorthy. The tomb is built up with sods and stones. On top of the mound is a large stone on which is written – 'John Reynolds shot and piked by the Rebels at Vinegar Hill.' He expressed a wish before he died to be buried in that field. For many years afterwards a light was seen near the spot at twelve o'clock at night. One night Moses Burns and his wife (they lived in Ballybreen in Ballindaggin parish) were coming home from Enniscorthy. As they were passing the grave a bright light shone across the road and the form of a pike appeared on the ditch. Mary Byrne fell off the car and died two days afterwards. (IFC S 892: 311)

<u>Historical Tradition</u> – About a mile from the Mile House there is a place called Monart. There is a grave of a man named Reynolds who was shot on Vinegar Hill in 1798. On the morning of the battle on Vinegar Hill he went to join the yoemen and he was shot by the insurgents on that day. His body was brought to a field owned by a man named Leslie now owned by Mr Shiel. The body was buried inside the ditch a few yards from the road. There was a tombstone erected over the grave and it is still to be seen. (IFC S 894: 12–13)

During the rebels' campaign to take the town of Enniscorthy a man named Reynold left his home in Monart and went to fight on Vinegar Hill. One morning the rebels saw Reynold looking over a wall. Suspecting him to be a spy they shot him. Next day his wife left her home and went to Vinegar Hill seeking her husband. When she found her husband she brought him home and buried him at Monart. (IFC S 893: 259)

Illustrations

1.1 Members of the steering group and others on Vinegar Hill, 31 Jan. 2014: Tony Larkin, Robert Shaw, Graham Cadogan, Tony Pollard, Ronan O'Flaherty, Jacqui Hynes, Rory O'Connor, Kieran Costello, Ian Kidd, Cathy Keane, Damian Shiels. Photo by Patrick Browne. Courtesy of the National 1798 Rebellion Centre.   8

2.1 'The [Rebel] Camp on Vinegar Hill', by George Cruikshank (Maxwell, 1866, p. 99). Courtesy of Wexford Public Library Service, Local Studies Collection.   17

2.2 The charismatic rebel leader Miles Byrne. Photograph taken in Paris in 1859.   21

3.1 British uniform style of the day.   39

3.2 Representation of 'defending the colours' at a Battle of Vinegar Hill re-enactment in 2013. Courtesy of the National 1798 Rebellion Centre.   43

3.3 Sketch plan of the battle, by Hardy after McGurk 1798. PD HP (1798) 21. Courtesy of the National Library of Ireland.   51

3.4 Illustration of crown forces and rebel positions for the Battle of Vinegar Hill. Map by Greg Walsh and Brian Ó Cléirigh.   52

3.5 'The Battle of Vinegar Hill'. Courtesy of Wexford Public Library Service, Local Studies Collection.   53

3.6 'Defeat of the Rebels at Vinegar Hill' by George Cruikshank (Maxwell, 1866, p. 145). Courtesy of Wexford Public Library Service, Local Studies Collection.   56

3.7 Vinegar Hill, charge of the 5th Dragoon Guards on the insurgents by William Sadler. PD 3176 TX1. Courtesy of the National Library of Ireland.   60

4.1 Oaths to be taken by the United Army.   77

5.1 British regimental baggage wagons, c.1802. Print after W.H. Pyne.   95

5.2 An army wagon train moves along a country road. Print after W.H. Pyne.   98

5.3 Route taken by Needham's column from Oulart to Solsborough and from Solsborough to Darby's Gap. Base map is by Valentine Gill, 1811. Reproduced with permission of Wexford County Council Archive Service.   100

5.4 Route taken during test march on 3 Sept. 2017, reconstructing the route taken from Oulart by Needham in 1798, first to Solsborough and then to Darby's Gap. Base map © Ordnance Survey Ireland/Government of Ireland. Copyright permit MP 001021.   102

5.5 Members of the Reserve Defence Forces, Lord Edward's Own and Enniscorthy Historical Re-enactment Group, who participated in our investigation. Photo by Jacqui Hynes.   103

6.1	Down Survey map of Enniscorthy showing a walled town at the junction of two rivers. L. Brown Collection of Digital Historic Maps.	106
6.2	Early road map by Taylor and Skinner showing Enniscorthy around 1777, with Vinegar Hill and its landmark windmill clearly visible.	107
6.3	Valentine Gill map of 1811. Reproduced with permission of Wexford County Council Archive Service.	108
6.4	Plan of the Battle of Vinegar Hill. Map by Greg Walsh and Brian Ó Cléirigh.	110
6.5	Enniscorthy *c.*1775, showing the castle and the bridge, which was hotly contested at both the Battle of Enniscorthy and the Battle of Vinegar Hill. From P. Sandby, *A collection of one hundred and fifty select views in England, Scotland and Ireland* (London, 1778). Private collection: Ronan O'Flaherty.	113
6.6	Detail from the Portsmouth estate map *c.*1822 showing the townscape of Enniscorthy and the Island that the rebels attempted to cross during the Battle of Enniscorthy. Courtesy of the earl of Portsmouth. Hampshire Record Office: 15M84/MP35.	117
6.7	Vinegar Hill, probably late nineteenth century. Robert French (Lawrence Collection), NLI L_CAB_07017. Courtesy of the National Library of Ireland.	118
6.8	Deep lane just below Vinegar Hill, probably one of the deep 'trenches' that rebels are described as occupying. Photo by Ronan O'Flaherty.	119
6.9	Electric Picnic 2018, where some 50,000 people were in attendance. Photo by An Garda Síochána, 2 Sept. 2018.	120
6.10	The windmill on Vinegar Hill – the iconic symbol of the rebellion in Wexford. Photo by Ronan O'Flaherty.	122
6.11a	Junction of the old Ferns and Clonhasten roads, where General Loftus broke away from the main force and made his dash to capture the all-important 'green hill'. Base image © Google.	127
6.11b	The outline of Vinegar Hill on the skyline, much as it would have appeared to General Loftus when he veered away from the main force to take 'the road to the fields'. Photo by Ronan O'Flaherty.	128
6.12a	Sketch plan of the battle, by Hardy after McGurk 1798. Location of Loftus indicated to the left of the Clonhasten Road. PD HP (1798) 21. Courtesy of the National Library of Ireland.	129
6.12b	The location of Loftus to the right of the Clonhasten Road (shown here as the 'road to the fields'). Contemporary map by Alexander Taylor of the Royal Engineers. Reproduced with permission of Wexford County Council Archive Service.	130
6.12c	The location of Loftus to the right of the Clonhasten Road. Reproduced with permission of Wexford County Council Archive Service.	131
6.13a	Aerial view of the modern road layout, showing location of junction where Loftus detached from the main column and the possible locations of the all-important 'green hill' per the contemporary records. Base image © Google.	132

Illustrations

6.13b First candidate for the 'green hill' occupied by Loftus – looking north-east, with the view south-west to Vinegar Hill inset. Photos by Ronan O'Flaherty. 133

6.13c Vinegar Hill as viewed from the top of our second candidate for the 'green hill' occupied by Loftus. Photo by Ronan O'Flaherty. 134

6.13d A view of our third candidate for the 'green hill' as it appears to the west of the Clonhasten Road, at the point where McGurk's map shows Loftus to have reached (but placing him on the opposite side of the road). Photo by Ronan O'Flaherty. 136

6.14 Beale's Barn, the notorious rebel prison at the foot of Vinegar Hill, as it appears today. Photo by Jacqui Hynes. 139

7.1 A 1793 view of 'Enniscorthy Castle and Bridge, Co. Wexford' (Grose, 1795). Private collection: Ronan O'Flaherty. 143

7.2 'Enniscorthy Castle, Co. Wexford.' By Francis Grose, 1792. Private collection: Ronan O'Flaherty. 143

7.3 Enniscorthy, oil on canvas, by Paul Sandby, *c*.1775. 145

7.4 'Vinegar Hill from the Bridge of Enniscorthy', *Gentleman's Journal,* 1801. Private collection: Ronan O'Flaherty. 146

7.5 Destruction of the church at Enniscorthy, engraved by George Cruickshank (Maxwell, 1845, p. 97). Courtesy of Wexford Public Library Service, Local Studies Collection. 147

8.1 Location of the search area. Image by James Bonsall and Cian Hogan, based on data collected by Earthsound Archaeological Geophysics. 159

8.2 Magnetometry survey results. 163

8.3 Earth resistance survey results. 164

8.4 Electrical resistivity imaging (ERI) survey and interpretation. Inset: Location of the ERI survey profiles across the pits. 165

8.5 Interpretive model of the search area, comprised of the backfilled quarry pit (northern pit) and pilot/trial pits or shallow graves (southern and south-western pits), along with stone deposits and disturbed soils. 167

9.1 Topographic map showing Enniscorthy at the centre of its landscape. ADCO. 172

9.2 View across the River Slaney in 2015, highlighting the dynamic water flow as it traverses Enniscorthy Bridge. ADCO. 173

9.3 View across the north end of the Island, highlighting its ruined building today with its curiously robust abutments. ADCO. 174

9.4 View looking from the Island towards Vinegar Hill obscured by the railway and its embankment that was built for its opening in 1872, and subsequent development. ADCO. 175

9.5 Down Survey, showing the town in 1654, with dashed line highlighting Enniscorthy. L. Brown Collection of Digital Historic Maps. 177

9.6	Detail from Ordnance Survey first-edition six-inch map sheet 20 highlighting the bridge in 1840, with overlay of modern river bank. © Ordnance Survey Ireland/Government of Ireland. Copyright permit MP 001021.	178
9.7	Different aspects of the bridge's stonework today: a) west-facing view of Enniscorthy Bridge (Arch 4) on its downstream side; b) view of composition of the intrados (arch ceiling) within Arch 4; c) north-facing example shot of triangular cutwaters located on the upstream side of Enniscorthy Bridge (1m scale); d) example of rounded cutwater located on the downstream side of Enniscorthy Bridge (1m scale). ADCO.	182–3
9.8	Archaeological survey of riverbed under Enniscorthy Bridge, showing principal observations. ADCO.	184
9.9	Underwater view of section of bonded masonry from the third section of collapsed masonry, identified under Arch 3, Section 8 (1m scale). ADCO.	185
9.10	Cast-iron bell-shaped object recovered from debris concentration upstream of Enniscorthy Bridge and considered to be a mud-anchor. ADCO.	186
10.1	Fields 1–8 assessed by the systematic licenced metal-detection survey across Vinegar Hill. Image by James Bonsall and Damian Shiels.	192
10.2	Distribution map of metal finds and lead bullets recovered from the systematic licensed metal-detection survey across Vinegar Hill. Image by James Bonsall and Damian Shiels.	198
10.3	Lead bullets fired from a musket and pistol, collected from Vinegar Hill during the systematic licensed metal-detection survey. Image: Michael Cahill.	200
10.4	Some of the lead bullets collected from Vinegar Hill during the systematic licensed metal-detection survey, exhibiting various rates of impaction. Image: Michael Cahill.	203
11.1	Locations of findspots of archaeological artefacts recovered during metal-detecting of stripped topsoil during the Vinegar Hill monitoring. © Stafford McLoughlin Archaeology.	206
11.2	Topsoil stripping of main pathway to summit of Vinegar Hill, looking west (western section). © Stafford McLoughlin Archaeology.	207
11.3	Musket balls recovered from pathways. © Stafford McLoughlin Archaeology.	208
11.4	Lead strips recovered from archaeological monitoring. © Stafford McLoughlin Archaeology.	208
11.5	Copper alloy objects recovered including a thimble, buttons and a George II or III coin dating to the eighteenth century. © Stafford McLoughlin Archaeology.	209
11.6	View of Clonhasten development site from the car park at Vinegar Hill. © Stafford McLoughlin Archaeology.	211
11.7	Location of the Clonhasten survey area in relation to the location of Vinegar Hill. Base map © Google Earth.	211

11.8	Fields surveyed at Clonhasten and general location of the lead shot and militaria uncovered during the survey (possible location of the 'green hill'). Base map © Google Earth.	212
11.9	Lead shot recovered from Field 2 during the survey at Clonhasten. © Stafford McLoughlin Archaeology.	214
11.10	Selection of militaria recovered from the Clonhasten survey. © Stafford McLoughlin Archaeology.	214
11.11	Two of the coins recovered from Clonhasten. © Stafford McLoughlin Archaeology.	216
12.1	View of Vinegar Hill from Corrig graveyard. Photo by Jacqui Hynes.	239
12.2	Tomb of Stephen William Reynells. Photo by Jacqui Hynes.	241
13.1	Location of the old bridge over the Boyne at Leinster Bridge, Clonard. Photo by Ciarán McDonnell.	252
13.2	Depiction of the attack on the tower at Clonard by George Cruickshank (Maxwell, 1845). Courtesy of Wexford Public Library Service, Local Studies Collection.	252
13.3	Map of the approximate route taken by the rebel army. Map drawn by Morogh O'Flaherty. Base map © Ordnance Survey Ireland/Government of Ireland. Copyright permit MP 001021.	253
13.4	a) 1796-pattern British light-cavalry sabre with b) close-up of hilt. Photo by Ciarán McDonnell.	255
13.5	Bogland at Knightstown. Photo by Ciarán McDonnell.	256
13.6	A croppy grave in Co. Meath. Photo by Ciarán McDonnell.	257
13.7	The 1798 memorial at Mountainstown. Photo by Ciarán McDonnell.	258

TABLES

TABLE 1:	Length of baggage train	99
TABLE 2:	March times	101

Abbreviations

ADC	aide-de-camp
aDNA	ancient DNA
ERI	Electrical resistivity imaging
GIS	Geographic Information System
GPR	ground-penetrating radar
IFC	National Folklore Collection Main Manuscript Collection
IFC S	National Folklore Collection Schools Folklore Collection
IT	institute of technology
JWHS	*Journal of the Wexford History Society*
NCO	non-commissioned officer
NLI	National Library of Ireland
NMS	National Monuments Service
OSI	Ordnance Survey Ireland
RA	Royal Artillery
RHA	Royal Horse Artillery
RIA	Royal Irish Artillery
XRF	X-ray flourescence

Contributors

Rex Bangerter MA is a leading maritime archaeologist with over twenty years' experience working in underwater archaeology throughout Ireland, Spain and the UK. He is also an experienced commercial diver, trained to the highest level of HSE certified diving (closed-bell/saturation diving) and is a director of the Archaeological Diving Company (ADCO).

Dr James Bonsall is an archaeologist specializing in geophysics and remote sensing. He led the forensic surveys for Earthsound Geophysics Ltd, and co-directed the metal-detection survey on Vinegar Hill. He is a lecturer at IT Sligo, director of Fourth Dimension Prospection Ltd and has previous publications on metal detection across battlefields in the UK.

Dr Niall Brady is a medievalist by training with special interests in agrarian technology, landscape archaeology and underwater archaeology. Co-founding director of the Archaeological Diving Company (ADCO) in 1999, Niall and his team continue to develop the company as Ireland's premier underwater archaeological consultancy.

Cian Hogan is an archaeologist based in the west of Ireland. He works with Earthsound Geophysics Ltd, carrying out archaeological geophysical surveys. He has his own practice conducting lithic analyses. His research interests revolve around prehistory in Ireland, with a focus on lithic traditions.

Jacqui Hynes is a member of the Longest Day Research Project, a teacher and former manager of the National 1798 Rebellion Centre. She has a master's of literature on the folklore of the 1798 Rebellion from University College Dublin and has written and published on this and wider folk traditions.

Edmund Joyce lectures at IT Carlow. His architectural work centres around architectural conservation and preservation of historic interiors. He has published extensively on material culture and architectural history. His MA thesis, *Borris House and elite Regency patronage*, was published in 2013 by Four Courts Press as part of the Maynooth Studies in Local History series.

Dr Ciarán McDonnell is a historian specialising in the long eighteenth century. He has published on Irishmen in the British army, the Irish militia and the Irish Brigade in France. He has also published on medieval Ireland and the Crusades.

Catherine McLoughlin is an archaeologist and partner in Stafford McLoughlin Archaeology, a heritage consultancy based in Wexford. A graduate of Queen's University Belfast and Trinity College Dublin, she has published widely on the archaeological landscapes of Co. Wexford.

Colm Moriarty, a graduate of University College Dublin, is an archaeologist and historian from Bree, Co. Wexford. He blogs about Irish archaeology and manages the website www.irisharchaeology.ie and its associated social-media channels.

Brian Ó Cléirigh, B.Agr.Sc., BA, is a native of Oulart, Co. Wexford. He is an NUIG history graduate and a retired senior translator in the houses of the Oireachtas, whose great great grand-uncle John Clary, Rathdrum, was one of gallant Michael Dwyer's men in 1798.

Rory O'Connor is a local historian with a particular interest in the 1798 rebellion. He has a B.Sc. degree in applied archaeology from IT Sligo and is a former manager of the National 1798 Rebellion Centre.

Dr Ronan O'Flaherty is an archaeologist and heritage consultant based in Wexford. He is a graduate of University College Dublin, a former CEO of the Discovery Programme (Centre for Archaeology and Innovation Ireland) and chair of the Longest Day Research Project.

Dr Tony Pollard is professor of conflict history and archaeology at the University of Glasgow, where he co-founded the *Journal of Conflict Archaeology* and the Centre for Battlefield Archaeology. His current projects include Waterloo Uncovered, which engages military veterans in the investigation of the 1815 battlefield.

Chris Robinson is a history graduate of the University of Limerick and has a lifelong interest in this area, particularly in weaponry and artillery. He has been involved in historical re-enactment for over forty years, focusing on the crown forces during the 1798 rebellion, Napoleonic Wars and American Civil War.

Dr Damian Shiels is a conflict archaeologist and historian who directed the archaeological fieldwork programme at Vinegar Hill and led the Rubicon Heritage Services Ltd team. He has published and lectured widely on Irish battlefield and conflict archaeology, and previously examined Vinegar Hill as part of the Irish Battlefields Project.

Emmet Stafford is an archaeologist, heritage consultant and partner in Stafford McLoughlin Archaeology. He has published on the history and archaeology of Ireland, with a focus on the archaeology of medieval Wexford and has a particular interest in the presentation and communication of heritage sites and spaces.

Barry Walsh is a re-enactor and living-history practitioner. Since 2004 he has been recreating the experience of participants in the 1798 rebellion, Napoleonic Wars, First World War and the Irish War of Independence with his group Lord Edward's Own Living History.

Bibliography

Alexander, J. 1800. *Some account of the first apparent symptoms of the late rebellion in the county of Kildare and an adjoining part of the King's County, with a succinct narrative of some of the most remarkable passages in the rise and progress of the rebellion in the County of Wexford, especially in the vicinity of Ross* (Dublin).

Anon. 1798. *An extract of a letter from a gentleman in Ireland to Mr William Thompson* (London).

Anon. 1805. *The history of the late grand insurrection or struggle for liberty in Ireland or, Struggle for liberty in Ireland impartially collected from Stephens, Hay, Jones &c.* (Carlisle).

Anon. 1806. *History of the rebellion in Ireland, in the year 1798* (Workington).

Anon. 2011. *Parkhead History*, http://parkheadhistory.com/vinegar-hill (accessed 9 Nov. 2020).

Anon. n.d. *Castle Hill rebellion*. National Museum Australia, https://www.nma.gov.au/defining-moments/resources/castle-hill-rebellion (accessed 9 Nov. 2020).

Bangerter, R. 2012. 'Underwater archaeological investigation, River Nore crossing point and Little Arrigle River, medieval settlement of Newtown Jerpoint, Thomastown, Co. Kilkenny', unpublished report for the Heritage Council, Grant RO2764.

Banim, M. 1865. *The croppy; a tale of the Irish rebellion of 1798* (Dublin).

Barrington, J. 1827. *Personal sketches of his own times* (London).

Bartlett, T. 1988–9. 'An officer's memoir of Wexford in 1798', *Journal of the Wexford Historical Society* 12, pp 72–85.

Bartlett, T. 1997. 'Counter-insurgency and rebellion' in T. Bartlett and K. Jeffery, *A military history of Ireland* (Cambridge).

Bartlett, T. & K. Jeffery. 1997. *A military history of Ireland* (Cambridge).

Bartlett, T., D. Dickson, D. Keogh & K. Whelan (eds). 2003. *1798: a bicentenary perspective* (Dublin).

Beatty, J.D. 2001. *Protestant women's narratives of the Irish rebellion of 1798* (Dublin).

Beck, J.D., L.T. Burds, R.J. Mataitis, H.M. Jol, R.A. Freund, A.F. McClymont & P. Bauman. 2018. 'Searching for Nazi mass execution trenches at Fort IX (Kaunas, Lithuania)', 17th International Conference on Ground Penetrating Radar (GPR), Rapperswil.

Beegan, M. 1820. *An impartial history of the Irish rebellion, in the year 1798*, vol. 1 (Manchester).

Beiner, G. 2006. *Remembering the Year of the French: Irish folk history and social memory* (Madison, WI).

Bennet, C. 1768. *A system for the complete interior management and economy of a battalion of infantry* (Dublin).

Binns, J. 1837. *The miseries and beauties of Ireland*, 2 vols (London).

Blackmore, H. 1969. *British military firearms, 1650–1850* (London).

Brady, C., E. Byrnes, G. Cooney & A. O'Sullivan. 2007. 'An archaeological study of the Battle of the Boyne at Oldbridge, Co. Meath' in I. Banks & T. Pollard (eds), *Scorched earth: studies in the archaeology of conflict*, *Journal of Conflict Archaeology*, 3, pp 53–78.

Brady, N. 2004. 'Archaeological investigation and excavation, John's Bridge, Kilkenny: River Nore Flood Alleviation Scheme, final report, 01E0036', unpublished report of the Archaeological Diving Company Ltd.

Burdy, Revd S. 1817. *The history of Ireland from the earliest ages to the Union* (Edinburgh).

Byrne, M. 1863. *Memoirs of Miles Byrne: chef de battalion in the service of France, officer of the Legion of Honour, knight of Saint-Louis, etc*, vol. 1 (Paris).

Byrne-Rothwell, D. 2010. *The Byrnes and the O'Byrnes*, vol. 2 (Isle of Colonsay).

Cahill, M. 2018. 'The archaeological evidence of crown artillery action at the battle site of Vinegar Hill (1798): a methodology for interrogating Fe (iron) finds of potential probability' (BA, Institute of Technology, Sligo).

Cantwell, B. 1992. 'Persons who died in 1798, &c: part 2', *The Past: The Organ of the Uí Cinseallaigh Historical Society*, 18.

Carman, J. & P. Carman. 2006. *Bloody meadows: investigating cultural landscapes of battle* (Cheltenham).

Castlereagh, R. 1848. *Memoirs and correspondence of Viscount Castlereagh, second marquess of Londonderry by Castlereagh, Robert Stewart, viscount, 1769–1822* (London).

Cavalcanti, M.M., M.P. Rocha, M.L. Bassay Blum & W.R. Borges. 2018. 'The Forensic Geophysical Controlled Research Site of the University of Brasilia, Brazil: results from methods GPR and electrical resistivity tomography', *Forensic Science International*, 293: e1–101.

Chambers, L. 2003. 'The 1798 rebellion in north Leinster' in T. Bartlett, D. Dickson, D. Keogh & K. Whelan (eds). 2003. *1798: a bicentenary perspective* (Dublin).

Charlotte-Elizabeth. 1838. *Letters from Ireland* (London).

Cleary, B. 1999. *The Battle of Oulart Hill, 1798: context and strategy* (Naas).

Cleary, B. 1992–3. 'Sowing the whirlwind', *Journal of the Wexford Historical Society*, 14.

Clements, B. 2011. *Martello towers worldwide* (Barnsley).

Cloney, T. 1832. *A personal narrative of those transactions in the County Wexford, in which the author was engaged, during the awful period of 1798* (Dublin).

Corrigan, S.L. 1844. *A new and improved history of the rebellion in Ireland in the year 1798* (Belfast).

Craig, M. 2020. *One day in April: the Scottish radical rising of 1820* (Edinburgh).

Cronin, J., F. Fitzsimons & D. Shiels. 2008. 'Report on the Battlefield of Vinegar Hill, Co. Wexford, 1798', unpublished client report for the Department of the Environment, Heritage & Local Government.

Crooks, J. 1914. *History of the Royal Irish Regiment of artillery* (Dublin).

Cullen, Revd Br L. 1959. *Personal recollections of Wexford and Wicklow insurgents of 1798* (Enniscorthy).

Curry, A. & G. Foard. 2016. 'Where are the dead of medieval battles? A preliminary survey', *Journal of Conflict Archaeology*, 11:2–3, pp 61–77.

Dargan, P. 2013. *The Georgian town house* (Stroud).

De Vál, S. 1998. 'George Taylor's experiences in the insurrection of 1798', *The Past: The Organ of the Uí Cinsealaigh Historical Society*, 21, pp 49–57.

Dickson, D. 1955. *The Wexford rising in 1798: its causes and its course* (Tralee).

Bibliography

Dickson, D., D. Keogh & K. Whelan. 1993. *The United Irishmen: republicanism, radicalism and rebellion* (Dublin).

Donnelly, L.J. & M. Harrison. 2013. 'Geomorphological and geoforensic interpretation of maps, aerial imagery, conditions of diggability and the colour-coded RAG prioritization system in searches for criminal burials' in D. Pirrie, A. Ruffell & L.A. Dawson (eds), *Environmental and criminal geoforensics* (London), pp 173–94.

Donohoe, P.A. 1998. *1798 rebellion: brave rebels all: Wexford, Wicklow, Carlow, Kildare* (Enniscorthy).

Doyle, E. 2011. *March into Meath: in the footsteps of 1798* (Dublin).

Doyle, E. 2013. 'The last of the storytellers: 1798 and Meath' in F. Tallon (ed.), *The field names of County Meath* (Drogheda), pp 230–44.

Duncan, F. 2012. *History of the Royal Regiment of artillery, vol II (1784–1815): compiled from original sources* (London).

'Dundas of Manour', http://www.dundasfamily.co.uk/dundas%20of%20manour.htm (accessed 7 June 2020).

Dunne, T. 2010. *Rebellions: memoir, memory and 1798* (Dublin).

Dunne, L. 2017. 'There's a buzz back and there's kids wanting to go to watch Wexford hurling again', *The 42*, 10 June 2017, available at the42.ie (accessed 28 Feb. 2018).

Eustace, R. 2009. *Eustace Family Association*, http://www.roneustice.com/Family%20History/IrishFamiliessub/Robertstown.html (accessed 19 Nov. 2017).

Field, H.M. 1851. *The Irish confederates, and the rebellion of 1798* (New York).

Fraser, J. 1844. *A hand book for travellers in Ireland* (Dublin).

Furlong, N. 1991. *Fr John Murphy of Boolavogue: 1753–1798* (Dublin).

Furlong, N. 1996. 'Wexford Bridge', Letters to the Editor, *Irish Times*, 23 Aug. 1996, https://www.irishtimes.com/opinion/letters/wexford-bridge-1.79399 (accessed 15 Jan. 2018).

Furlong, N. 2003. *A history of County Wexford: a comprehensive study of Wexford's history, culture and people* (Dublin).

Gahan, D. 1995. *The people's rising: Wexford, 1798* (Dublin).

Gahan, D. 2010. 'Rebellion and atrocity in an Irish town: Enniscorthy, 28th May–20 June, 1798' in C. Toibin (ed.), *Enniscorthy: a history* (Wexford).

Gibney, J. 2009. 'Sir Richard Musgrave, 1746–1818: ultra-Protestant ideologue', *History Ireland*, https://www.historyireland.com/18th-19th-century-history/sir-richard-musgrave-1746–1818-ultra-protestant-ideologue (accessed 1 Feb. 2018).

Gilbert, J. 1893. *Documents relating to Ireland, 1795–1804* (Dublin).

Gordon, J. 1801. *History of the rebellion in Ireland in the year 1798* (London).

Gordon, J. 1803. *History of the rebellion in Ireland in the year 1798* (Dublin).

Gordon, J. 1803. *History of the rebellion in Ireland, in the year 1798* (2nd ed., London).

Gordon, J. 1805. *History of the civil war in Ireland containing an impartial account of the proceedings of the Irish revolutionists from the year 1782 until the suppression of the intended revolution* (Baltimore).

Gorton, J. 1833. *A topographical dictionary of Great Britain and Ireland*, 3 vols (London).

Graham, T. 2000. 'The shift in United Irish leadership from Belfast to Dublin, 1796 to 1798' in J. Smith, *Revolution, counter-revolution and Union: Ireland in the 1790s* (Cambridge).

Grattan Flood, W.H. 1898. *History of Enniscorthy and the neighbourhood with interesting chronicles of Co. Wexford* (Enniscorthy).

Grose, F. 1795. *The antiquities of Ireland*, 2 vols (London).

Gurley, L.B. 1854. *Memoir of Rev William Gurley late of Milan, Ohio, a local minister of the Methodist Episcopal Church: including a sketch of the Irish insurrection and martyrs of 1798* (Cincinnati).

Harwood, P. 1844. *History of the Irish rebellion of 1798* (London).

Hay, E. 1803. *History of the insurrection of the County of Wexford, A.D. 1798* (Dublin).

Haythornthwaite, P. 1994. *The armies of Wellington* (London).

Haythornthwaite, P. 1999. *Weapons and equipment of the Napoleonic Wars* (London).

Holmes, R. 2002. *Redcoat: the British soldier in the age of horse and musket* (London).

Holst, M. & T. Sutherland. 2014. 'Towton revisited – analysis of the human remains from the Battle of Towton 1461', *Schlachtfeld und Massengrab: Spektren Interdisziplinärer Auswertung von Orten der Gewalt (Zossen)*, pp 97–129.

Hotham, G. 1837. 'Report upon the proposed municipal boundary of the borough of Enniscorthy' in *Reports from commissioners*, ix (London).

Irish Folklore Commission, Schools Folklore Scheme, online at https://www.duchas.ie/en, and also available in the Main Manuscript Collection, Department of Irish Folklore, UCD.

Jeffrey Jarrett, M. 2006. *Castlereagh, Ireland and the French restorations of 1814–1815*, vol. 1 (Stanford).

Jones, J. 1800. *An impartial narrative of the most important engagements which took place between His Majesty's forces and the rebels during the Irish rebellion 1798* (Dublin).

Jones, J. 1834. *An impartial narrative of the most important engagements which took place between His Majesty's forces and the rebels during the Irish rebellion 1798* (2nd ed., New York).

Joyce, J. 1922. *Ulysses* (Paris).

Joyce, P.W. 1891–1913. *The origin and history of Irish names of places*, 3 vols (Dublin).

Kavanagh, P. 1874. *A popular history of the insurrection of 1798: derived from every available written record and reliable tradition* (Dublin).

Kavanagh, P. 1898. *A popular history of the insurrection of 1798: derived from everyday record and reliable tradition* (Cork).

Kavanagh, P.F. 1918. *A popular history of the insurrection of 1798: derived from every available record and reliable tradition* (Dublin).

Kavanagh, P. 1920. *A popular history of the insurrection of 1798: derived from everyday record and reliable tradition* (Cork).

Keogh, D. & N. Furlong. 1996. *The mighty wave: the 1798 rebellion in Wexford* (Dublin).

Keogh, D. & N. Furlong. 1998. *The women of 1798* (Dublin).

Keogh, D. & K. Whelan (eds). 2001. *Acts of union: the causes, contexts and consequences of the Act of Union* (Dublin).

Kirby, R.I. 2018. *Historical notes relating to Bideford's East-the-Water Shore*, http://thewharves.org/wp-content/uploads/2020/02/Historical-Notes-relating-to-Bidefords-East-the-Water-Shore-2018-09-09.pdf (accessed 9 Nov. 2020).

Komar, D. 2008. 'Patterns of mortuary practice associated with genocide: implications for archaeological research', *Current Anthropology*, 49, pp 123–33.

Larsson, Å.M. 2013. 'Participate or perish: why archaeology must gain confidence', *Archaeological Dialogues*, 20:1, pp 29–35.

Lender, M. & G. Stone. 2016. *Fatal Sunday: George Washington, the Monmouth Campaign, and the politics of battle* (Norman, OK).

Lett, B.N. 1949. 'A '98 diary by Mrs Barbara Newton Lett, Killaligan, Enniscorthy', *The Past: The Organ of the Uí Cinsealaigh Historical Society*, 5, pp 117–78.

Lewis, S. 1849. *A topographical dictionary of Ireland*, 2 vols (London).

Le Biez, G. 1993. 'Irish news in the French press 1789–98' in D. Dickson et al. (eds), *The United Irishmen: republicanism, radicalism and rebellion*, pp 256–68.

Luckombe, P. 1783. *A tour through Ireland: wherein the present state of that kingdom is considered; and the most noted cities, towns, seats, buildings, loughs, &c. described ...* (2nd ed., London).

Maxwell, W.M. 1845. *History of the Irish rebellion in 1798: with memoirs of the union and Emmett's insurrection in 1803* (London).

M'Laren/MacLaren, A. 1798. *A minute description of the battles of Gorey, Arklow and Vinegar-Hill*.

McConnell, D. 1988. *British smooth-bore artillery: a technological study to support identification, acquisition, restoration, reproduction, and interpretation of artillery at national historic parks in Canada* (Ottowa), sha.org (accessed 5 Feb. 2018).

McClymont, A., P. Bauman, R. Freund, J. Seligman, H. Jol, K. Bensimon & P. Reeder. 2017. 'The forgotten Holocaust in Lithuania – geophysical investigations at the Ponary Extermination Site', *European Association of Geoscientists & Engineers: conference proceedings*, 23rd European Meeting of Environmental and Engineering Geophysics.

McDonnell, C. 2017. 'Insurgency and counter-insurgency in royal Meath: the Battle of Tara, 1798', *Journal of the Navan and District Historical Society*, 4, pp 333–52.

McDonnell, C. 2019. 'From the Boyne to Waterloo: military identity in Meath during the long eighteenth century', *Ríocht na Mídhe: Journal of Meath Archaeological and History Society*, 30, pp 158–81.

McGuigan, R. 2003. 'The forgotten army: fencible regiments of Great Britain 1793–1816', *The Napoleon Series*, https://www.napoleon-series.org/military-info/organization/Britain/fencibles/c_fencibles1.html (accessed 9 Nov. 2020).

McLoughlin, C. 2015. 'Archaeological monitoring report, Vinegar Hill, Templeshannon, Enniscorthy, Co. Wexford', unpublished report submitted to the National Monuments Service.

Madders, A. 1997. *'98 diary: Wexford in rebellion* (2nd ed., Wexford).

McLoughlin, C. 2020. 'Preliminary survey and excavation report, Clonhasten, Enniscorthy, Co. Wexford', unpublished report submitted to the National Monuments Service.

Maxwell, W.H. 1845 and 1866. *History of the Irish rebellion in 1798; with memoirs of the Union and Emmett's insurrection in 1803* (London).

Maxwell, W.H. 1871. *History of the Irish rebellion in 1798: with memoirs of the union, and Emmet's rebellion in 1803* (9th ed., London).

Misterek, K. 2012. 'Ein Massengrab aus der Schlacht von Alerheim am 3. August 1645', *Berichte der bayerischen Bodendenkmalpflege*, 53, pp 361–91.

Moore, J. 1904. *The diary of Sir John Moore,* vol. 1 (London).

Moore, R. 2009–17. *Napoleonic Guide*, http://www.napoleonguide.com/weapcav.htm (accessed 25 Nov. 2017).

Mullen, J. 2013. 'Irish history reflected in Meath fields' in F. Tallon (ed.), *The field names of County Meath* (Drogheda), pp 230–44.

Munnelly, T. 1988. *The great Irish rebellion of 1798* (Dublin), pp 160–71.

Musgrave, R. 1802. *Memoirs of the different rebellions in Ireland*, vol. 1 (3rd ed., Dublin).

Musgrave, R. 1802. *Memoirs of the different rebellions in Ireland*, vol. 2 (3rd ed., Dublin).

Musgrave, R. 1802. *Memoirs of the different rebellions in Ireland from the arrival of the English* (3rd ed., Dublin).

Musgrave, R. 1995. (eds Myers and McKnight) *Memoirs of the Irish rebellion of 1798* (Fort Wayne, IN).

National Inventory of Architectural Heritage. 2020. www.buildingsofireland.ie.

Nelson, I. 2007. *The Irish militia, 1793 to 1802: Ireland's forgotten army* (Dublin).

Newkirk, V.R. 2017. 'Black Charlottesville has seen this all before', *The Atlantic*, 18 Aug. 1817, https://www.theatlantic.com/politics/archive/2017/08/black-community-charlottesville-response/537285 (accessed 9 Nov. 2020).

Newton, J. & W. n.d. [early nineteenth century]. *A rough sketch of the earl of Portsmouth's estates in the baronies of Scarawelsh and Ballakeen or manors of Kilhobuck and Enniscorthy* (Hampshire Record Office, 15M84/MP35).

Nicklisch N., F. Ramsthaler, H. Meller, S. Friederich & K.W. Alt. 2017. 'The face of war: trauma analysis of a mass grave from the Battle of Lützen (1632)', *PLoS ONE*, 12:5: e0178252.

Ní Shéaghdha, N. 1939–40. 'Maidean Luain Chíngcíse', *Éigse*, 1, pp 191–5.

Ó Crualaoich, C. & A. Mac Giolla Chomhghaill. 2016. *Townland names of Co. Wexford*, vol. 1 (Dublin).

O'Donnell, R. 1998a. *1798 diary* (Dublin).

O'Donnell, R. 1998b. *The rebellion in Wicklow, 1798* (Dublin).

O'Donnell, R. 2015. 'Revolutionary Meath, 1791–1798' in A. Crampsie & F. Ludlow (eds), *Meath: history and society* (Dublin), pp 397–443.

O'Keeffe, P. & T. Simington. 1991. *Irish stone bridges: history and heritage* (Dublin).

O'Kelly, P. 1842. *General history of the rebellion of 1798 with many interesting occurrences of the two preceding years* (Dublin).

O'Neill, J. & P. Logue. 2010. 'Investigations at the site of the Battle of the Yellow Ford' in E. Murray & P. Logue (eds), *Battles, boats and bones: archaeological discoveries in northern Ireland, 1987–2008* (Belfast), pp 94–7.

Pakenham, T. 1972. *The year of liberty: the great Irish rebellion of 1798* (3rd ed., London).

Pearse, H. 1908. *Memoir of the life and military services of Viscount Lake, Baron Lake of Delhi and Laswaree, 1744–1808* (Edinburgh).

Pearson, P. 2010. 'Enniscorthy: townscape and architecture' in C. Toibin & C. Rafferty (eds), *Enniscorthy: a history* (Wexford), pp 369–97.

Phillips, R. 1801. *The British Military Library or Journal: comprehending a complete body of military knowledge; and consisting of original communications; with selections from the most approved and respectable foreign military publications* (London).

Pollard, T. (ed.). 2009. *Culloden: the history and archaeology of the last clan battle* (Barnsley).

Pounden, A. 2001 'Alicia Pounden' in J. Beatty, *Protestant women's narratives of the Irish rebellion of 1798* (Dublin).
Price, L. 1946. *The placenames of County Wicklow* (Dublin).
Quade, L. & M. Binder. 2018. 'Life on a Napoleonic battlefield: a bioarchaeological analysis of soldiers from the Battle of Aspern, Austria', *International Journal of Paleopathology*, 22, pp 23–38.
Rayner, S. n.d. 'British marching discipline in the 18th century: the evolution of "The Long March" into the "Route Step"', https://www.scribd.com/document/130573182/British-Marching-Discipline-in-the-18th-Century-The-Evolution-of-The-Long-March-into-the-Route-Step (accessed 16 Feb. 2018).
Renshaw, L. 2013. 'The dead and their public: memory campaigns, issue networks and the role of the archaeologist in the excavation of mass graves', *Archaeological Dialogues*, 20:1, pp 35–47.
Roche, R. 1979. 'Links with 1798 – Rathangan and the rising', *Rathangan Journal*.
Rogers, H.C.B. 1977. *The British army of the eighteenth century* (London).
Ross, C. (ed.). 1859. *Correspondence of Charles, first Marquis Cornwallis* (2nd ed., London).
Rothwell, J.S. 1891. *Military administration staff duties tables and data* (London).
Rubio-Melendi, D., A. Gonzalez-Quirós, D. Roberts, M. del Carman García García, A. Caunedo Domínguez, J.K. Pringle & J-P. Fernández-Álvarez. 2018. 'GPR and ERT detection and characterization of a mass burial, Spanish Civil War, Northern Spain', *Forensic Science International*, 287, pp e1–e9.
Ruffell, A., A. McCabe, C. Donnelly & B. Sloan. 2009. 'Location and assessment of an historic (150–160 years old) mass grave using geographic and ground penetrating radar investigation, NW Ireland', *Journal of Forensic Sciences*, 54:2, pp 382–94.
Shelbourn, C.H. 2015. 'Remains, research and respect: some reflections on burial archaeology and the treatment of the "anciently dead"' in R. Redmond-Cooper (ed.), *Heritage, ancestry and law: principles, policies and practices in dealing with historical human remains* (Builth Wells).
Saunders, J.R. & R.N. Shackelford. 1998. *Urban renewal and the end of Black culture in Charlottesville, Virginia* (Jefferson, NC).
Scallan, E. & D. Rowe. 2004. *Houses of Wexford* (Ballinakella).
Scott, D. & R. Fox. 1987. *Archaeological insights into the Custer battle: an assessment of the 1984 field season* (Norman, OK).
Shaffery, P. & M. 1983. *Buildings of Irish towns: treasures of everyday architecture* (Dublin).
Sheldon, R. 1904. *The army on the march*.
Shiels, D. 2008. 'Identifying and interpreting Ireland's post-medieval conflict archaeology', *Journal of Irish Archaeology*, 17, pp 137–52.
Sidney, J. 1999. 'The folklore of the 1798 rebellion in Wexford and surrounding counties' (MA, NUI Dublin).
Smith, C.H. & P.J. Haythornthwaite. 2002. *Wellington's army: the uniforms of the British soldier, 1812–1815* (London).
Soulsby, I. 2018. 'The Irish military establishment, 1796–1798: a study in the evolution of military effectiveness' (MA, NUI Cork).

Stafford, E. 2006. 'Slaney Place, Enniscorthy, Wexford', Excavations.ie, record 2006:2102, https://excavations.ie/report/2006/Wexford/0016855 (accessed 21 Jan. 2020).

Steele, C. 2008. 'Archaeology and the forensic investigation of recent mass graves: ethical issues for a new practice of archaeology', *Archaeologies* 4:3, pp 414–28.

Steen, L.J. 1991. *The Battle of the Hill of Tara, 26th May 1798* (Trim).

Sutherland, T. & A. Schmidt. 2003. 'Towton, 1461: an integrated approach to battlefield archaeology', *Landscapes* 4:2, pp 15–25.

Sweetman, W. 2013. *County Wexford trials of 1798* (Wexford).

Taylor, G. 1800. *A history of the rise, progress, and suppression of the rebellion in the county of Wexford, in the year 1798: to which is annexed the author's account of his captivity, and merciful deliverance* (3rd ed., Dublin).

Teeling, C.H. 1832. *Sequel to personal narrative of the Irish rebellion of 1798* (Belfast).

Thompson S. 1949. *Motif-index of folk literature: a classification of narrative elements in folktales, ballads, myths, fables, mediaeval romances,* exampla, fabliaux, *jest-books, and local legends* (Manhattan, KS).

Tully, D. 2008. 'The Slaney cot' in C. MacCárthaigh (ed.), *Traditional boats of Ireland: history, folklore and construction* (Cork).

Turner, L. 1903. *The memories of Sir Llewelyn Turner*, ed. J.E. Vincent (London).

Turner, P. 2017. *Paul Dwight Turner's family genealogy and genealogical resources*, www.paulturner.ca/Phillips/Gowan/gowan-dossiers.htm (accessed 1 Mar. 2018).

Urban, S. 1801. *The Gentleman's Magazine and Historical Chronicle for the year 1801* (London).

Walsh, D. 2010. 'Enniscorthy: industry and trade' in C. Toibin & C. Rafferty (eds), *Enniscorthy: a history* (Wexford), pp 191–209.

Wexford Freeholder. c.1803. *Observations on Edward Hay's history of the insurrection in the county of Wexford AD 1798* (pamphlet).

Wheeler, H.F.B. & A.M. Broadley. 1910. *The war in Wexford: an account of the rebellion in the south of Ireland in 1798 told from original documents* (London).

Whelan, K. 1997. 'The Wexford priests in 1998' in L. Swords, *Protestant, Catholic and Dissenter: the clergy and 1798* (Dublin).

Whelan, K. 1998. 'The Wexford Republic, June 1798' in R. Roche (ed.), *The French Revolution and Wexford.* Souvenir Record, Comoradh '98 (Enniscorthy), pp 19–22.

Wilbers-Rost, S. 2001. 'Archäologische Forschungen zur Varusschlacht in Kalkriese Bei Osnabrück', *Revue Archéologique*, 1, pp 187–91.

Manuscripts and maps

Barber, Jane. n.d.. 'Recollections of the summer of 1798', typescript, Wexford Library (Wexford).

Gough, G. 1798. 'Gough to Col. Verecher, 12 July', manuscript, National Archives of Ireland, Rebellion Papers: 620/436/1 (Dublin).

Moll, H. 1728. 'The Counties of Wicklow, Catherlogh, and Wexford', Bibliothèque Nationale de France, Département Cartes et Plans, CPL GE DD-2987 (2668), http://www.europeana.eu/portal/record/9200365/BibliographicResource_1000055653176.html.

Munday Map: William Munday, 'A survey of all and singular the lands and estates belonging to Viscount Lymington in the baronies of Scarawelth and Ballakenn and manors of

Killhobuck and Enniscorthy, county of Wexford and kingdom of Ireland, 1729, Hampshire Record Office, 15M84/MP34.
Newton Map: Copied by J. and W. Newton, 66 Chancery Lane, 'A rough sketch of the earl of Portsmouth's estates in the baronies of Scarawelsh and Ballakeen or manors of Kilhobuck and Enniscorthy, early 19th century', Hampshire Record Office, 15M84/MP35.
Wemyss, W. 1798. 'Wemyss to Capt. Taylor, 15 July', manuscript, National Archives of Ireland, Rebellion Papers: 620/39/85.

Newspapers, journals and directories
All the Year Round – A weekly journal, 17 (1867), p. 207
Anti-Jacobin Review and Magazine, 27 (1807), pp 515–16.
Bell's Weekly Messenger, 14 (1798).
Bradshaw's Railway Manual, Shareholders' Guide and Official Directory for 1867.
Gentleman's Magazine, 1 (1731), p. 130; 71 (1801), p. 977.
Methodist Magazine, 22 (1799).
New Annual Register or General Repository of History, Politics and Literature for the year 1798 (1799).
Penny Cyclopaedia of the Society for the Diffusion of Useful Knowledge (1843).
Protestant Advocate (1813).
Terrific Register; or Record of, Crimes, Judgements, Providences, and Calamities, 2 (1825), p. 722.
Universal Magazine of Knowledge and Pleasure for July 1798.

Parliamentary proceedings, rules and regulations etc
Parliamentary register: or, history of the proceedings and debates of the House of Commons of Ireland, 1782–1801 (Dublin).
Rules and regulations for the formations, field-exercise, and movements, of His Majesty's Forces, 1798 (London).
Speech of the Right Honourable John, earl of Clare in the House of Lords of Ireland …, 1800 (Dublin).

Oral histories
Longest Day Research Project
LDRP. Informant: Linda Gethings, Killoughrim, Caim. Collector: Leo Durnan, St Mary's National School, Enniscorthy, 15 June 2015.

National Folklore Collection Main Manuscript Collection (All records from Co. Wexford unless otherwise stated.)
IFC 54: 152–3. Informant: James Sinnott, Duncormick, aged 65. Collector: Tomás Carey, Woodgraigue, Duncormick on 9 Mar. 1935.
IFC 107: 171. Informant: Willie Cox, Duncormick, aged 82. Collector: Tomás Carey, Woodgraigue, Duncormick, May 1935.
IFC 107: 171. Written by Robert Dwyer Joyce, '98 Commemoration Association (1938).
IFC 437: 196–7. Collector: Seán Butler, Little Cullenstown, Foulksmills.

National Folklore Collection Schools' Folklore Collection (All records from Co. Wexford unless otherwise stated)

IFC S 647: 273. School: Tooraneena, Clonmel, Co. Waterford. Informant: Micheal Breathnach, Reid na dTeampán, Baile Mhic Cairbre. Collector: Padraig Teidhirs, Cathair na Leige.

IFC S 703: 130–1. School: Clochar na Trócaire, Ceannanus Mór. Collector: Teresa Stone, aged 12, 12 May 1938.

IFC S 708: 7. School: Carlanstown, Co. Meath.

IFC S 714: 235. School: Rathkenny, Co. Meath. Informant: Joseph Price, Ladyrath, aged 64. Collector: Sheila Price, Ladyrath.

IFC S 771: 272. School: Castletown, Co. Meath. Collector: Margaret Farrelly, Leggagh.

IFC S 865: 348–9. School: Coone, Leighlinbridge. Informant: Paul Miskella, Coan, Co. Kilkenny. Collector: Eamonn de Paor, teacher.

IFC S 871: 22–5. School: San Leonard, Ballycullane. Informant: Mr J. Gleson, St Kierans. aged 60, farmer. Collector: Mary B. Dunphy, teacher.

IFC S 878: 54–5. School: Montfield, Ballymore.

IFC S 880: 95–6. School: St Brigid's (B), Wexford. Informant: His mother. Collector: Patrick Lacey.

IFC S 880: 424. School: Christian Brothers, Wexford. Informant: Mr Murphy, 9 Selskar St., Wexford, aged 47. Collector: James Murphy, 9 Selsker St., Wexford.

IFC S 880: 433. School: Scoil na mBráthar, Loch Garman, Wexford. Informant: Mr Fortune, Bree, aged 89. Informant: Sean Foley, Crossabeg.

IFC S 880: 434. School: Christian Brothers, Wexford. Informant: Mrs Duggan, 21 High St., Wexford, aged 57. Collector: Brendan Redmond, 30 High St., Wexford.

IFC S 881: 341. School: Clochar N. Muire, Loch gCarman. Collector: Mary A. Goold.

IFC S 884: 44–5. School: Castlebridge. Informant: Thomas Ryan Ballytramont, Castlebridge, aged 63, grandparent. Collector: Kathleen Morris.

IFC 884: 46. School: Castlebridge (C). Informant: Thomas Ryan, Ballycramont, aged 63, grandfather. Collector: Kathleen Morris, Castlebridge GNS, 16 June 1938.

IFC S 884: 47–9. School: Castlebridge (C). Informant: George Dixon. Collector: Nancy O'Connor.

IFC 884: 52–4. School: Castlebridge (C). Informant: Nick Rossiter, Ardcavan, aged 69. Collector: Evelyn Shortall.

IFC S 884: 59. School: Castlebridge (C). Informant: George Dixon. Collector: Kathleen Murphy, aged 41.

IFC S 885: 197. School: Screen.

IFC S 886: 122–3. School: Naomh Bríghid, Blackwater. Informant: Reddy Fitzimons.

IFC S 887: 53. School: Kilmuckridge. Collector: Anna Murphy, aged 12.

IFC S 888: 16. School: Riverchapel. Informant: Patrick Ryan, Ballybracken. Collector: Betty Ryan.

IFC S 888: 185. School: Hollyfort. Informant: M. Vaughan, Kilcashel, Co. Wicklow.

IFC S 891: 21–3. Collector: John Doyle, Camolin, Ferns. Informant: Mr M. Breen, Ferns, Co. Wexford.

Bibliography

IFC S 891: 21–3. School: Guaire (Xtian Bros), Gorey. Informant: Mr M. Breen, Ferns, Co. Wexford. Collector: John Doyle, Camolin, Ferns.

IFC S 891: 26–31. School: Guaire (Xtian Bros.), Gorey. Informant: Mrs Kinsella, Bolacreen, grandparent. Collector: Martin Kinsella.

IFC S 892: 311. School: Baile an Daingin (Ballindaggin). Informant: William Redmond, Woodlands, Ballindaggin.

IFC S 893: 4–5. School: Caime. Informant: Mrs Denton, Moneyhore, aged 75, grandparent. Collector: Edward Barnes, same address, aged 12.

IFC S 893: 35. School: Caime.

IFC S 893: 177. An Mhódh-Scoil, Enniscorthy (St. Mary's). Informant: Mrs Russell, Templescoby, aged 83, grandparent. Informant: Lillian Russell.

IFC S 893: 178–9. An Mhódh-Scoil, Enniscorthy (St Mary's). Informant: his parent, aged 58. Collector: David McDermott, written 9 Mar. 1938.

IFC S 893: 206–7. An Mhódh-Scoil, Enniscorthy (St Mary's). Informant: Mr Ormond, Jamestown, aged 64.

IFC S 893: 214. School: Scoil na mBráthar, Informant: Aidan Hendrick, Enniscorthy. Collector: James Hendrick, Enniscorthy.

IFC S 893: 216. School: Scoil na mBráthar. Informant: Mrs Murphy, 12 St Johns Villas, aged 45, housekeeper. Collector: Felix Murphy, Enniscorthy.

IFC S 893: 217. School: Scoil na mBráthar. Informant: James Guilfoyle, 55 St Johns Villas, aged 50, cook. Collector: Thomas Guilfoyle.

IFC S 893: 250. School: Scoil na mBráthar. Informant: Philip Murphy, 1 O'Neill's Terrace, Enniscorthy, postman. Collector: Peadar Ó Murchú.

IFC S 893: 250–1. School: Scoil na mBráthar. Informant: Aidan Hendrick, 7 Duffry St., labourer. Collector: James Hendrick.

IFC S 893: 256–7. Scoil na mBráthar, Enniscorthy. Informant: Mrs Foley, 51 St John's Villas, aged 39, housekeeper. Collector: Laurence Foley.

IFC S 893: 259. School: Scoil na mBráthar, Enniscorthy. Informant: Aidan Hendrick, 7 Duffry St., aged 48, labourer. Collector: James Hendrick.

IFC S 893: 263. School: Scoil na mBráthar, Enniscorthy. Informant: Bill Devereux, 23 Court Street, aged 58, dealer in bicycles. Collector: Eamon Devereux.

IFC S 893: 264. School: Scoil na mBráthar, Enniscorthy. Informant: Thomas Walsh, 18 Court Street, aged 48, solicitor's clerk. Collector: Samuel Walsh.

IFC S 893: 264–5. School: Scoil na mBráthar, Enniscorthy. Informant: Mr Mooney, Bestmount, The Still, aged 50, farmer. Collector: Liam Mooney.

IFC S 894: 11–12. School: Enniscorthy (Pres. Convent). Informant: Mr Fenlon, Enniscorthy. Collector: Eilish Fenlon. Note inclusion of Motif F991.5 – Bleeding Rocks.

IFC S 894: 12. School: Enniscorthy (Pres. Convent). Informant: Mr Fenlon, Milehouse, Enniscorthy. Collector: Eilis Fenlon.

IFC S 894: 13. School: Enniscorthy (Pres. Convent). Informant: Mr Fenlon, Enniscorthy. Collector: Eilish Fenlon.

IFC S 894: 16. School: Enniscorthy (Pres. Convent). Informant: Mr John Tobin, Clavass, Enniscorthy. Collector: Theresa Cooper.

IFC S 894: 26. School: Enniscorthy (Pres. Convent). Informant: Mr Thomas Walsh, Court Street, Enniscorthy. Collector: Mollie Walsh.

IFC S 894: 27. School: Enniscorthy (Pres. Convent). Informant: Mrs Murphy, Enniscorthy. Collector: Cissie Murphy.

IFC S 894: 65–6. School: Enniscorthy (Pres. Convent). Collector: Kathleen Murphy.

IFC S 894: 67–8. School: Enniscorthy (Pres. Convent). Collector: Kathleen Murphy.

IFC S 894: 69–70. School: Enniscorthy (Pres. Convent). Informant: Mr James Mythen, Duffry Gate, grandparent. Collector Teresa Mythen.

IFC S 896: 41–2. School: Ferns (C).

IFC S 896: 246. School: Monagear.

IFC S 900: 136–7. School: Rathnure (C). Informant: John Timmins, Forrestalstown, aged 44, postman.

IFC S 901: 2 & 5. School: Rathnure (B). Informant: James Whyte, farmer/old-age pensioner, aged 95, living in Killanne since he was born, dated 25 May 1934.

IFC S 901: 120. School: Templeudigan. Collector: Mary Ann Redmond.

IFC S 902: 21. School: Galbally, Co. Wexford. Informant: Patrick Jackman, Barmoney, Bree, Co. Wexford, aged 65. Collector: John Jackman, same address.

IFC S 904: 265. School: Rathanna, Borris, Co. Carlow. Collector: Revd Brother Luke, Bagenalstown.

IFC S 904: 269–70. School: Rathanna, Borris, Co. Carlow.

IFC S 909: 140. School: Cluain Mór (1), Baile an Droichid (Clonmore, Co. Carlow).

IFC S 911: 84. School: Cloneygall, Co. Carlow. Informant: Pádraig Ó Nualain, Clonegal, Co. Carlow, aged 50, farmer. December 1938.

Sidney, J. 1997. Recordings at Ár mBreacha Storytelling House, with Mr Rory Murphy, Bunclody, 11 Mar. 1997 (cassette recordings); Mr Seamus Corrigan, Ross Road, Enniscorthy (4 Jan. 2018).

Index

Page numbers in **_bold italics_** refer to illustrations.

1798 rebellion, vii, 1–2
   bicentenary commemorations, 246
   centenary commemorations, 245
   epicentre in Enniscorthy, 10
   failure in Dublin, 62
   memorials, **_258_**, 259

Acts of Union (1800), 34, 35
ADCO Ltd, 189
   cast-iron bell-shaped object, **_186_**
   Down Survey, Enniscorthy, **_177_**
   Enniscorthy Bridge, **_173_**, **_182–3_**
   Island, The, 173–4, **_174_**, **_175_**
   Ordnance Survey, Enniscorthy, **_178_**
   topographic map, **_172_**
   underwater survey, 6, **_184_**, **_185_**
Alexander, J., 16, 96
America, 1, 71, 234
American War of Independence (1775–83), 8, 34, 37, 89
Antijacobean Review, 148
archaeological monitoring of groundworks, 205–11, 216–17
   additional pathway, 210
   artefacts and finds-retrieval strategy, 210
   artefacts recovered, ix, 7, 205, **_206_**, **_208_**, **_209_**, 210, 216–17
   coins, **_209_**
   copper-alloy objects, **_209_**
   horseshoes/nails/iron objects, 210
   lead strips recovered, **_208_**
   medieval pottery sherd, 210
   musket balls recovered, **_208_**, **_209_**, 216–17
   new pedestrian pathway, 207, 209
   trench for stone kerbing, 210

archaeological survey at Clonhasten, 211–16, 217
   artefacts recovered, 213, 215, 215–16, 217
   coins, 215–16, **_216_**
   copper-alloy buttons, 215
   development site, **_211_**, 212
   Global Positioning System (GPS), 195, 196, 210, 212
   methodology, 212
   militaria, 213, **_214_**, 215, 217
   musket balls, 213, **_214_**, 215, 217
   pistol ball, **_214_**, 215
   survey area, **_211_**, 212
Arklow, Co. Wicklow, 15, 16–17
   see also Battle of Arklow
Army in Ireland Act (1768), 36
artillery, 16, 20, 24–5, 35
   Board of Ordnance and, 40
   bombardment/assault phase, 2, 18, 54–6
   field artillery, 41–2, 47–50
   rebels and, 15
   role of, 25, 41
Asgill, Major General Sir Charles, 45, 46
atrocities, 3–4
   'Black Mob' and, 243
   crown forces and, 3–4, 79
   pitchcapping, 3, 228, 230
   Scullabogue massacre, 78, 81
   Wexford bridge massacre, 17, 26, 75, 84
Australia, vii
Aylmer, Major, 45, 50
Aylmer, William, 250–1

Ballaghkeene Unitedmen, 67n3, 68, 85
Ballinahallen Wood, 231, 237, 238
Ballygullen, 250
Ballyorill Hill, 13

Banim, John, 158
Banim, Michael, 33, 158
   Croppy, The: a tale of the Irish rebellion of 1798, 32, 123, 158
Barber, Jane, 25–6, 30, 113–14, 149–50, 237
Barber, Samuel, 25, 149
Barber, William, 26
Barker, William, 3, 18, 53, 55, 109
   William Barker Bridge, 6, 111
Barrington, Sir Jonah, 4, 30–1, 35
Bartlett, T., et al., 125, 128
   1798: a bicentenary perspective, 4, 29
Bath Chronicle and Weekly Gazette, viii–viv
Battle of Alerheim, Germany, 157
Battle of Arklow, 15, 16, 17, 47, 48–9
   aftermath, 79
   Needham and, 16, 17, 47, 48–9, 89
Battle of Aspern (Austria), 169
Battle of Ballinamuck, 61
Battle of Ballyellis, 49, 228, 250
Battle of Bonnymuir (Scotland), x
Battle of the Boyne, 25, 191
Battle of Culloden (Scotland), x, 120
Battle of Enniscorthy, 10–11, 12–14, 77, 111–15, 173
   Abbey Square, 115
   aftermath, 27
   Battle of Castle Hill, 115
   bridge, 6, 13, 29, 111–12, **113**, 179–80
   Byrne's recollection of, 19–20
   Castle Street, 115
   casualties, 14
   Cathedral Street, 115
   cattle driven through battle, 19–20, 222–3
   Court Street, 115
   crown forces, 13–14
   Duffry Gate area, 13–14, 53, 55, 106, 113
   Duffry Hill, 115
   house-to-house fighting, 3
   insurgents, 12–13
   Irish Street, 13, 14
   Island, The, 116, **117**
   Island Road, 115
   Johnson's attack, 111
   Jones' (insurgent) account of, 29
   loyalist townspeople, 13
   Main Street, 115
   Market House, 113–14
   Market Square, 14, 109, 115
   military eyewitness accounts, 18–20
   oral histories/folklore, 222–3
   Rafter Street, 115
   rebels killed/wounded, 180
   River Slaney, attempts to cross, 115–16, 180, 181
   St John's Road, 14
   St John's Street, 13, 14, 115
   yeoman cavalry, 138
Battle of Foulksmills, 17, 23, 42, 49–50
Battle of Horetown, 75, 83, 84, 226–7
Battle of Little Bighorn (USA), 190
Battle of Lützen (Germany), 168, 169, 170
Battle of New Ross, 227, 228, 246
Battle of the Three Rocks, 15, 23, 64, 65, 77
Battle of Towton (England), 161, 168, 170
Battle of Vinegar Hill, 1–2, 10, 18, **51**, **52**, **53**, **60**, **110**, **129**
   aftermath, 22, 24, 60–1, 249–50
   approach phase, 52–4
   bombardment/assault phase, 54–6, 109, 121
   bridge, defence of, 112, 181
   'Cannon Banks, The', 236
   casualties, 29–30, 61, 124
   civilians killed, 4
   crown forces, positions, **52**
   Darby's Gap, 53, 55, 57, 58, 59, 88, **100**, 107
   eve of the battle, 50
   explosive canister shot used, 122–3
   eyewitness accounts, 25–7, 223
   field artillery for the battle, 47–50
   field of battle, 105–40
   general overview, 108–110
   'green hill', capture of, 126–36
   historical accounts of, 4–5, 11–12

Index 323

intense fighting, areas of, 124–6
light battalions, 46
military eyewitness accounts, 18–25
'mopping up' phase, 57–8
'Needham's Gap', 3, 55, 88, 93, 109
Northern Army's retreat, 85
number of people involved, 120
officers for, 44–5
oral history/folklore, 223
order of battle, 45–7
ordnance used by British Army, 41, 49, 194
plan of the battle, *110*
preparation for battle, 43–4
re-enactment (2013), *43*
rebel defence and retreat, 124–6
rebels' pike charges, 124, 125
retreat of rebels, 124–6, 249–50
rifle-equipped troops, 42
sequence of battle, 50–8
sketch plan of the battle, *129*
troop movements, 44
United Irishmen, defensive positions, *52*, 191, 193, 194, 199, 201, 202
weapons, United Irishmen and, 194–5
see also 'green hill'
battlefield
   area encompassed by, 120
   landscape, intact since 1798, 7, 119–20, 140, 191, *192*, 193
   preservation of, 7–8
   threats to area, 203
battlefield archaeology, 190–204
   artefacts, distribution patterns, 194, 195, *198*, 201–2
   artefacts recovered, 195, 197, 199–203, *200*, *203*
   bullets recovered, 197, *198*, 199–201, *200*, 202, *303*
   contamination, 199
   GPS and, 195, 196
   gridded metal-detection surveys, 195
   illegal detection, impact of, 197, *198*, 199, 200, 204

Irish Battlefields Project, 5, 7, 134, 191–3
landscape, survival of, 191, 193, 199, 201, 203, 204
Little Bighorn, 190
metal objects, identification, 193–5
metal-detection survey, *192*, 195–6
metal-detection survey, results, 197–201
postgraduate programmes, 190
results, interpretation of, 201–4
survey, approach, 195–6
Templeshannon townland, *192*, 196, 197
United Irishmen camp, 196, 197
battlefield sites, illegal metal detection, 195, 197
battlefield tourism, 7–8
Beale, George, 138, 140
Beale, John, 138, 155
Beale's Barn, 6, 120, 138–40, *139*, 155
Beatty, J.D., 114, 137, 237
Beiner, Guy, 28, 219
   Remembering the Year of the French, 4
Bell's Weekly Messenger, 47
Bien Informé, Le (periodical), 110
Binns, Jonathon, *Miseries and beauties of Ireland, The*, 144
Blacker, Colonel William, 71
blacksmiths, 230–1
Blackstoops townland, 13, 115, 116, 180, 181
Blaney, Brigadier General, 45, 58, 112
Bloomfield townland, 13, 137
Board of Ordnance, 36, 40–2
   cavalry weapons, 42
   field artillery, 41
   infantry weapons, 42
Bond, Oliver, 12
Boolavogue parish, 12
Botany Bay, 75
Bourke, Lieutenant, 79–80, 81
Boyd, James (magistrate), 62, 78
Brennan, Isaac, 230–1
Brennan, John, 76

British Army
    Ancient Britons cavalry regiment, 250
    atrocities, Wexford-Wicklow border, 79
    baggage train, *95*, 97–8, *99*
    Board of Ordnance, 40–2
    Brown Bess muskets, 36–7, 38, 42, 194, 215
    charms carried by soldiers, 216
    colours, 42–3, *43*
    Dumbarton fencibles, 46, 47, 50, 61, 89
    Durham cavalry, 256
    field formations, 38–9
    garrison in Ireland, 36–8
    Irish Board of Ordnance, 36, 40
    kingdom of Ireland, 35–8
    knapsacks, 97
    light-cavalry sabre, *255*
    'long march' or 'route march', 95–6
    Midlothian fencibles, 46, 47, 48, 50
    ordnance/weaponry, 34, 35, 194
    organization and structure, 36–8
    Royal Artillery (RA), 40, 41, 47
    Royal Foot Artillery, 41
    Royal Horse Artillery (RHA), 34, 46, 47, 48
    Royal Irish Artillery (RIA), 34, 40, 41, 47
    Royal Irish Dragoons, 47, 111
    Scottish fencibles, 253–4
    War Office, 36
    see also Board of Ordnance; militia; yeomanry
British Army in Ireland, 36–8
    cavalry, 36
    cavalry weapons, 42
    fencibles, 37
    infantry, 36–7
    infantry weapons, 42
    mercenary units, 37–8
    militia, 37
    regimental uniforms, 39–40, *39*
    regular army, 38–9
    rifles, 37
    yeomanry, 37
Brownrigg, Mrs, 67, 69
Buildings of Ireland database, 153

Bunclody *see* Newtownbarry
Burrowes, Peter, 73
Byrne, Billy, 16, 18, 19–20, **21**, 181
Byrne, Fanny, 19
Byrne, Miles, 2, 10–11, 13
    ammunition shortage, 257
    attack on Newtownbarry, 15
    Battle of Enniscorthy, 19–20
    Battle of Vinegar Hill, 10, 55, 109, 119, 121, 124
    death, 19
    Irish Legion and, 19
    memoirs, 19, 52, 55
    Needham's diversion to Solsborough, 90, 91
    rebel ambush of regiment, 250
    Taylor's print shop, views on, 69
    United Irishmen and, 19
Byrne-Rothwell, D., 12
Byrnes of Coolalug, 224

Cadogan, James and Nellie, 232
Camack, Lieutenant, 92
Campbell, Colonel, 138
    Battle of Vinegar Hill, 45, 54, 55, 58, 124, 125
    Light Brigade and, 46, 91, 124, 125
Canning, Thomas, 226
Cantwell, B., 242
Carnew, Co. Wicklow, 17, 83, 225, 231, 250
Carrickbyrne Camp, 70–1
Carty, Mr and Mrs, 231–2
Carty, Robert, 82
Carty, William, 74
Castlecomer, Co. Kilkenny, 19, 249
Castlereagh, Robert Stewart, Viscount, 18, 43–4
    General Lake and, 18, 24, 54–5, 121
Catholic clergy
    insurrection and, 43–4, 64, 235
    see also Clinch, Fr Thomas; Kearns, Fr Mogue; Murphy, Fr John; Murphy, Fr Michael; Murphy, Fr Thomas; Roche, Fr Philip

Catholics
>   insurrection and, 4, 22–3, 220
>   militia and, 37, 254
>   yeomanry and, 254

Caulfield, James, Bishop of Ferns, 62
Centre for Battlefield Archaeology, Glasgow, 190
Champitt, William, 148
Chichester, Thomas Pelham, 2nd earl of, 43–4
Clinch, Fr Thomas, 3, 64, 109, 249
Clonhasten House, 155
Clonard, Co. Meath, 251
>   attack on Leinster Bridge, 251, **252**
>   Leinster Bridge, 251, **252**

Clonbullogue, Co. Offaly, 258
Clonegal, Co. Carlow, 228
Cloney, Thomas, 11, 18, 22–4, 64, 66
>   Battle of the Three Rocks, 65
>   Battle of Vinegar Hill, 23, 24
>   Cromwellian settlers, views on, 74
>   delegation to General Lake, 23–4
>   Keugh, perception of, 69
>   memoirs, 22–3
>   Needham, reason for lateness, 90
>   proclamation issued by, 78
>   Senate meetings in Wexford, 67
>   trial of, 72–3

Clonhasten townland
>   archaeological survey, 205, 211–16
>   artefacts recovered, 205
>   development site, **211**
>   Global Positioning System (GPS), 195, 196, 210, 212
>   survey area, **211**, **212**

Coastway Ltd, 6
Coates of Tankerley, 224
Cogley, Fr Patrick, 235
Colclough, John Henry, 14
Commons Journal, 27
Comóradh '98, 222
Connors, James, 230–1
Cooper, Richard, 247

Cooper, William, 31
Cornwallis, General Charles, 27, 35, 254
Corrig (Carrig) graveyard, 238, 239–40, **239**, 244
Corrigan, S.L., 54
Council for Directing the Affairs of the People of the County of Wexford, 66, 70, 82–3, 87
Cox, John, 226–7
Cromwellian settlers, 74, 233, 236
croppy graves, **257**, 258, 259
croppy/croppies, 89, 90, 120, 124, 245
Cruikshank, George, **17**, 28, **56**, **147**, **252**
Cullen, Brother Luke, 28–9, 112
Cullen, Thomas, 228–9
Cunningham, Philip, vii
Curry, A., and G. Foard, 157, 166–7, 168

Daphne Castle, 120, 137, 237, 238
Dargan, Pat, 154
Davis, Charles, 30, 158
Davis, Ciarán, 162
De Renzy, Captain, 228
de Vál, Seamus, 27
Department of Culture, Heritage and Gaeltacht, 205
Department of Defence, 88
Department of the Environment, Heritage and Local Government, 4–5, 191
Dickson, Charles, 27
Dickson, D., et al., 110, 242
>   *United Irishmen, The: republicanism, radicalism and rebellion*, 4, 29

Dixon, Madge (*née* Roche), 232–4, 245
Dixon, Thomas, 17, 75, 81, 232, 233
Donohoe, Dick, 31
Donohoe, P.A., 158, 159
Donovan, Tom, 63
Down Survey, 106, **106**, 176, **177**, 178
Doyle, E., 253, 254, 255, 256–7, 258–9
>   Ballygullen battle, 250
>   Leinster Bridge, Clonard, 251
>   retreat from Vinegar Hill, 249

Doyle, Fr James, 79
Doyle, Ian, 5
Drakestown Bridge, Meath, 259
Drumgoold House, 146, 155
Drumgoold townland, 138, 196, 199, 201, 203–4
Dublin Castle, 37, 70
Duff, Major General Sir James, 17, 45, 46, 47
    Ballygullen battle, 250
    Battle of Vinegar Hill, 3, 48, 54, 55–6, 57, 109
    Loftus and, 126
Duffry Gate, 13–14, 53, 55, 106, 113, 149, 152
Duncan, F., 41
Duncannon Fort, 15, 78
Dundas, Lieutenant General Ralph, 17, 44
    Battle of Vinegar Hill, 3, 45, 46, 48, 55, 109, 124, 125
    Hacketstown, pursuit of rebels, 48
    insurgents and, 196
    rebels' retreat, 125
    Solsborough House and, 138
Dunne, Liam, 245–6
Dwyer, Michael, 224, 232

earth-resistance survey (2D), 162, 164–5, **164**, 166, 170
Earthsound Geophysics Ltd, 6, *159*, 162, 197
Electric Picnic (2018), 120, **120**
electrical-resistivity imaging (ERI), 161, 162, 164–5, **165**, 170
Emmet, Robert, 19, 21, 65–6
Enniscorthy, 10, *107*, *113*
    in 1798, 106–8, **106**
    abbey site, 144, 151
    arcades, ground floors and, 152
    architectural survey of, 5–6, 141–56
    atrocities, 3–4
    battles during 1798 rebellion, 10–11
    'Bloody Bridge, The', 234–5
    building date stones, 152, 154
    businesses prior to 1798, 151
    Committee of Public Safety, 73–5
    country houses on outskirts, 155–6
    Courthouse, 112, 114–15
    destruction/damage (1798), 148–9, 150
    Down Survey, 106, **106**, 176, ***177***
    Duffry Gate, 149
    during the battle, 147–50
    early development of, 176–9
    eighteenth-century buildings, 141–2, 144, 150, 153, 155
    epicentre of 1798 rebellion, 10
    Fr Cullen Terrace, ***159***, 160, 235
    Georgian-style house (*c*.1775), 154
    golf course, *159*, 160
    granaries, 151
    Holohan's, 153
    Irish Street, 13, 14, 154
    Island Street, 153, 154
    letters intercepted by rebels, 79–80
    Market House, 111, 112, 113–14, 149, 151–2, 237
    Market Square, 141, 151, 152
    Market Street, 152
    Mary Street, 153
    Mill Park Road, 144, 153–4
    Mill Parks, 145
    Nineteenth-century changes, 141–2, 150, 151–2
    Nineteenth-century streets, 153–4
    'Old Brewery', 155
    'old' bridge, 6, 29, 111–12, *113*, ***143***, 151
    Old Church Road, 156
    Pig Market, 152
    P.J. Kenny Cycle Repairs, 153
    population, 154
    premises extant (1798), 150–6
    Pye Lane (Spout Lane), 227–8
    quays, 145–6, 151, 179
    railway, introduction of, 153
    rebel hospital, burning of, 4, 22, 57, 86, 114, 115
    St Aidan's Cathedral, 155
    St Mary's Church of Ireland, 111, 112, 114, 147–8, ***147***

Index 327

sectarian attacks, St Mary's Church and, 114
Slaney Place, 142, 144
Society of Friends' Meeting House, 154–5
streetscape, surviving, 115–17, 154–5, 156
Templeshannon, 146–7, **146**, 150, 154, 176, 180, 181
thatched roofs, 142, 144, 146, 149, 150
topographic map, **172**
topographical analysis of, 142–7
Water Lane, 154
Weafer Street, 153–4
yeoman infantry, 13
see also Battle of Enniscorthy; Enniscorthy Bridge; Enniscorthy Castle; Portsmouth estate
Enniscorthy Bridge, **143**, **145**, **172**, **173**, 179
archaeological survey of riverbed, 117, 184–5, **184**
cast-iron bell-shaped object, **186**, 187
clay pipe recovered, 187
cutwaters, **178**, 179, **183**, 184, **184**
earlier bridge components, 6, 184–5, **185**
forged iron pieces recovered, 187
glassware/ceramics/clay pipes, 187
intrados (arch ceiling), **183**
items identified on riverbed, 187
length and width, 178
metal-detection, 185, 187
Ordnance Survey (1840), **178**
riverbed underneath, 175–6
stone work, **182**–3
Enniscorthy Castle, 111, **113**, 142, **143**, 144, **145**
built on earlier ruins, 150
castle garden, 144
folk narrative and, 237–8
location, **172**
prisoners held in, 111, 237–8
Enniscorthy Historical Re-enactment Group, 88, **103**
Enniscorthy Town Council, 5
Eustace, Major General Charles, 17, 45, 94

Eustace, William Cornwallis, 45
exploding shell, 2, 18, 54, 109

Fenian rising (1867), 220, 245, 247
Fenlon, William, 139
Fields of Conflict, 190
Finglas, Paule (carpenter), 177
Fitzgerald, Edward, 14, 67, 73, 251
Ballaghkeene Unitedmen, 67n3, 68
folk tradition and, 224, 225–6
Forth Mountain, 44, 110
Three Rocks camp, 15, 17, 59, 86
Foules, Colonel Sir James, 45
France, 1, 12, 61, 77, 233, 242
Fraser, James, 146, 151, 152–3
French Army, 1, 12, 61
Irish Legion, 8, 19
French Revolution, 62, 72
French, Robert, Vinegar Hill, **118**
Furlong, Nicholas, 148, 154, 223, 233

Gahan, Daniel, 29, 30, 64, 74
People's rising, The, 13, 14, 15, 16, 17, 18, 233–4
Gentleman's Magazine, 31–2
Enniscorthy, **146**, 147, 150
Vinegar Hill mass grave, 158
geophysical survey, 160–7
George III, King, 35, 202
Germany
Battle of Alerheim, 157
Battle of Lützen, 168, 169, 170
Varus battlefield, 190
Gibney, J., 28
Gilbert, J., 44
Gill, Valentine (surveyor), **100**, 107, **108**
Glebe House, Enniscorthy, 155, 181
Global Positioning System (GPS), 195, 196, 210, 212
Gordon, Revd James, 28, 55, 63, 91, 92, 93, 113
Battle of Enniscorthy, 180
'green hill', Loftus and, 127, 129, 131
Hacketstown, rebels and, 250
Goresbridge, Co. Kilkenny, 249

Gorey, Co. Wexford, 15, 17, 27, 120
    crown forces in, 55, 59, 79, 83, 91
Gorton, John, 145
Gough, Lieutenant Colonel, 254
Gowan, Hunter (magistrate), 62, 78, 230
Grattan Flood, W.H., 105
graves
    at Tara, 254
    burial practices, 169–70
    croppy graves in Meath, *257*, 258, 259
    oral histories and, 238–42
    Reynells/Rennells/Reynolds grave, 240–2
    see also mass graves
Gray, Betsy, 233
Gray, Nicholas, 66, 73, 77, 82, 83
'green hill', 126–36, *129*, *130*, *131*, *192*
    Clonhasten townland, 131–6, *131*, *132*, *133*, *134*, *136*, 193, 217
    developments in vicinity, 203
    location, 6, *127*, *128*, 131–6, *132*, *133*, *134*, *136*
    Loftus and, 126–9, 131, 134–5, 136, 213
Greene, Thomas, 73
Grey de Wilton, Arthur Grey, 14th baron, 177
Griffin, Liam, 245–6
Grogan, Cornelius, 68, 73, 75, 76
Grose, Francis, 179
    Antiquities of Ireland, The, 142, *143*, 144
ground-penetrating radar (GPR), 161
Gurley, L.B., 121

Hacketstown, Co. Carlow, 48, 224, 250
Hall, Mary, 139, 240, 242
Hardy-McGurk Map, *129*, 131, *132*, 133, 135, 136
Harpar brothers, 227–8
Harvey, Bagenal Beauchamp, 15, 64, 65, 73
    commander-in-chief, 65, 66–7, 68, 70–1
    last Senate meeting, 87
    New Ross and, 16
    oaths and, 82
    president of the Council, 82
    United Army, oaths and, 77

Harwood, P., 115
Hatton, Henry, 239
Hatton, William, 82
Hay, Edward, 11, 18, 22, 50, 57, 65–6
    capitulation terms, Kingsborough and, 84, 85
    Commissariat, establishment of, 75–6
    Committee House (Cullimore's), 66
    Enniscorthy council and, 74
    Harvey as commander-in-chief, 66–7, 70
    History of the insurrection of the county of Wexford AD1798, 4, 22
    king's mail and, 79–80
    last Senate meeting, 84–5, 87
    member of the Council, 82
    prisoners in Enniscorthy Castle, 111
    proclamation issued by, 78
    rebel hospital, burning of, 115
    rebels' attempt to cross the river, 116
    return of plundered property, 72
    'secretary of state', 70
    Wexford Navy, 71
    Wexford town's surrender notice, 57
Hay, John, 22, 50
Hay, Philip, 22, 74
Heaney, Seamus, 'Requiem for the croppies', 235
Hendrick, Mary, 236
Heritage Council, 5
Holt, Joseph, 250, 253
Hompesch, Colonel Ferdinand von, 38
Hompesch Mounted Rifles, 38, 47, 49, 137
Hore, Philip, 150
hospital (rebel), 4, 22, 57, 86, 114–15
Hotham, George, 151
Howlin, John, admiral of the Wexford Navy, 71
Humbert, General Jean Joseph Amable, 68

Innis, Lieutenant Colonel, 6n46
Irish Battlefields Project, 5, 7, 134, 191–3, 203, 212
Irish Folklore Commission, 220, 244–7, 248

Index

Island, The, 116, 117, **117**, 173–5, **174**, **175**, 180–1

Jacob, Archibald Hamilton (magistrate), 62, 78, 85
Johnson, Major General, 2, 3, 16, 17, 45, 46, 53, 55
    attack on Enniscorthy, 111, 112
    Battle of Vinegar Hill, 17, 47, 49, 52, 58, 90, 109
    march against Vinegar Hill, 96
Jones, John, 29, 111, 116
Jordan, Brian, 222
Journal of Conflict Arachaeology, 190
Joyce, James, *Ulysses*, 245
Joyce, P.W., 105
Joyce, Robert Dwyer, 245

Kane, Esmond, 250
Kavanagh, Fr Patrick F., 28, 231
    Popular history of the insurrection of 1798, A, 4, 35, 220
Kearney, Edward, 82
Kearney, William, 75
Kearns, Fr Mogue, 3, 15, 53, 55, 64, 109, 181
    attack at Knockderrig, 254
    execution, 258
    march through Kildare, 250–1
Keegan, Hugh, 228
Keegan, Michael, 228
Kelly, John, 16, 224, 225, 238, 248
Keogh, D. and N. Furlong
    Mighty wave, The, 29
    Women of 1798, The, 29
Keogh, Matthew (governor of Wexford), 242
Kerr, William (6th marquess of Lothian), 18, 48
    aide-de-camp to General Loftus, 25
    Battle of Vinegar Hill, account of, 25, 55, 57–8, 125
    'green hill', Loftus and, 127–8, 129, 131, 134–5, 136

Midlothian fencible regiment, 48, 50
    rebels' retreat on Vinegar Hill, 125
Kervin, Dan, 124
Keugh, Matthew, 65, 67, 68–9, 80
    Battle of Horetown, 75, 83
    capitulation, 85
    chairman, Committee of Public Safety, 72
    last meeting of Senate, 84–5, 87
    member of the Council, 82
    perception of, 69
    residence in Lower George Street, 84
    Wexford Bridge massacre, 84
Kilcashel graveyard, Co. Wicklow, 242
Kilcock, Co. Kildare, 250
Kildare, rebel march through, 250–1
Killoughrim Wood, 229, 235, 243
Kilmuckridge, Co. Wexford, 229
Kilthomas Hill, 12–13
King, Colonel, 45, 49
Kingsborough, Colonel, 71, 79–80
    capitulation terms, Hay and, 84–5
    surrender of Wexford town, 85–6
Knightstown Bog, Co. Meath, **253**, 256, **256**
Kyan, Richard, 242

Lake, General Gerard, 2, 3, 12, 16
    American War of Independence, 89
    Battle of Ballinamuck, 61
    Battle of Vinegar Hill, 16, 45, 46, 48, 55, 60, 108–9
    Castlereagh, correspondence with, 18, 25, 121
    delegation sent to, 23–4
    eve of the battle, Vinegar Hill, 50
    folk memory of command post, 222
    'gaps' in his net, 59
    general advance ordered by, 83
    humanitarian intent, 93
    initial plans, 120–1
    Needham, orders given to, 89–90, 91–4, 95
    ordnance, 35, 44
    rebel hospital, burning of, 86
    rebels' request terms, response to, 94–5

Lake, General Gerard (*continued*)
   report, Battle of Vinegar Hill, 25, 54–5
   Solsborough House and, 138, 236
   surrender terms, rejection of, 86
   troops at his disposal, 34–5, 44
Landscape and Geophysical Services (LGS), 6, 161
Larsson, Å.M., 168
Lett, Barbara Newtown, 25, 26, 137
Loftus, Major General William, 3, 17, 45, 46, 47–8, 54, 55–6
   Battle of Vinegar Hill, 109
   'green hill' captured by, 126–9, *129*, *130*, *131*
Logue, Paul, 191
Longest Day Research Project, 1, 5, 195, 203, 204, 205
   architectural survey of Enniscorthy, 6
   Beale's Barn, location of, 139–40
   budget, 5
   geophysical surveys, 6, 32
   key stakeholders, 5
   metal-detection survey, 190
   photogrammetric survey of the Windmill, 6, 123n2
   project team, 5, 6
   research highlights, 6–7
   steering group, 5, *8*
   underwater investigation, 6
Lord Edward's Own, 88, *103*

McCall, P.J., 245
McDonald, Billy, 227, 248
McGurk's map, *129*, 131, *132*, 133, 135, 136
M'Laren, Sergeant Archibald, 18
   Battle of Vinegar Hill, 24, 45, 50, 55, 61, 125–6
   casualties at Vinegar Hill, 124
   march to Solsborough, 99
   Minute description of the battles of Gorey, Arklow and Vinegar-Hill, 120
   Needham's orders from Lake, 89–90, 96
McManus, Captain, 57

magnetometer survey, 162–3, 166
mass graves, 29, 30, 31–3, 157–70
   2D earth-resistance survey, 162, 164–5, *164*, 166, 170
   aDNA analysis, 169
   bioarchaeological data, 169
   burials in the Barley Field, 158–9
   creation of, 157–8
   'diggability' of the soil, 159–60
   documentary sources, 158–9
   electrical resistivity imaging (ERI), 161, 162, 164–5, *165*, 170
   excavations, the case for, 168–70
   folklore and, 159
   geophysical survey, 160–1
   geophysical survey results, 162–5
   geophysical survey results, implications of, 165–7
   ground-penetrating radar (GPR), 161
   identification, 158
   location of search area, *159*
   magnetometer survey, 162–3, *163*, 166
   non-intrusive techniques to assess, 160–1
   osteoarchaeological data, 169
   quarry pits, 160, 166, 167, *167*, 170
   social and/or ritual customs, 169–70
   typical location of, 157
Maxwell, William Hamilton
   Battle of Arklow, 49
   Battle of Foulksmills, 49–50
   Battle of Vinegar Hill, 28, 44, 58, 60–1
   History of the Irish rebellion, 4, 28, 147
   illustrations by Cruikshank, *17*, 28, *56*, *147*, *252*
   Needham, 88
   St Mary's Church of Ireland, 147–8, *147*
Maynooth, Co. Kildare, 250
Meánscoil Gharman, Brownswood, 221
Meath
   'Cnoc an áir', 259
   'Croppy Field', 259
   croppy graves, *257*, 258, 259
   Knightstown Bog, defeat at, *253*, 256, *256*

Leinster Bridge, Clonard, attack on, 251, **252**
metal-detection surveys, 7, 185, 187, **192**, 195–6
  results, 197–201
Methodist Magazine, 123
Meyler, Robert, 82
militia, 37, 47
  Antrim militia, 49, 92
  Armagh militia, 49, 55, 71
  Donegal militia, 137
  Meath militia, 14, 253–4
  North Cork militia, 13, 24, 71, 81, 111, 116, 179, 180
  South Cork militia, 202
  South Devon militia, viii–ix
  see also yeomanry
Minchin, Henry, 72–3
Missionary Magazine, 31
Moll, Herman, *New Map of Ireland*, 179
Moore, Captain Hugh, 45
Moore, Brigadier General Sir John, 16–17, 45, 46, 47, 49
  advance towards Wexford town, 83
  Battle of Foulksmills, 49–50
  Battle of Horetown, 226–7
  Dunbarton fencibles, 302
  Forth Mountain position, 59–60
  Peninsular War and, 83
  Vinegar Hill, condition of, 61
Mountainstown House, Meath, 258–9
Mullen, J., 259
Munday Map, 142, 145, 146, 148, 151, 152, 154
Munday, William, 145
Munnelly, T., 244
Murphy, John, 74
Murphy, Fr John, 2, 12, 13, 28, 64
  Battle of Vinegar Hill, 109, 223, 224
  burial place, 225
  Byrne, Myles and, 19
  folk tradition and, 224–5
  retreat from Vinegar Hill, 86, 225, 229, 249
  Tubberneering ambush, 15
Murphy, Fr Michael, 13, 16

Murphy, Rory, 230–1
Murphy, Fr Thomas, 259
Musgrave, Sir Richard, 28, 64–5
  banknotes, rebels and, 78–9
  Battle of Enniscorthy, 14
  Battle of Vinegar Hill, 47–8, 58, 59, 128–9
  bridge in Enniscorthy, crown forces and, 112
  Commissariat, representatives of, 76
  'embryo republic', views on, 62, 78
  Enniscorthy, description of, 10
  'green hill', Loftus and, 128–9, 131, 132, 133, 134, 135
  Harvey appointed commander-in-chief, 70
  Loftus, green hill occupied by, 213
  Memoirs of the different rebellions in Ireland, 4, 10, 28, 47
  Needham's baggage train, 98, 99
  Needham's lateness, reasons for, 91–3
  Needham's route march, 96
  rebels' attempt to cross the river, 116
  Solsborough, crown forces at, 138
Myler, Stephen, 76

Naas, Co. Kildare, 49
Napoleonic Wars, 19, 42
National 1798 Rebellion Centre, Enniscorthy, ix, 1, 5, 29, **43**, 171
National Folklore Collection, 219–20, 248
  Main Manuscript Collection (IFC), 220
  Schools' Collection (IFC S), 220–1
  see also Schools' Folklore Scheme
National Inventory of Architectural Heritage, 152, 153, 154, 155, 156
National Library of Ireland, 150
National Monuments (Amendment) Act (1987), 161
National Monuments Service (NMS), 161
Needham, Hon. Major General Francis, 83, 88–104
  American War of Independence, 89
  arrival at Vinegar Hill, 109–10

Needham, Hon. Major General Francis (*continued*)
  baggage train, 89, 91, 92, 94, 95, 98–9, 103–4
  Battle of Arklow, 16, 17, 47, 48–9, 89
  Battle of Vinegar Hill, 3, 24, 45, 46, 47, 53, 57, 109
  Darby's Gap area, 55, 57, 58, 59
  humanitarian intent and, 93, 94, 102–4
  Lake's orders, 89–90, 91–4
  lateness, reasons for, 6, 59, 88–9, 99–104, 138
  nickname, 94
  route march, 95–6, **100**
  route march, research field trials of, 100–2, **102**
  soldiers, knapsacks and, 97
  Solsborough, diversion to, 59, 90, 91–2, 94, 95, 103
'Needham's Gap', 3, 55, 88, 93, 109, 138, 222, 230, 236
New Annual Register or General Repository of History, Politics and Literature for the Year 1798, 55
New Ross, Co. Wexford, 14
  rebel forces and, 15–16, 77–8
  Three Bullet Gate, 16
New Zealand, viii
Newton, J. and W., 142, 144, 146, 148
Newton Map, 142, 144, 146, 148, 154, 155
Newtownbarry (now Bunclody), 15, 16
Nicholson, Captain (ADC of General Lake), 45

O'Brien, Flann, *Béal bocht, An*, 245
O'Connor, Jasper, 228–9
Ó Crualaoich, C. and A. Mac Giolla Chomhghaill, 236
O'Flaherty, Morogh, **253**
Ogle, George, MP, 148
O'Hea, Captain, 24
O'Keeffe, P. and T. Symington, 178, 179
O'Kelly, P., 50, 76, 237–8

Ó Longáin, Mícheál Óg, 105
O'Neill, James, 191
oral histories of 1798, 219–48
  1798 general participants, 226–9
  1798 leaders, 224–6
  artefacts/signs of battle, 243–4
  'Babes' Glen', 235
  'Babes in the Wood', 229, 243
  Ballinahallen Wood, 238
  'Barley Field, The', 235
  Battle of Enniscorthy, 222–3
  Battle of Horetown, 226–7
  Battle of Vinegar Hill, 221, 222, 223
  blacksmith, role of, 230–1
  'Bloody Bridge, The', 234–5
  'Cannon Banks, The', 236
  crown forces, members of, 230
  Daphne Castle, 238
  Enniscorthy Castle, 237–8
  eyewitness account, 223
  ghostly encounters, 243
  ghostly white horse, 234
  graves/graveyards, 238–42
  international motifs, 236
  landmarks/features/place-names, 234–8
  Murphy, Fr John, 224–5
  'Needham's Gap', 236
  River Slaney, 224
  Riverchapel, 238
  Scollough Gap, 237, 238
  'Soldier's Hole, The', 236–7
  sources of information, 220–1
  women of the rebellion, 231–4
Ordnance Survey maps, 118, 155, 167
  abbey site, Enniscorthy, 144
  Enniscorthy, 145, **178**
  Island, The, structure on, 173
  quarry pits, 160, 166
  River Slaney, 172
  Templeshannon, 191
Oriel Brothers, Hampshire, 181
Oulart Hill, 12–13, 63, 64, 77, 226
Ovidstown, Co. Kildare, 250

Pakenham, Thomas, *Year of liberty, The*, 1, 4, 80, 249, 250, 251, 253
Pearse, H., 89, 94
Pearse, Padraig, 235
Pearson, Peter, 144, 152, 154
Peninsular Wars, 8, 83
Perry, Anthony, 2, 19, 250, 258
    assault on Arklow, 16
    attack on Gorey and Arklow, 15
    Battle of Vinegar Hill, 109
    retreat from Vinegar Hill, 86
photogrammetric survey, 6, 123n2
pogrom, magistrates and, 62–3, 74, 75, 78, 84
Pollard, Tony, vii–x, 5, **8**, 216
Pollock, John, 258–9
Portsmouth estate, **117**, 156
    bridge, remedial works, 181
    Munday Map, 142, 145, 146, 148, 151, 152, 154
    Newton Map, 142, 144, 146, 148, 154, 155
    quays, contribution towards, 151
    rental records, 151
Pounden, Alicia, 26–7, 137
Pounden, John, 26, 238n6
Pounden, Joshua, 26, 238n6
Pyne, W.H., British regimental baggage wagons, **95**

Quirke, Raymond, 158–9, 235

Rayner, S., 96
Redmond, Fr Edward, 235
Redmond, Fr John, 235
Redmond, Fr Michael, 235
Redmond, Fr Nicholas, 235
Redmond, Peter, 74
Regan, Darren, 162
Report on Irish prisons, 27
republic
    attempt to establish, 62, 78
    Wexford Republic, 2, 80, 86
Republic of Connacht, 68
Reserve Defence Forces, 6, 88, **103**

Reynells, Catherine, 242
Reynells, William Stephen, 30, 158, **241**, 242
Reynells/Rennells/Reynolds (yeoman), 230, 238, 240
Richards, Captain Solomon, 116, 138, 236
River Nore, 188, 188n1
River Nore Flood Alleviation Scheme, 188
River Slaney
    1798 events and, 179–81
    archaeological assessment, 181
    bedrock, 171
    bodies thrown into, 30
    course, 171
    Enniscorthy Bridge, 172, **173**, 174, 175–6, 178, **178**, 179, 181
    Enniscorthy Bridge, stone work, **182–3**
    first stone bridge, Enniscorthy, 179
    frontage, Enniscorthy, 176–9
    Island, The, 173–6, **174**, **175**, 181
    Island, The, structure on, 173–4, **174**
    Railway Bridge, Enniscorthy, 174
    riverbed at bridge, 117, 175–6
    Seamus Rafter Bridge, 176
    tidal limit, 176
    timber bridge, contract for, 176–9
    timber trade/pipe staffs, 176
    topography, 174–5
    underwater surveys, 117, 171–89, **184**
Riverchapel, 238
Roche, Edward, 3, 13, 20, 71, 73
    assault on Arklow, 16
    Battle of Vinegar Hill, 110
    folk tradition and, 222, 224, 225
    Oulart Hill, role on, 71
    proclamation issued by, 78
Roche, Fr Philip, 64, 79, 82, 83
Rogers, H.C.B., 97
Rosslare Fort, bombardment of, 85
Rothwell, J.S., 96, 98, 99
Rowe, David, 155

Sadler, William, *Vinegar Hill*, **60**
St Mary's National School, Enniscorthy, 221

St Senan's graveyard, 238, 239
Sandby, Paul, Enniscorthy, *113*, 144, **145**
Scallan, Eithne, 155
Scallan, John, 71
Schools' Folklore Scheme, 220–1, 243, 244, 258, 259
Scollough Gap, 58, 229, 237, 238
Scott, Douglas, 190
Scottish Radical Rising (1820), x
Scullabogue Barn, 78, 81, 87
Segrave, Mrs, 76
Shaffery, Patrick and Maura, *Buildings of Irish towns*, 141
Shelmalier, 85, 222, 224, 226
Sinnot, Anthony, 31, 33, 158, 166
Snowe, Captain William, 13–14, 19, 20, 116, 179, 180, 237
Society of United Irishmen *see* United Irishmen
Solsborough House, 138, 236
songs/poems, 244–7
    'Boolavogue', 220, 245
    'Father Dwyer', 247
    'I had a dream the other day', 246–7
    'Kelly the boy from Killanne', 16, 220, 225
    'O'Rourke the blacksmith', 247
    'The boys of the flail', 247
    'The boys of Wexford', 232, 245–6
Spanish Civil War, 161, 169
Sparrows, J., Enniscorthy, 142, *143*, 144
Stafford from Littlegraigue, 227
Stafford McLoughlin Archaeology, 6, 136, 195, 201, 205, 215
    artefacts recovered, **208**, **209**, **214**
    Clonhasten area, **211**, **212**
Stewart, Lieutenant Colonel, 45, 46
Storey, Martin, 246
Sutton, Matthew, 74–5, 79
Synnott, Thomas, 20

Tara, Co. Meath, 253–4
Taylor, Alexander, **130**
Taylor, Christopher (printer), 68, 69
Taylor, George, 27, 30, 66, 69, 82, 83, 86, 232
Taylor, Iseult, 68n5
Taylor and Skinner Map, 106–7, **106**, 123
Teeling, C.H., 34, 44, 51, 54
Thompson, William, 122–3, 224
Tone, Theobald Wolfe, 12
Tubberneering, Co. Wexford, 15, 19, 224, 225
Turner, Sir Llewelyn, 94
Turner, P., 243
Tyrell, John, 251
Tyrell, Thomas (high sheriff of Kildare), 251

underwater surveys *see* River Slaney
United Irishmen, x, 2, 16
    arrests, 12
    battle at Tara, 253–4
    call-up in Wexford, 63
    Dublin, failure of rebellion, 62
    French support, 12
    leadership, 14
    role, Vinegar Hill and, 4
    Ulster uprisings, 16
    weaponry, 194–5
    see also Wexford Army; Wexfordmen
University College Dublin (UCD), School of Archaeology, 191

Varus battlefield, Germany, 190
Vesey, Colonel, 45, 58, 112
Vinegar Hill, *118*, *128*, *133*, *134*, *136*, *146*
    aerial views, **127**, **132**
    archaeological monitoring, 205–17
    archaeological surveys, ix–x, 4–5, **134**, 136, 190–204
    Beale's Barn, 6, 120
    burial activity, phases of, 29
    Cnoc Fhiodh na gCaor, Irish name for, 105–6
    deep ditches, 119–20
    deep lane below, **119**
    earthen banks, 191
    historical background, 11–12
    illegal metal detection, 7

Index

international legacy, vii–x
landscape of the hill, 118–23
location, 2
mass graves, 29, 30, 31–3, 157–70
metal-detector survey, ix, 7
paths/trails, upgrading of, 205
preservation of the battlefield, 7–8, 157
rebel camp, 2, 14, *17*
refuge for families/non-combatants, 14
report on (2008), 5
shallow graves, 31
strategic position of, 106–7, *107*
terrain surrounding, 99
see also Battle of Vinegar Hill; 'green hill'; mass graves; Windmill
Vinegar Hill Battlefield research team, 220
Vinegar Hill place names, viii–viv

Walpole, Lieutenant Colonel, 15, 44
Walsh, Greg, and Brian Ó Cléirigh, *110*
Walsh, Mrs (née Murphy), 235
Walsh, Nicholas, 240
Walsh, Paul, 5
Warren, Joseph, Jnr, 228
Warren, Joseph, Snr, 228
Waterloo Uncovered, ix
Weekly Journal, 147
Wemyss, General, 255, 256
Wexford Army, 70–1
    Fr Roche as commander-in-chief, 82
    Harvey as commander-in-chief, 65, 66–7, 68, 70–1
    leaders, 109
    Northern Army, 62, 70, 72, 76, 77, 78, 81, 86
    oaths to be taken, 77, 82
    proclamation issued by Roche, 78
    Protestants and, 70, 78
    recruitment, 83
    Southern Army, 62, 70, 77, 79, 82, 83
Wexford Bridge massacre, 17, 26, 75, 84
Wexford, Co., 77–81
    course of the rebellion, 14–17

    pogrom, magistrates and, 62–3, 74, 75, 78, 84
    rebel control of, 15
    Vinegar Hill camp, 14
    war, 77–81
Wexford County Council, 8
    archaeological monitoring, 205
    archaeological work, 195, 204
    Longest Day Research Project, 1, 5
    ownership of area near/around summit, 7
    projects supported by, 221
    underwater survey, 171
Wexford Herald, 68
Wexford Navy, 71–2
Wexford Prisons Committee, 75
Wexford Public Library Service, *17*, *53*, *56*, *147*
Wexford Republic, 2, 80, 86
    see also Wexford Senate
Wexford Senate, 69–77
    Commissariat, 75–7
    Committee of Public Safety, 72–3
    first meeting, 66–9, 87
    first meeting, decisions of, 69–77
    judiciary, 72–3
    last meeting of, 84–6, 87
    Scullabogue, enquiry proposal, 81, 87
    second meeting, 81–5
    Senate House (Cullimore's), 66–9
    Wexford Army, 70–1
    Wexford Navy, 71–2
    Wexford Prisons Committee, 75
Wexford town, 14
    Borough Corporation, 72
    British forces advance towards, 83
    Confederate Navy, 71
    Cullimore's premises, meeting at, 65–6
    execution of informers, 72
    garrison, 15
    munitions factory, 76
    pike production, 76–7
    surrender notice, 57, 85–6
    wards, division into, 72
    see also Wexford Senate

Wexfordmen
- flight, 256–9
- Knightstown Bog, defeat at, **253**, 256, **256**
- Leinster Bridge, Clonard, attack on, 251, **252**
- march through Kildare, 250–1
- march to Meath, 251
- Meath, shelter given in, 258–9
- Meath/Louth border skirmishes, 255
- retreat from Leinster Bridge, 251
- route taken by, **253**

Wheeler, H.F.B. and A.M. Broadley, 67
Whelan, K., 235
Whelp Rock, Wicklow, 250
White, Hawtry (magistrate), 62, 78
White, John, 155
Whyte, James, 248
Wicklow
- retreat through, 250
- see also Arklow; Battle of Arklow

Wide Streets Commissioners, 152
Wilford, General Richard R., 45, 46, 54, 124, 138
Wilkinson, Lieutenant Colonel, 50
William III, King, 216
Williamson, Lieutenant Colonel, 45, 46
Windmill, 7, 120, 121, **122**, 123–4
- photogrammetric survey of, 6, 123n2
- used as rebel prison, 123

witness evidence at trials, 27
women (in the rebellion), 11, 226, 231–4
- Battle of Vinegar Hill and, 4, 18, 22, 24, 57, 88
- see also Barber, Jane; Dixon, Madge; Lett, Barbara Newtown; Pounden, Alicia

Wynne, Revd Dr, 142
Wynne, Colonel Sir W., 45

Yellow Ford, Co. Armagh, 191
yeomanry, 37, 224
- 'Black Mob', 243
- Camolin, 12
- cavalry, 12, 138, 243, 254
- Clonegal area, 228
- Meath, 254
- perception of, 254
- Scarawalsh infantry, 13
- Tinahely, 'True Blues', 48, 224

Young Ireland movement, 244